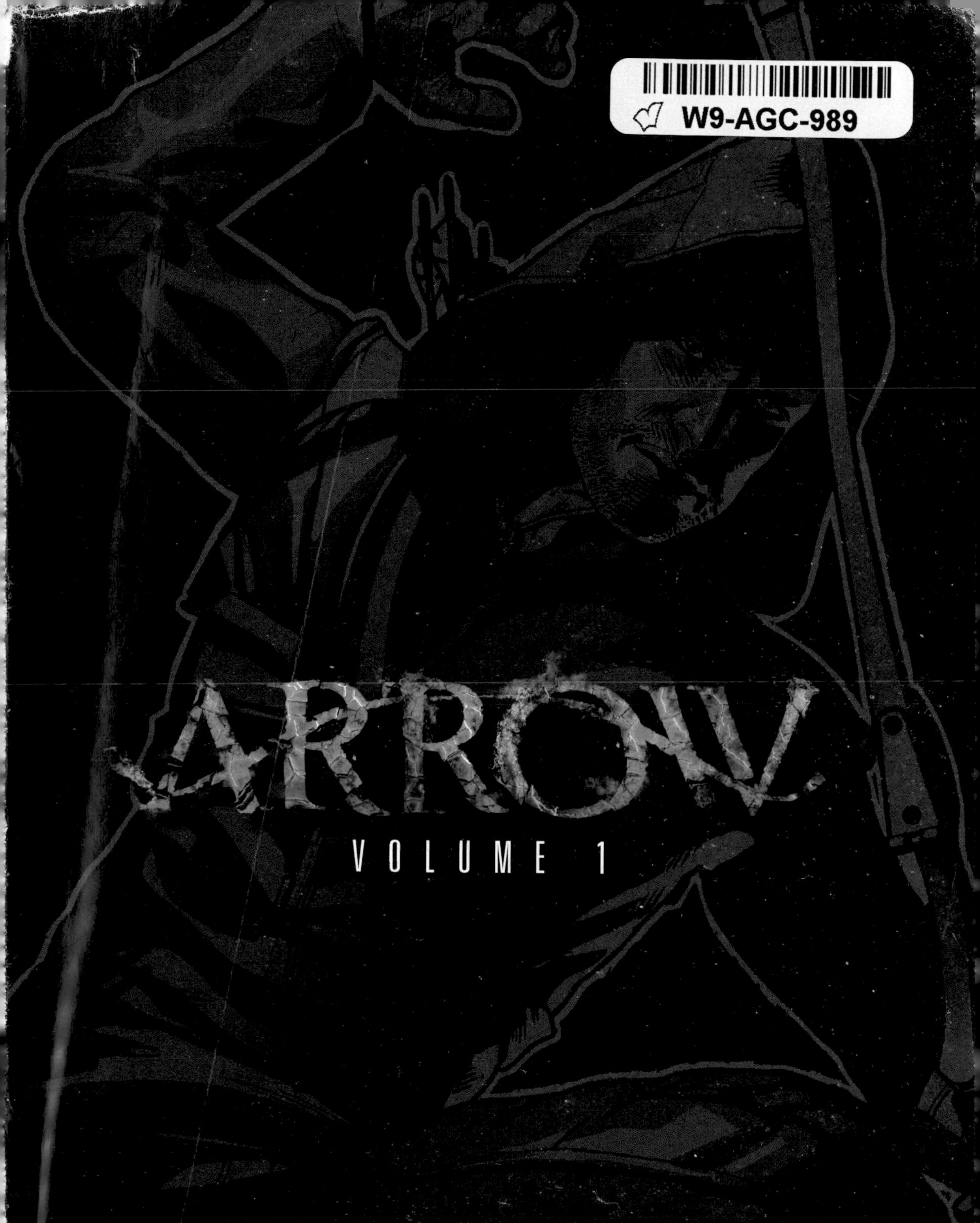

ARROW

VOLUME 1

ALEX ANTONE BEN ABERNATHY Editors–Original Series ROBIN WILDMAN Editor ROBBIN BROSTERMAN Design Director–Books DAMIAN RYLAND Publication Design

Hank Kanalz Senior VP–Vertigo and Integrated Publishing

DIANE NELSON President DAN DIDIO and JIM LEE Co-Publishers GEOFF JOHNS Chief Creative Officer JOHN ROOD Executive VP–Sales, Marketing and Business Development AMY GENKINS Senior VP–Business and Legal Affairs NAIRI GARDINER Senior VP–Finance JEFF BOISON VP – Publishing Planning MARK CHIARELLO VP–Art Direction and Design JOHN CUNNINGHAM VP–Marketing TERRI CUNNINGHAM Editorial Administration ALISON GILL Senior VP–Manufacturing and Operations HANK KANALZ Senior VP–Digital JAY KOGAN VP–Business and Legal Affairs, Publishing JACK MAHAN VP–Business Affairs, Talent NICK NAPOLITANO VP–Manufacturing Administration SUE POHJA VP–Book Sales COURTNEY SIMMONS Senior VP–Publicity BOB WAYNE Senior VP–Sales

ARROW VOLUME 1

Published by DC Comics. Copyright © 2013 DC Comics. All Rights Reserved.

Originally published in single magazine form in ARROW #1-6, ARROW: SPECIAL ISSUE #1 Copyright © 2012, 2013 DC Comics. All Rights Reserved. All characters, their distinctive likenesses and related elements featured in this publication are trademarks of DC Comics. The stories, characters and incidents featured in this publication are entirely fictional. DC Comics does not read or accept unsolicited ideas, stories or artwork.

DC Comics, 1700 Broadway, New York, NY 10019. A Warner Bros. Entertainment Company. Printed by RR Donnelley, Salem, VA, USA. 8/16/13. First Printing. ISBN: 978-1-4012-4299-2

Library of Congress Cataloging-in-Publication Data

Guggenheim, Marc.
Arrow. Volume 1 / Marc Guggenheim, Andrew Kreisberg, Mike Grell.
pages cm
"Originally published in single magazine form in Arrow 1-6 and Arrow: Special Issue 1."
ISBN 978-1-4012-4299-2
1. Graphic novels. I. Kreisberg, Andrew, 1971- II. Grell, Mike, III. Title.
PN6728.G725G84 2013
741.5'973–dc23
2013016903

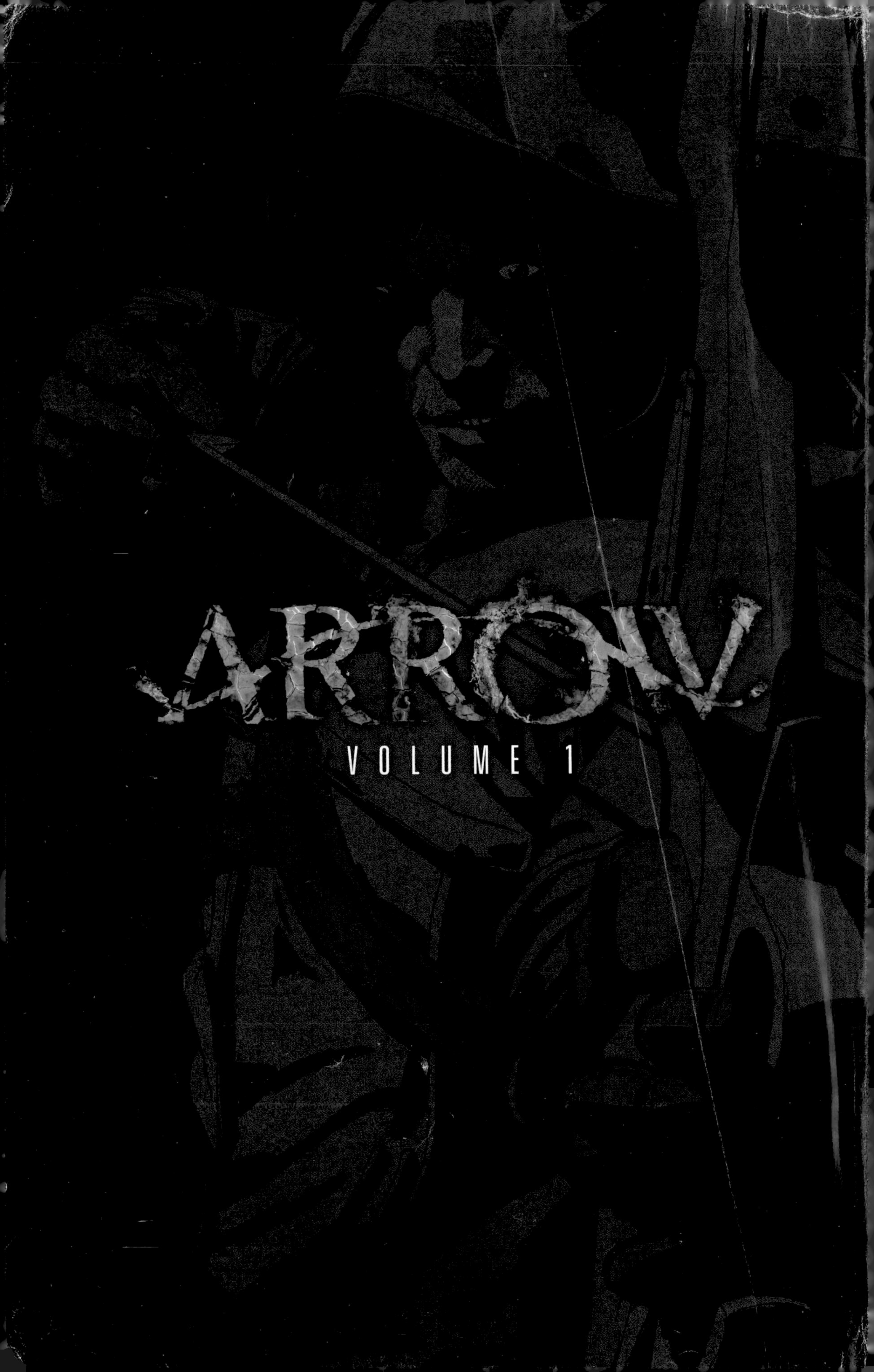
ARROW
VOLUME 1

Story by **Marc Guggenheim & Andrew Kreisberg**

PROLOGUE: TEST DRIVE
Script: **Andrew Kreisberg, Marc Guggenheim**
Greg Berlanti & Geoff Johns
Art: **Omar Francia**

CHAPTER 1: TIME'S ARROW
Script: **Marc Guggenheim & Andrew Kreisberg**
Art: **Mike Grell**

CHAPTER 2: PREY
Script: **Ben Sokolowski**
Pencils: **Sergio Sandoval**
Inks: **Pol Gas**

CHAPTER 3: FEAR
Script: **Beth Schwartz**
Art: **Jorge Jimenez**

CHAPTER 4: DIGGLE
Script: **Lana Cho**
Art: **Eric Nguyen**

CHAPTER 5: FATHOMS
Script: **Wendy Mericle**
Pencils: **Sergio Sandoval**
Inks: **Pol Gas**

CHAPTER 6: MOSCOW
Script: **Ben Sokolowski & Lana Cho**
Art: **Mike Grell**

CHAPTER 7: BOYS NIGHT
Script: **Beth Schwartz**
Art: **Jorge Jimenez**

CHAPTER 8: [REC]
Script: **Wendy Mericle & Mary Iacono**
Pencils: **Sergio Sandoval**
Inks: **Pol Gas**

CHAPTER 9: FALLING
Script: **Beth Schwartz &**
Katherine Walczak
Art: **Mico Suayan**

CHAPTER 10: CAGED
Script: **Ben Sokolowski & Moira Kirland**
Art: **Eric Nguyen**

CHAPTER 11: HUNTRESS YEAR ONE
Script: **Marc Guggenheim**
Art: **Mike Grell**

CHAPTER 12: LIMBO
Script: **Emilio Aldrich**
Art: **Julian Totino Tedesco**

CHAPTER 13: SHANGHAI
Script: **Tiffany Williams**
Pencils: **Sergio Sandoval**
Inks: **Pol Gas**

CHAPTER 14: CALL TO THE BAR
Script: **Mary Iacono**
Art: **Xermanico**

CHAPTER 15: 6:15 TO STARLING CITY
Script: **Katherine Walczak**
Art: **Omar Francia**

CHAPTER 16: SINS OF THE FATHER
Script: **Emilio Aldrich**
Art: **Mike Grell**

CHAPTER 17: TWO-MINUTE WARNING
Script: **Jake Coburn**
Art: **Xermanico**

CHAPTER 18: KEEP 'EM COMING
Script: **Mary Iacono & Tiffany Williams**
Pencils: **Sergio Sandoval**
Inks: **Pol Gas**

Colors by **David Lopez &**
Santi Casas of Ikari Studio
Rex Lokus
Letters by **Wes Abbott**
Special thanks to **Ben Sokolowski**

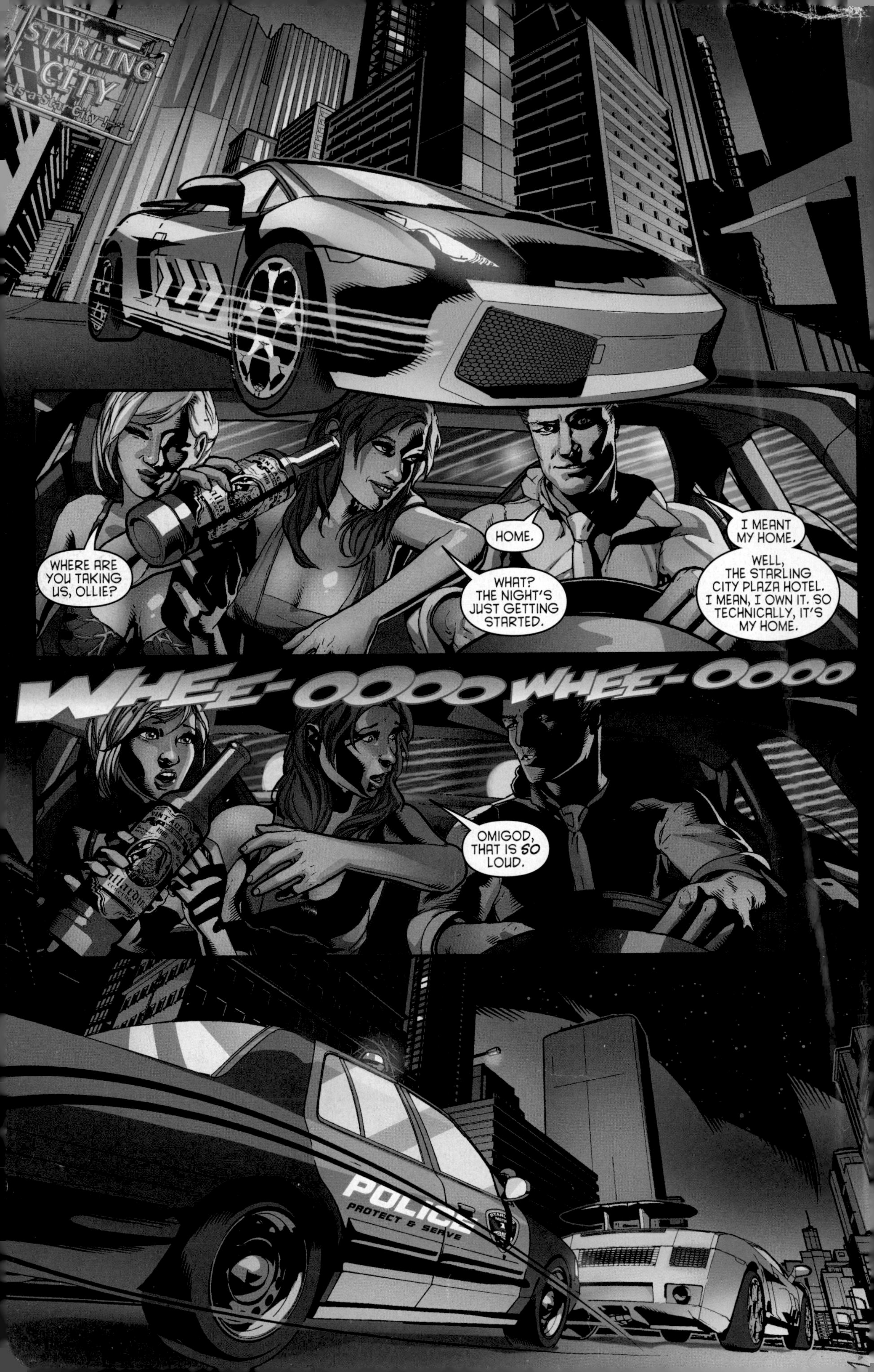
STARLING CITY
is a Star city
WHERE ARE YOU TAKING US, OLLIE?
HOME.
WHAT? THE NIGHT'S JUST GETTING STARTED.
I MEANT MY HOME.
WELL, THE STARLING CITY PLAZA HOTEL. I MEAN, I OWN IT. SO TECHNICALLY, IT'S MY HOME.
WHEE-OOOO WHEE-OOOO
OMIGOD, THAT IS SO LOUD.
POLICE
PROTECT & SERVE

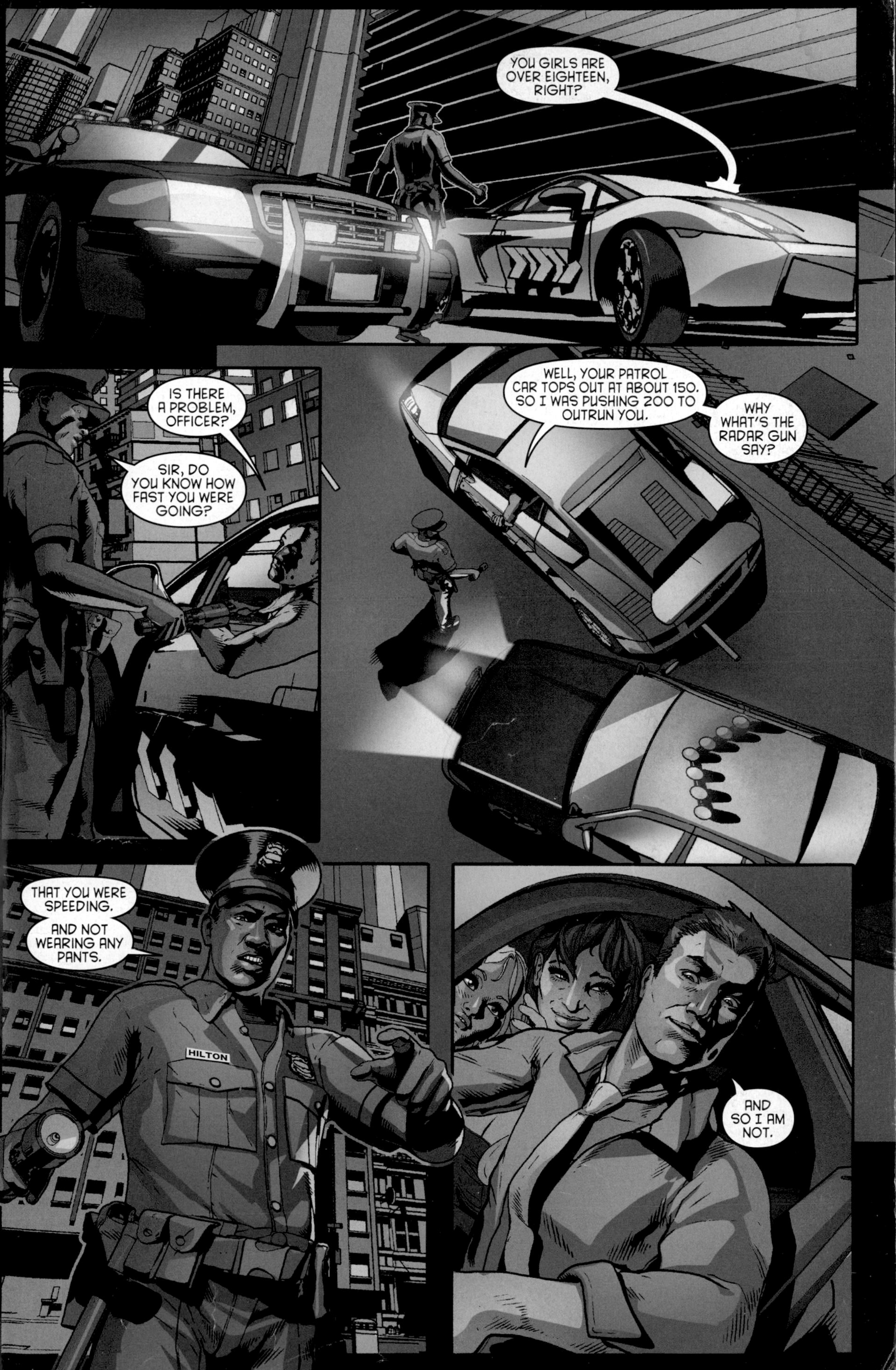
YOU GIRLS ARE OVER EIGHTEEN, RIGHT?
IS THERE A PROBLEM, OFFICER?
SIR, DO YOU KNOW HOW FAST YOU WERE GOING?
WELL, YOUR PATROL CAR TOPS OUT AT ABOUT 150. SO I WAS PUSHING 200 TO OUTRUN YOU.
WHY WHAT'S THE RADAR GUN SAY?
THAT YOU WERE SPEEDING.
AND NOT WEARING ANY PANTS.
HILTON
AND SO I AM NOT.

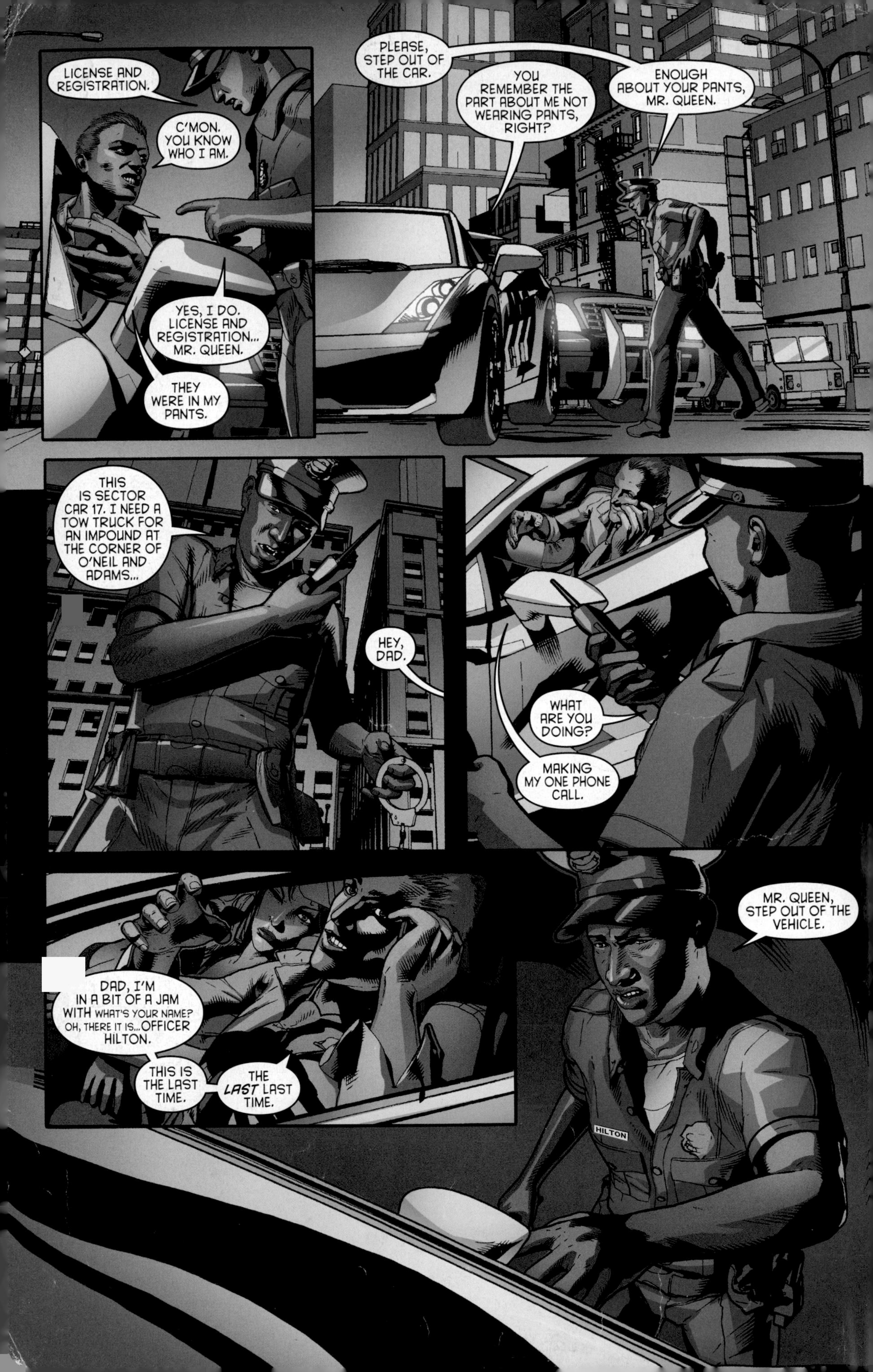
LICENSE AND REGISTRATION.
C'MON. YOU KNOW WHO I AM.
YES, I DO. LICENSE AND REGISTRATION... MR. QUEEN.
THEY WERE IN MY PANTS.
PLEASE, STEP OUT OF THE CAR.
YOU REMEMBER THE PART ABOUT ME NOT WEARING PANTS, RIGHT?
ENOUGH ABOUT YOUR PANTS, MR. QUEEN.
THIS IS SECTOR CAR 17. I NEED A TOW TRUCK FOR AN IMPOUND AT THE CORNER OF O'NEIL AND ADAMS...
HEY, DAD.
WHAT ARE YOU DOING?
MAKING MY ONE PHONE CALL.
DAD, I'M IN A BIT OF A JAM WITH WHAT'S YOUR NAME? OH, THERE IT IS...OFFICER HILTON.
THIS IS THE LAST TIME.
THE LAST LAST TIME.
MR. QUEEN, STEP OUT OF THE VEHICLE.
HILTON

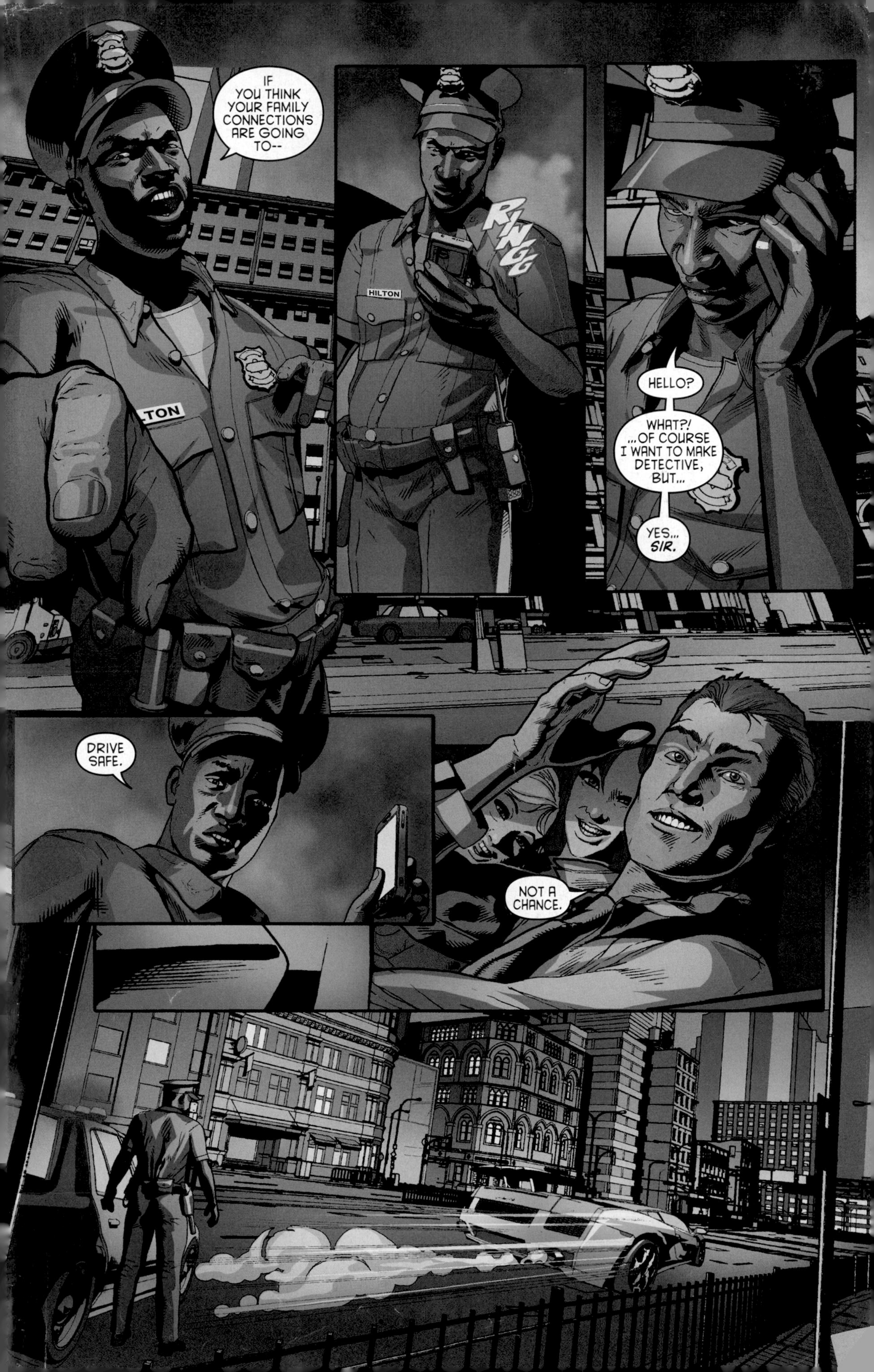

IF YOU THINK YOUR FAMILY CONNECTIONS ARE GOING TO--
HILTON
RINGG
HILTON
HELLO?
WHAT?! ...OF COURSE I WANT TO MAKE DETECTIVE, BUT...
YES... SIR.
DRIVE SAFE.
NOT A CHANCE.

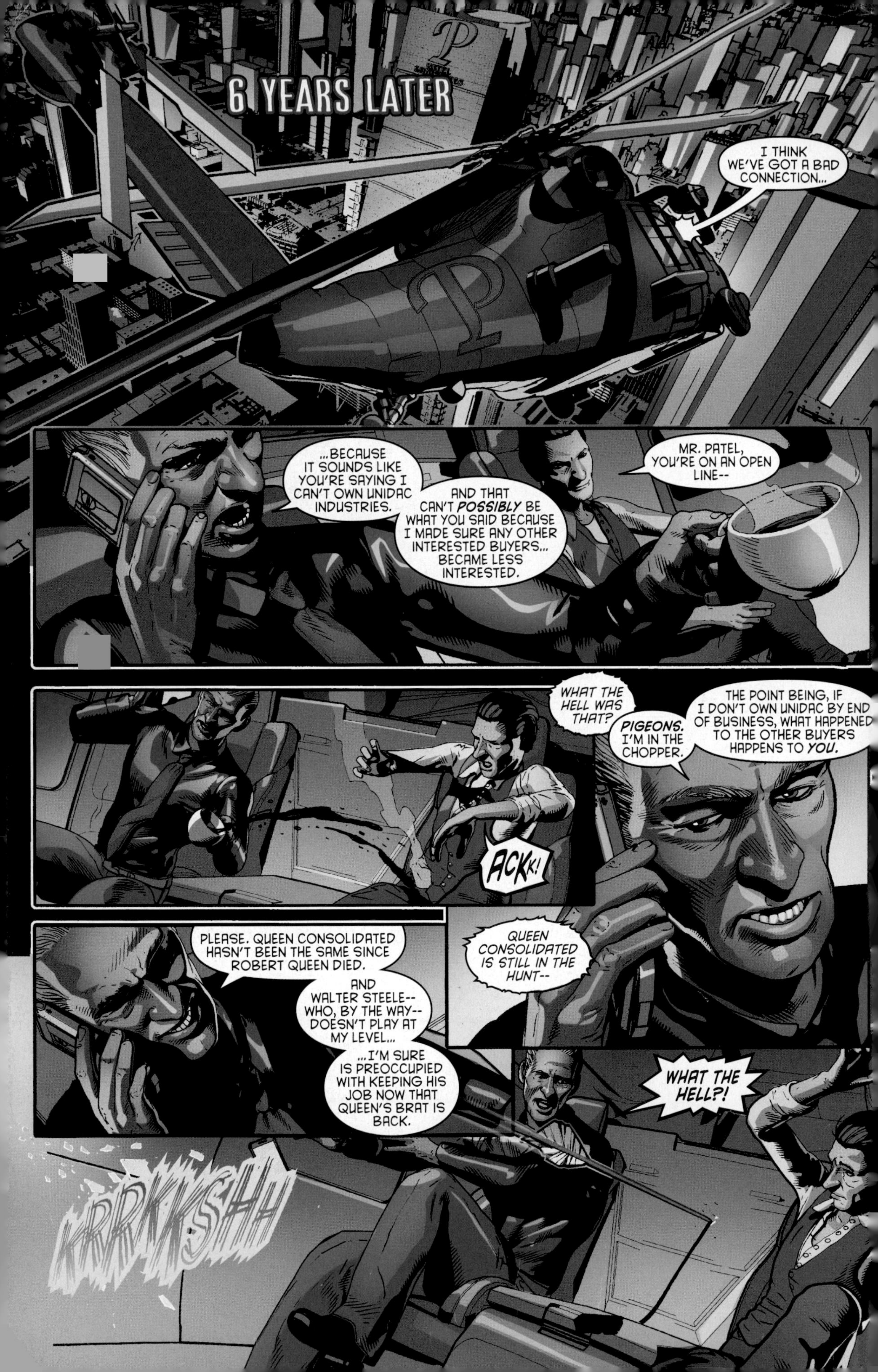
6 YEARS LATER
I THINK WE'VE GOT A BAD CONNECTION...
...BECAUSE IT SOUNDS LIKE YOU'RE SAYING I CAN'T OWN UNIDAC INDUSTRIES.
AND THAT CAN'T POSSIBLY BE WHAT YOU SAID BECAUSE I MADE SURE ANY OTHER INTERESTED BUYERS... BECAME LESS INTERESTED.
MR. PATEL, YOU'RE ON AN OPEN LINE--
WHAT THE HELL WAS THAT?
PIGEONS. I'M IN THE CHOPPER.
THE POINT BEING, IF I DON'T OWN UNIDAC BY END OF BUSINESS, WHAT HAPPENED TO THE OTHER BUYERS HAPPENS TO YOU.
ACKK!
QUEEN CONSOLIDATED IS STILL IN THE HUNT--
PLEASE. QUEEN CONSOLIDATED HASN'T BEEN THE SAME SINCE ROBERT QUEEN DIED.
AND WALTER STEELE-- WHO, BY THE WAY-- DOESN'T PLAY AT MY LEVEL...
...I'M SURE IS PREOCCUPIED WITH KEEPING HIS JOB NOW THAT QUEEN'S BRAT IS BACK.
WHAT THE HELL?!
KRRKKSHH

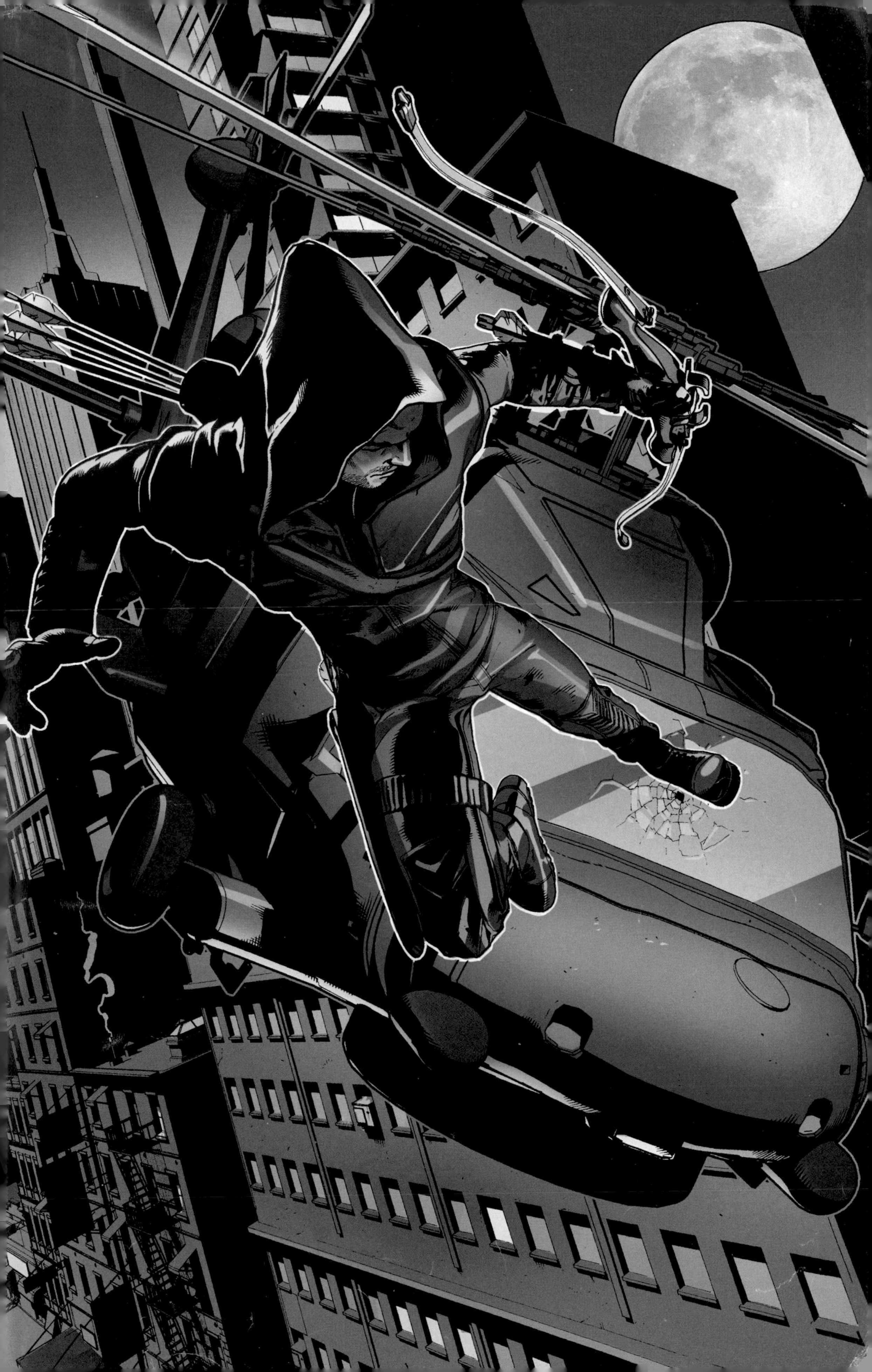

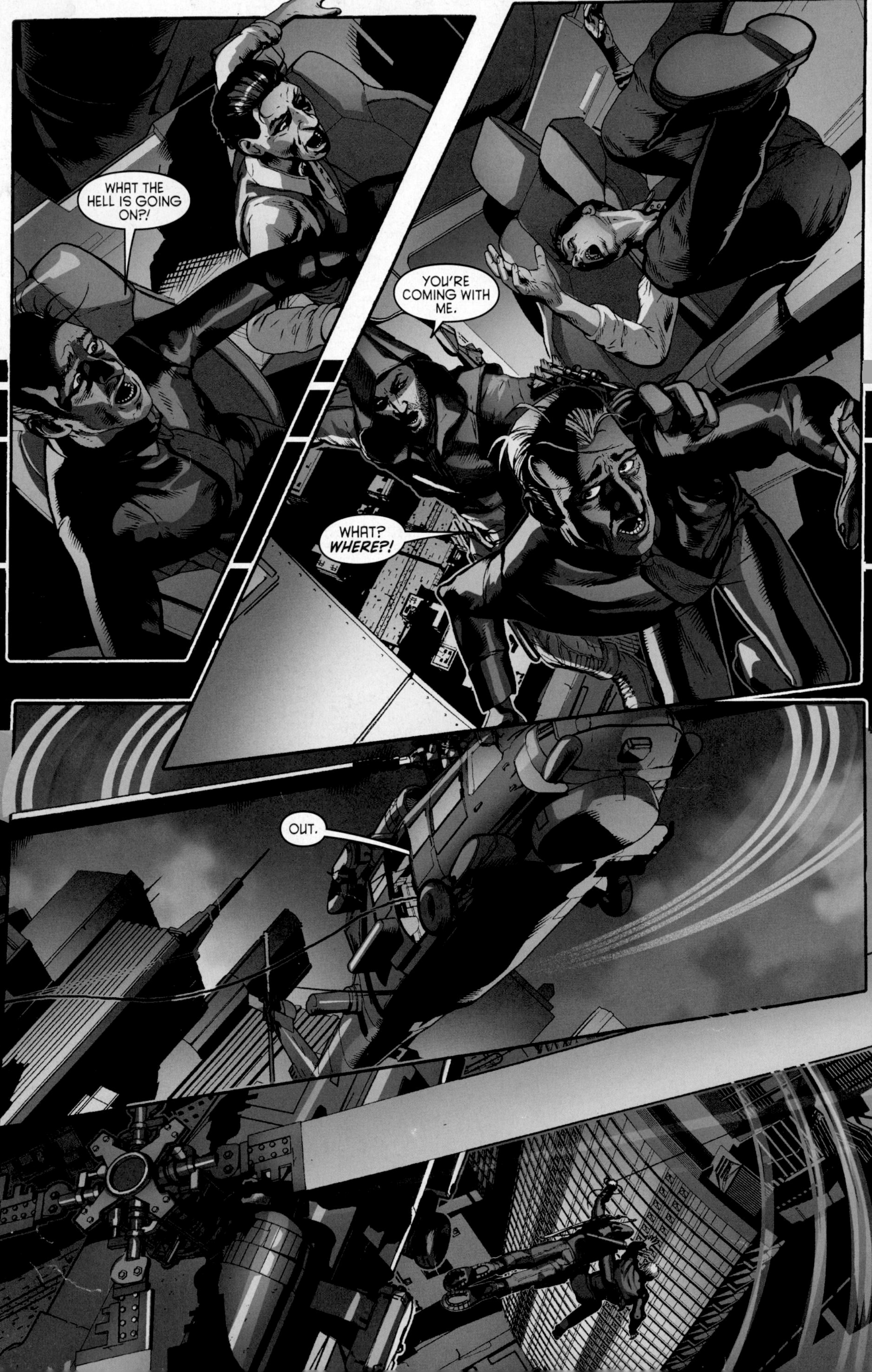
WHAT THE HELL IS GOING ON?!
YOU'RE COMING WITH ME.
WHAT? *WHERE?!*
OUT.

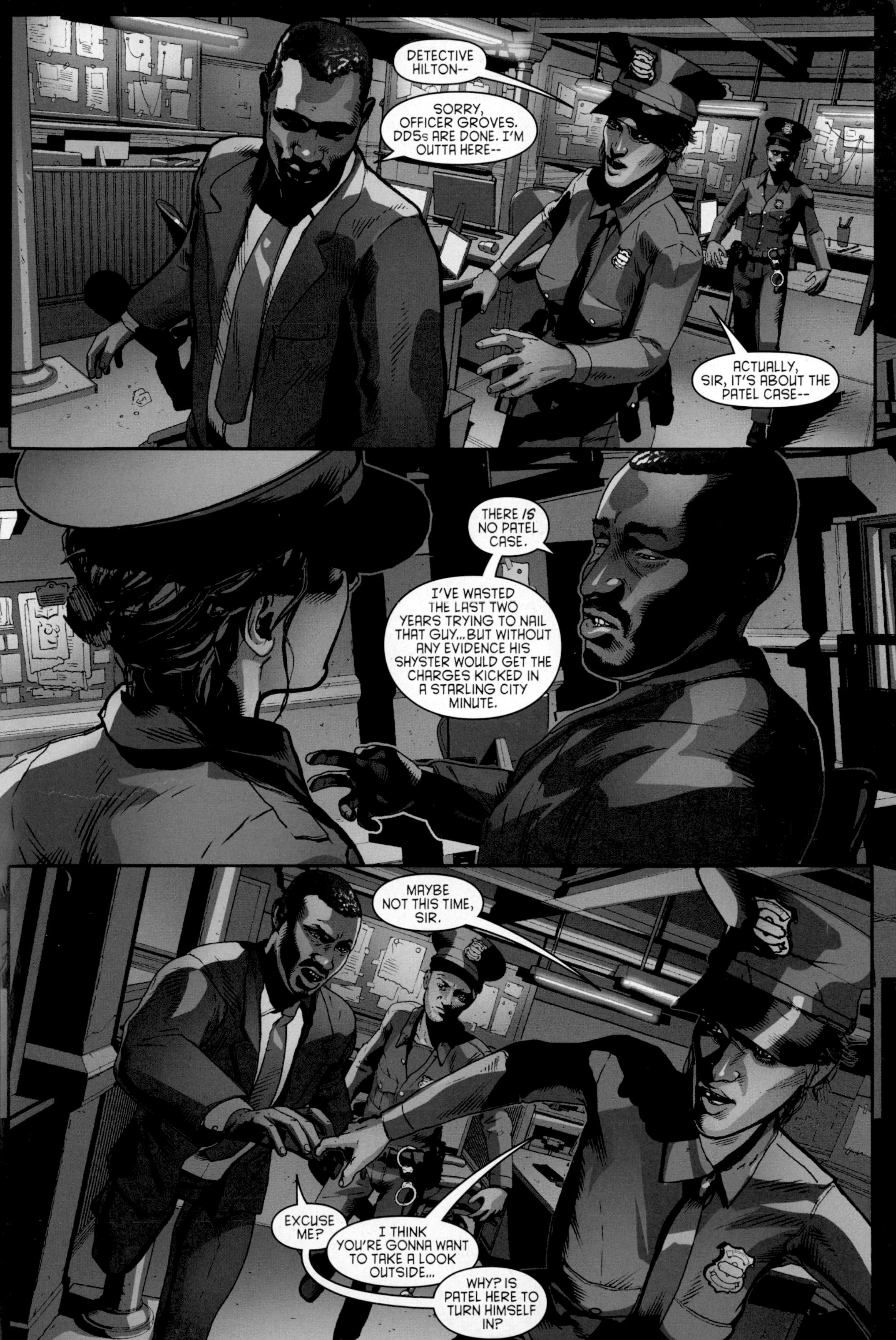
DETECTIVE HILTON--
SORRY, OFFICER GROVES. DD5s ARE DONE. I'M OUTTA HERE--
ACTUALLY, SIR, IT'S ABOUT THE PATEL CASE--
THERE IS NO PATEL CASE.
I'VE WASTED THE LAST TWO YEARS TRYING TO NAIL THAT GUY...BUT WITHOUT ANY EVIDENCE HIS SHYSTER WOULD GET THE CHARGES KICKED IN A STARLING CITY MINUTE.
MAYBE NOT THIS TIME, SIR.
EXCUSE ME?
I THINK YOU'RE GONNA WANT TO TAKE A LOOK OUTSIDE...
WHY? IS PATEL HERE TO TURN HIMSELF IN?

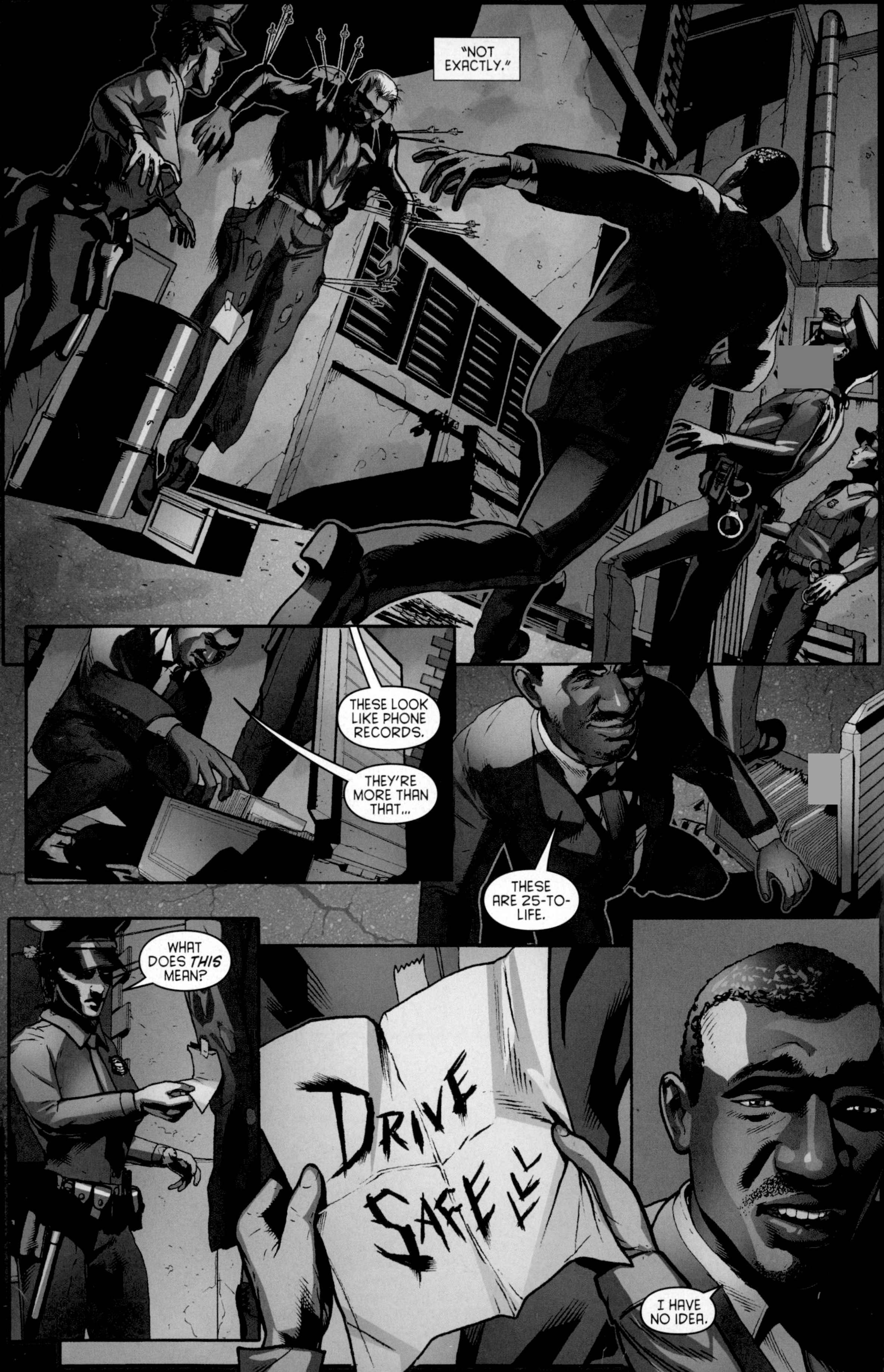
"NOT EXACTLY."
THESE LOOK LIKE PHONE RECORDS.
THEY'RE MORE THAN THAT...
THESE ARE 25-TO-LIFE.
WHAT DOES *THIS* MEAN?
DRIVE SAFE
I HAVE NO IDEA.

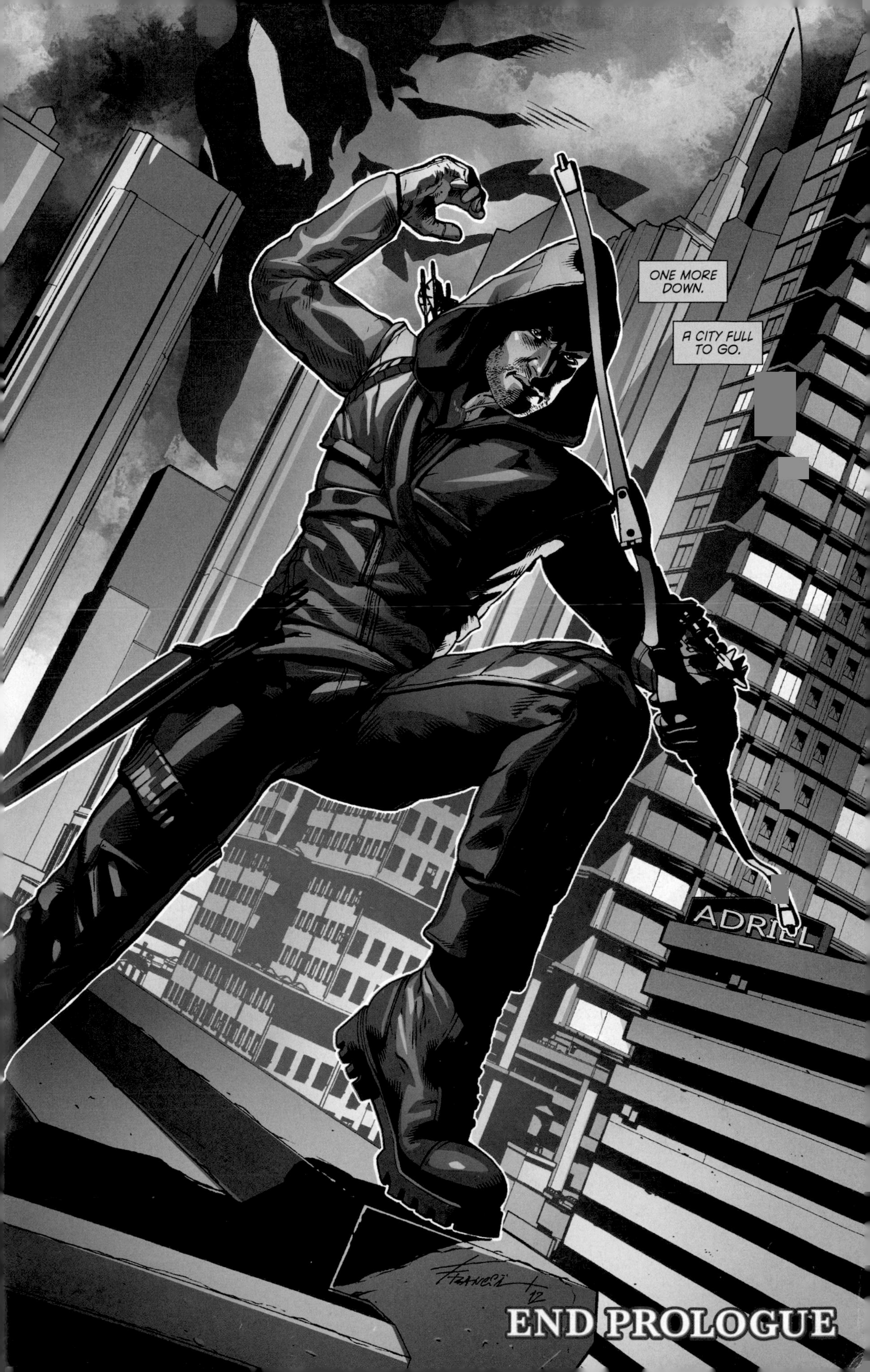
ONE MORE DOWN.
A CITY FULL TO GO.
ADRIEL
END PROLOGUE

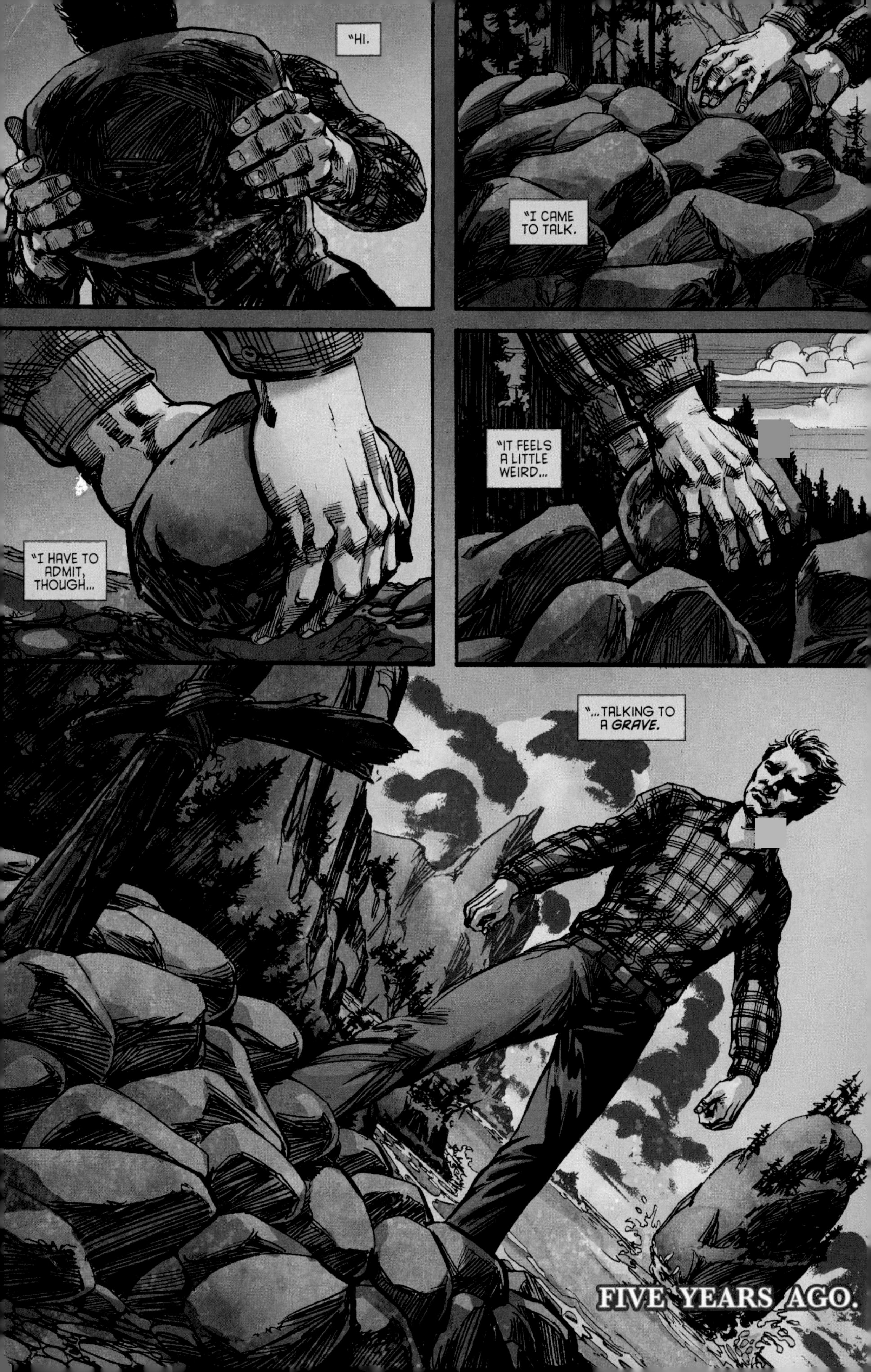
"HI.
"I CAME TO TALK.
"I HAVE TO ADMIT, THOUGH...
"IT FEELS A LITTLE WEIRD...
"...TALKING TO A *GRAVE.*
FIVE YEARS AGO.

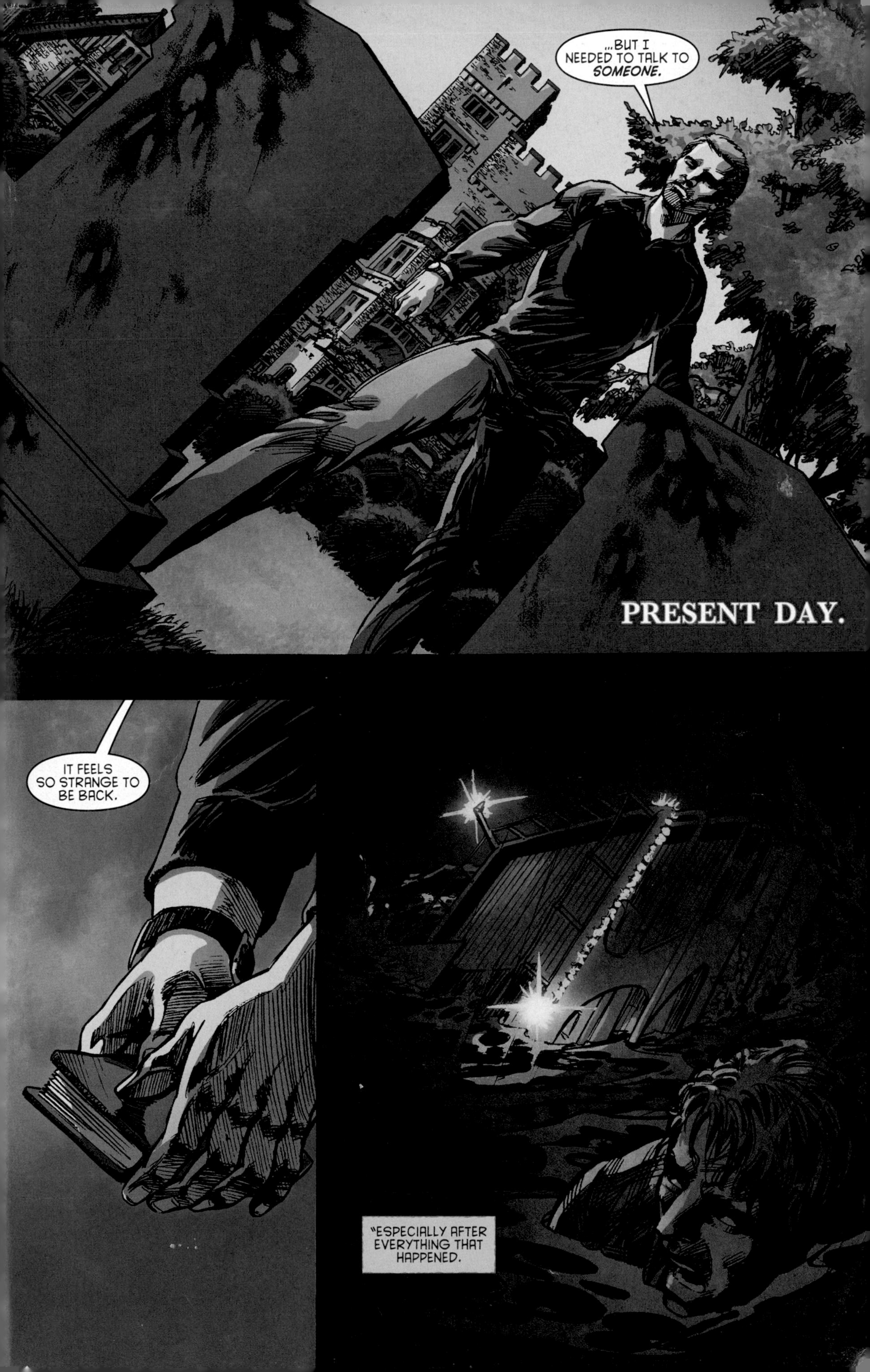
...BUT I NEEDED TO TALK TO SOMEONE.
PRESENT DAY.
IT FEELS SO STRANGE TO BE BACK.
"ESPECIALLY AFTER EVERYTHING THAT HAPPENED.

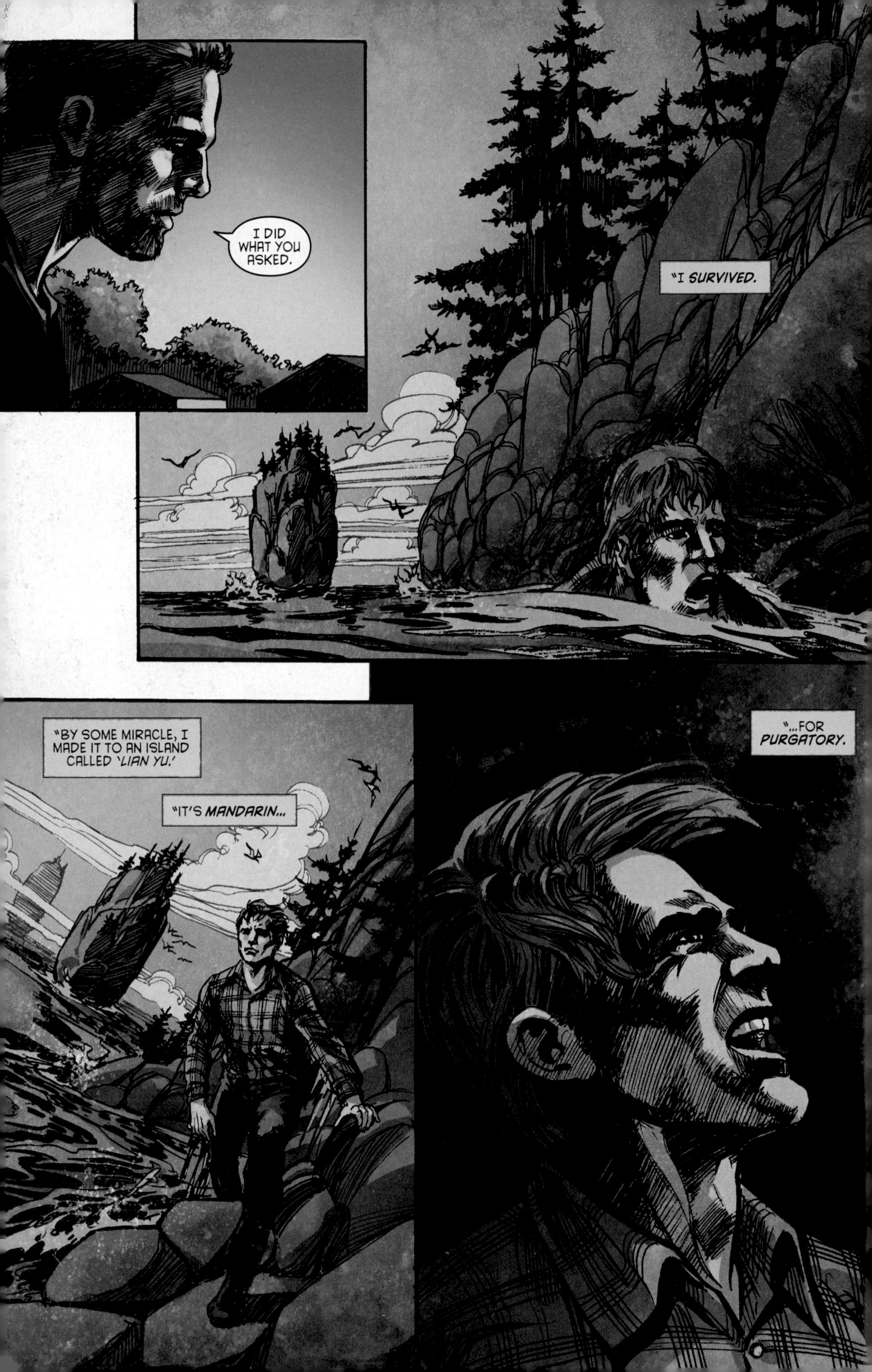
I DID WHAT YOU ASKED.
"I SURVIVED.
"BY SOME MIRACLE, I MADE IT TO AN ISLAND CALLED 'LIAN YU.'
"IT'S MANDARIN...
"...FOR PURGATORY.

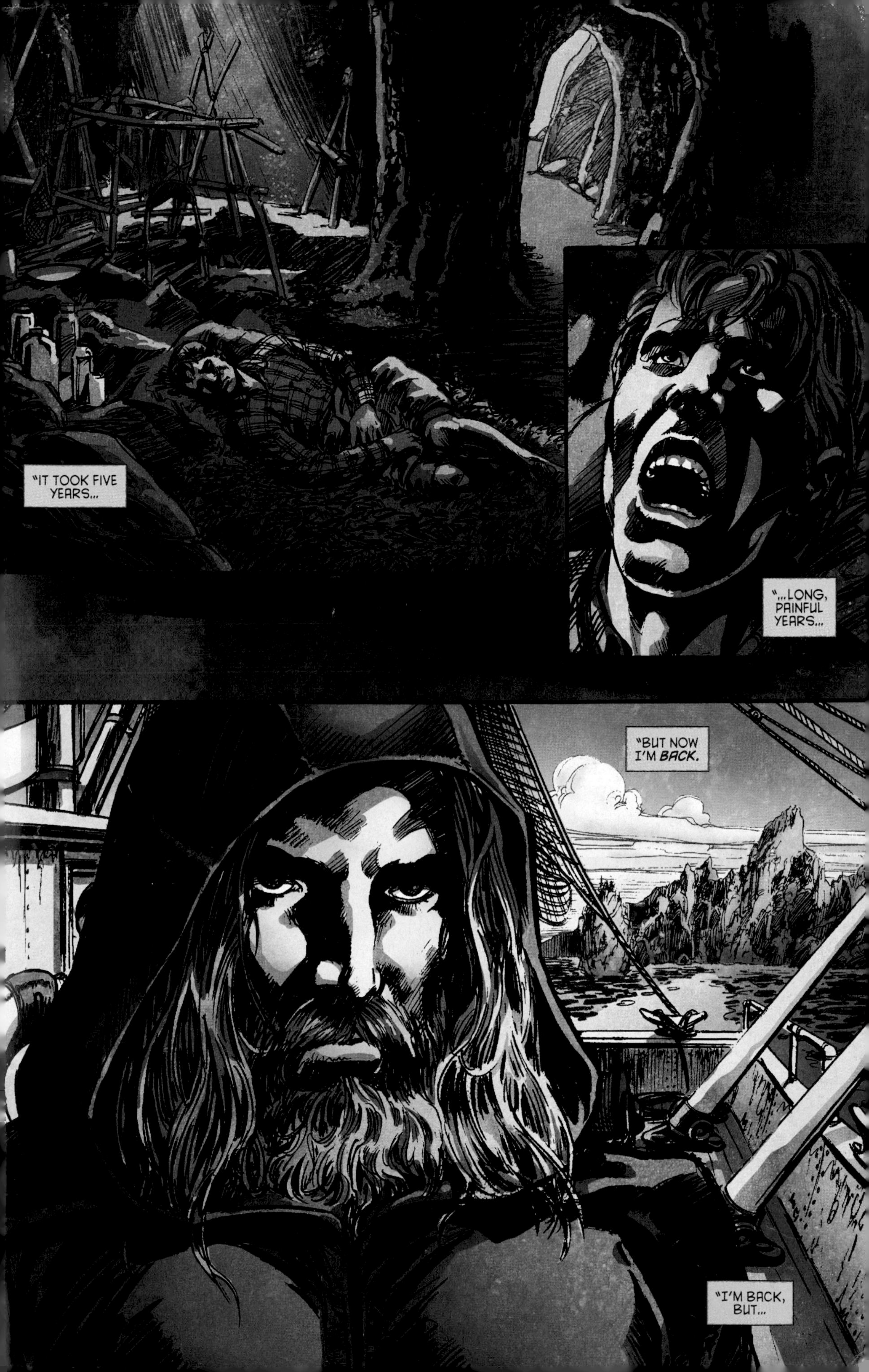
"IT TOOK FIVE YEARS...
"...LONG, PAINFUL YEARS...
"BUT NOW I'M *BACK*.
"I'M BACK, BUT...

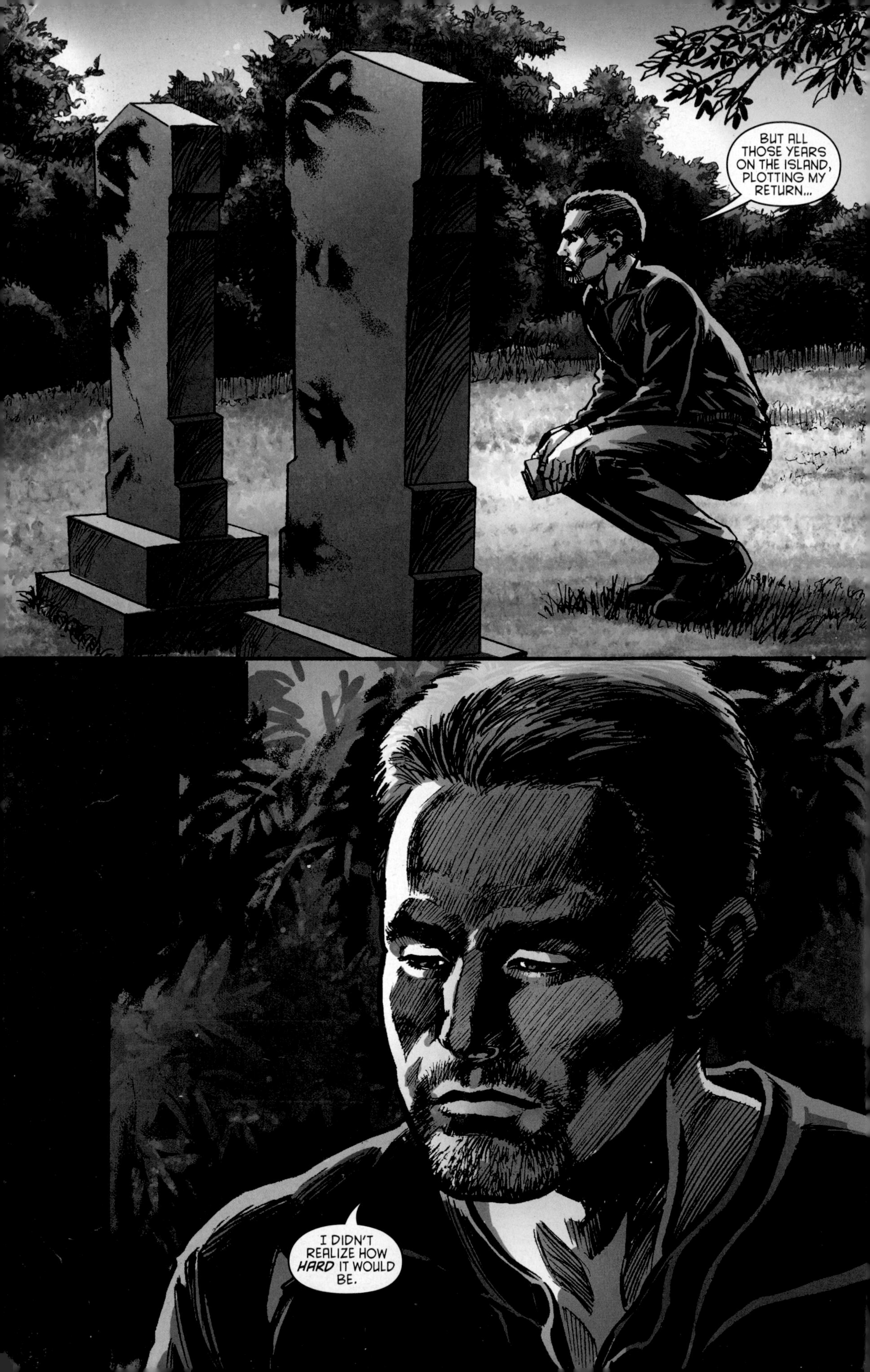
BUT ALL THOSE YEARS ON THE ISLAND, PLOTTING MY RETURN...
I DIDN'T REALIZE HOW *HARD* IT WOULD BE.

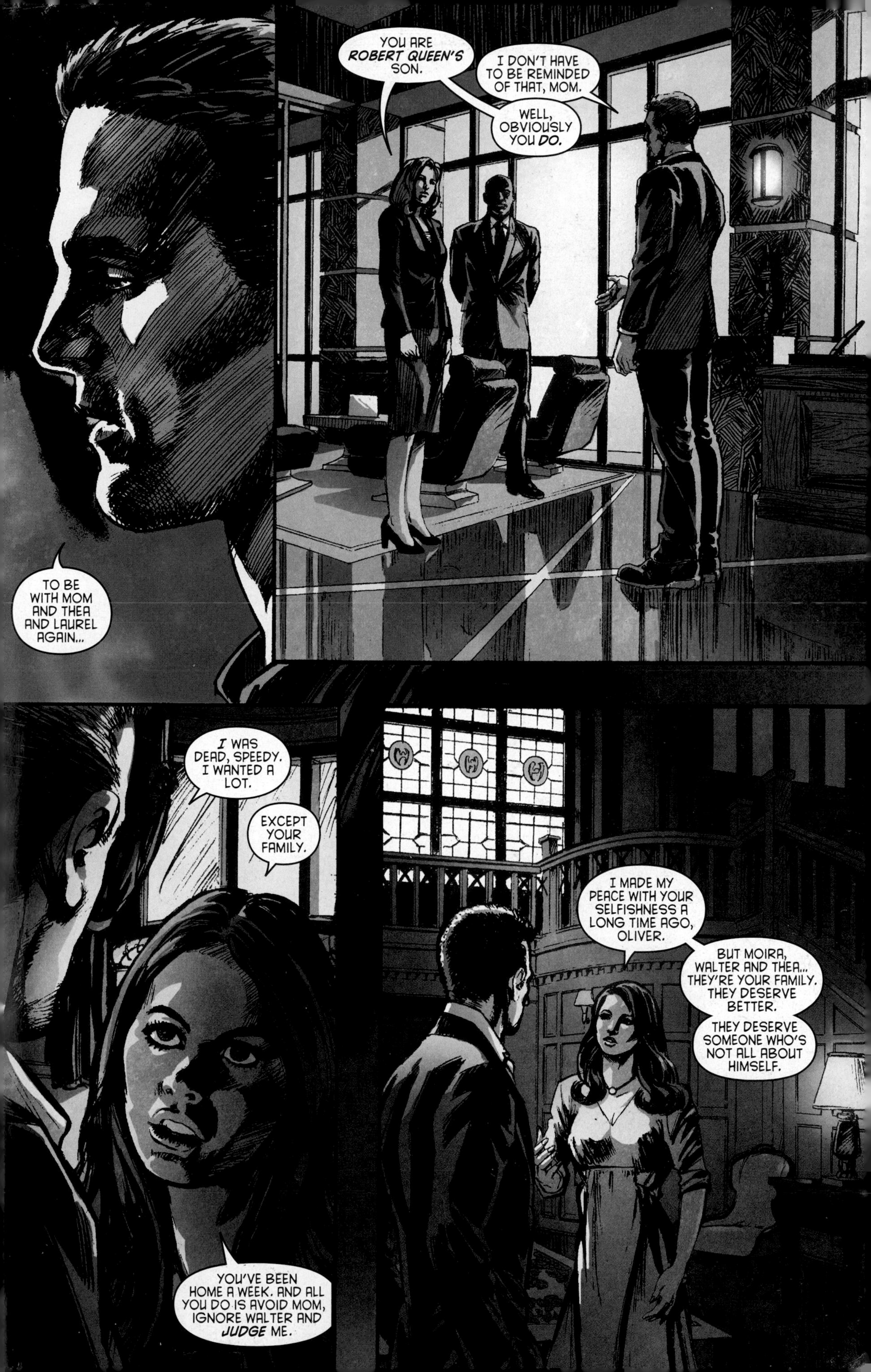

YOU ARE ROBERT QUEEN'S SON.
I DON'T HAVE TO BE REMINDED OF THAT, MOM.
WELL, OBVIOUSLY YOU DO.
TO BE WITH MOM AND THEA AND LAUREL AGAIN...
I WAS DEAD, SPEEDY. I WANTED A LOT.
EXCEPT YOUR FAMILY.
YOU'VE BEEN HOME A WEEK. AND ALL YOU DO IS AVOID MOM, IGNORE WALTER AND JUDGE ME.
I MADE MY PEACE WITH YOUR SELFISHNESS A LONG TIME AGO, OLIVER.
BUT MOIRA, WALTER AND THEA... THEY'RE YOUR FAMILY. THEY DESERVE BETTER.
THEY DESERVE SOMEONE WHO'S NOT ALL ABOUT HIMSELF.

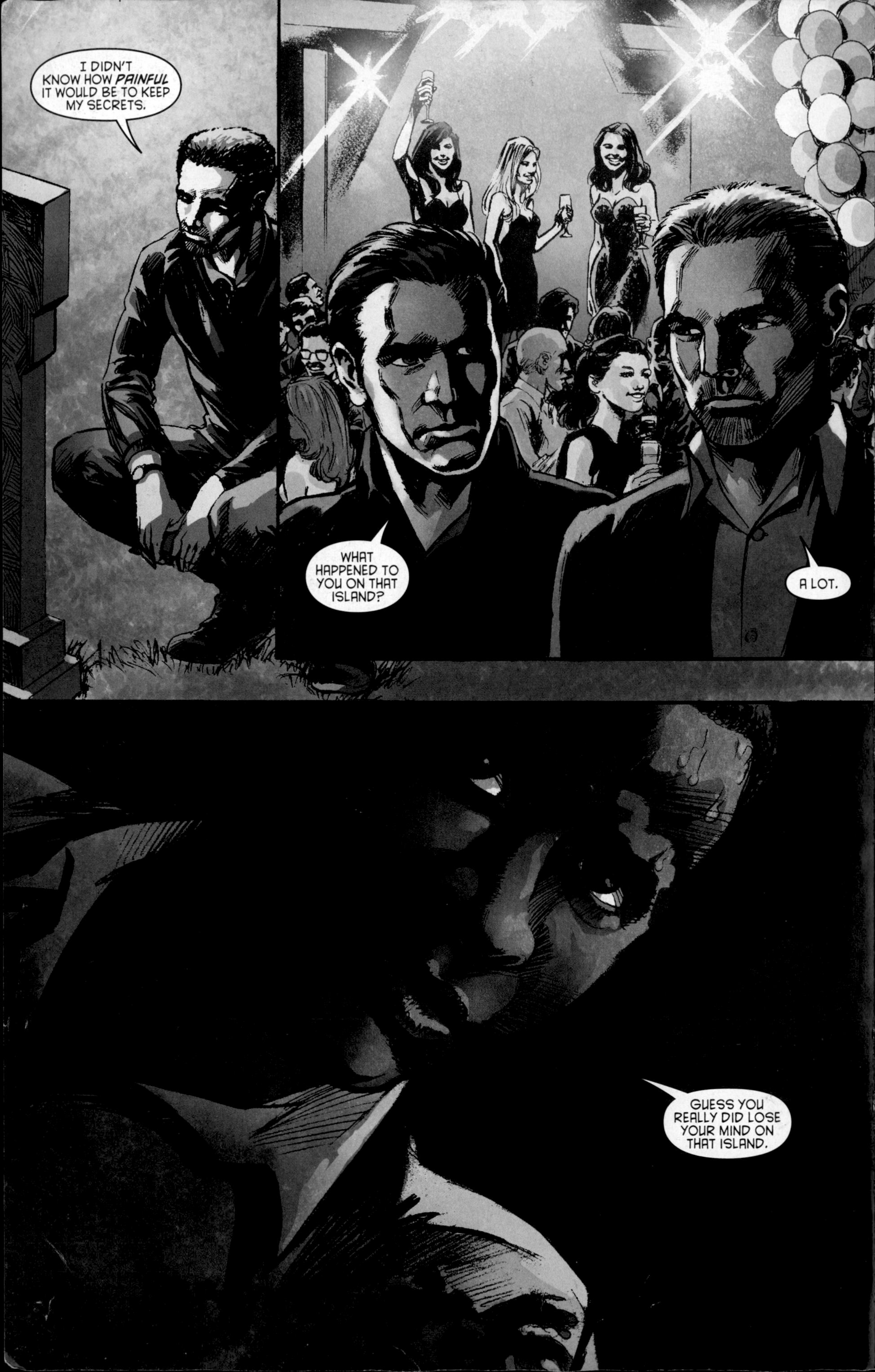
I DIDN'T KNOW HOW PAINFUL IT WOULD BE TO KEEP MY SECRETS.
WHAT HAPPENED TO YOU ON THAT ISLAND?
A LOT.
GUESS YOU REALLY DID LOSE YOUR MIND ON THAT ISLAND.

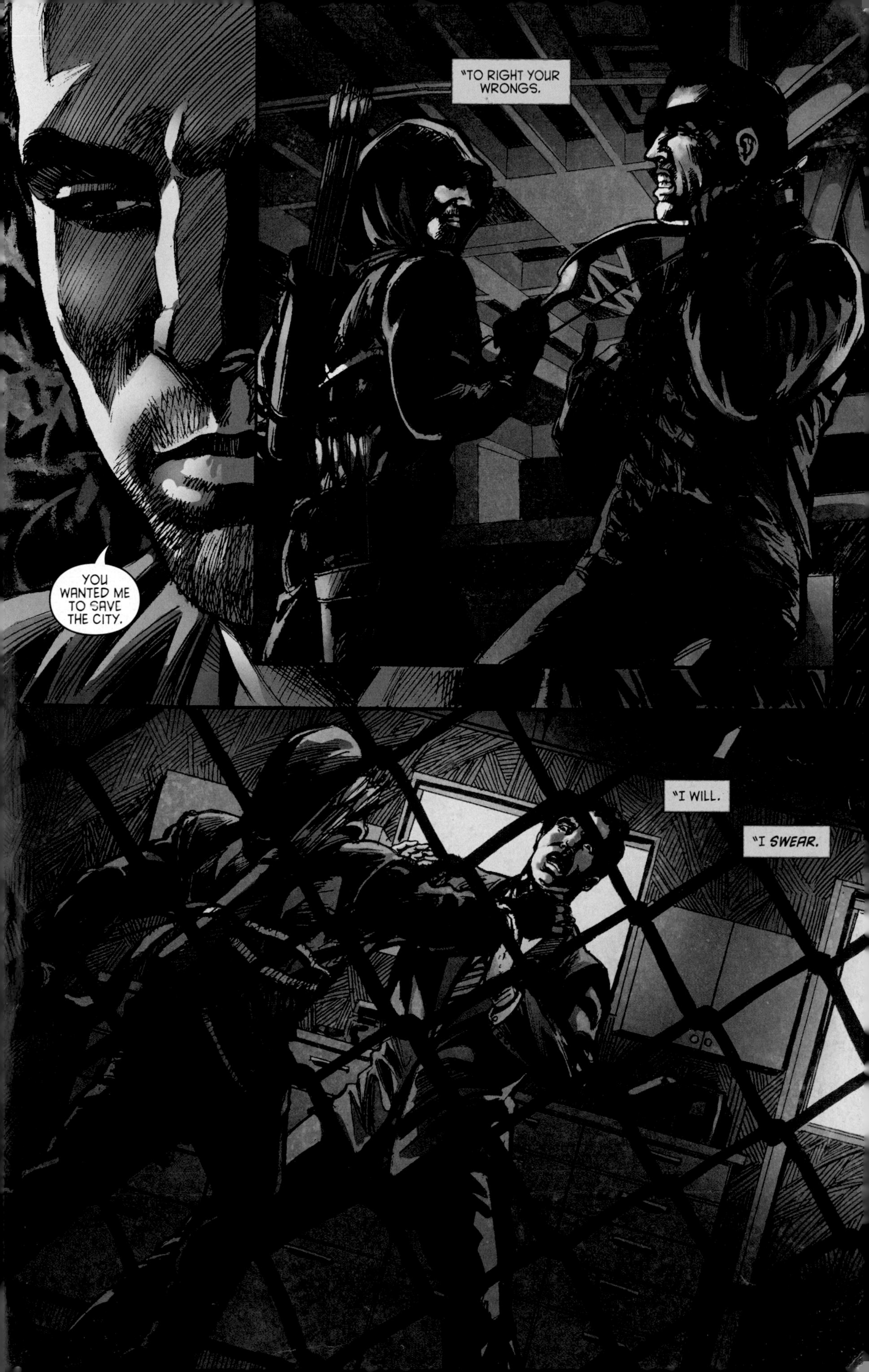
"TO RIGHT YOUR WRONGS.
YOU WANTED ME TO SAVE THE CITY.
"I WILL.
"I SWEAR.

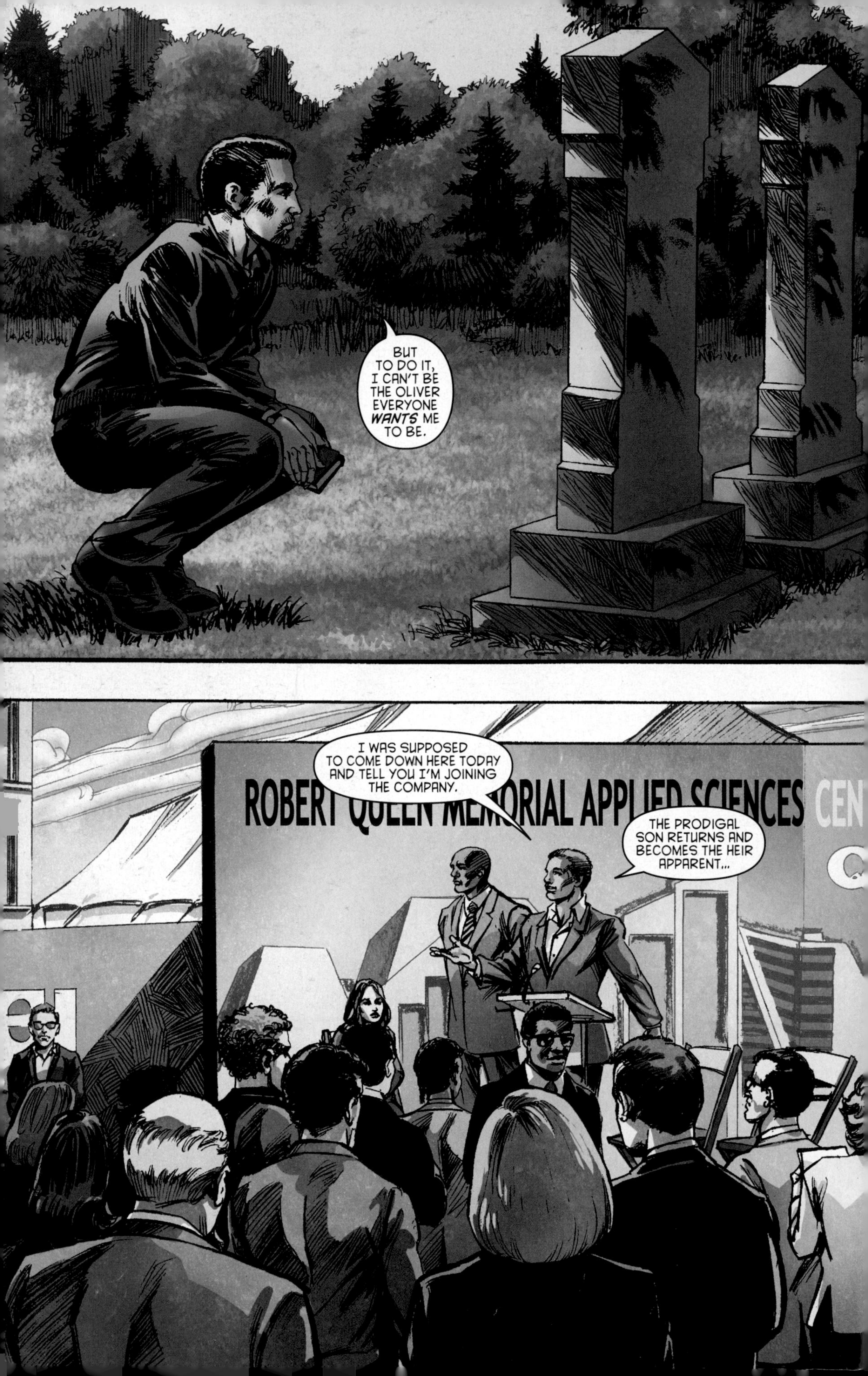
BUT TO DO IT, I CAN'T BE THE OLIVER EVERYONE *WANTS* ME TO BE.
I WAS SUPPOSED TO COME DOWN HERE TODAY AND TELL YOU I'M JOINING THE COMPANY.
ROBERT QUEEN MEMORIAL APPLIED SCIENCES CEN
THE PRODIGAL SON RETURNS AND BECOMES THE HEIR APPARENT...

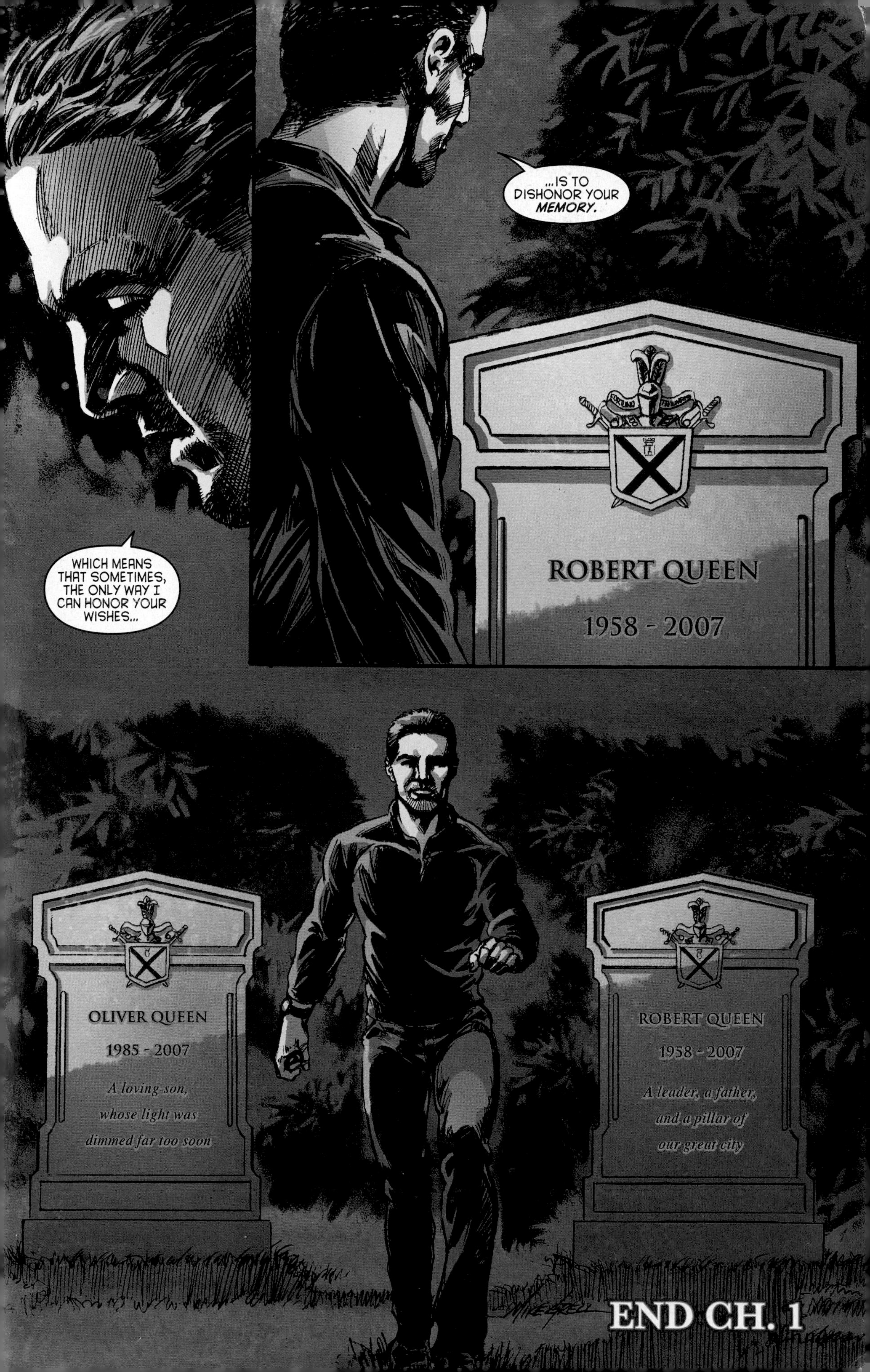
WHICH MEANS THAT SOMETIMES, THE ONLY WAY I CAN HONOR YOUR WISHES...
...IS TO DISHONOR YOUR MEMORY.
ROBERT QUEEN
1958 - 2007
OLIVER QUEEN
1985 - 2007
A loving son, whose light was dimmed far too soon
ROBERT QUEEN
1958 - 2007
A leader, a father, and a pillar of our great city
END CH. 1

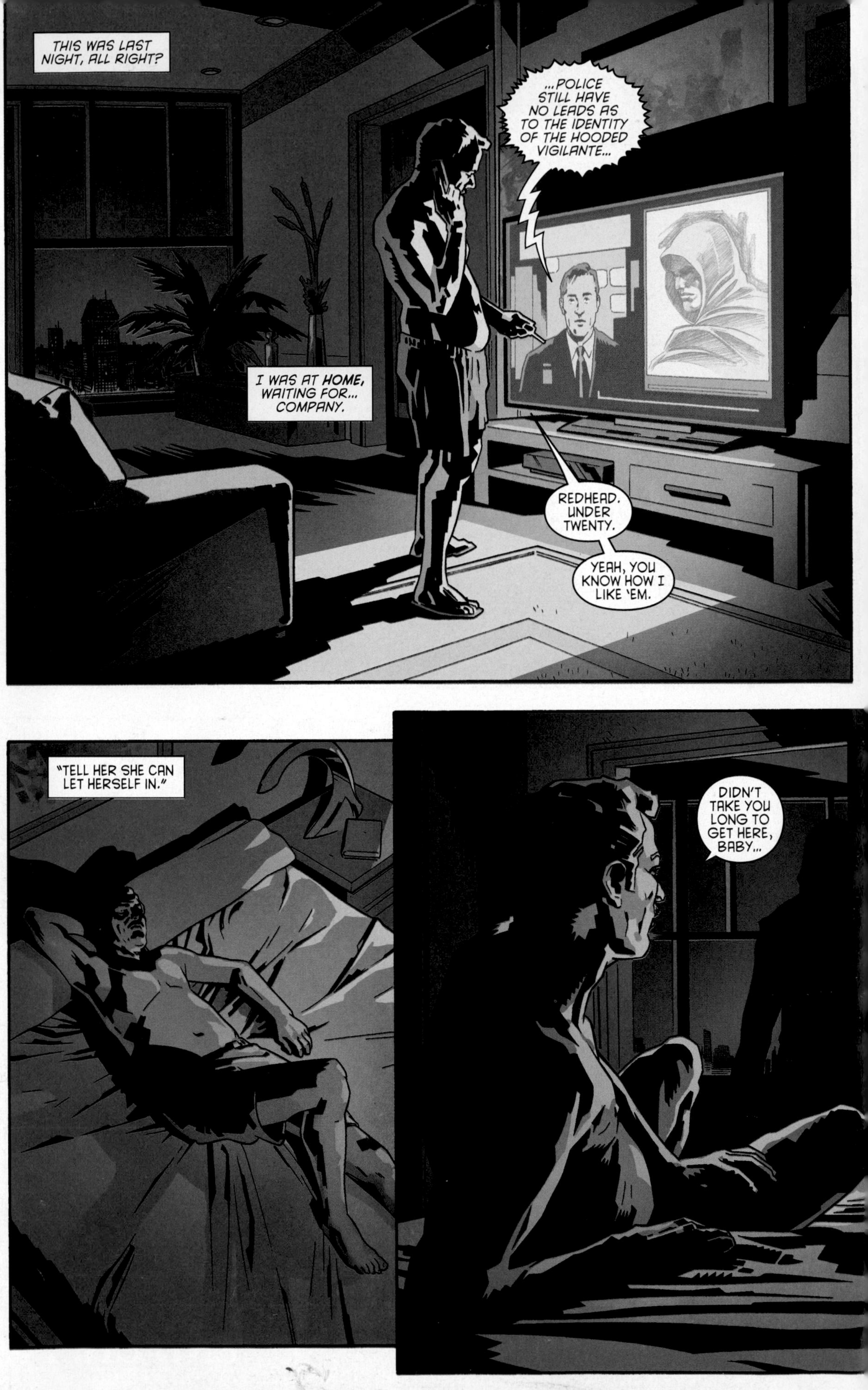
THIS WAS LAST NIGHT, ALL RIGHT?
...POLICE STILL HAVE NO LEADS AS TO THE IDENTITY OF THE HOODED VIGILANTE...
I WAS AT HOME, WAITING FOR... COMPANY.
REDHEAD. UNDER TWENTY.
YEAH, YOU KNOW HOW I LIKE 'EM.
"TELL HER SHE CAN LET HERSELF IN."
DIDN'T TAKE YOU LONG TO GET HERE, BABY...

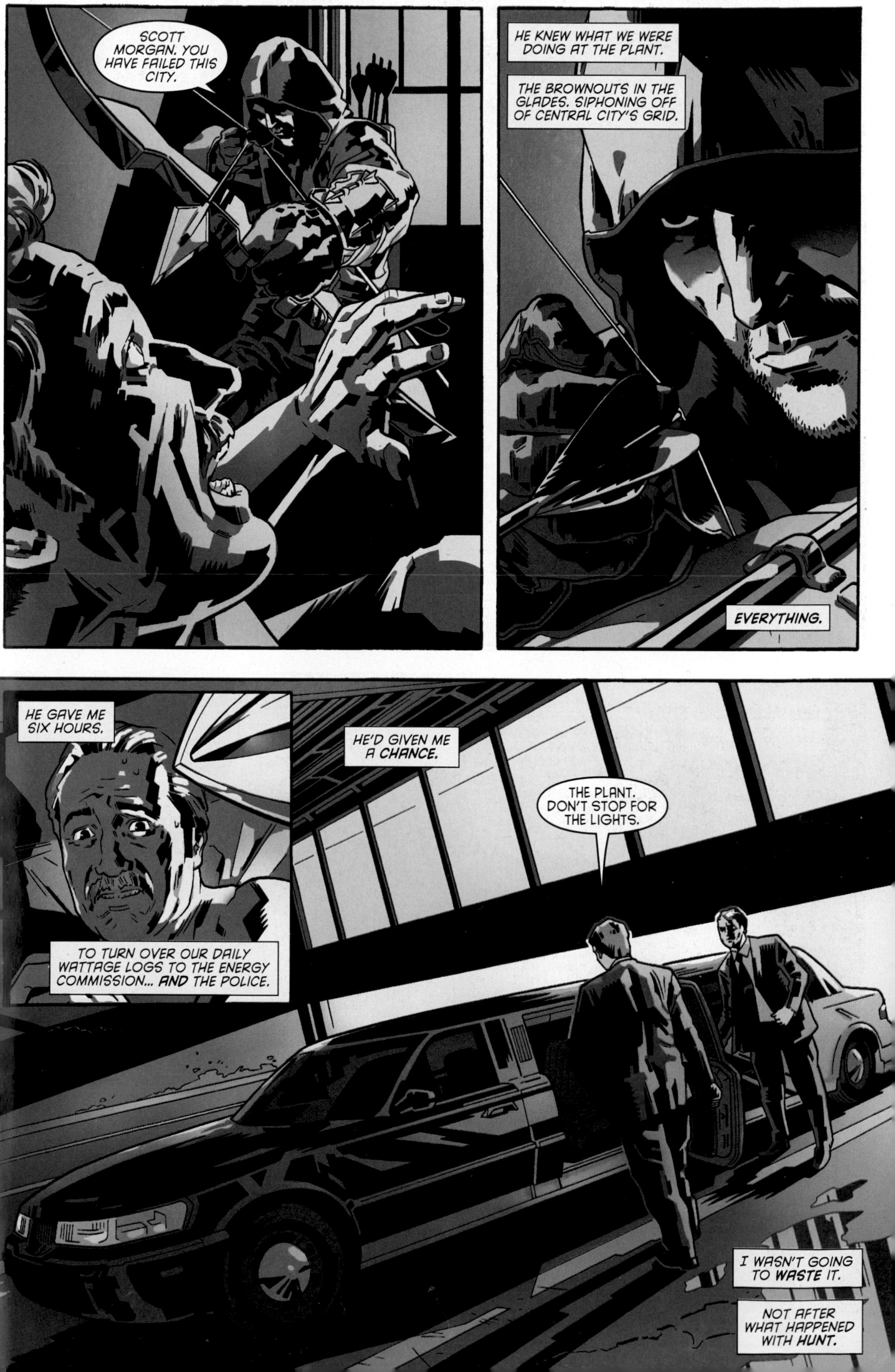
SCOTT MORGAN. YOU HAVE FAILED THIS CITY.
HE KNEW WHAT WE WERE DOING AT THE PLANT.
THE BROWNOUTS IN THE GLADES. SIPHONING OFF OF CENTRAL CITY'S GRID.
EVERYTHING.
HE GAVE ME SIX HOURS.
TO TURN OVER OUR DAILY WATTAGE LOGS TO THE ENERGY COMMISSION... AND THE POLICE.
HE'D GIVEN ME A CHANCE.
THE PLANT. DON'T STOP FOR THE LIGHTS.
I WASN'T GOING TO WASTE IT.
NOT AFTER WHAT HAPPENED WITH HUNT.

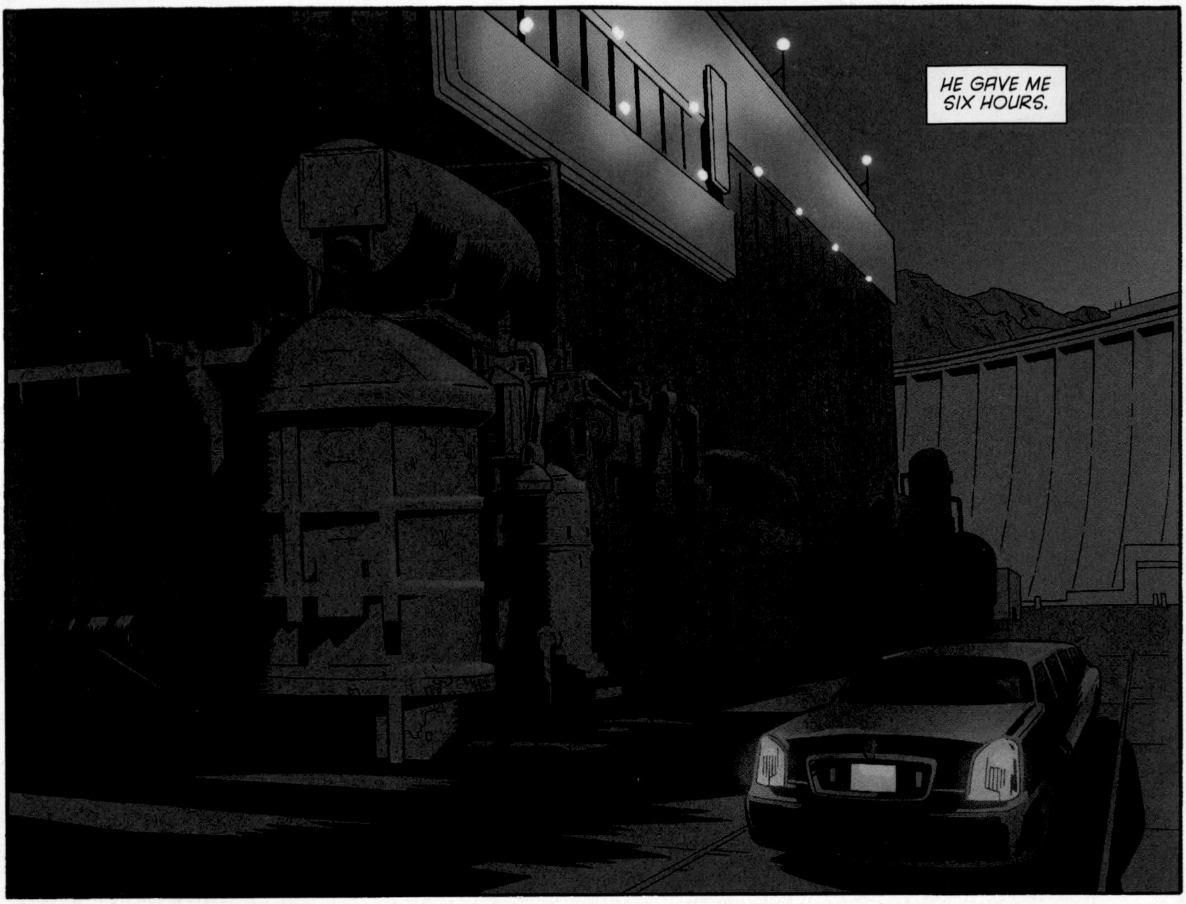
HE GAVE ME SIX HOURS.

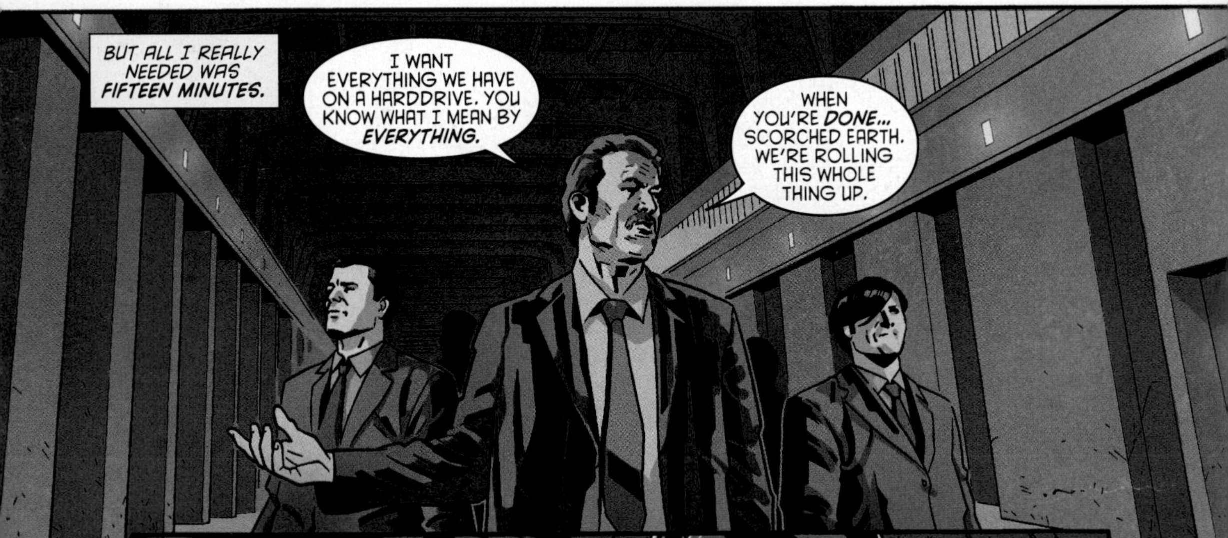
BUT ALL I REALLY NEEDED WAS FIFTEEN MINUTES.
I WANT EVERYTHING WE HAVE ON A HARDDRIVE. YOU KNOW WHAT I MEAN BY EVERYTHING.
WHEN YOU'RE DONE... SCORCHED EARTH. WE'RE ROLLING THIS WHOLE THING UP.

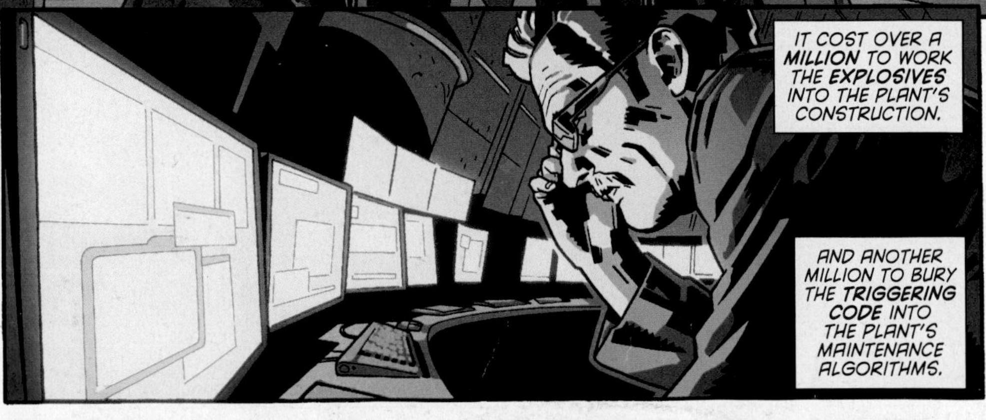
IT COST OVER A MILLION TO WORK THE EXPLOSIVES INTO THE PLANT'S CONSTRUCTION.
AND ANOTHER MILLION TO BURY THE TRIGGERING CODE INTO THE PLANT'S MAINTENANCE ALGORITHMS.

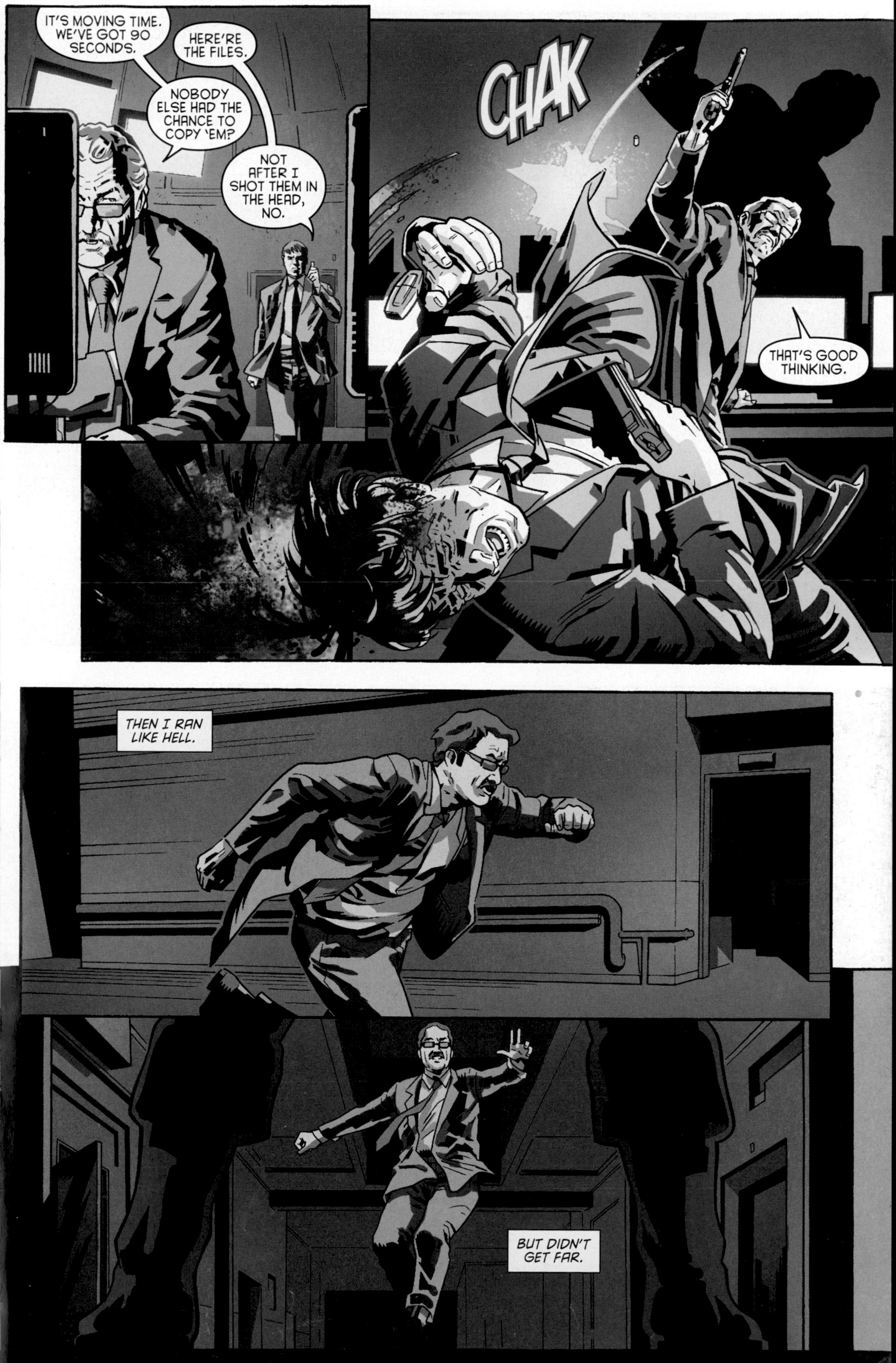
IT'S MOVING TIME. WE'VE GOT 90 SECONDS.
HERE'RE THE FILES.
NOBODY ELSE HAD THE CHANCE TO COPY 'EM?
NOT AFTER I SHOT THEM IN THE HEAD, NO.
CHAK
THAT'S GOOD THINKING.
THEN I RAN LIKE HELL.
BUT DIDN'T GET FAR.

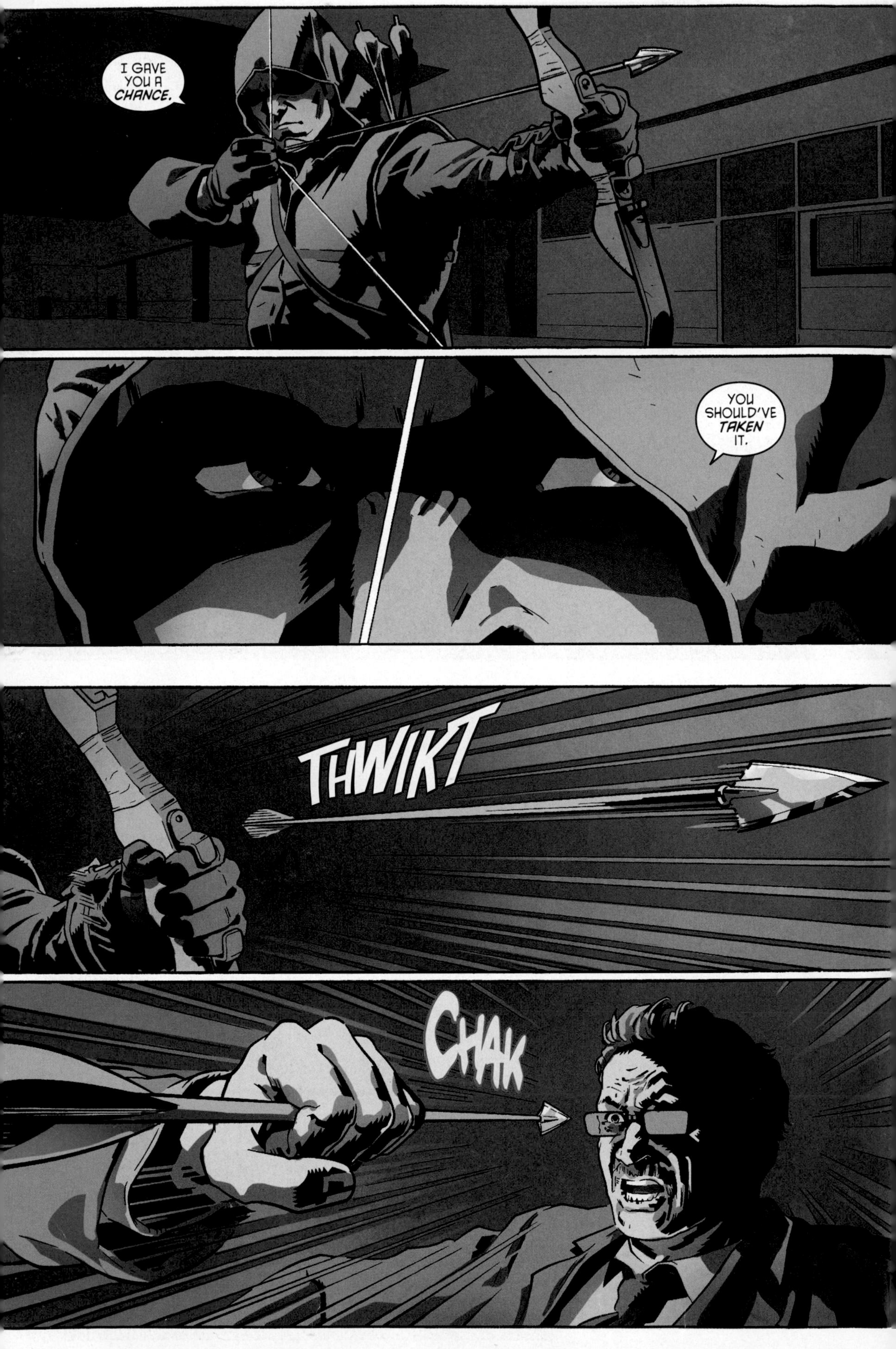
I GAVE YOU A *CHANCE.*
YOU SHOULD'VE *TAKEN* IT.
THWIKT
CHAK

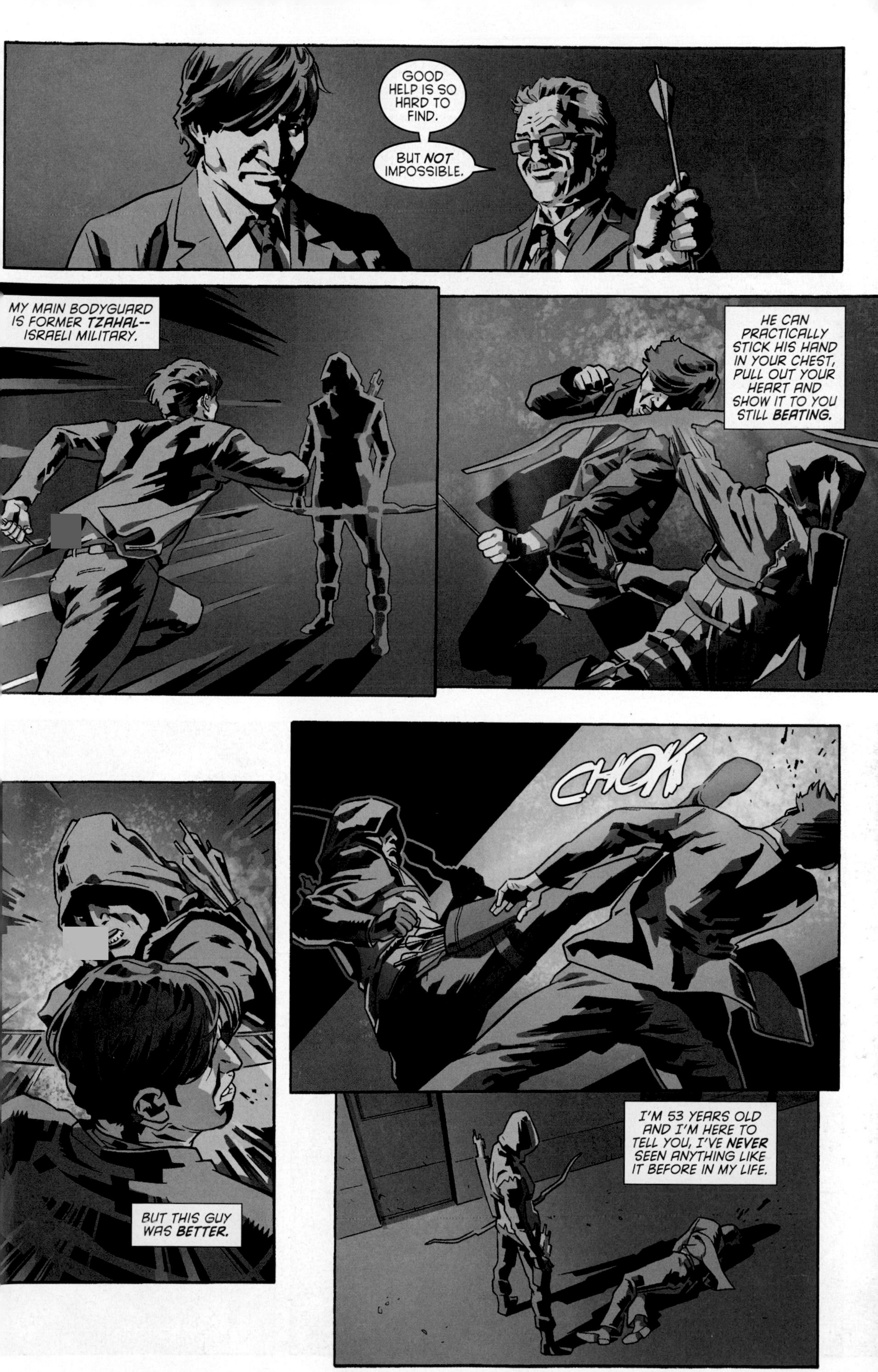
GOOD HELP IS SO HARD TO FIND.
BUT NOT IMPOSSIBLE.
MY MAIN BODYGUARD IS FORMER TZAHAL-- ISRAELI MILITARY.
HE CAN PRACTICALLY STICK HIS HAND IN YOUR CHEST, PULL OUT YOUR HEART AND SHOW IT TO YOU STILL BEATING.
BUT THIS GUY WAS BETTER.
CHOK
I'M 53 YEARS OLD AND I'M HERE TO TELL YOU, I'VE NEVER SEEN ANYTHING LIKE IT BEFORE IN MY LIFE.

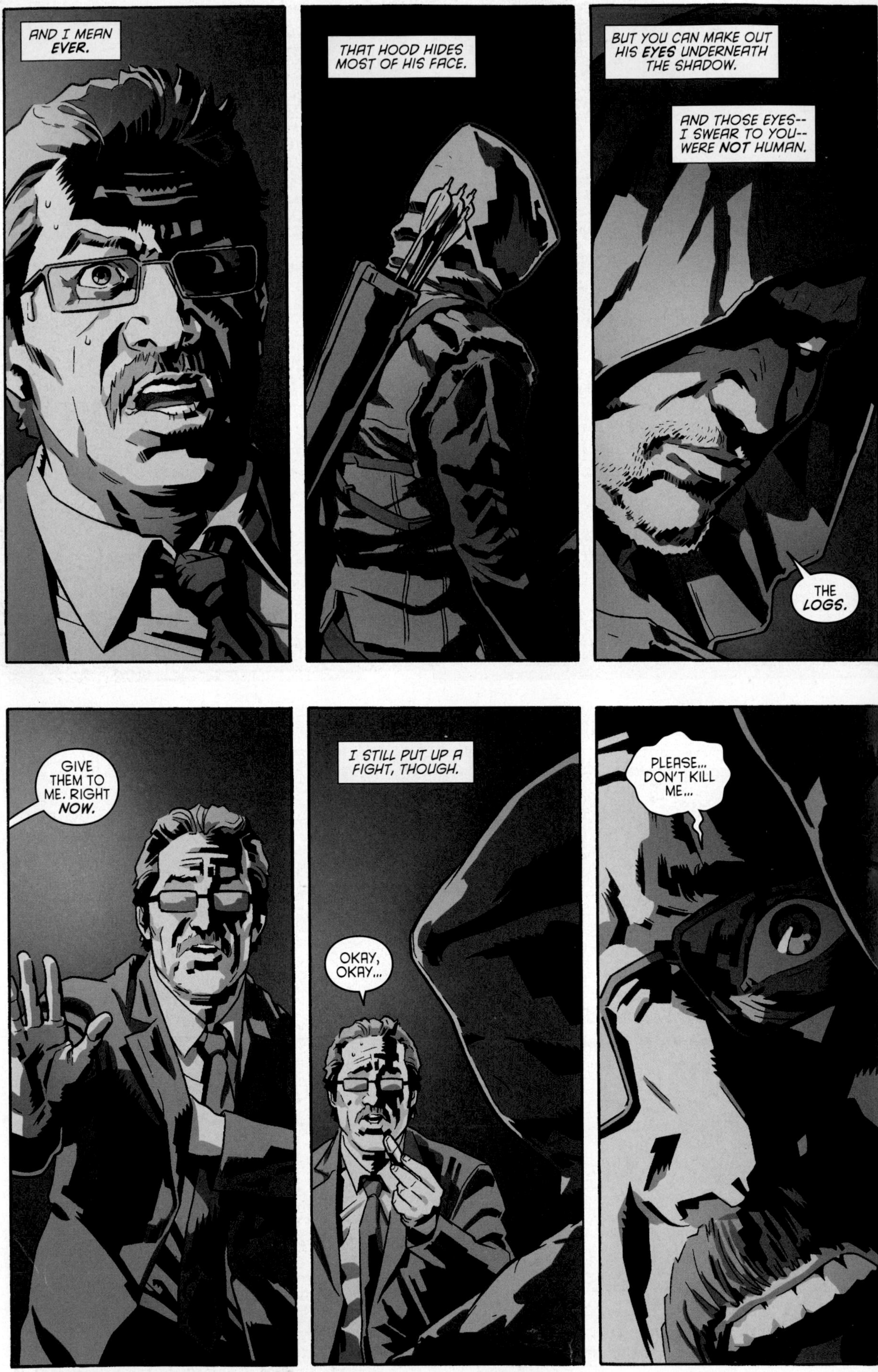
AND I MEAN EVER.
THAT HOOD HIDES MOST OF HIS FACE.
BUT YOU CAN MAKE OUT HIS EYES UNDERNEATH THE SHADOW.
AND THOSE EYES-- I SWEAR TO YOU-- WERE NOT HUMAN.
THE LOGS.
GIVE THEM TO ME. RIGHT NOW.
I STILL PUT UP A FIGHT, THOUGH.
OKAY, OKAY...
PLEASE... DON'T KILL ME...

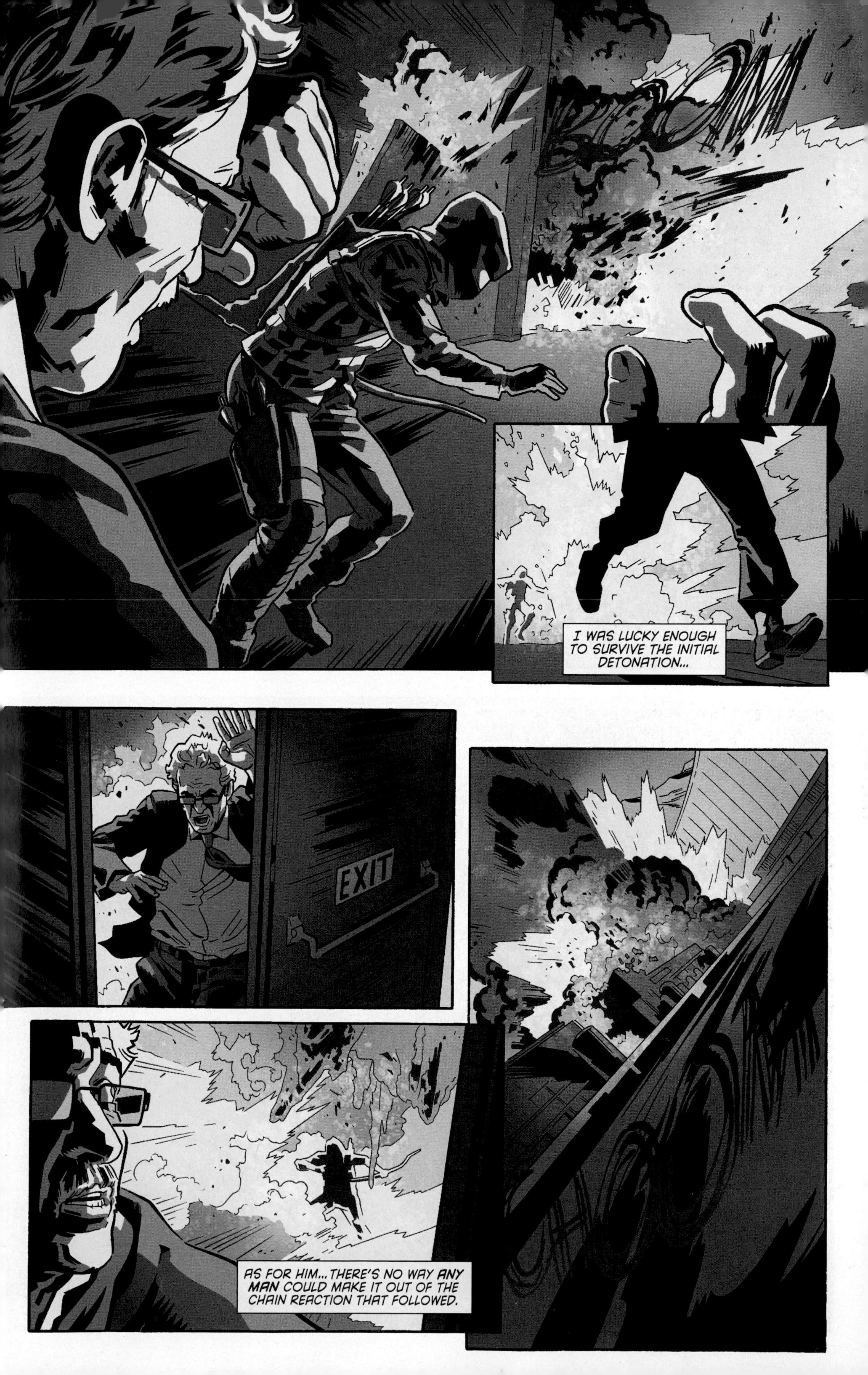
I WAS LUCKY ENOUGH TO SURVIVE THE INITIAL DETONATION...
EXIT
AS FOR HIM... THERE'S NO WAY ANY MAN COULD MAKE IT OUT OF THE CHAIN REACTION THAT FOLLOWED.

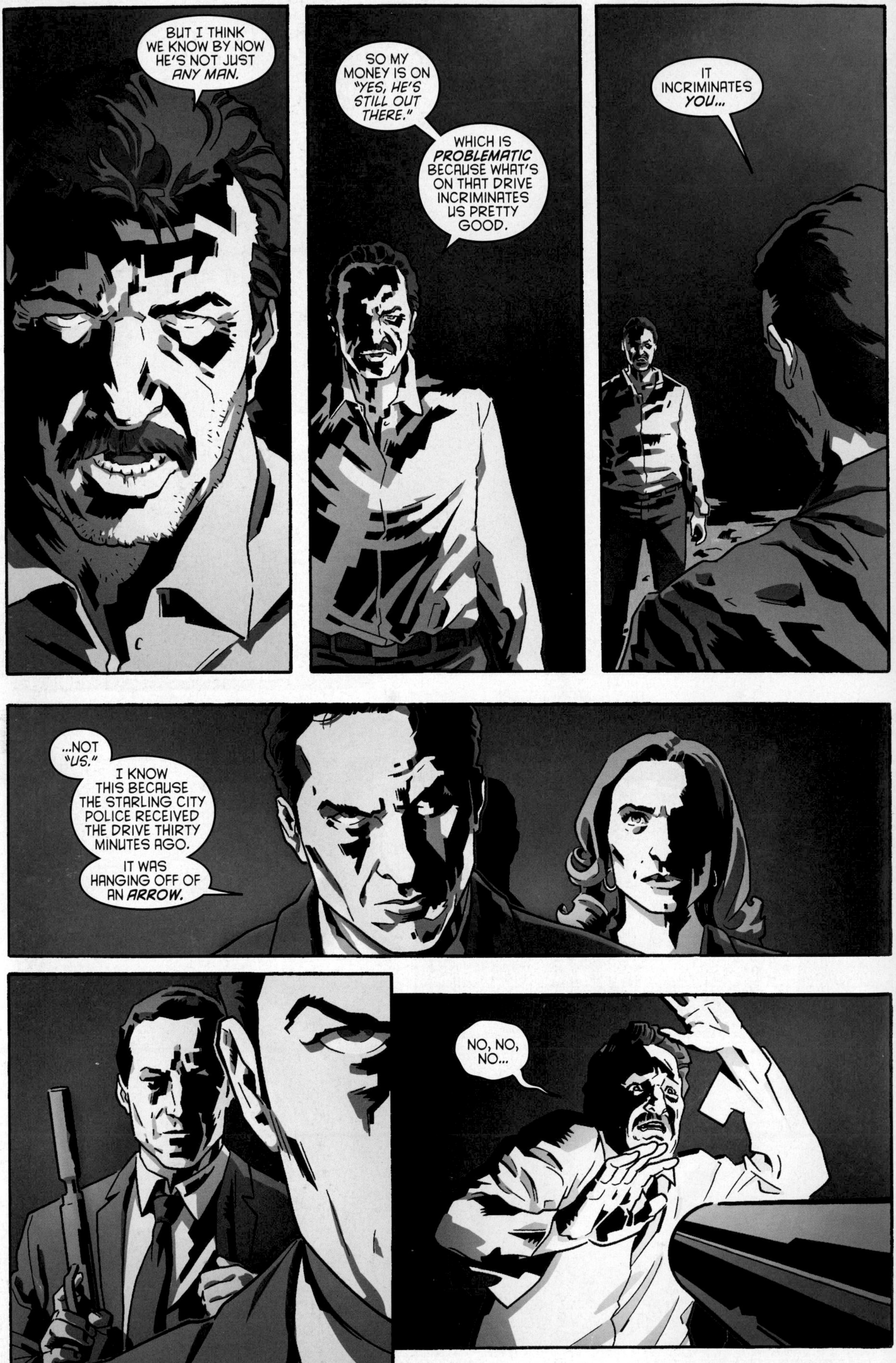
BUT I THINK WE KNOW BY NOW HE'S NOT JUST *ANY MAN.*
SO MY MONEY IS ON *"YES, HE'S STILL OUT THERE."*
WHICH IS ***PROBLEMATIC*** BECAUSE WHAT'S ON THAT DRIVE INCRIMINATES US PRETTY GOOD.
IT INCRIMINATES ***YOU...***
...NOT *"US."*
I KNOW THIS BECAUSE THE STARLING CITY POLICE RECEIVED THE DRIVE THIRTY MINUTES AGO.
IT WAS HANGING OFF OF AN ***ARROW.***
NO, NO, NO...

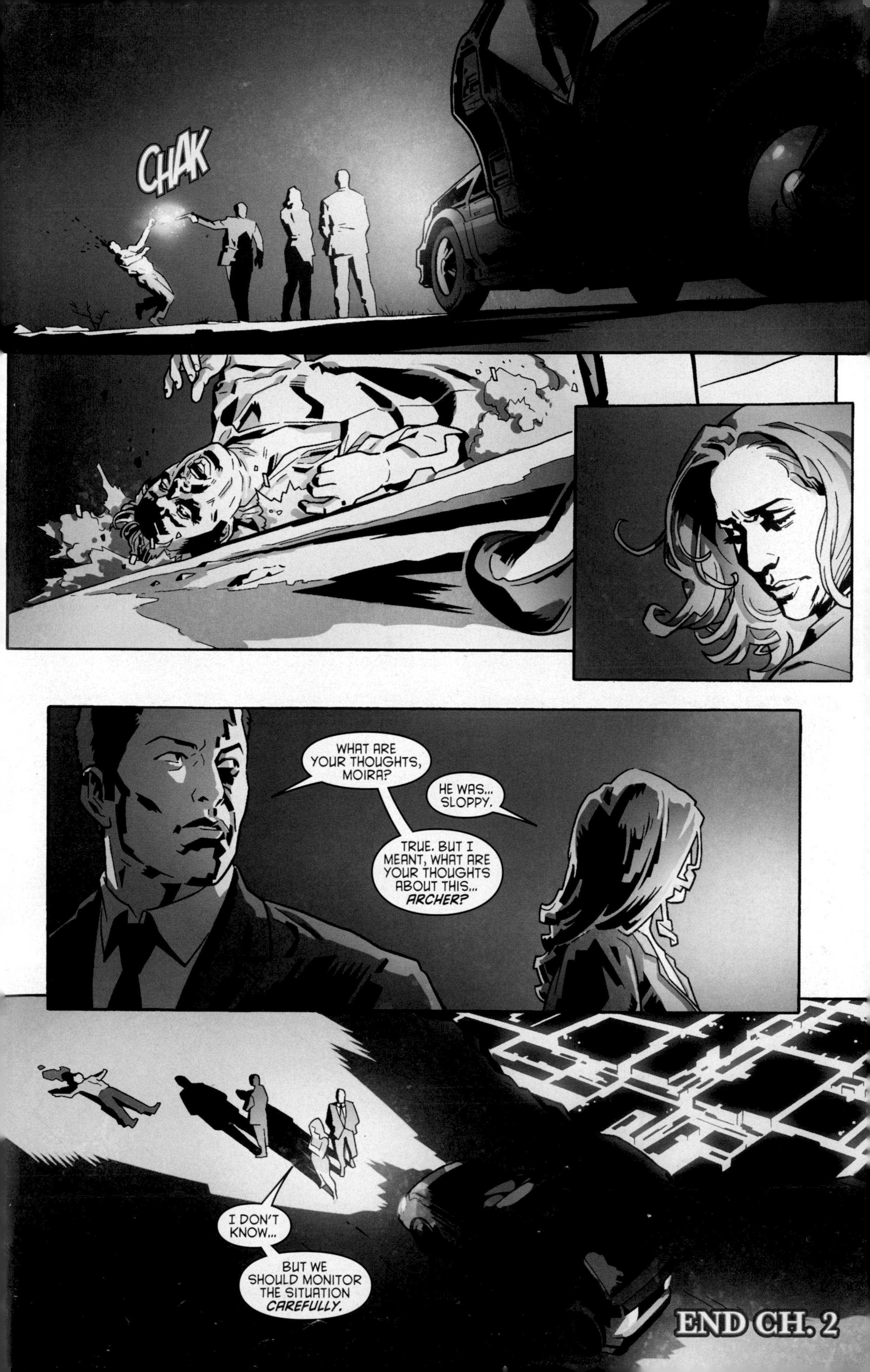
CHAK
WHAT ARE YOUR THOUGHTS, MOIRA?
HE WAS... SLOPPY.
TRUE. BUT I MEANT, WHAT ARE YOUR THOUGHTS ABOUT THIS... ARCHER?
I DON'T KNOW...
BUT WE SHOULD MONITOR THE SITUATION CAREFULLY.
END CH. 2

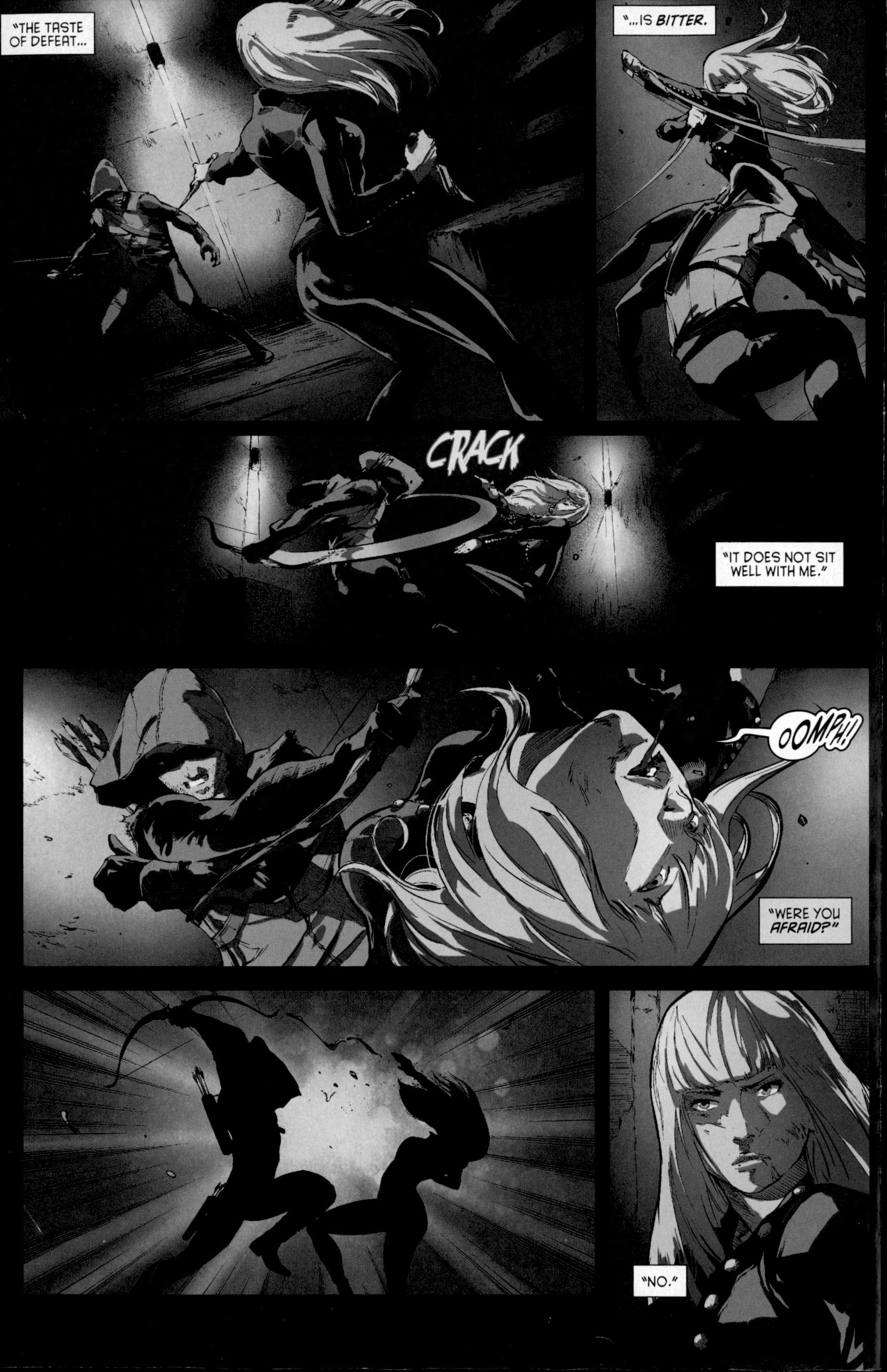
"THE TASTE OF DEFEAT...
"...IS BITTER.
CRACK
"IT DOES NOT SIT WELL WITH ME."
OOMPH!
"WERE YOU AFRAID?"
"NO."

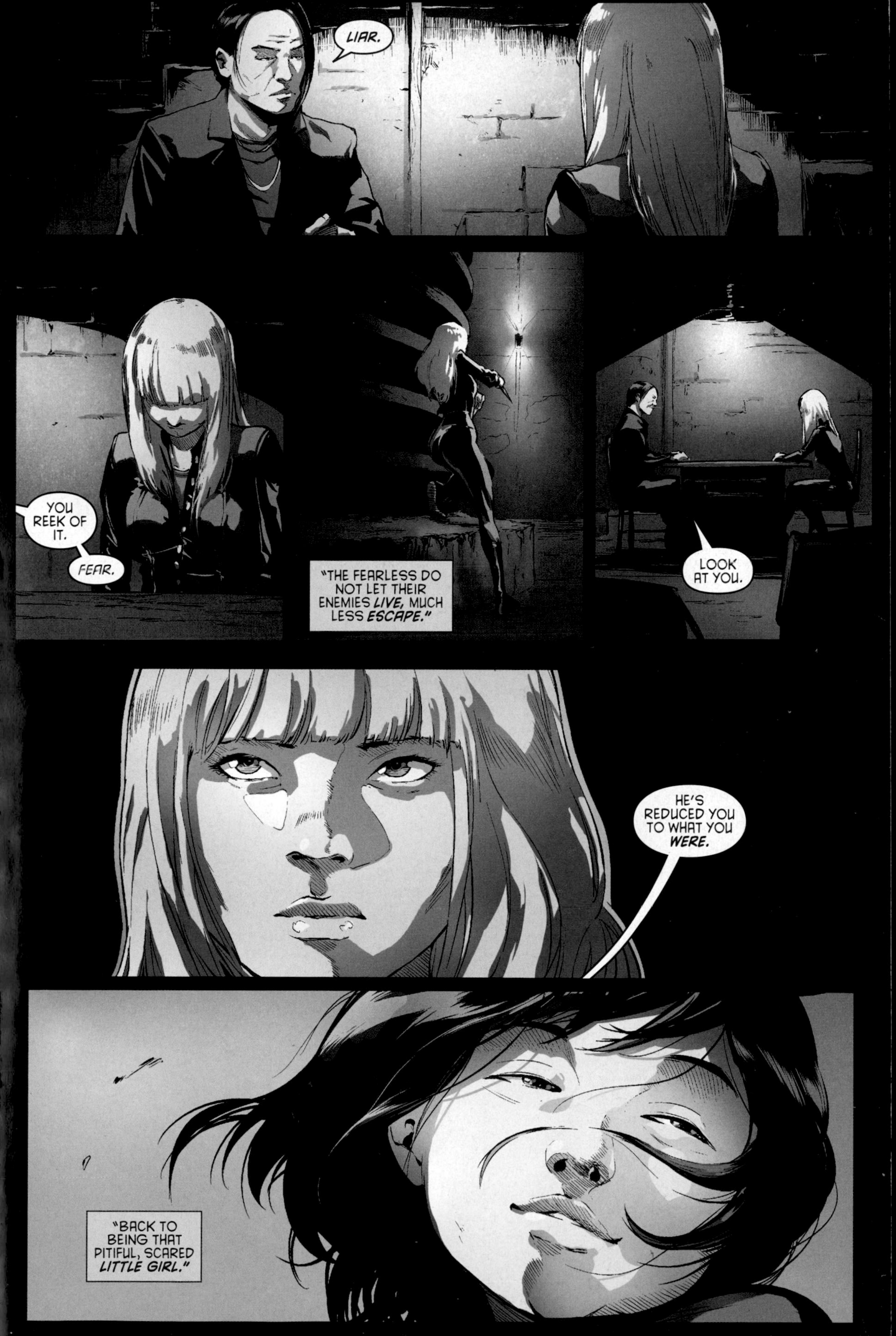
LIAR.
YOU REEK OF IT.
FEAR.
"THE FEARLESS DO NOT LET THEIR ENEMIES LIVE, MUCH LESS ESCAPE."
LOOK AT YOU.
HE'S REDUCED YOU TO WHAT YOU WERE.
"BACK TO BEING THAT PITIFUL, SCARED LITTLE GIRL."

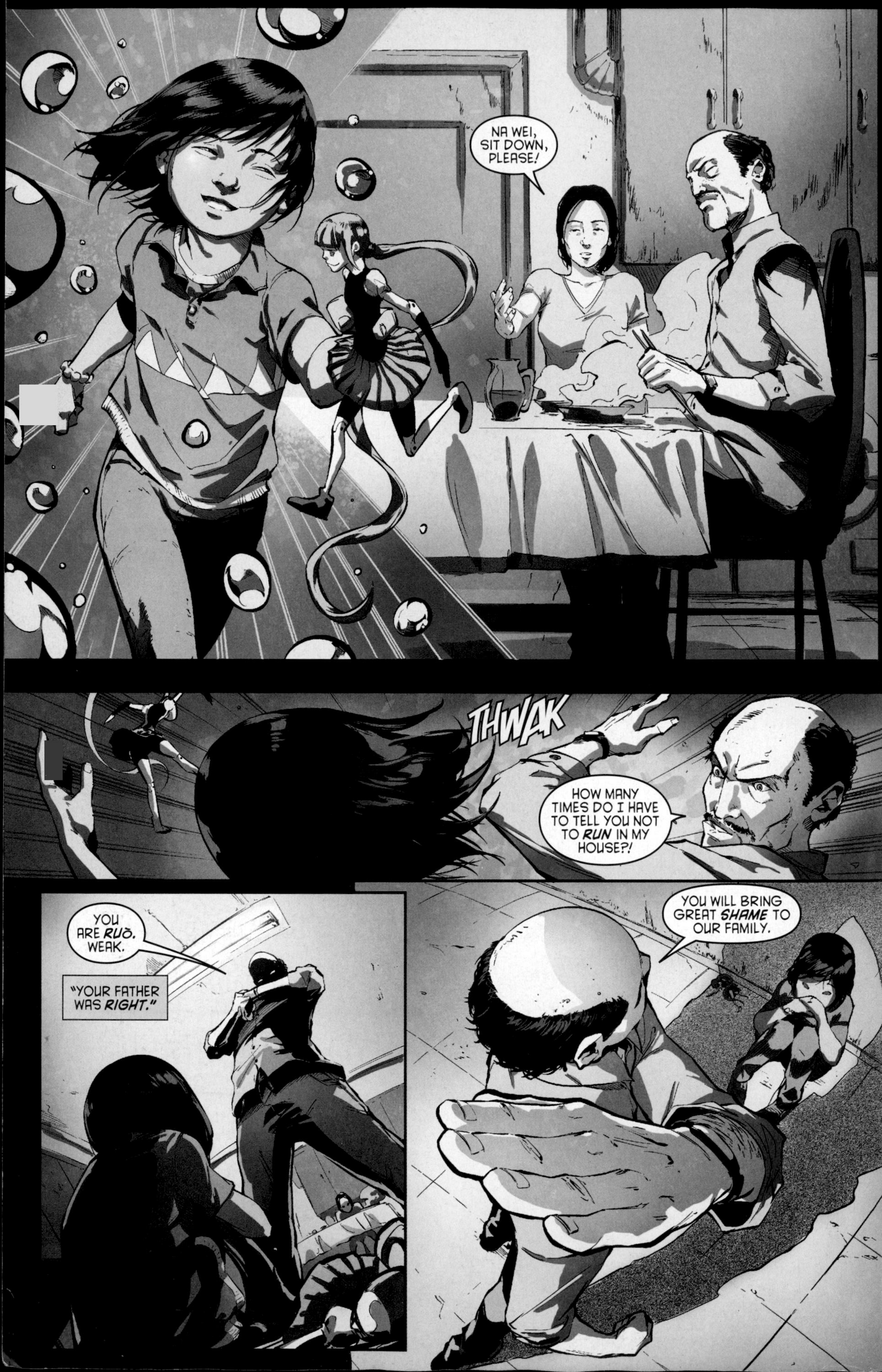

NA WEI, SIT DOWN, PLEASE!
THWAK
HOW MANY TIMES DO I HAVE TO TELL YOU NOT TO RUN IN MY HOUSE?!
YOU ARE RUÒ. WEAK.
"YOUR FATHER WAS RIGHT."
YOU WILL BRING GREAT SHAME TO OUR FAMILY.

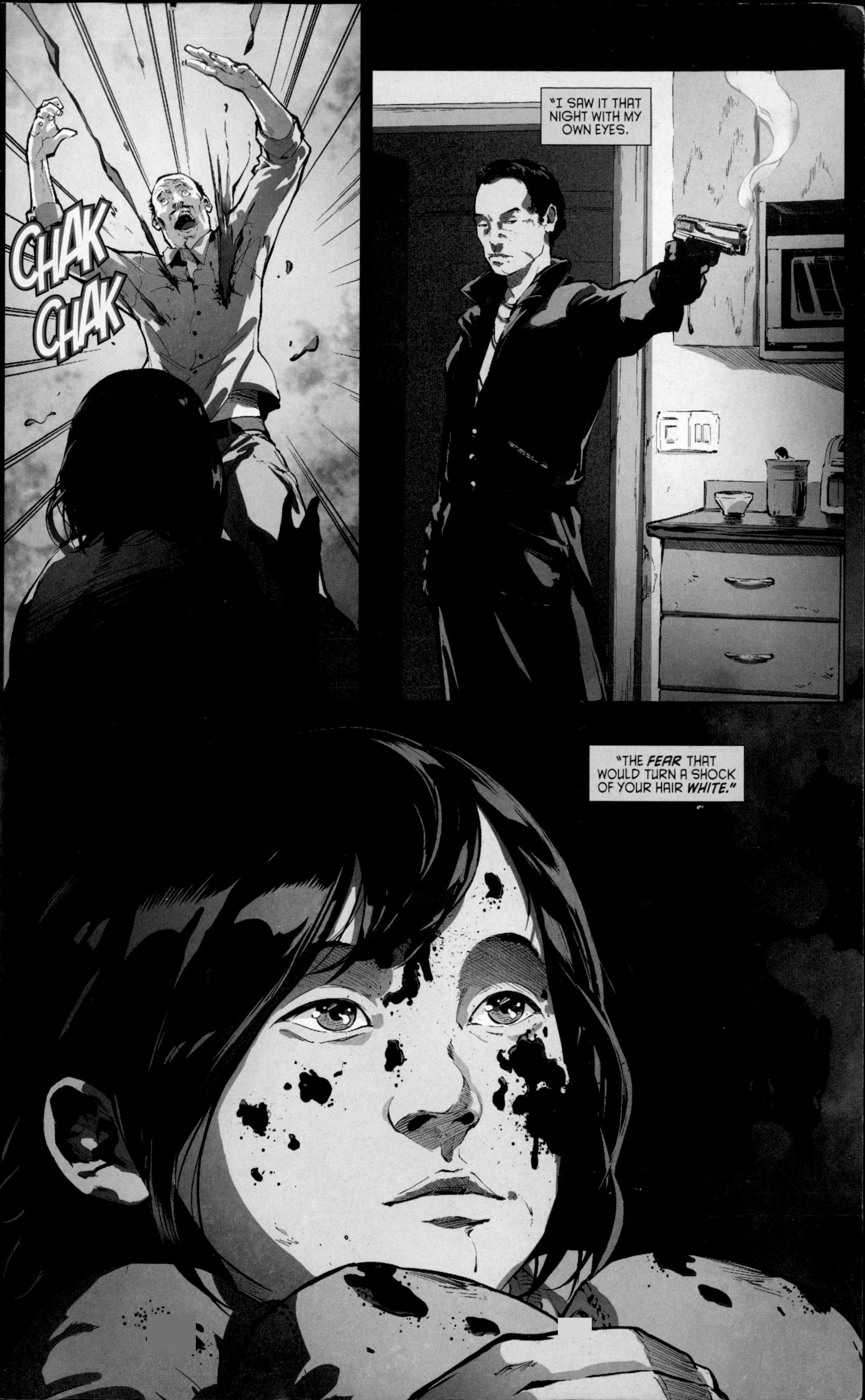
CHAK
CHAK
"I SAW IT THAT NIGHT WITH MY OWN EYES.
"THE FEAR THAT WOULD TURN A SHOCK OF YOUR HAIR WHITE."

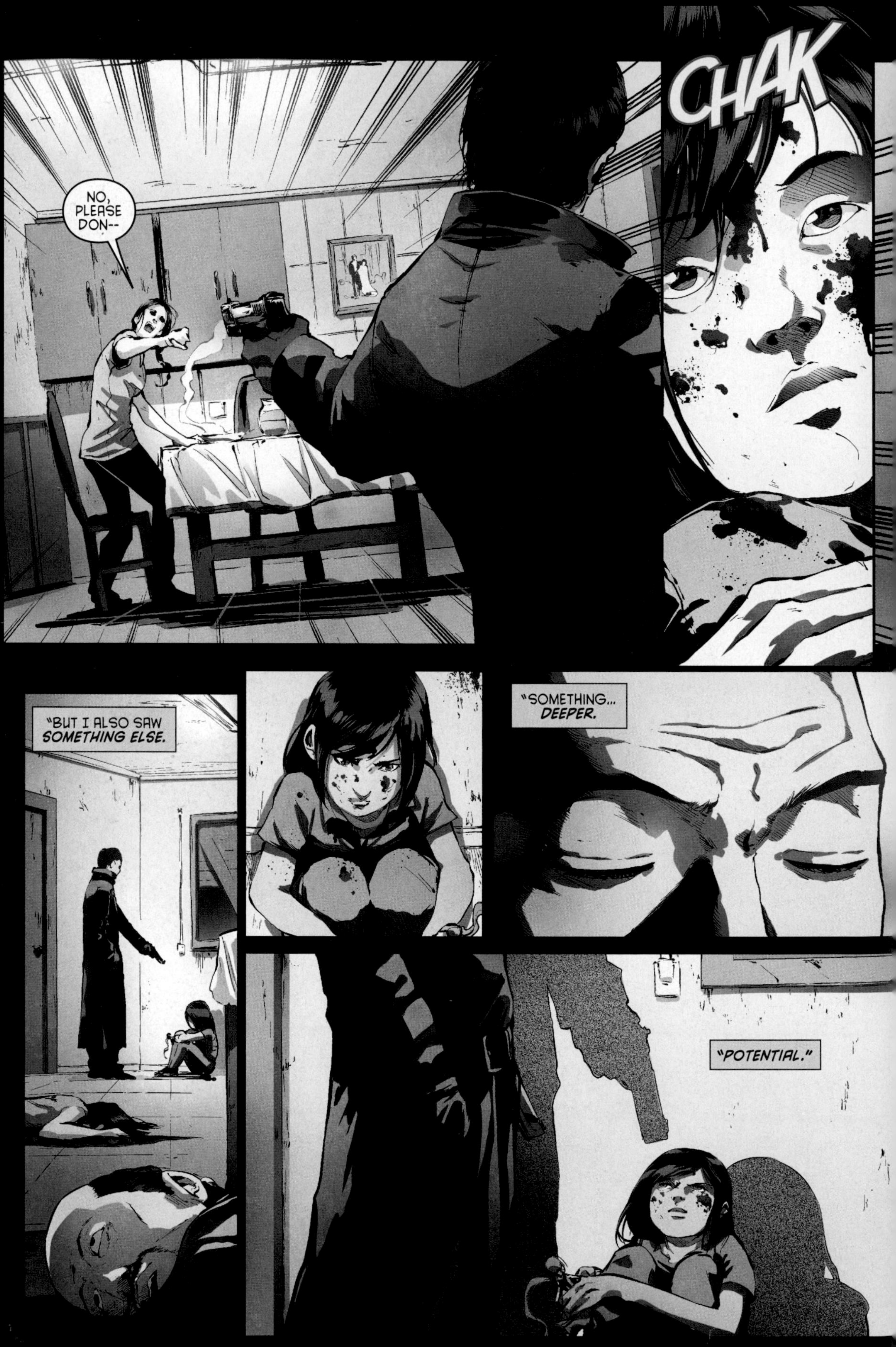
NO, PLEASE DON--
CHAK
"BUT I ALSO SAW *SOMETHING ELSE.*
"SOMETHING... *DEEPER.*
"*POTENTIAL.*"

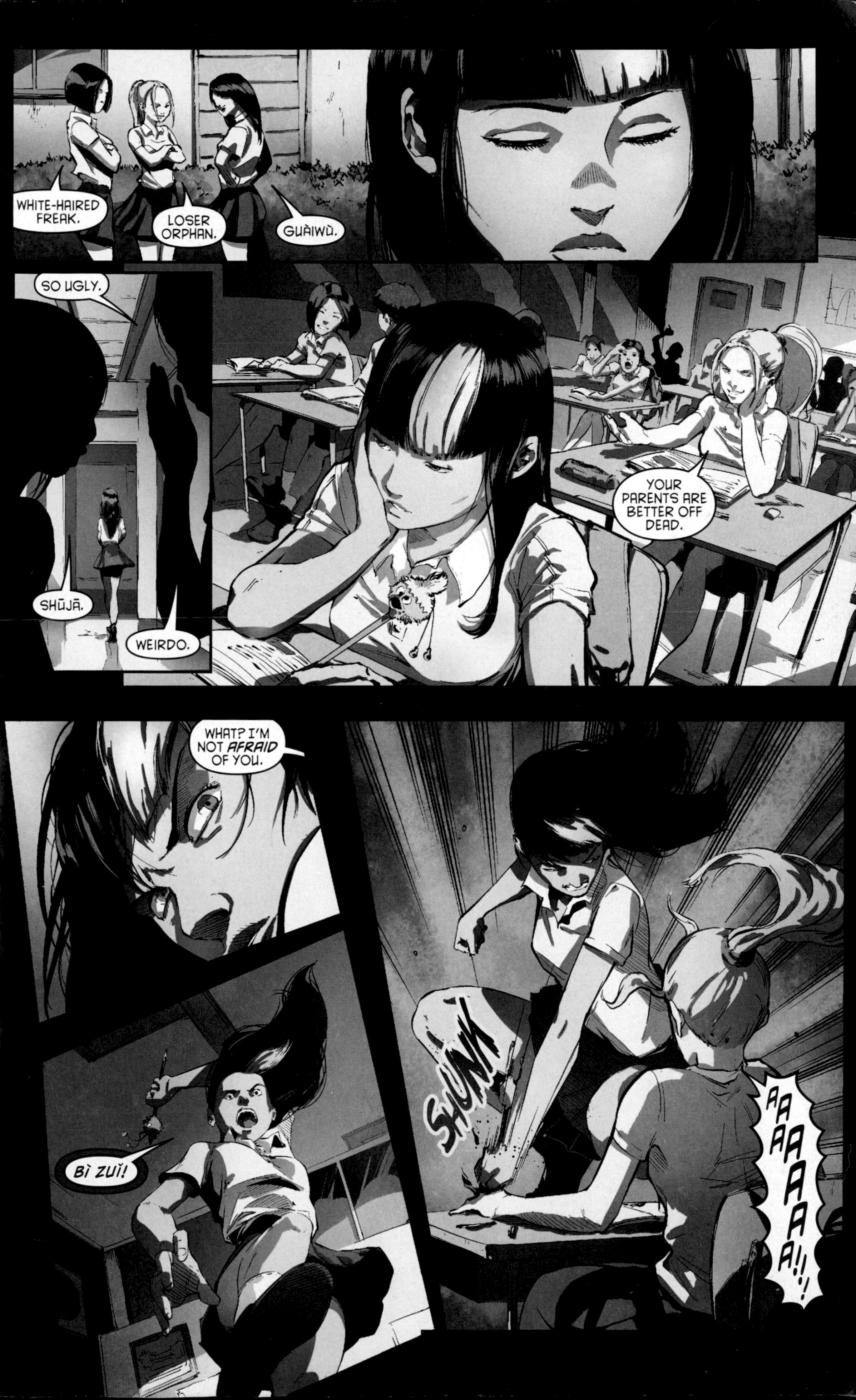

WHITE-HAIRED FREAK.
LOSER ORPHAN.
GUÀIWÙ.
SO UGLY.
SHŪJĀ.
WEIRDO.
YOUR PARENTS ARE BETTER OFF DEAD.
WHAT? I'M NOT AFRAID OF YOU.
BÌ ZUǏ!
SHUNK
AAAAAAAAA!!!

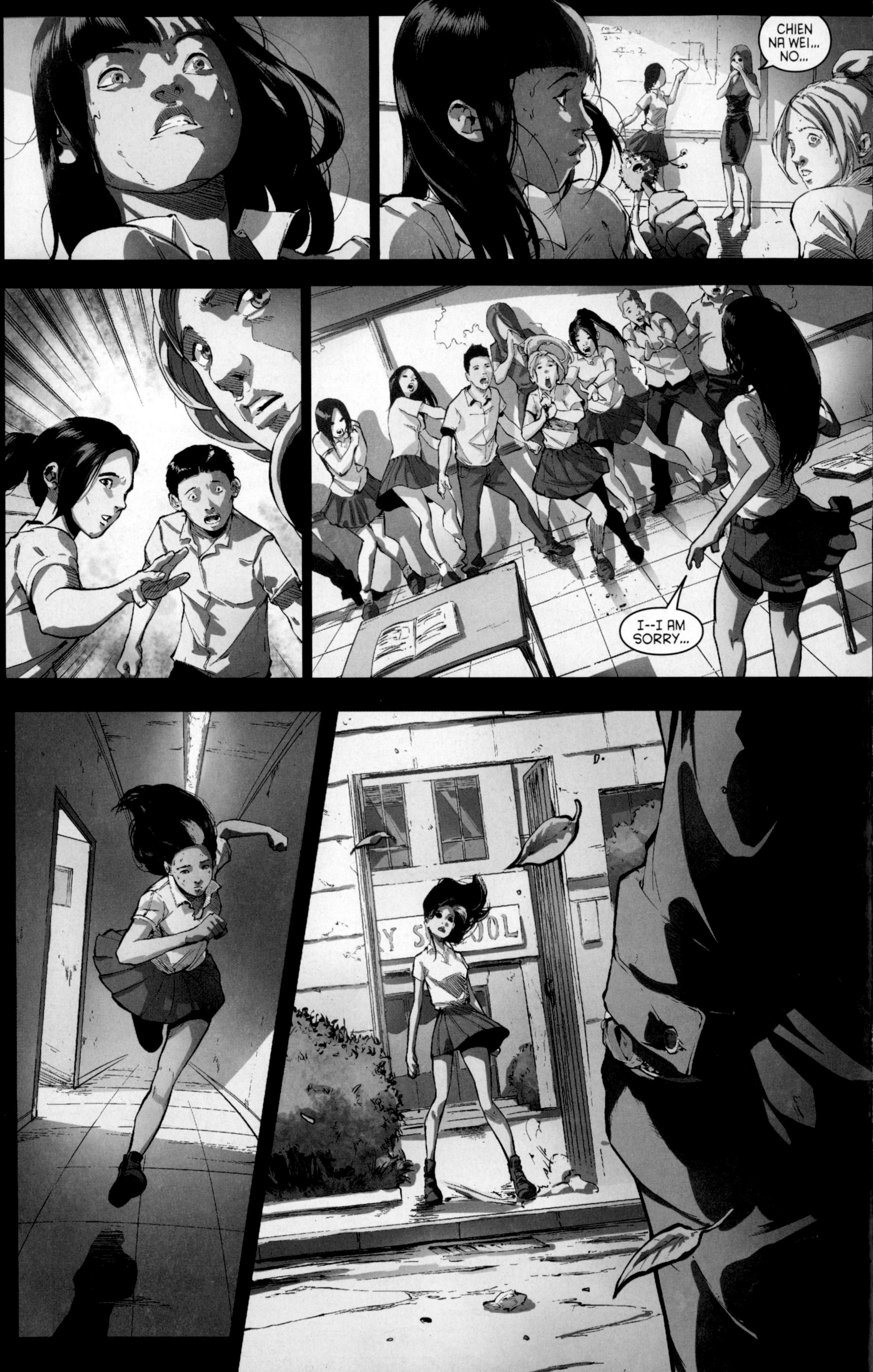
CHIEN NA WEI... NO...
I--I AM SORRY...
Y SCHOOL

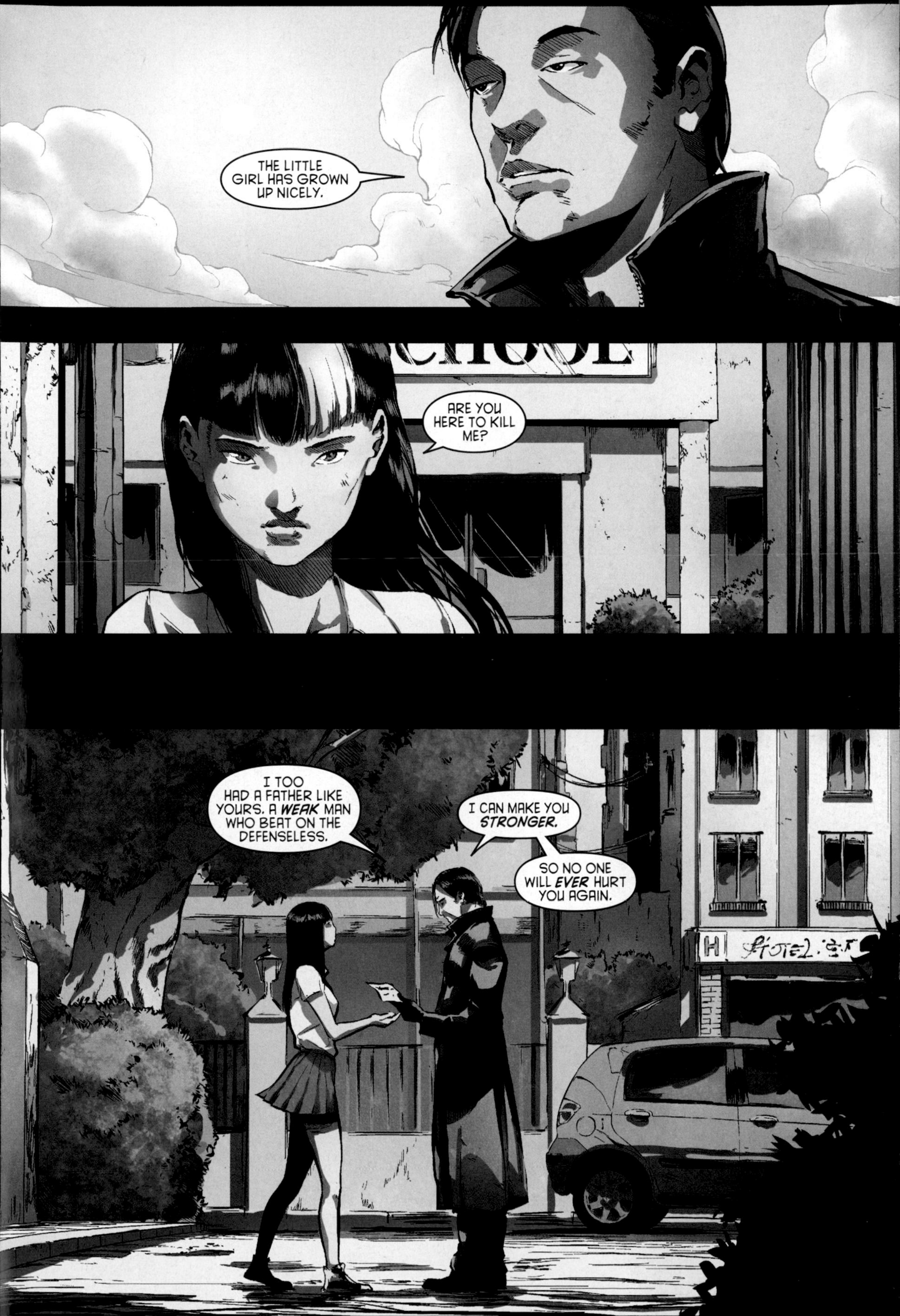
THE LITTLE GIRL HAS GROWN UP NICELY.
CHOOL
ARE YOU HERE TO KILL ME?
I TOO HAD A FATHER LIKE YOURS. A *WEAK* MAN WHO BEAT ON THE DEFENSELESS.
I CAN MAKE YOU *STRONGER.*
SO NO ONE WILL *EVER* HURT YOU AGAIN.
H

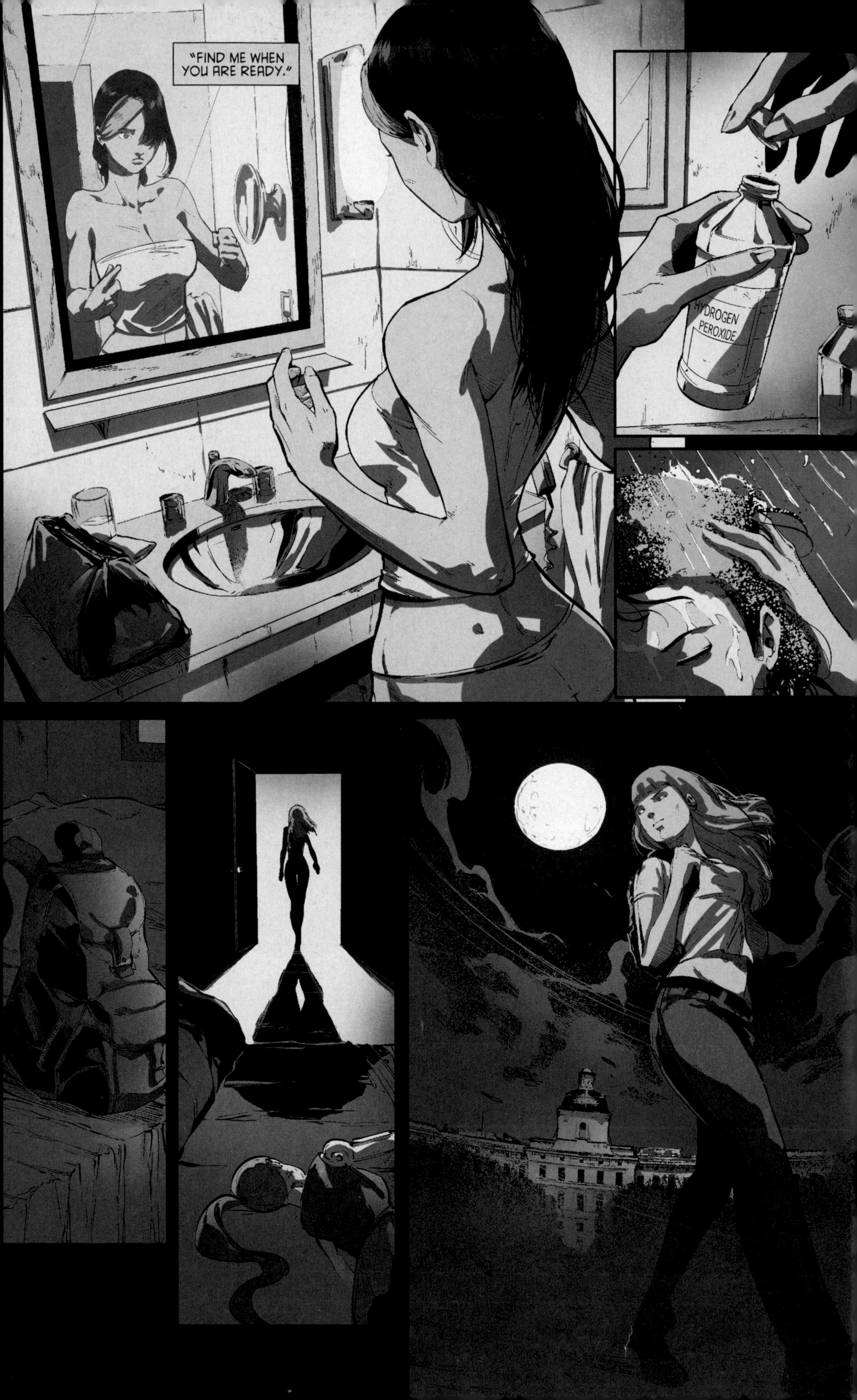
"FIND ME WHEN YOU ARE READY."
HYDROGEN PEROXIDE

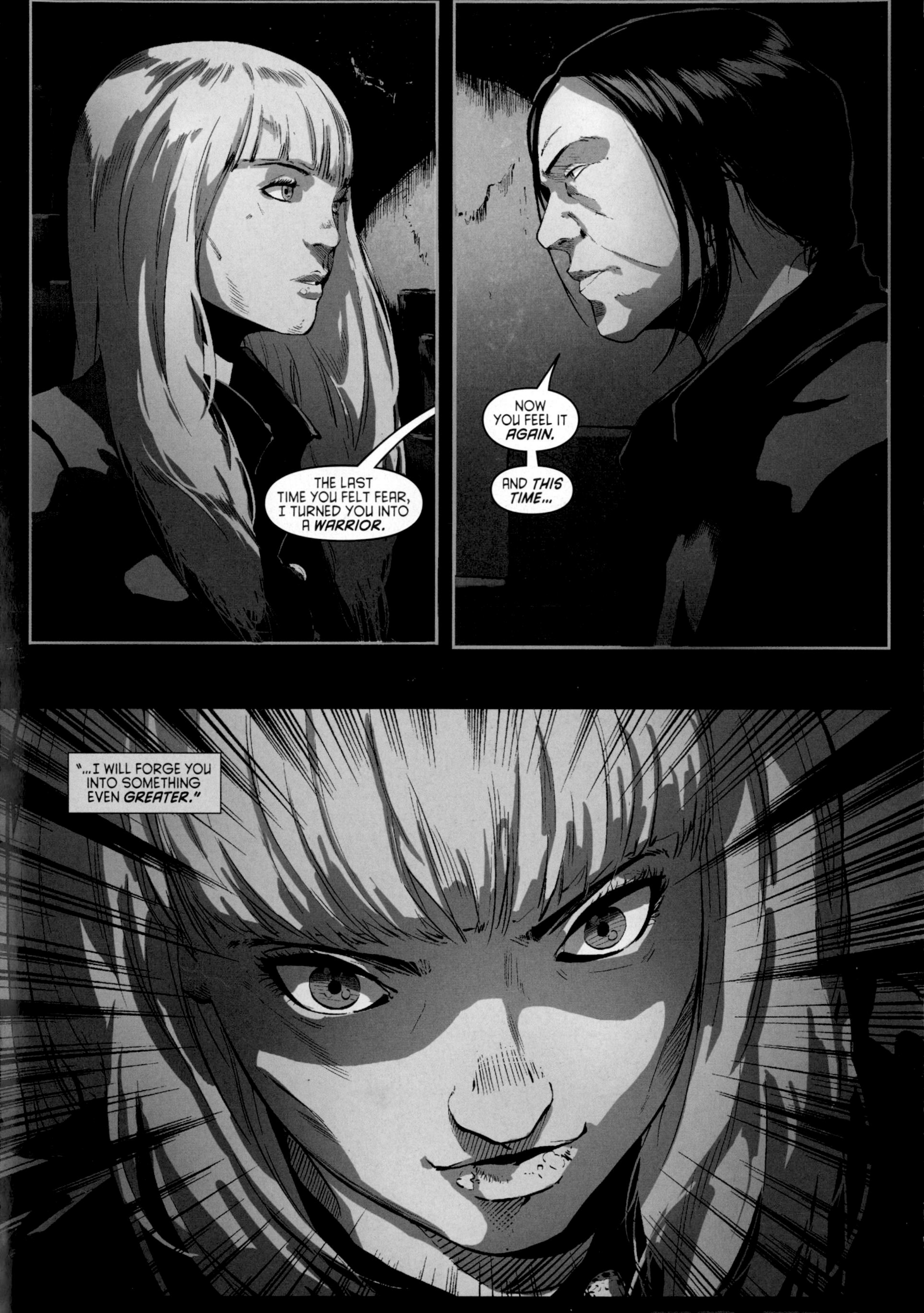

THE LAST TIME YOU FELT FEAR, I TURNED YOU INTO A *WARRIOR.*
NOW YOU FEEL IT *AGAIN.*
AND *THIS TIME...*
"...I WILL FORGE YOU INTO SOMETHING EVEN *GREATER.*"

END CH. 3

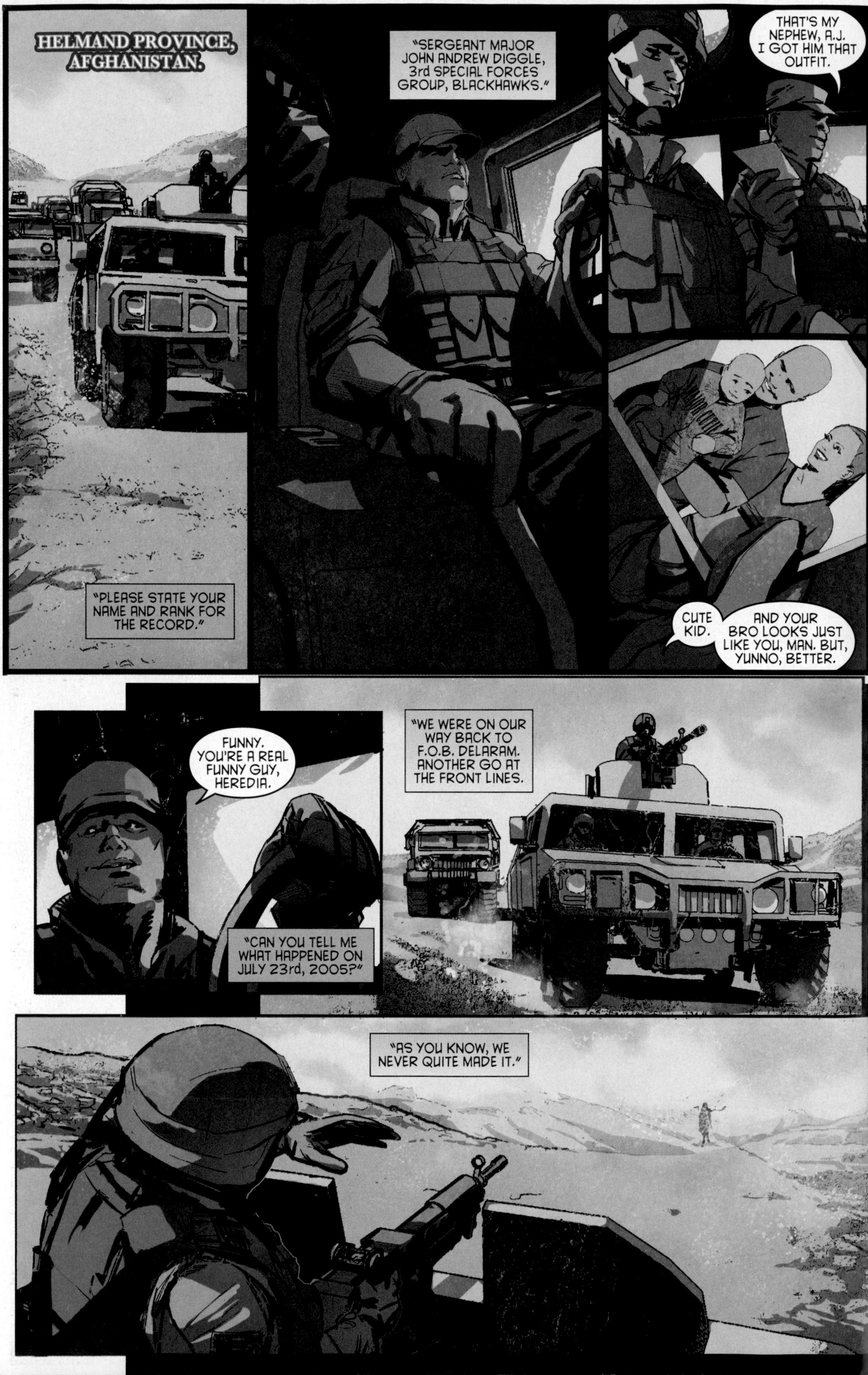
HELMAND PROVINCE, AFGHANISTAN.
"PLEASE STATE YOUR NAME AND RANK FOR THE RECORD."
"SERGEANT MAJOR JOHN ANDREW DIGGLE, 3rd SPECIAL FORCES GROUP, BLACKHAWKS."
THAT'S MY NEPHEW, A.J. I GOT HIM THAT OUTFIT.
CUTE KID.
AND YOUR BRO LOOKS JUST LIKE YOU, MAN. BUT, YUNNO, BETTER.
FUNNY. YOU'RE A REAL FUNNY GUY, HEREDIA.
"CAN YOU TELL ME WHAT HAPPENED ON JULY 23rd, 2005?"
"WE WERE ON OUR WAY BACK TO F.O.B. DELARAM. ANOTHER GO AT THE FRONT LINES.
"AS YOU KNOW, WE NEVER QUITE MADE IT."

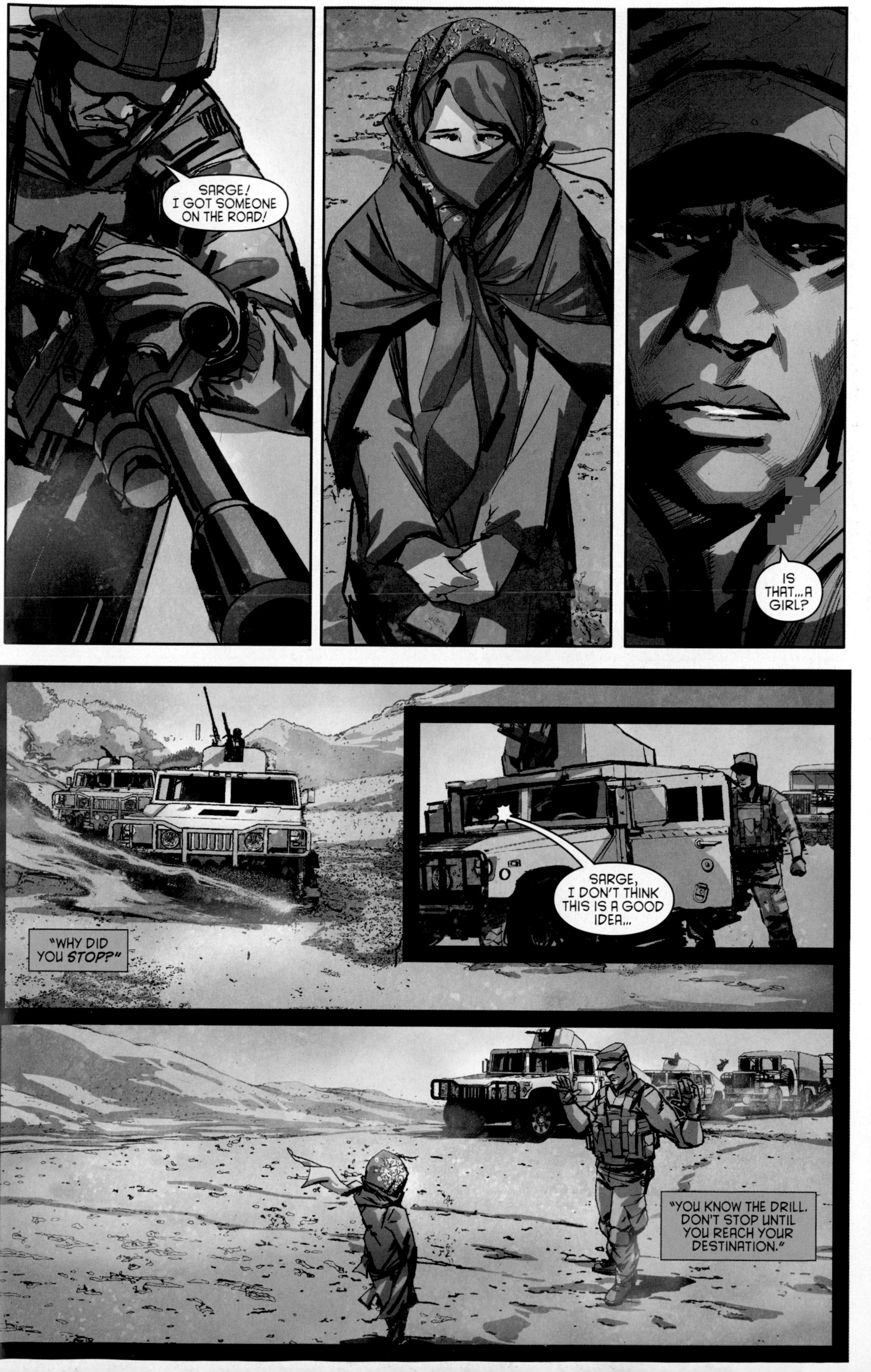
SARGE! I GOT SOMEONE ON THE ROAD!
IS THAT... A GIRL?
"WHY DID YOU *STOP?*"
SARGE, I DON'T THINK THIS IS A GOOD IDEA...
"YOU KNOW THE DRILL. DON'T STOP UNTIL YOU REACH YOUR DESTINATION."

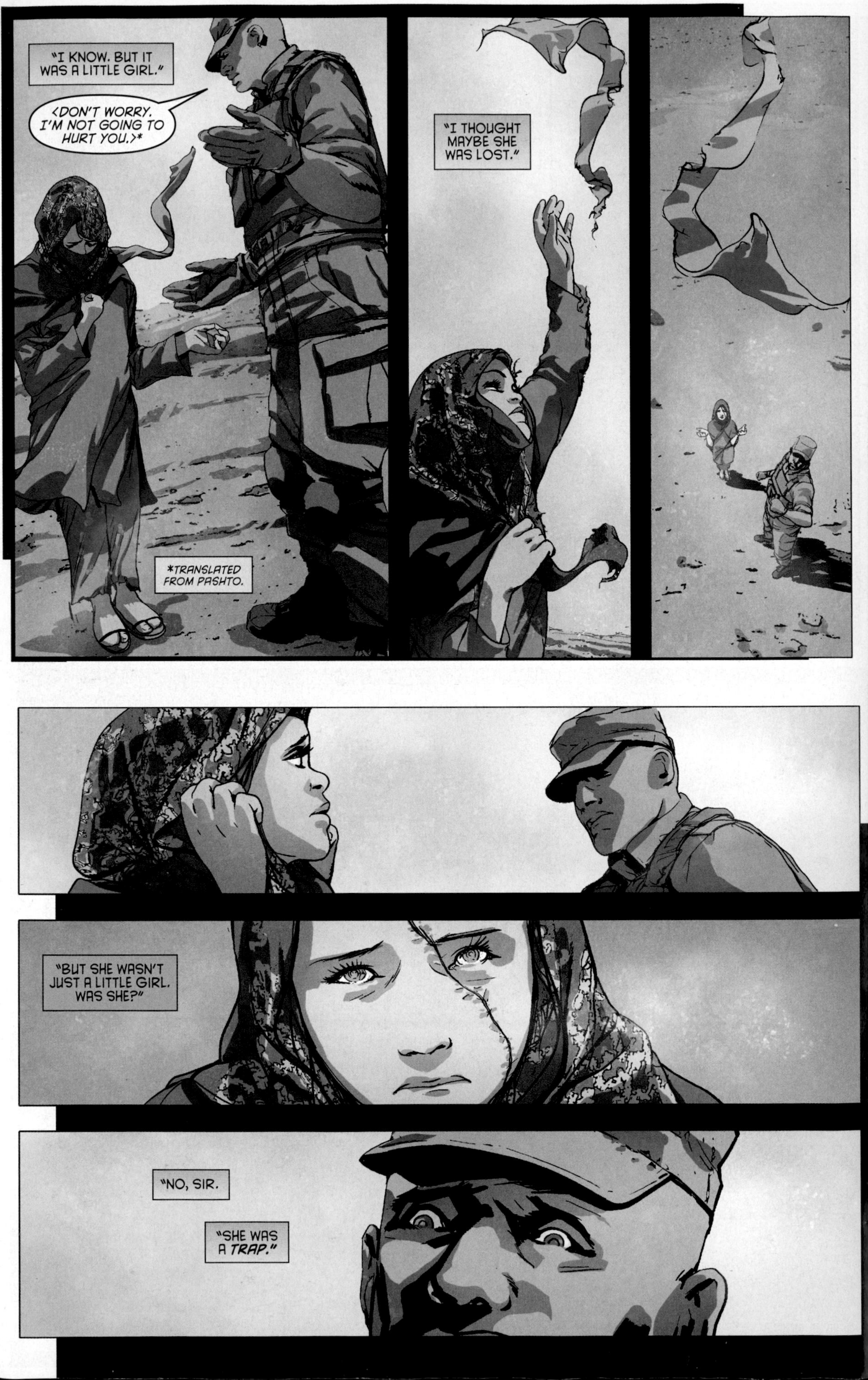
"I KNOW. BUT IT WAS A LITTLE GIRL."
<DON'T WORRY. I'M NOT GOING TO HURT YOU.>*
*TRANSLATED FROM PASHTO.
"I THOUGHT MAYBE SHE WAS LOST."
"BUT SHE WASN'T JUST A LITTLE GIRL. WAS SHE?"
"NO, SIR.
"SHE WAS A TRAP."

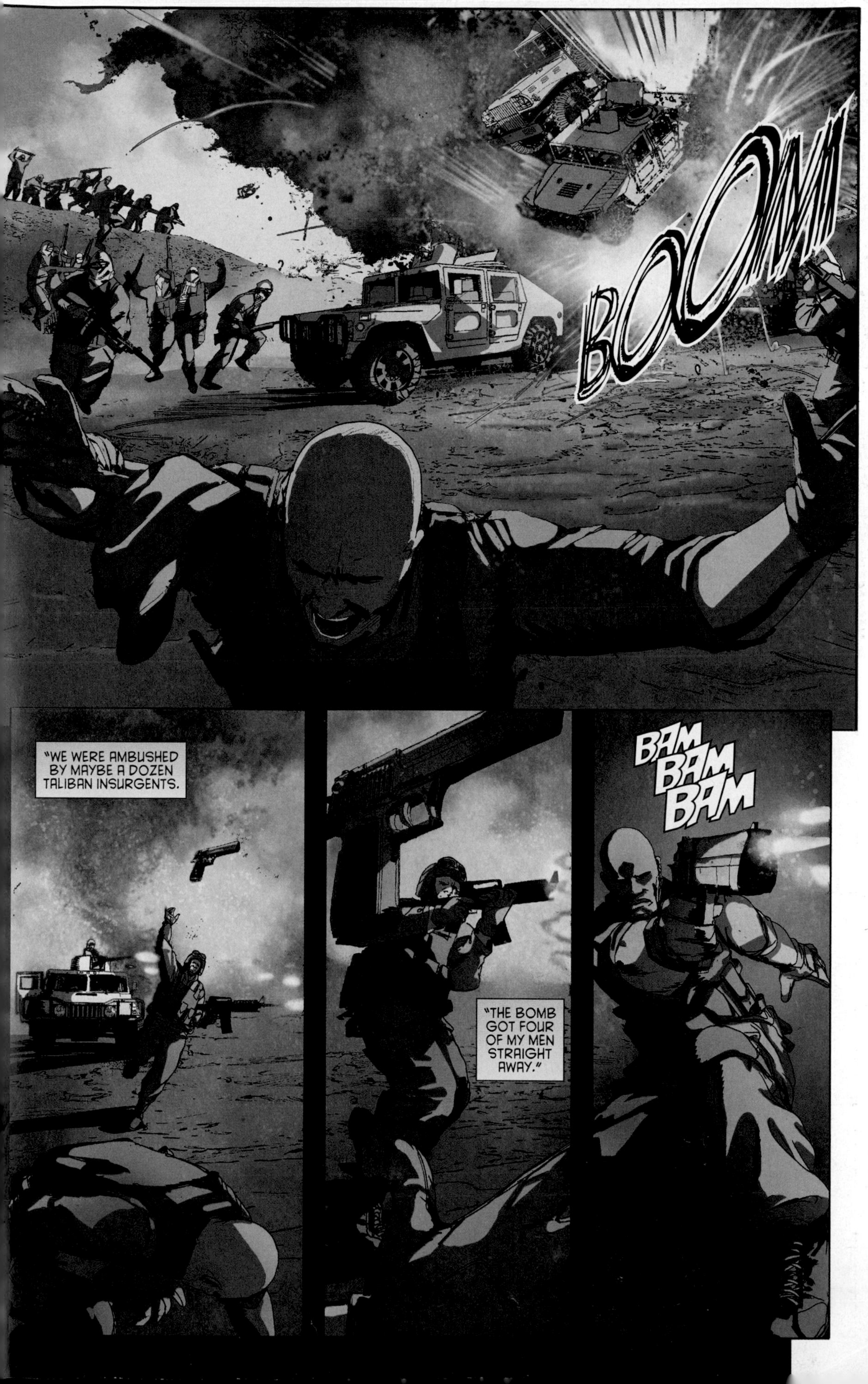
BOOM!!
"WE WERE AMBUSHED BY MAYBE A DOZEN TALIBAN INSURGENTS.
"THE BOMB GOT FOUR OF MY MEN STRAIGHT AWAY."
BAM BAM BAM

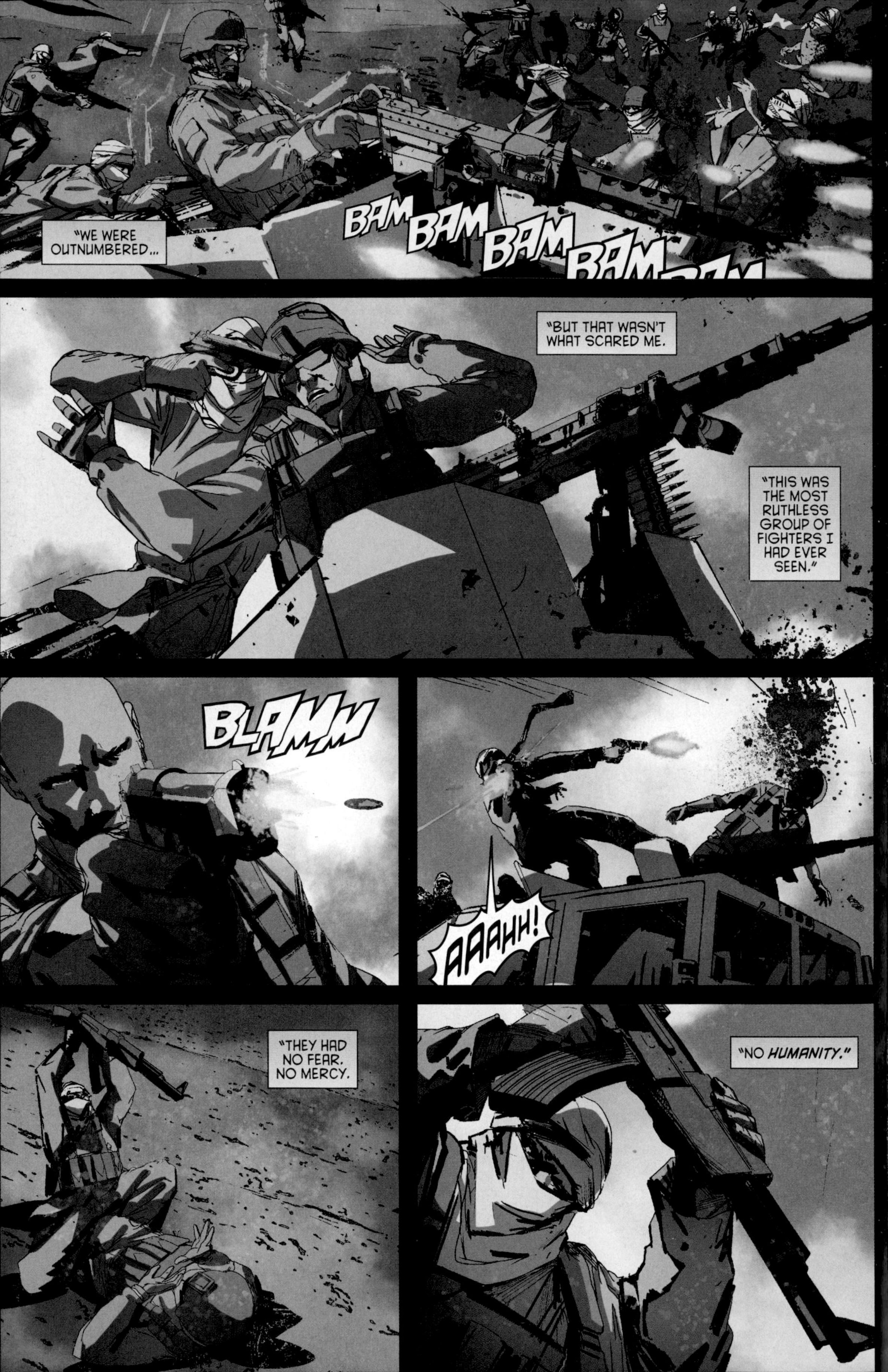

"WE WERE OUTNUMBERED...
BAM BAM BAM
"BUT THAT WASN'T WHAT SCARED ME.
"THIS WAS THE MOST RUTHLESS GROUP OF FIGHTERS I HAD EVER SEEN."
BLAMM
AAAHH!
"THEY HAD NO FEAR. NO MERCY.
"NO HUMANITY."

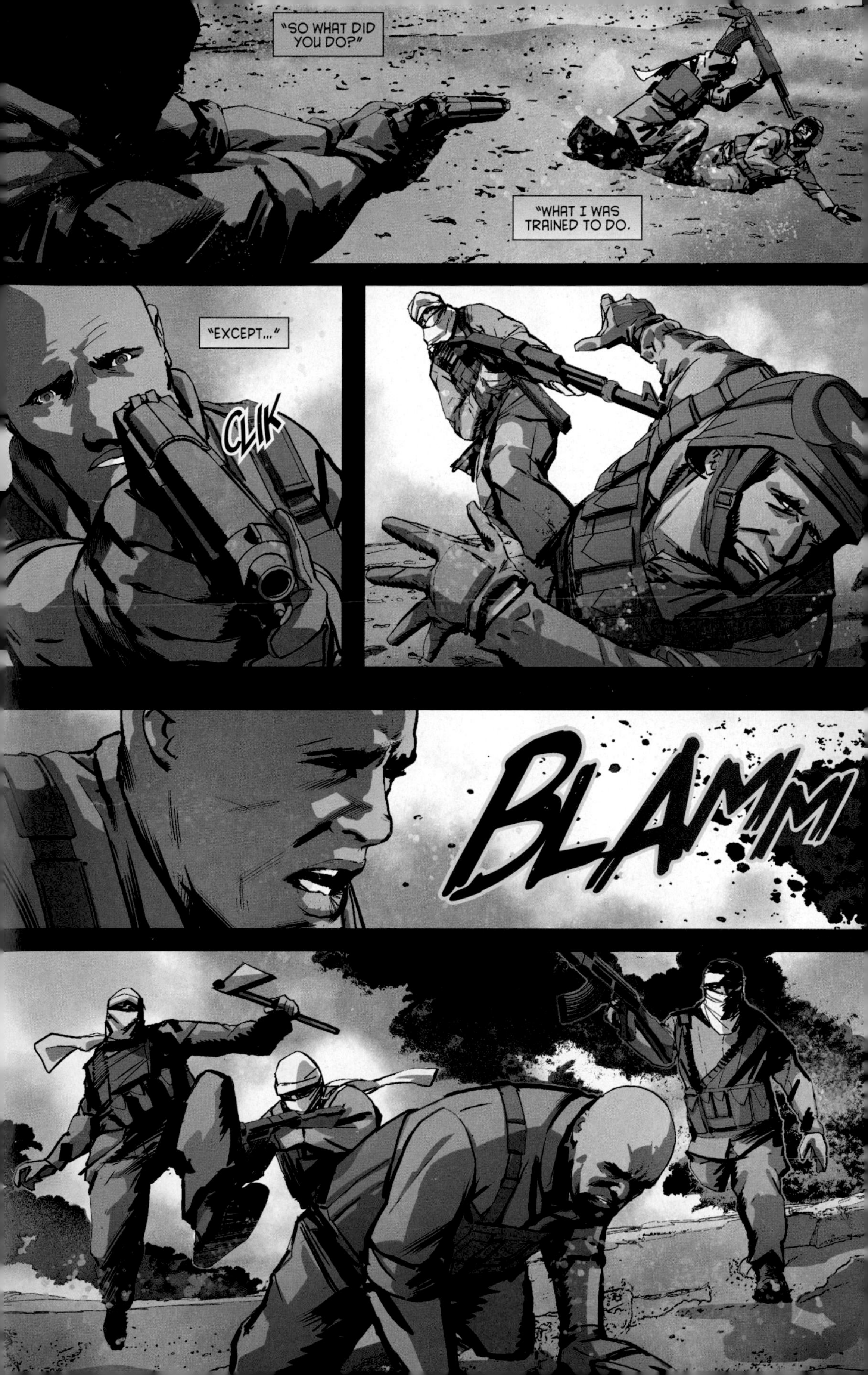
"SO WHAT DID YOU DO?"
"WHAT I WAS TRAINED TO DO.
"EXCEPT..."
CLIK
BLAMM

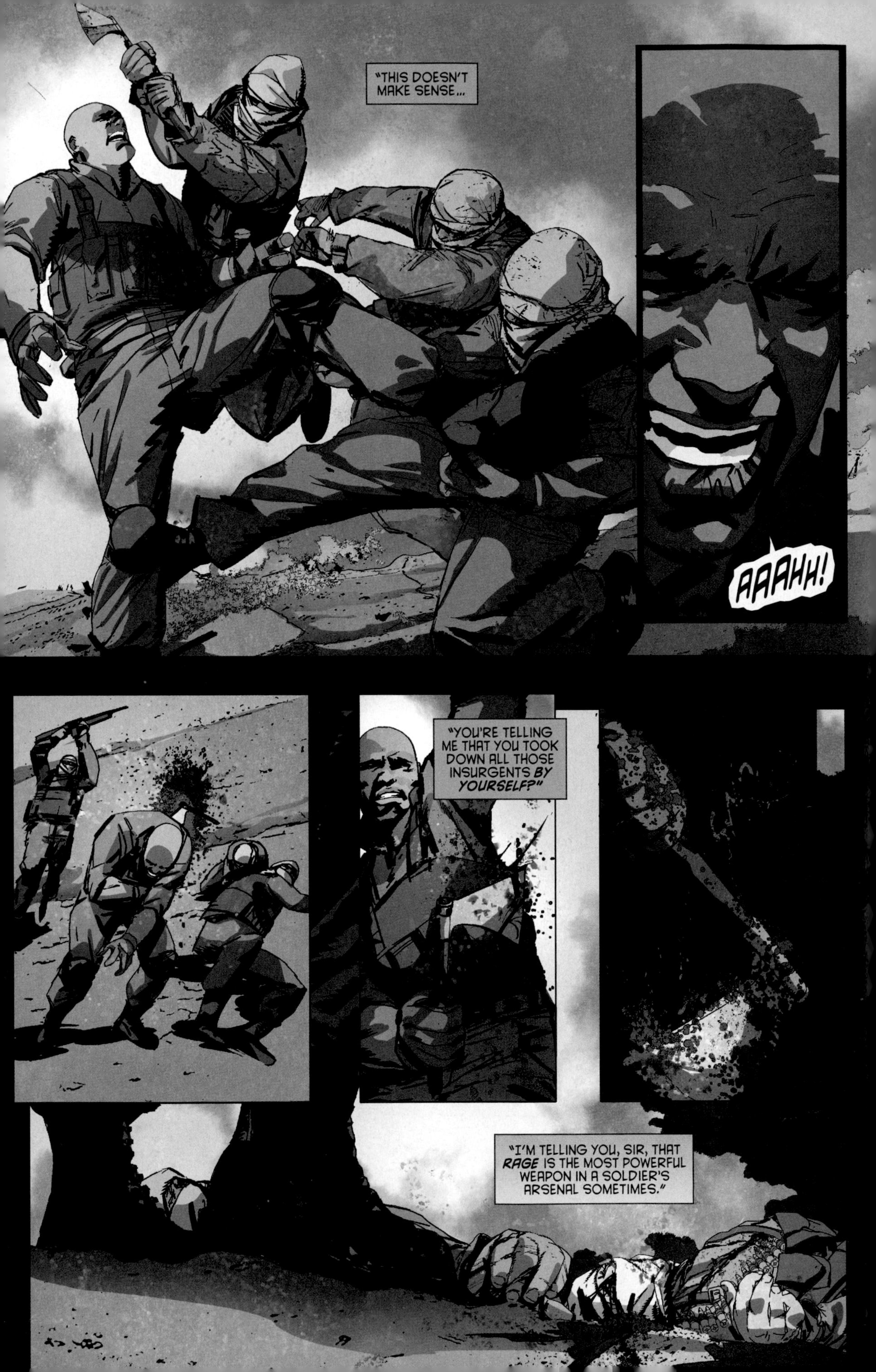
"THIS DOESN'T MAKE SENSE...
AAAHH!
"YOU'RE TELLING ME THAT YOU TOOK DOWN ALL THOSE INSURGENTS BY YOURSELF?"
"I'M TELLING YOU, SIR, THAT RAGE IS THE MOST POWERFUL WEAPON IN A SOLDIER'S ARSENAL SOMETIMES."

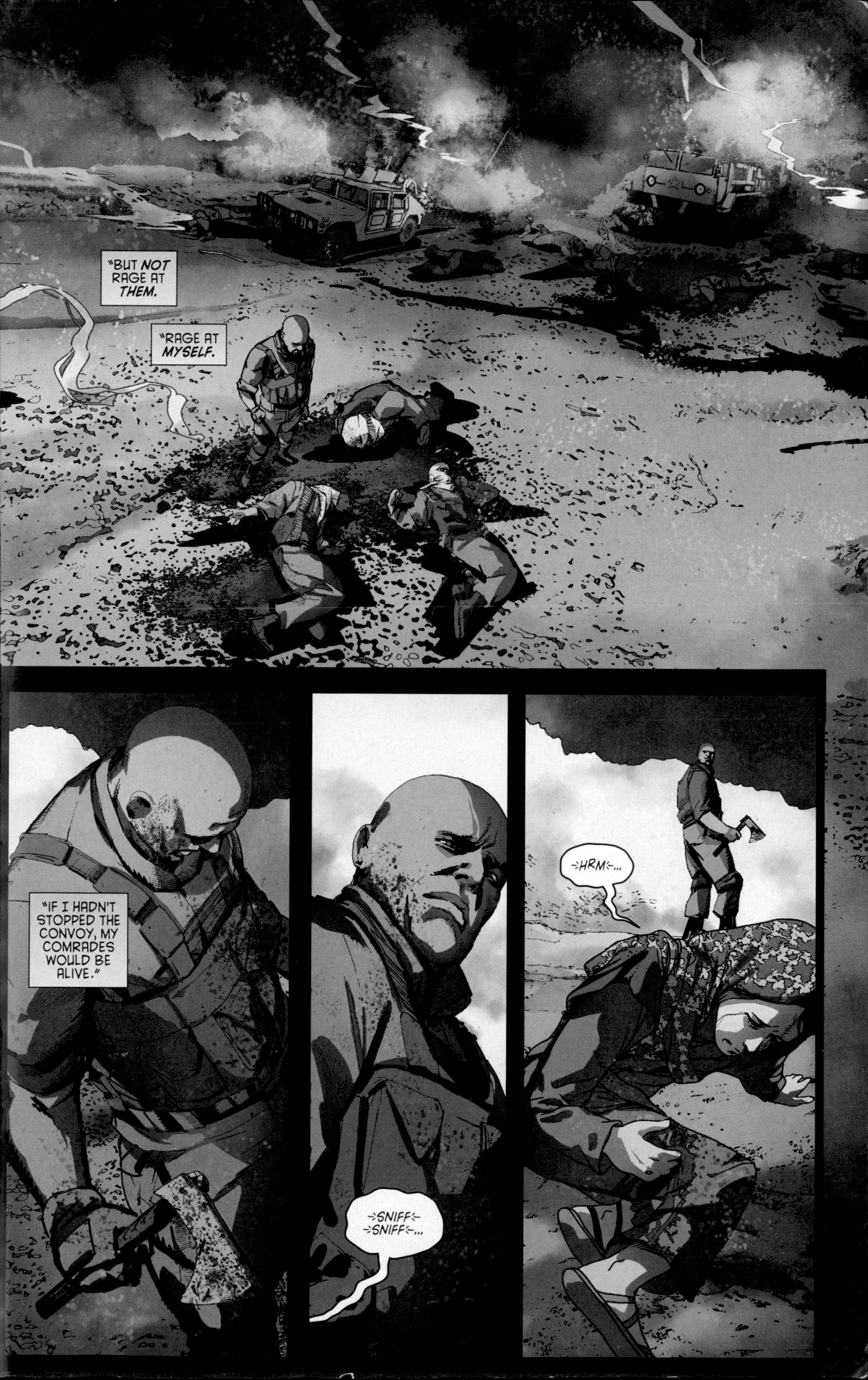
"BUT NOT RAGE AT THEM.
"RAGE AT MYSELF.
"IF I HADN'T STOPPED THE CONVOY, MY COMRADES WOULD BE ALIVE."
SNIFF SNIFF...
HRM...

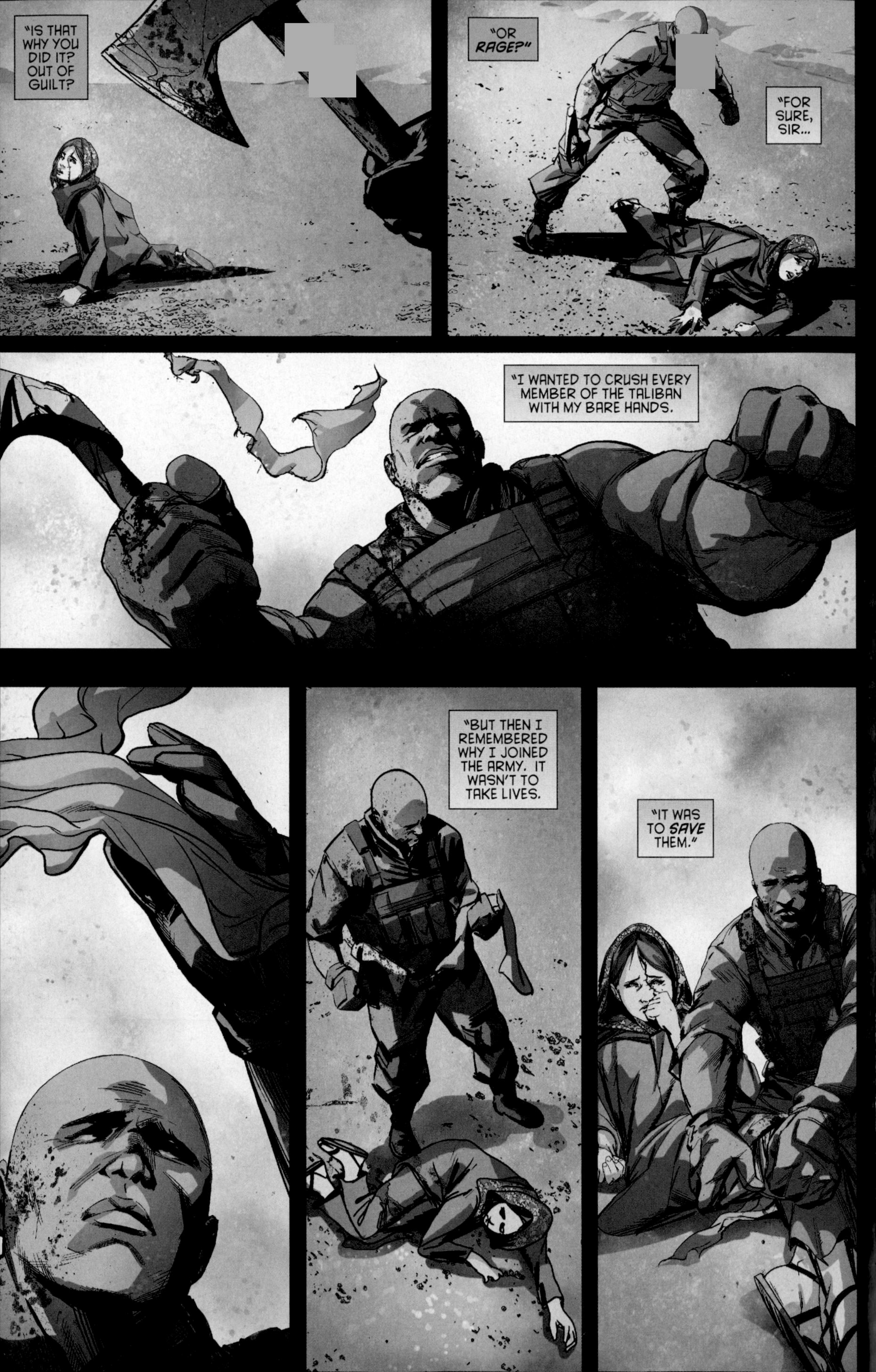
"IS THAT WHY YOU DID IT? OUT OF GUILT?
"OR RAGE?"
"FOR SURE, SIR...
"I WANTED TO CRUSH EVERY MEMBER OF THE TALIBAN WITH MY BARE HANDS.
"BUT THEN I REMEMBERED WHY I JOINED THE ARMY. IT WASN'T TO TAKE LIVES.
"IT WAS TO SAVE THEM."

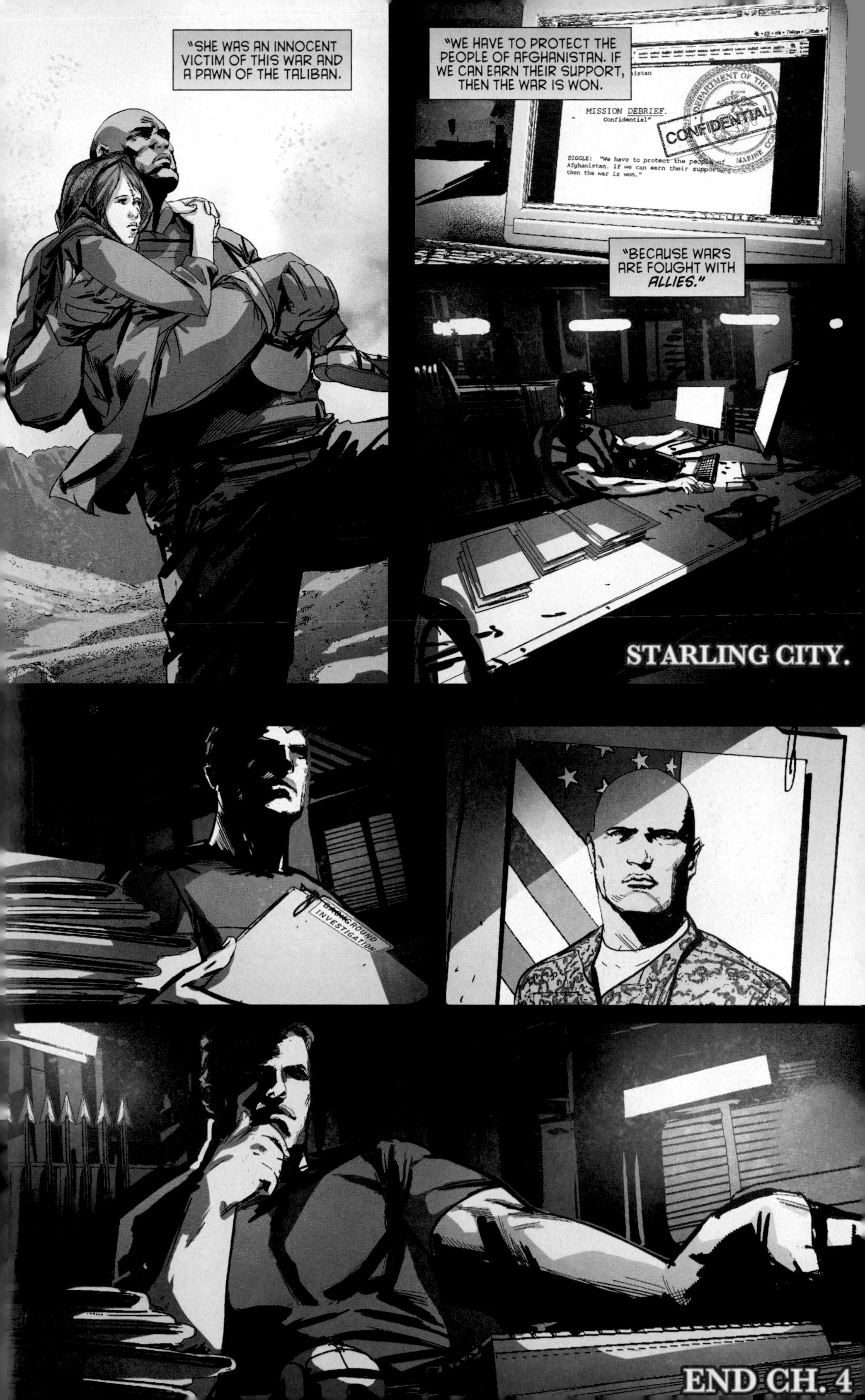
"SHE WAS AN INNOCENT VICTIM OF THIS WAR AND A PAWN OF THE TALIBAN.
"WE HAVE TO PROTECT THE PEOPLE OF AFGHANISTAN. IF WE CAN EARN THEIR SUPPORT, THEN THE WAR IS WON.
MISSION DEBRIEF.
CONFIDENTIAL
DIGGLE: "We have to protect the people of Afghanistan. If we can earn their support, then the war is won."
"BECAUSE WARS ARE FOUGHT WITH ALLIES."
STARLING CITY.
INVESTIGATION
END CH. 4

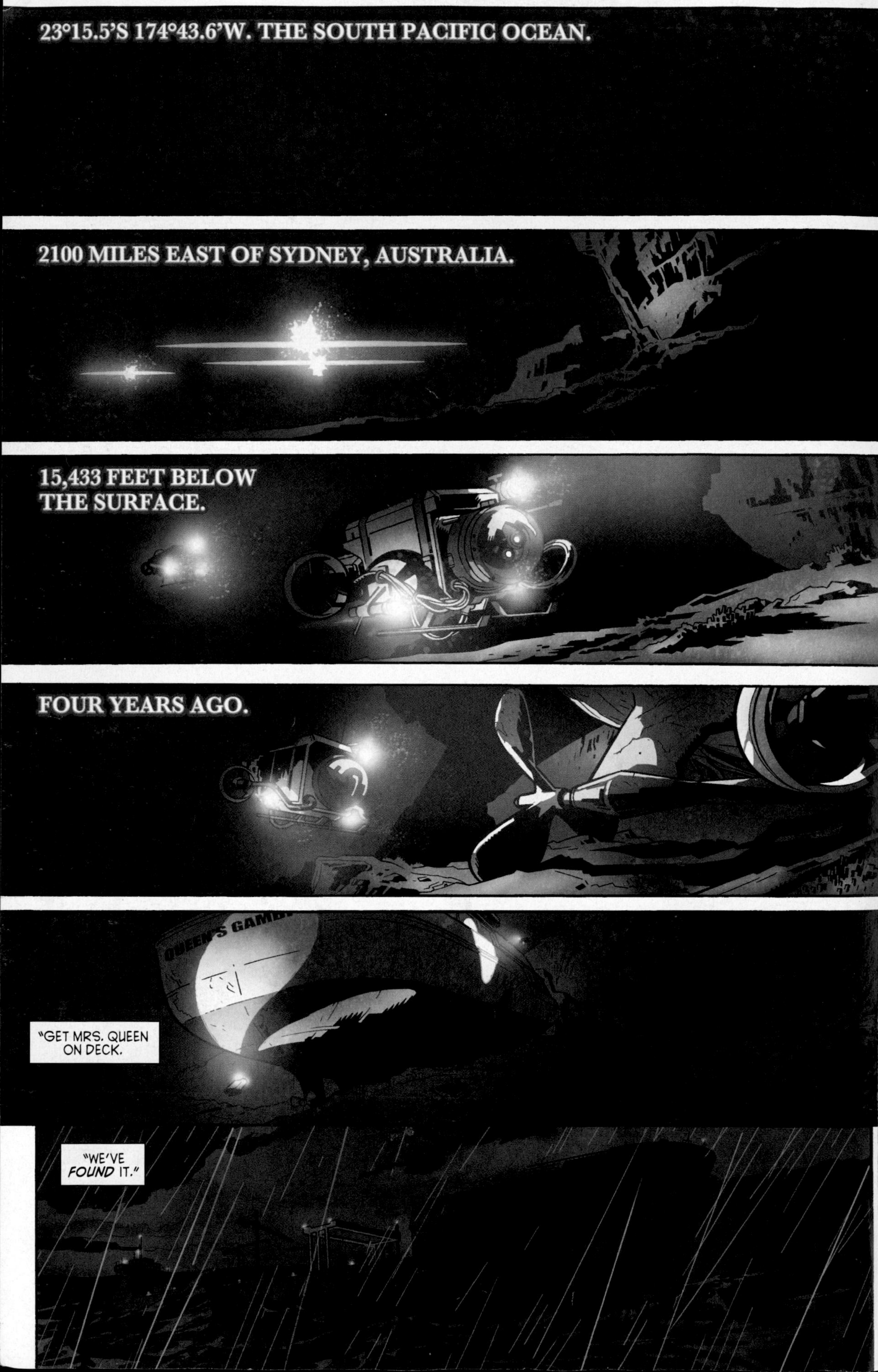
23°15.5'S 174°43.6'W. THE SOUTH PACIFIC OCEAN.
2100 MILES EAST OF SYDNEY, AUSTRALIA.
15,433 FEET BELOW THE SURFACE.
FOUR YEARS AGO.
QUEEN'S GAMB
"GET MRS. QUEEN ON DECK.
"WE'VE FOUND IT."

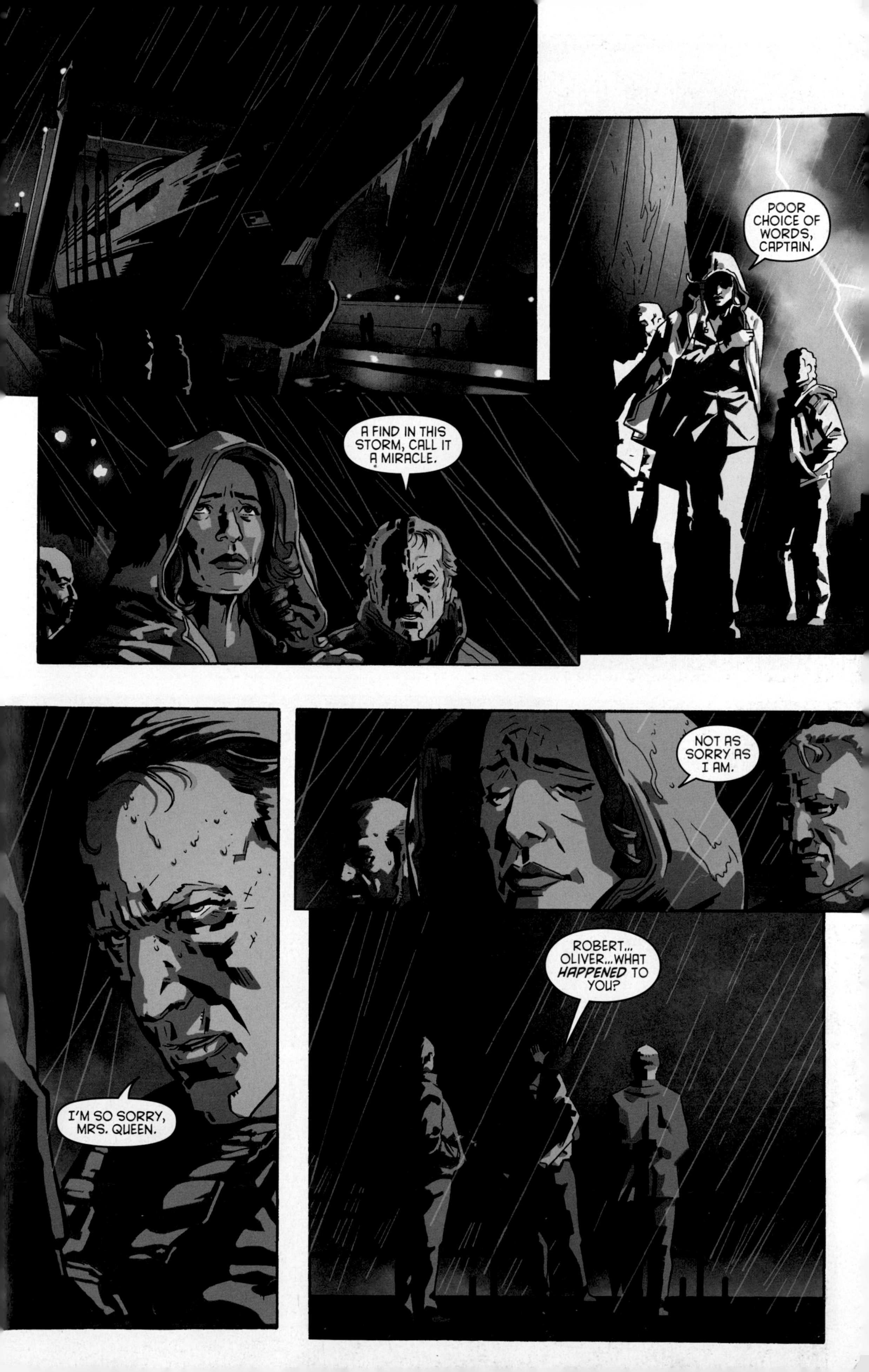
A FIND IN THIS STORM, CALL IT A MIRACLE.
POOR CHOICE OF WORDS, CAPTAIN.
I'M SO SORRY, MRS. QUEEN.
NOT AS SORRY AS I AM.
ROBERT... OLIVER...WHAT HAPPENED TO YOU?

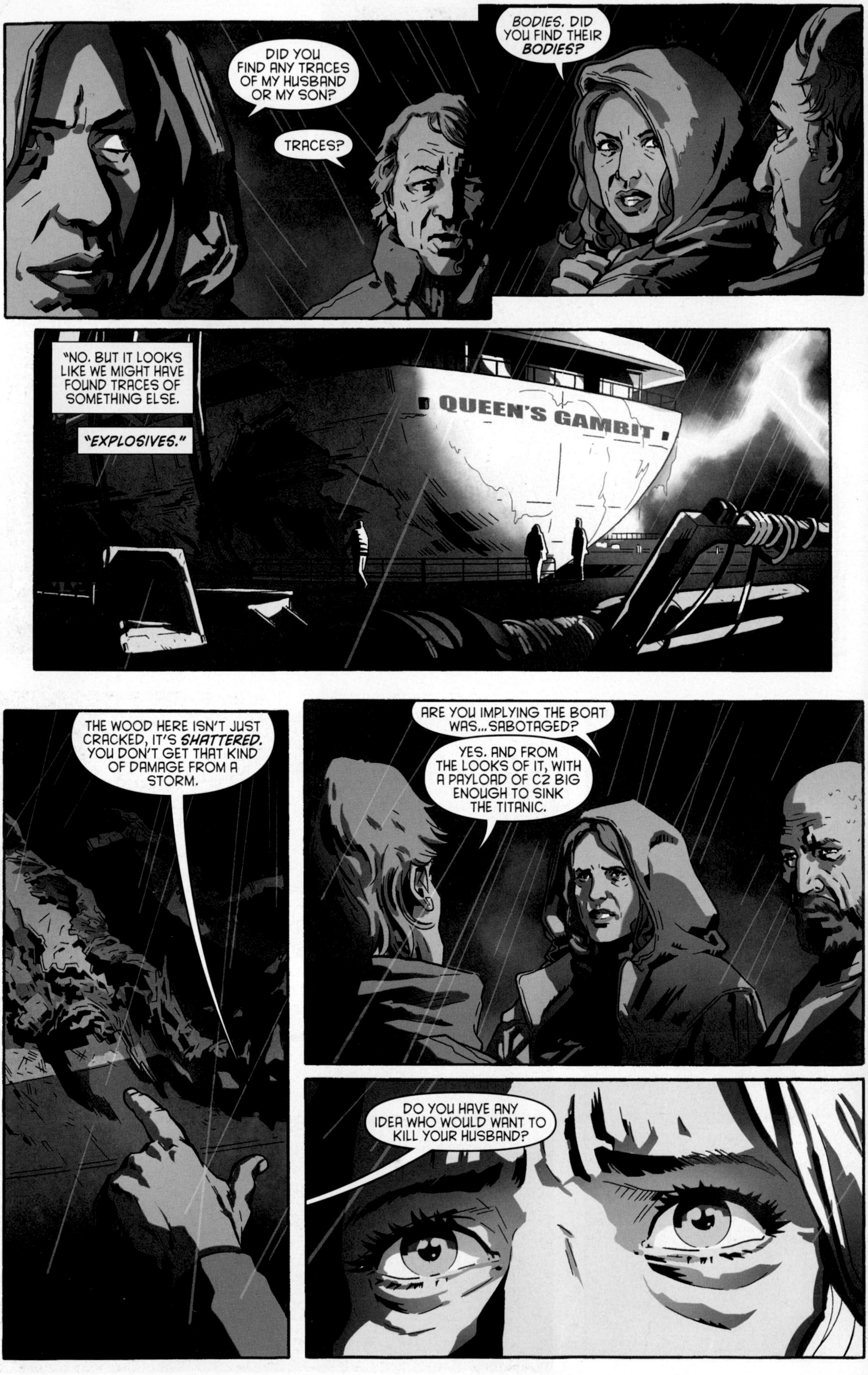
DID YOU FIND ANY TRACES OF MY HUSBAND OR MY SON?
TRACES?
BODIES. DID YOU FIND THEIR BODIES?
"NO. BUT IT LOOKS LIKE WE MIGHT HAVE FOUND TRACES OF SOMETHING ELSE.
"EXPLOSIVES."
QUEEN'S GAMBIT
THE WOOD HERE ISN'T JUST CRACKED, IT'S SHATTERED. YOU DON'T GET THAT KIND OF DAMAGE FROM A STORM.
ARE YOU IMPLYING THE BOAT WAS... SABOTAGED?
YES. AND FROM THE LOOKS OF IT, WITH A PAYLOAD OF C2 BIG ENOUGH TO SINK THE TITANIC.
DO YOU HAVE ANY IDEA WHO WOULD WANT TO KILL YOUR HUSBAND?

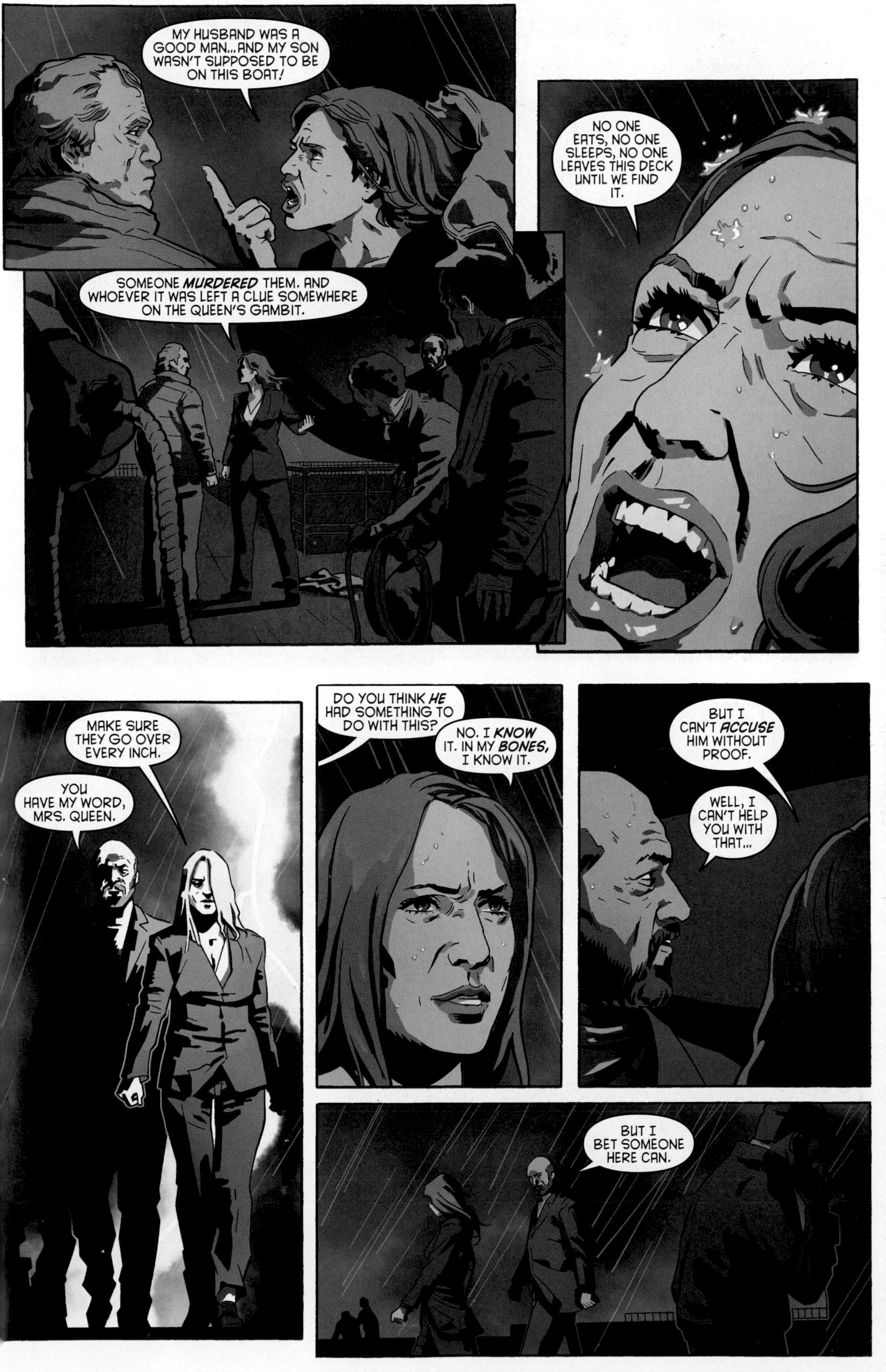
MY HUSBAND WAS A GOOD MAN...AND MY SON WASN'T SUPPOSED TO BE ON THIS BOAT!
SOMEONE MURDERED THEM. AND WHOEVER IT WAS LEFT A CLUE SOMEWHERE ON THE QUEEN'S GAMBIT.
NO ONE EATS, NO ONE SLEEPS, NO ONE LEAVES THIS DECK UNTIL WE FIND IT.
MAKE SURE THEY GO OVER EVERY INCH.
YOU HAVE MY WORD, MRS. QUEEN.
DO YOU THINK HE HAD SOMETHING TO DO WITH THIS?
NO. I KNOW IT. IN MY BONES, I KNOW IT.
BUT I CAN'T ACCUSE HIM WITHOUT PROOF.
WELL, I CAN'T HELP YOU WITH THAT...
BUT I BET SOMEONE HERE CAN.

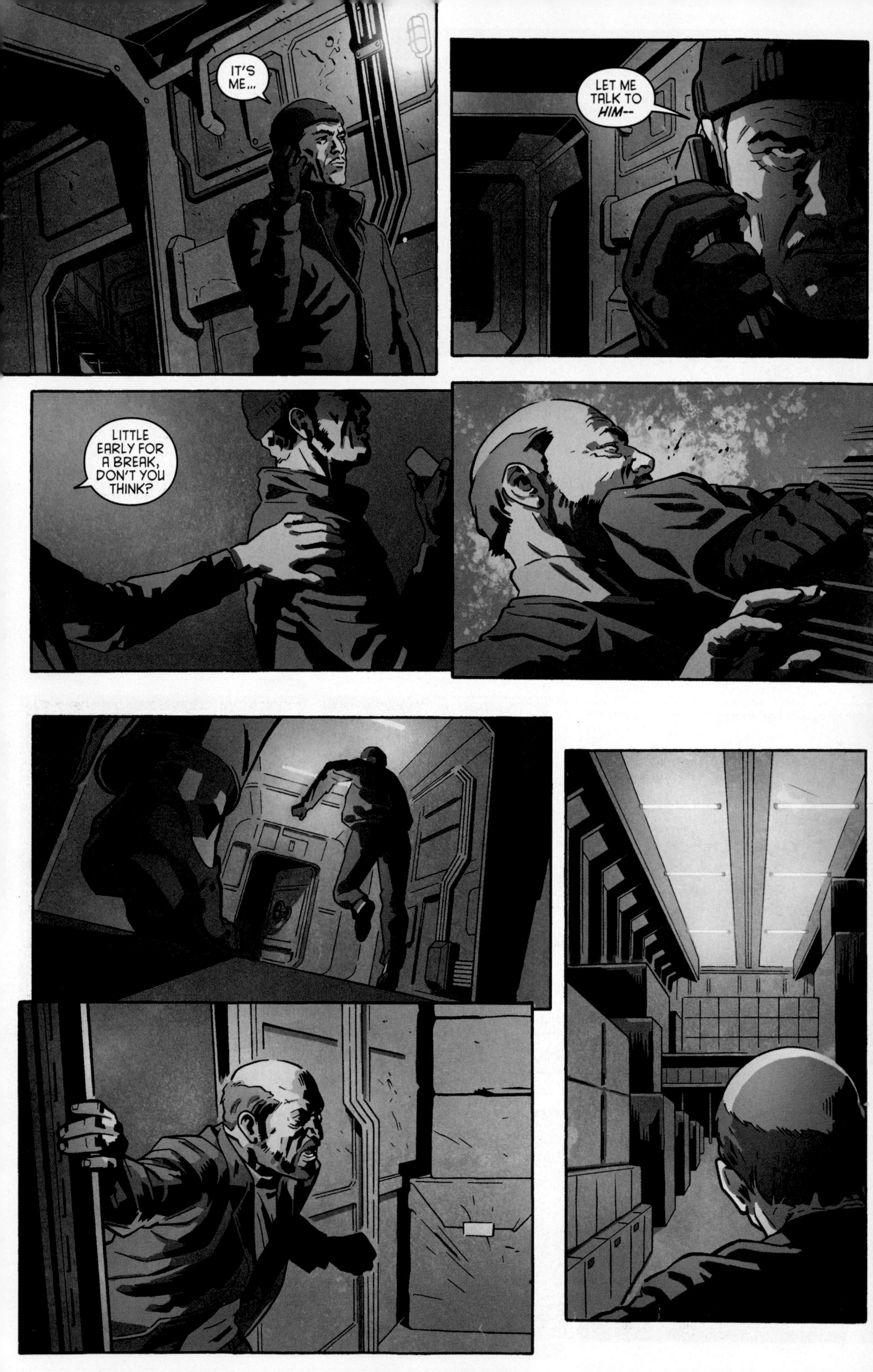
IT'S ME...
LET ME TALK TO *HIM*--
LITTLE EARLY FOR A BREAK, DON'T YOU THINK?

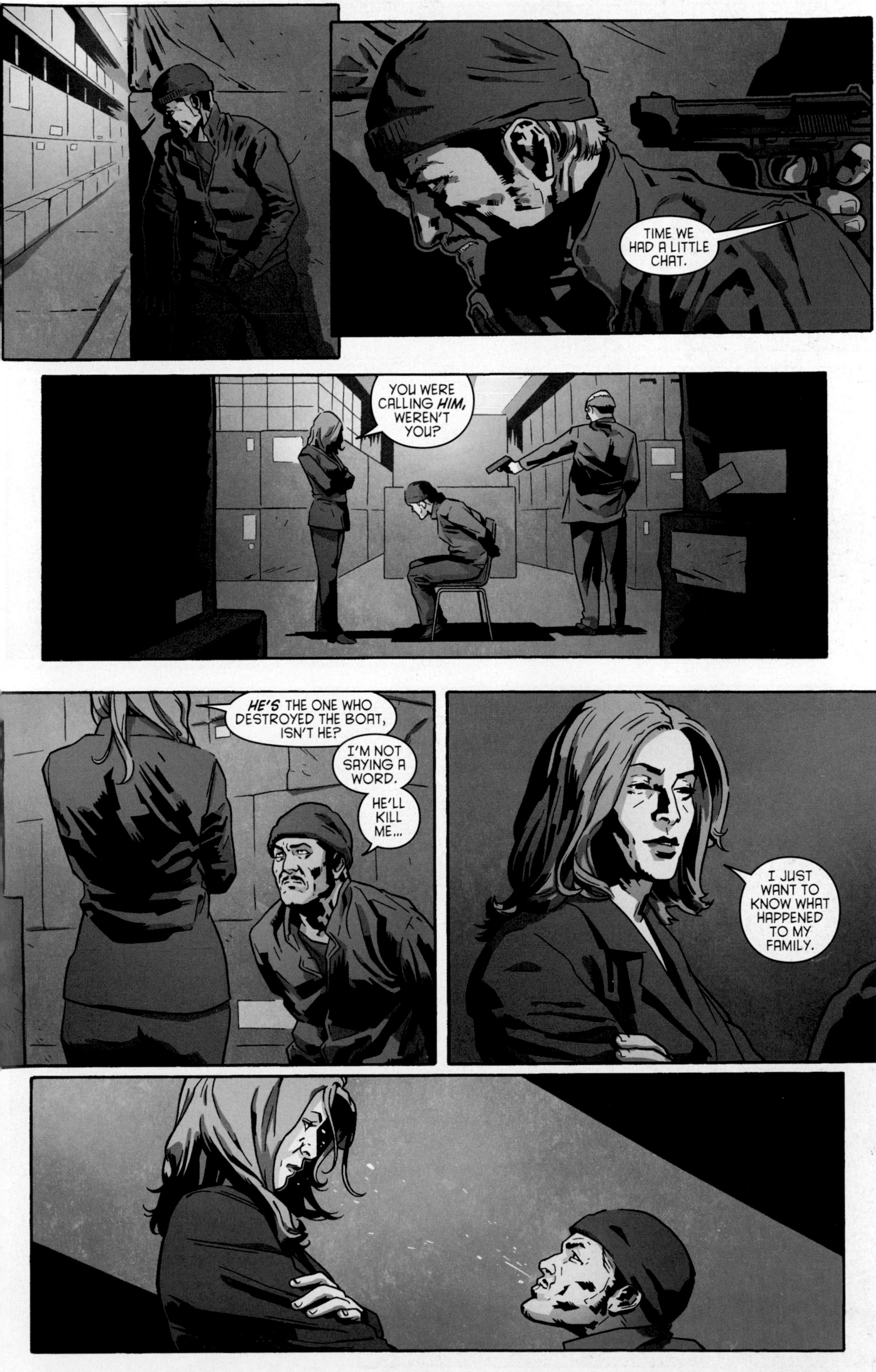
TIME WE HAD A LITTLE CHAT.
YOU WERE CALLING *HIM*, WEREN'T YOU?
HE'S THE ONE WHO DESTROYED THE BOAT, ISN'T HE?
I'M NOT SAYING A WORD.
HE'LL KILL ME...
I JUST WANT TO KNOW WHAT HAPPENED TO MY FAMILY.

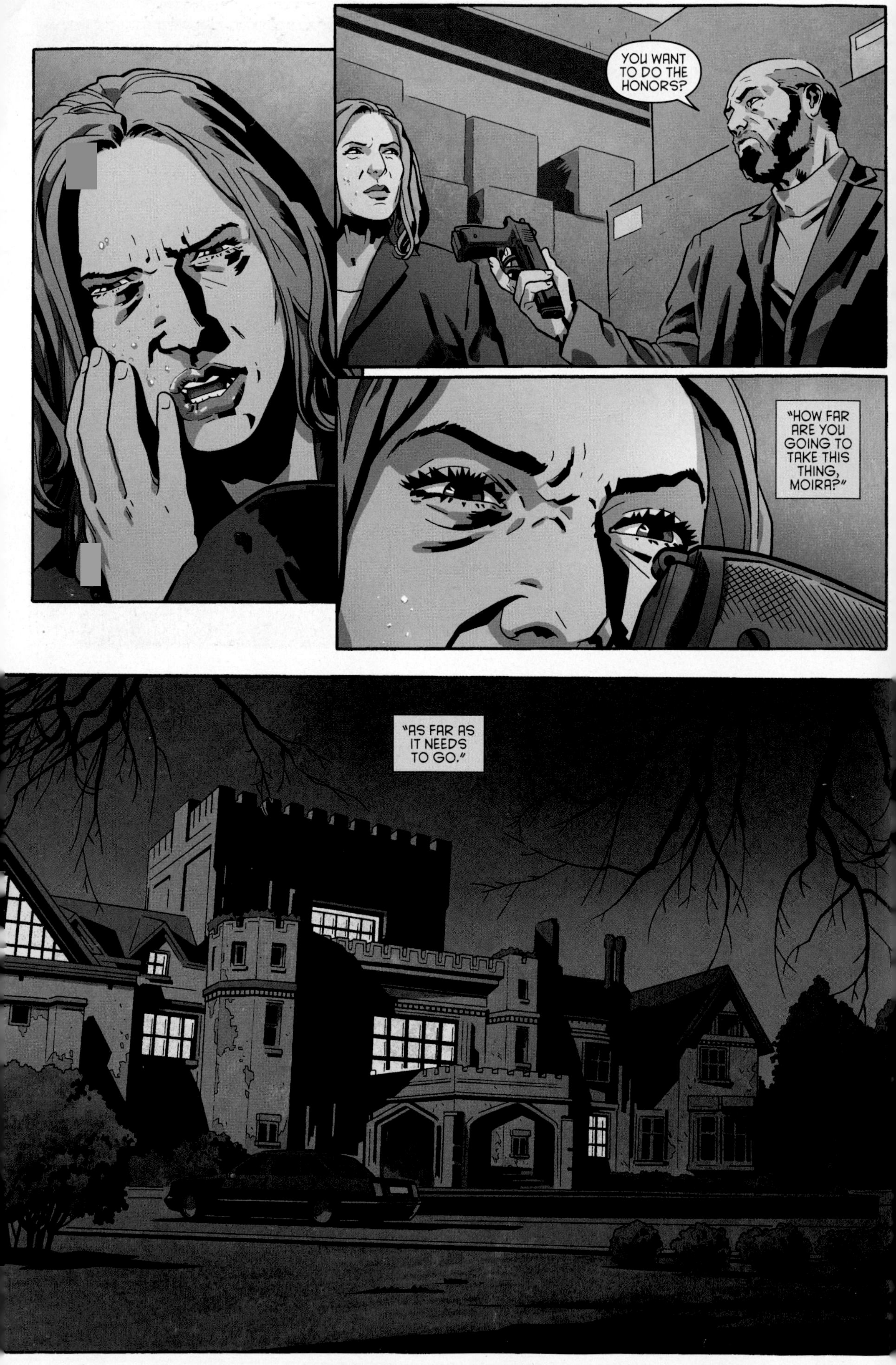
YOU WANT TO DO THE HONORS?
"HOW FAR ARE YOU GOING TO TAKE THIS THING, MOIRA?"
"AS FAR AS IT NEEDS TO GO."

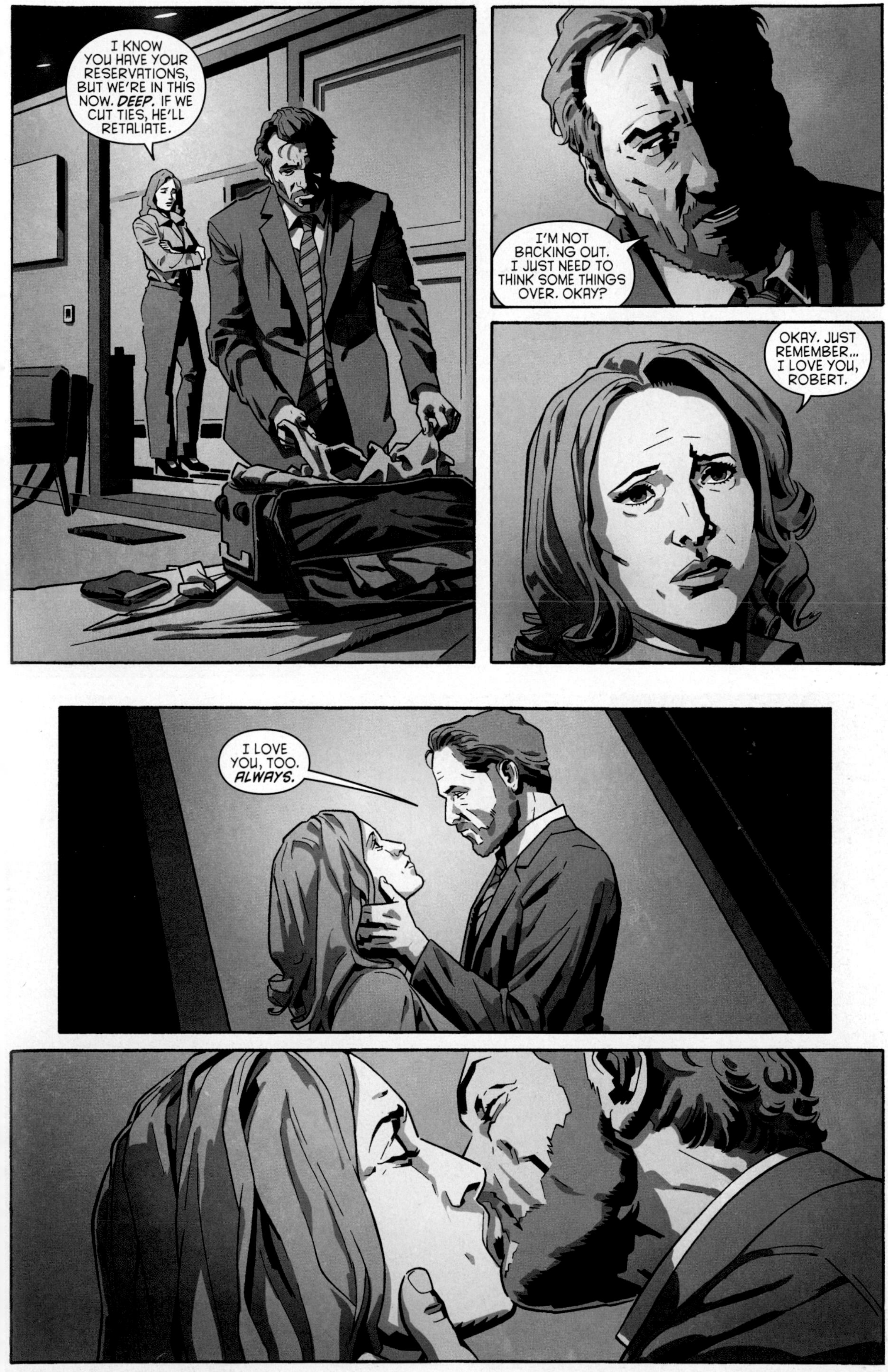
I KNOW YOU HAVE YOUR RESERVATIONS, BUT WE'RE IN THIS NOW. DEEP. IF WE CUT TIES, HE'LL RETALIATE.
I'M NOT BACKING OUT. I JUST NEED TO THINK SOME THINGS OVER. OKAY?
OKAY. JUST REMEMBER... I LOVE YOU, ROBERT.
I LOVE YOU, TOO. ALWAYS.

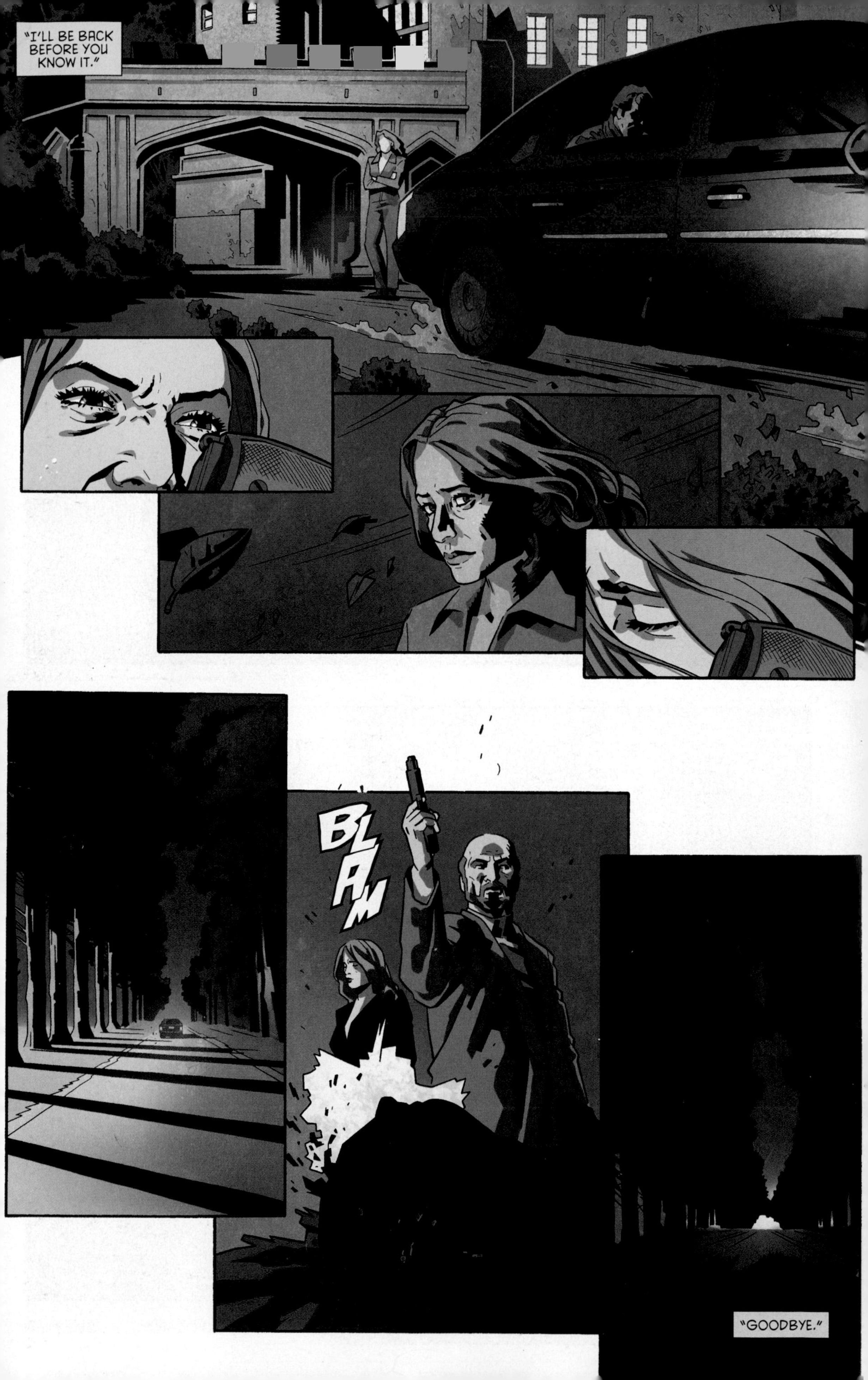
"I'LL BE BACK BEFORE YOU KNOW IT."
BLAM
"GOODBYE."

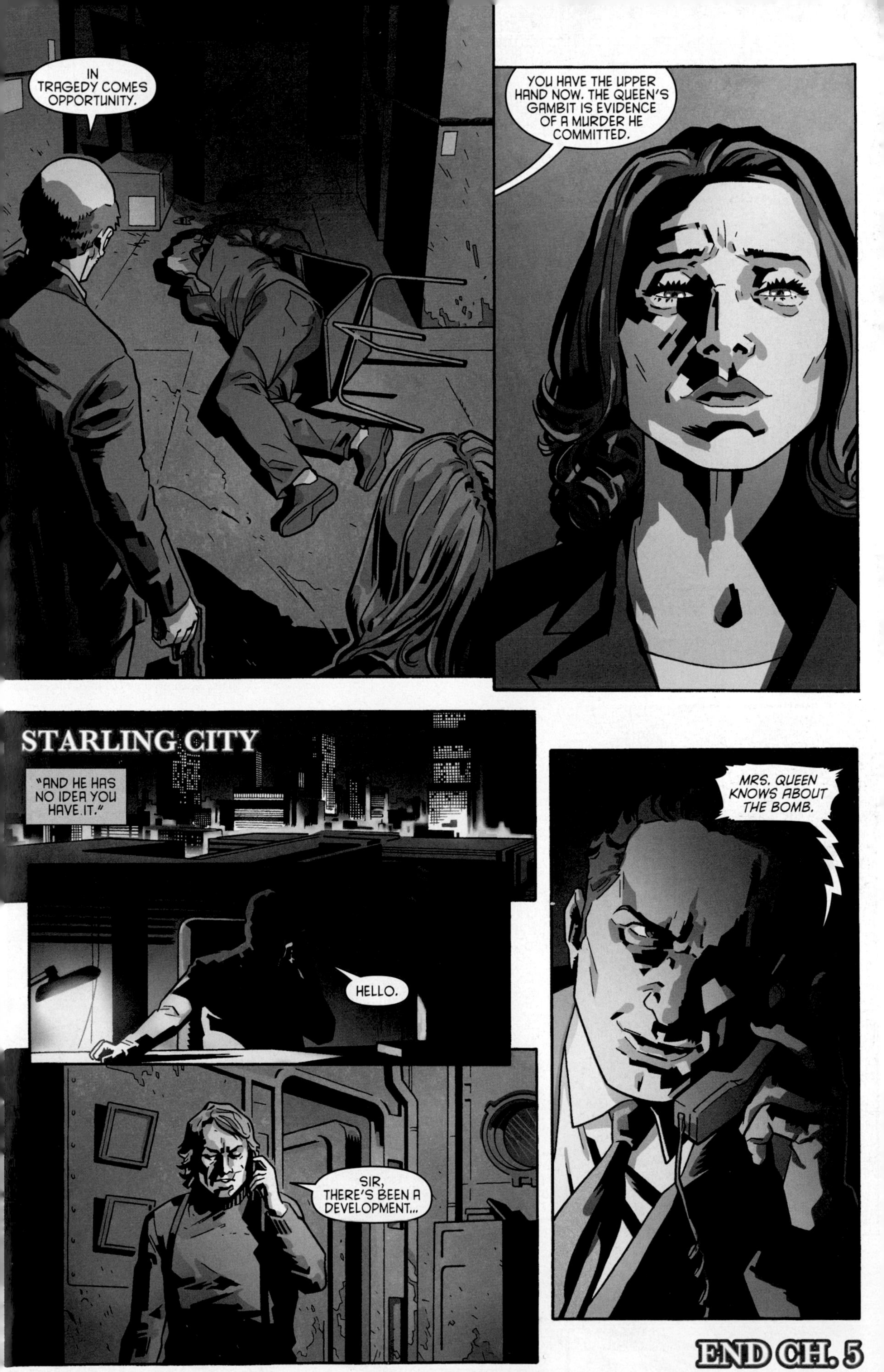
IN TRAGEDY COMES OPPORTUNITY.
YOU HAVE THE UPPER HAND NOW. THE QUEEN'S GAMBIT IS EVIDENCE OF A MURDER HE COMMITTED.
STARLING CITY
"AND HE HAS NO IDEA YOU HAVE IT."
HELLO.
SIR, THERE'S BEEN A DEVELOPMENT...
MRS. QUEEN KNOWS ABOUT THE BOMB.
END CH. 5

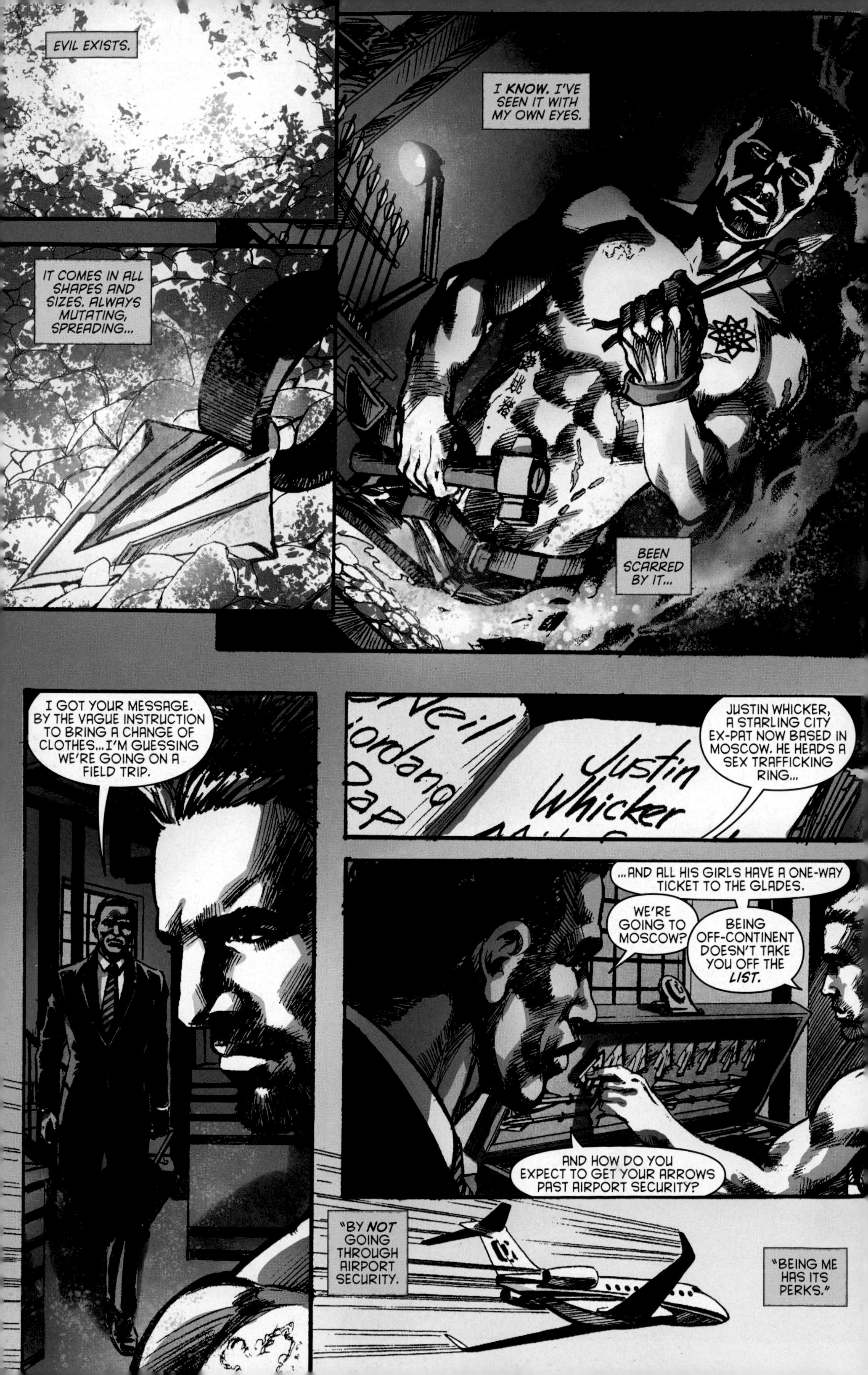
EVIL EXISTS.
I KNOW. I'VE SEEN IT WITH MY OWN EYES.
IT COMES IN ALL SHAPES AND SIZES. ALWAYS MUTATING, SPREADING...
BEEN SCARRED BY IT...
I GOT YOUR MESSAGE. BY THE VAGUE INSTRUCTION TO BRING A CHANGE OF CLOTHES...I'M GUESSING WE'RE GOING ON A FIELD TRIP.
Justin Whicker
JUSTIN WHICKER, A STARLING CITY EX-PAT NOW BASED IN MOSCOW. HE HEADS A SEX TRAFFICKING RING...
...AND ALL HIS GIRLS HAVE A ONE-WAY TICKET TO THE GLADES.
WE'RE GOING TO MOSCOW?
BEING OFF-CONTINENT DOESN'T TAKE YOU OFF THE LIST.
AND HOW DO YOU EXPECT TO GET YOUR ARROWS PAST AIRPORT SECURITY?
"BY NOT GOING THROUGH AIRPORT SECURITY.
"BEING ME HAS ITS PERKS."

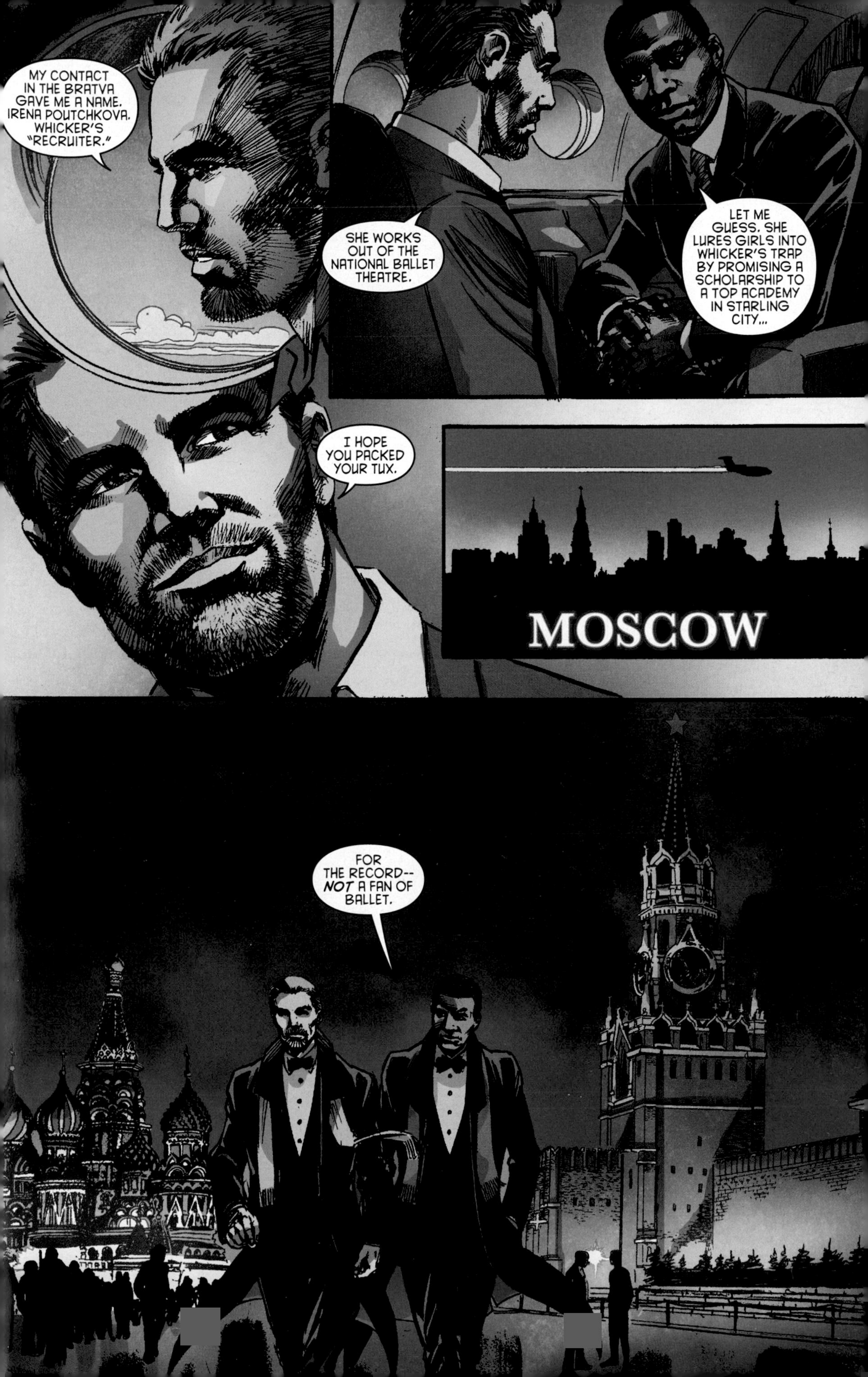
MY CONTACT IN THE BRATVA GAVE ME A NAME. IRENA POUTCHKOVA. WHICKER'S "RECRUITER."
SHE WORKS OUT OF THE NATIONAL BALLET THEATRE.
LET ME GUESS. SHE LURES GIRLS INTO WHICKER'S TRAP BY PROMISING A SCHOLARSHIP TO A TOP ACADEMY IN STARLING CITY...
I HOPE YOU PACKED YOUR TUX.
MOSCOW
FOR THE RECORD-- *NOT* A FAN OF BALLET.

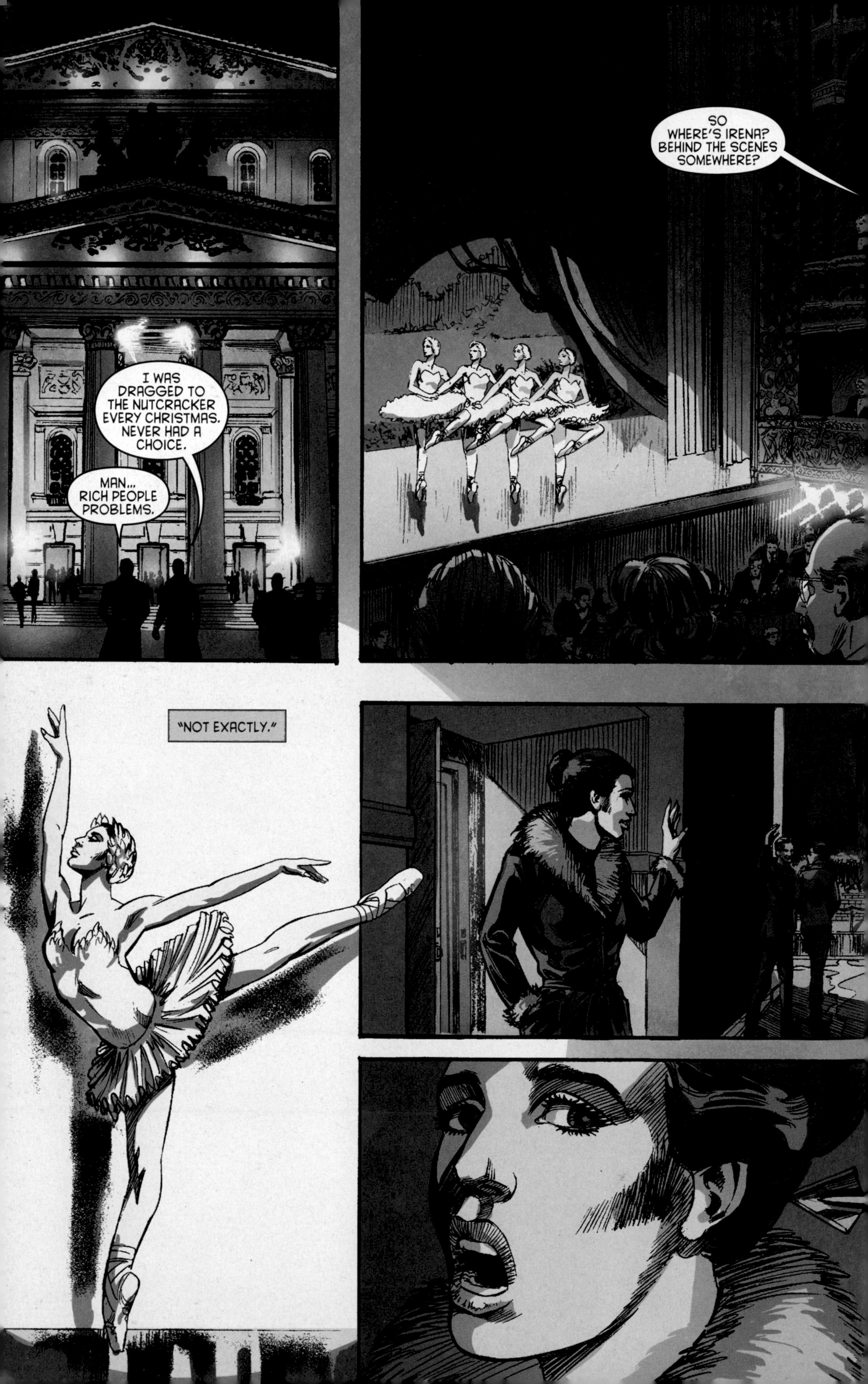
I WAS DRAGGED TO THE NUTCRACKER EVERY CHRISTMAS. NEVER HAD A CHOICE.
MAN... RICH PEOPLE PROBLEMS.
SO WHERE'S IRENA? BEHIND THE SCENES SOMEWHERE?
"NOT EXACTLY."

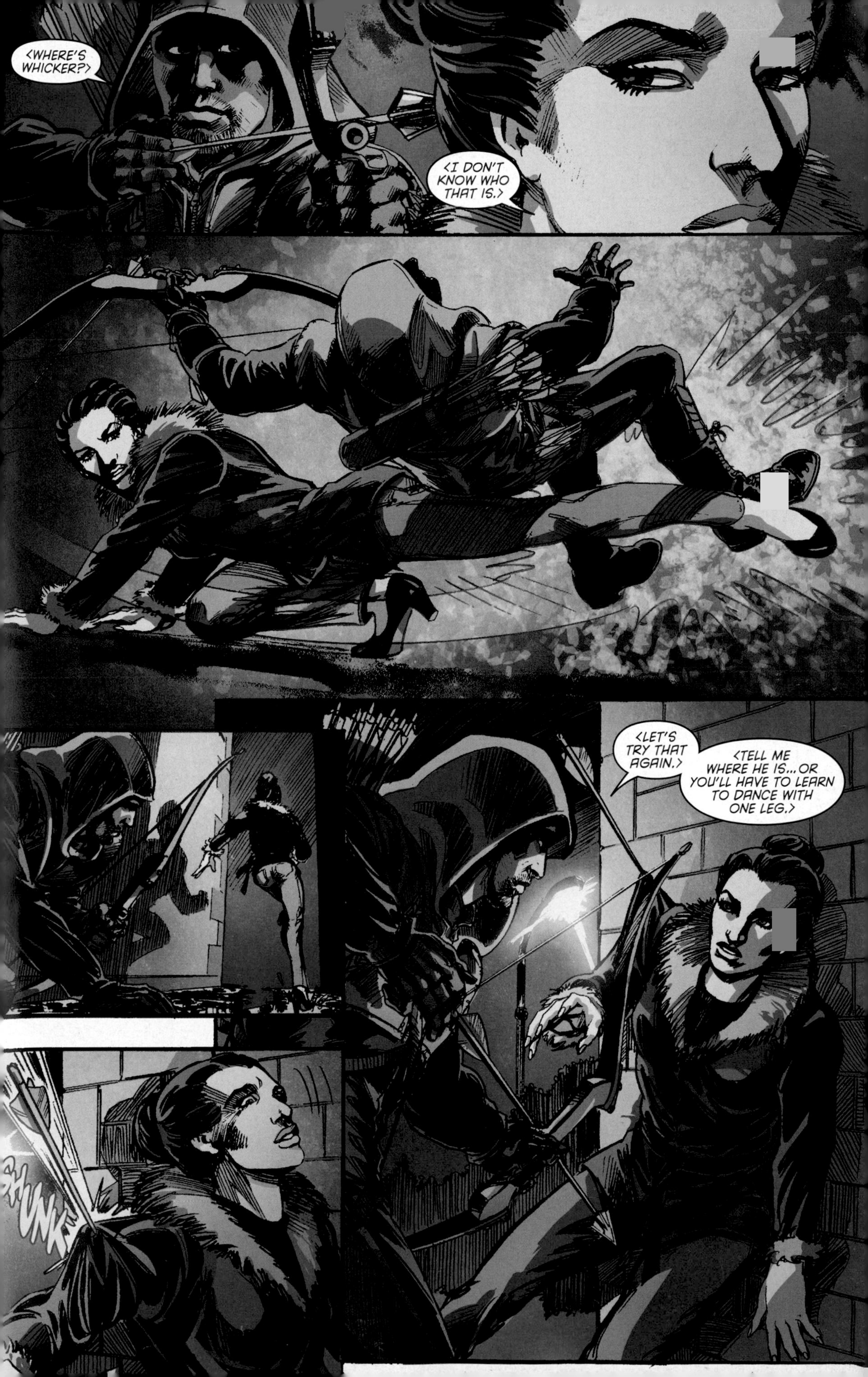
<WHERE'S WHICKER?>
<I DON'T KNOW WHO THAT IS.>
<LET'S TRY THAT AGAIN.>
<TELL ME WHERE HE IS...OR YOU'LL HAVE TO LEARN TO DANCE WITH ONE LEG.>
SHUNK

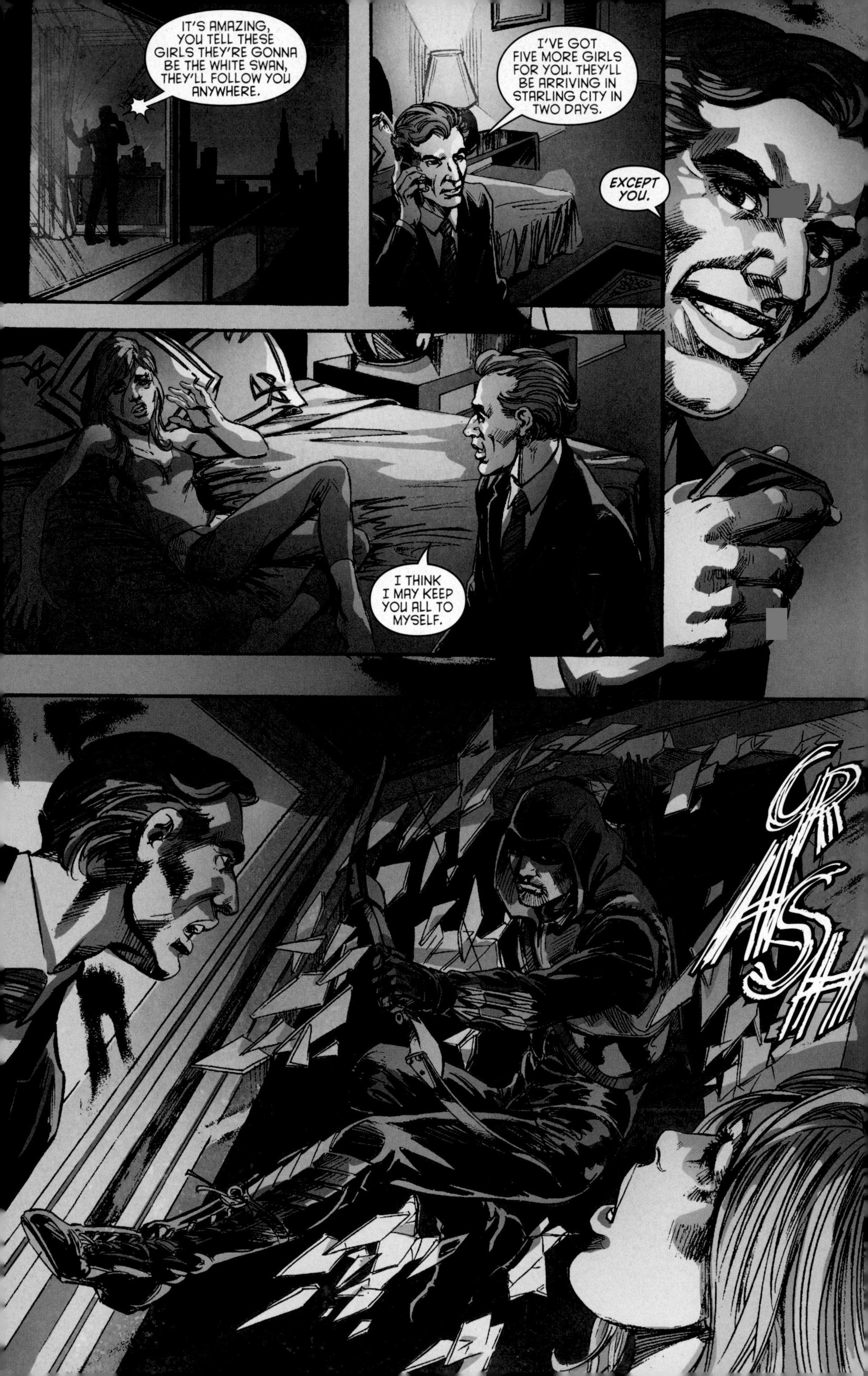
IT'S AMAZING, YOU TELL THESE GIRLS THEY'RE GONNA BE THE WHITE SWAN, THEY'LL FOLLOW YOU ANYWHERE.
I'VE GOT FIVE MORE GIRLS FOR YOU. THEY'LL BE ARRIVING IN STARLING CITY IN TWO DAYS.
EXCEPT YOU.
I THINK I MAY KEEP YOU ALL TO MYSELF.
CRASH

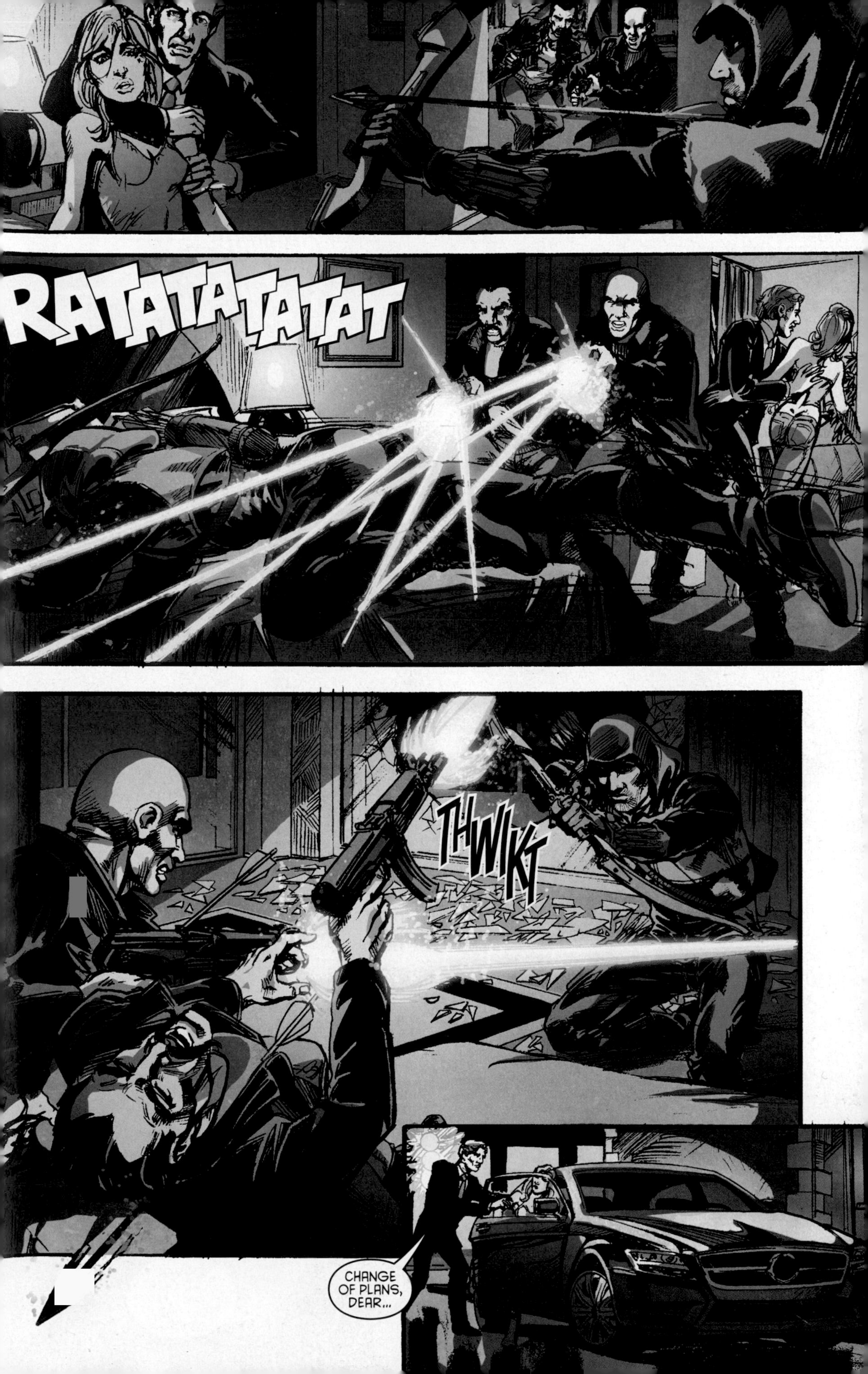
RATATATATAT
THWIKT
CHANGE OF PLANS, DEAR...

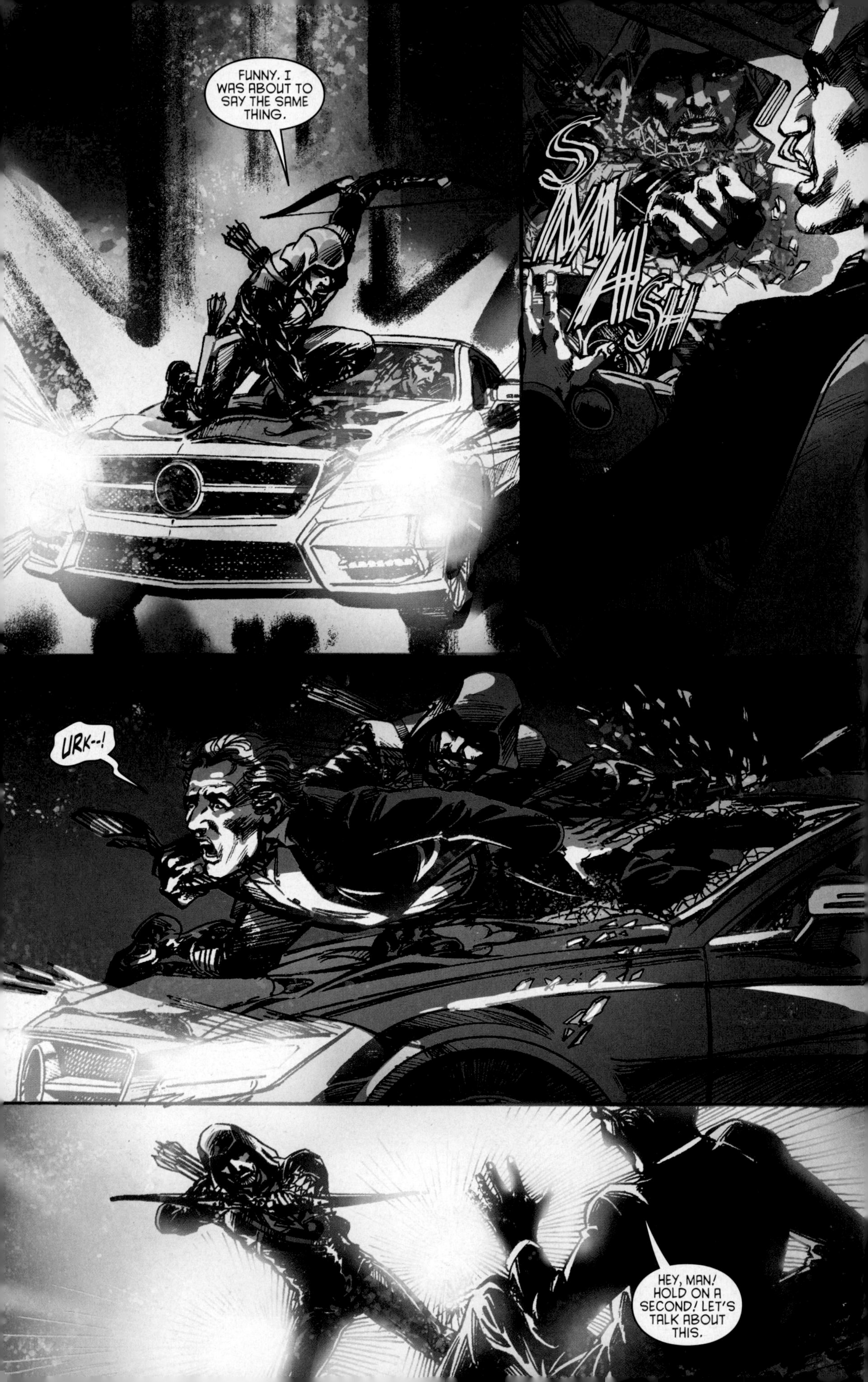
FUNNY. I WAS ABOUT TO SAY THE SAME THING.
SMASH
URK--!
HEY, MAN! HOLD ON A SECOND! LET'S TALK ABOUT THIS.

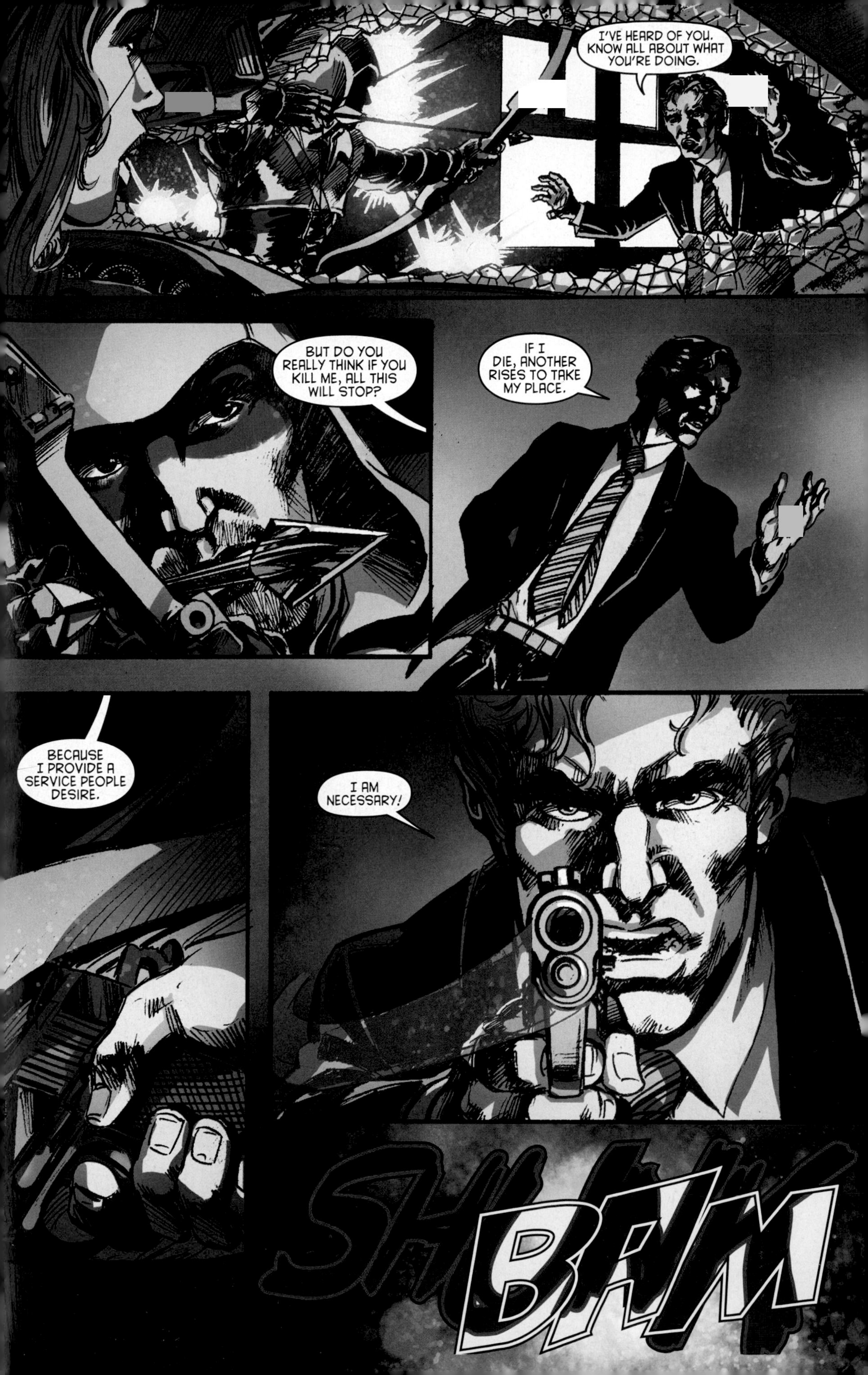
I'VE HEARD OF YOU. KNOW ALL ABOUT WHAT YOU'RE DOING.
BUT DO YOU REALLY THINK IF YOU KILL ME, ALL THIS WILL STOP?
IF I DIE, ANOTHER RISES TO TAKE MY PLACE.
BECAUSE I PROVIDE A SERVICE PEOPLE DESIRE.
I AM NECESSARY!
BAM

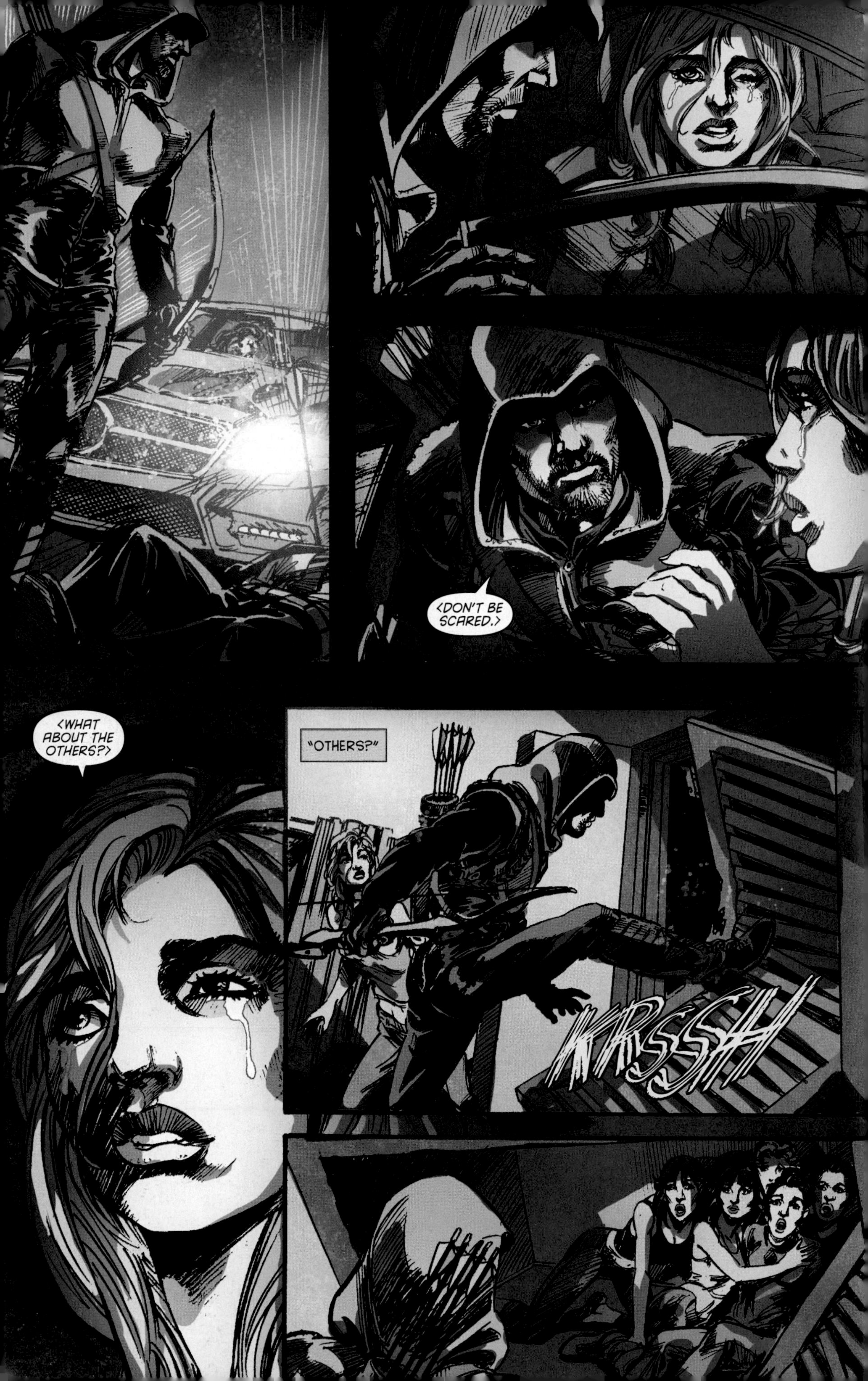

<DON'T BE SCARED.>
<WHAT ABOUT THE OTHERS?>
"OTHERS?"
KRSSSH

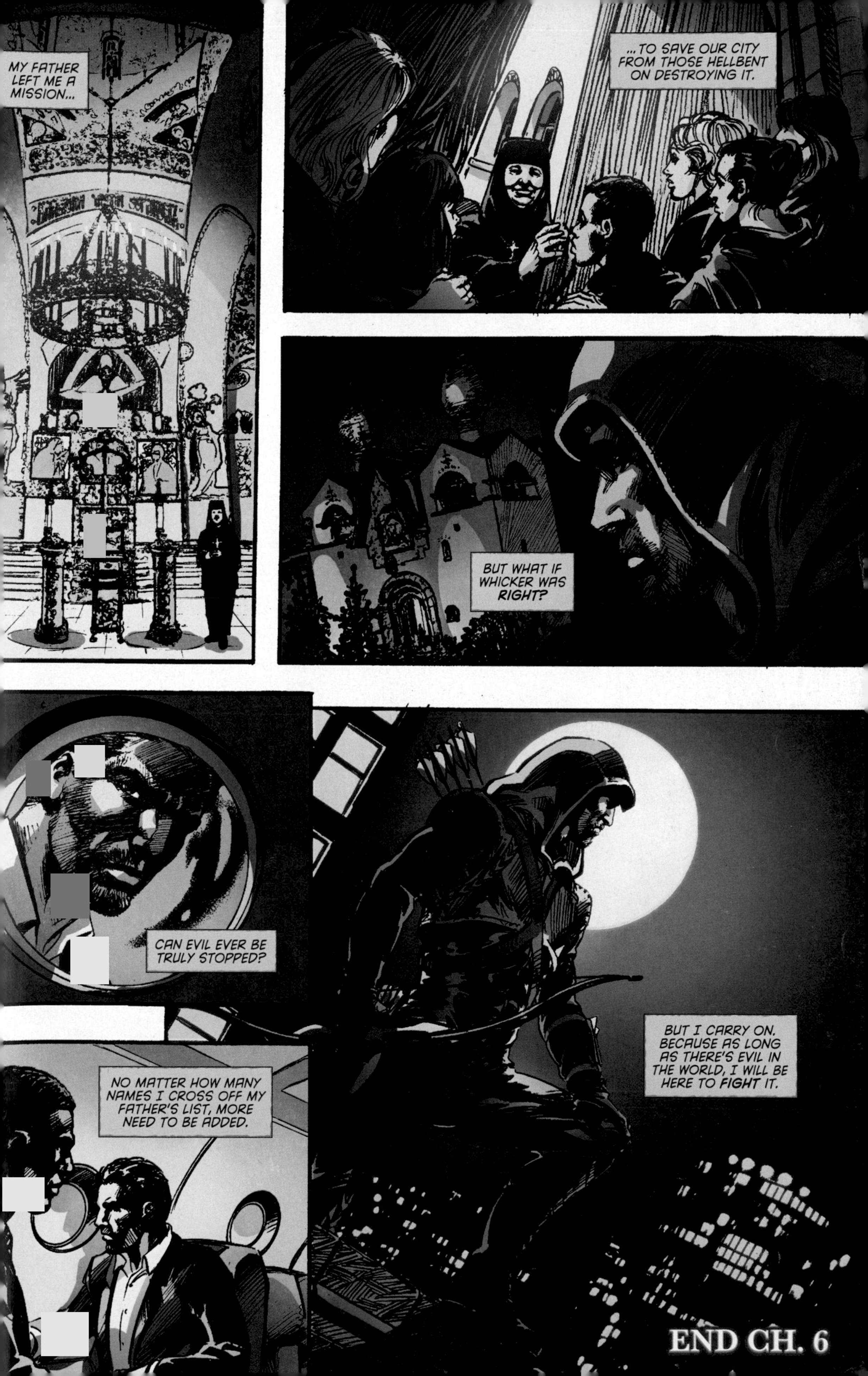
MY FATHER LEFT ME A MISSION...
...TO SAVE OUR CITY FROM THOSE HELLBENT ON DESTROYING IT.
BUT WHAT IF WHICKER WAS RIGHT?
CAN EVIL EVER BE TRULY STOPPED?
NO MATTER HOW MANY NAMES I CROSS OFF MY FATHER'S LIST, MORE NEED TO BE ADDED.
BUT I CARRY ON. BECAUSE AS LONG AS THERE'S EVIL IN THE WORLD, I WILL BE HERE TO FIGHT IT.
END CH. 6

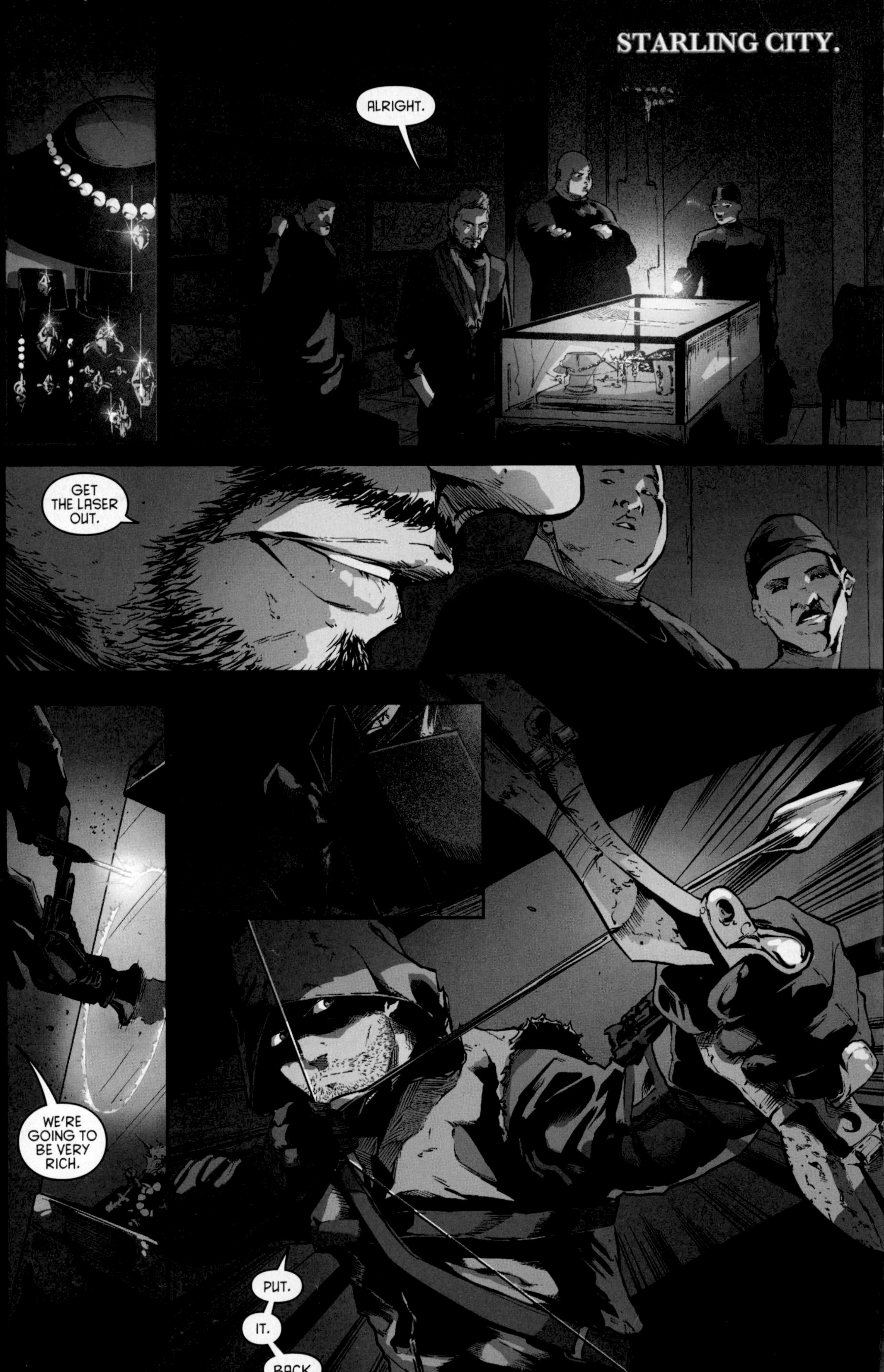
STARLING CITY.
ALRIGHT.
GET THE LASER OUT.
WE'RE GOING TO BE VERY RICH.
PUT.
IT.
BACK.

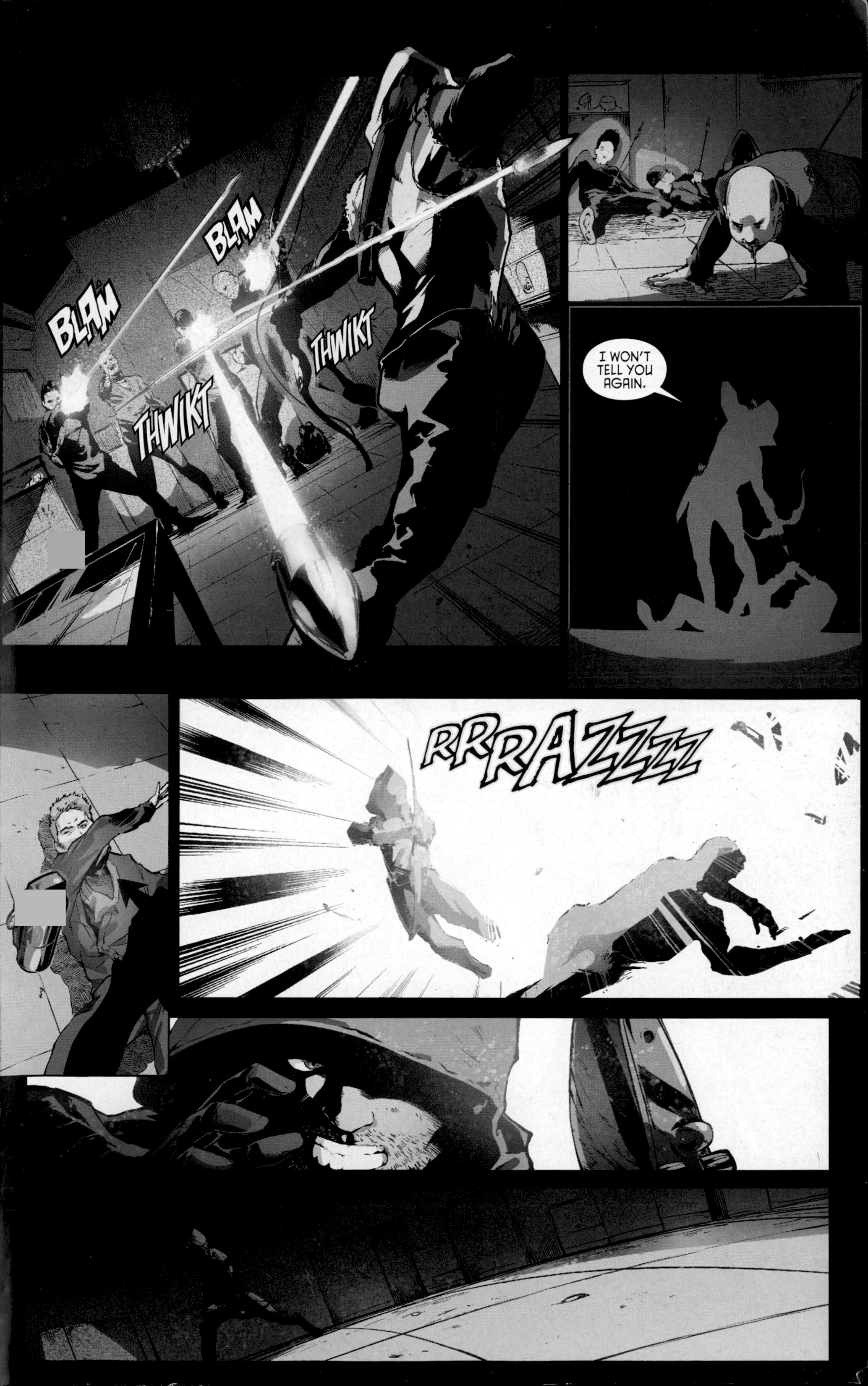
BLAM
BLAM
BLAM
THWIKT
THWIKT
I WON'T TELL YOU AGAIN.
RRRAZZZZ

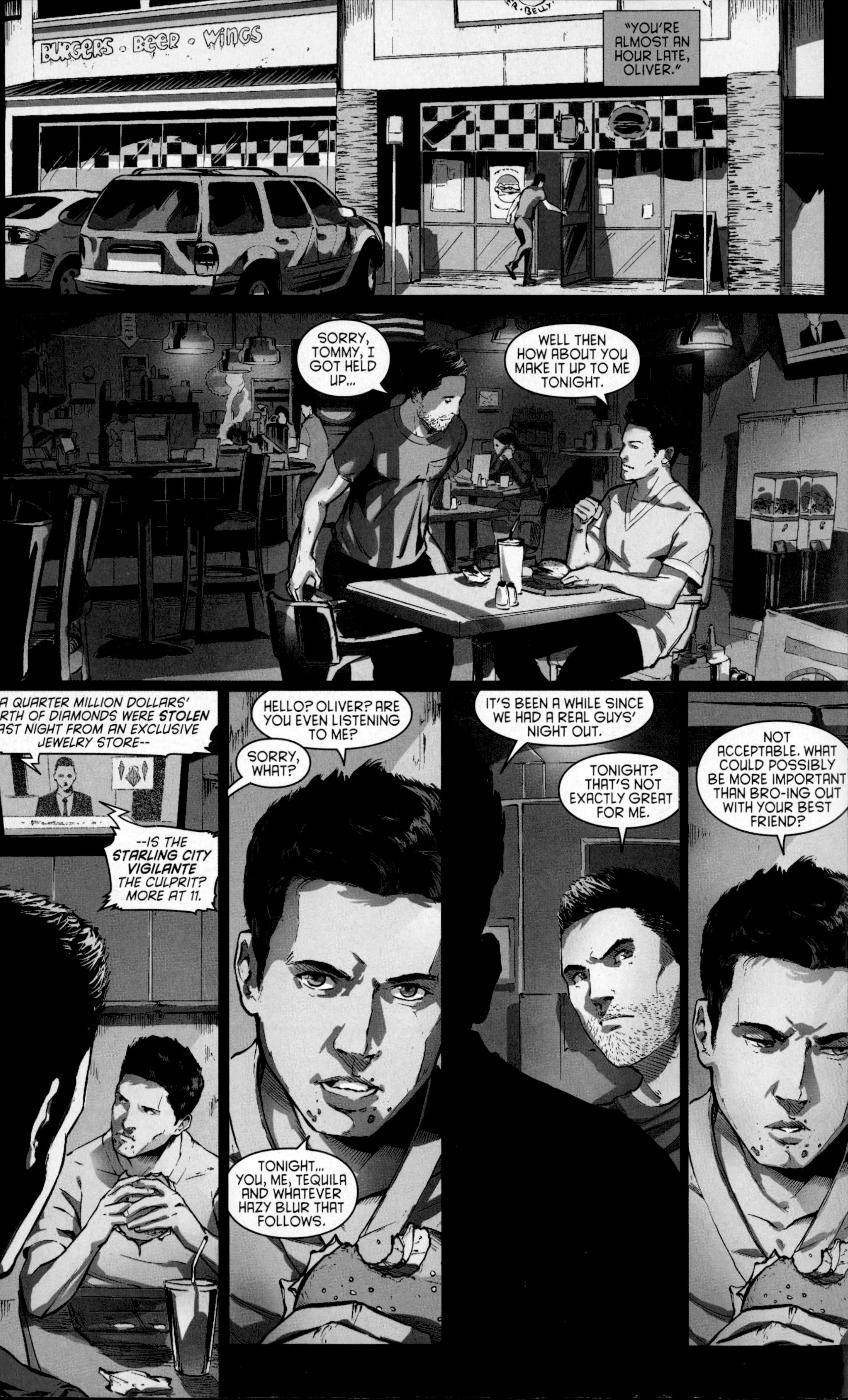
BURGERS · BEER · WINGS
"YOU'RE ALMOST AN HOUR LATE, OLIVER."
SORRY, TOMMY, I GOT HELD UP...
WELL THEN HOW ABOUT YOU MAKE IT UP TO ME TONIGHT.
A QUARTER MILLION DOLLARS' WORTH OF DIAMONDS WERE STOLEN LAST NIGHT FROM AN EXCLUSIVE JEWELRY STORE--
--IS THE STARLING CITY VIGILANTE THE CULPRIT? MORE AT 11.
HELLO? OLIVER? ARE YOU EVEN LISTENING TO ME?
SORRY, WHAT?
TONIGHT... YOU, ME, TEQUILA AND WHATEVER HAZY BLUR THAT FOLLOWS.
IT'S BEEN A WHILE SINCE WE HAD A REAL GUYS' NIGHT OUT.
TONIGHT? THAT'S NOT EXACTLY GREAT FOR ME.
NOT ACCEPTABLE. WHAT COULD POSSIBLY BE MORE IMPORTANT THAN BRO-ING OUT WITH YOUR BEST FRIEND?

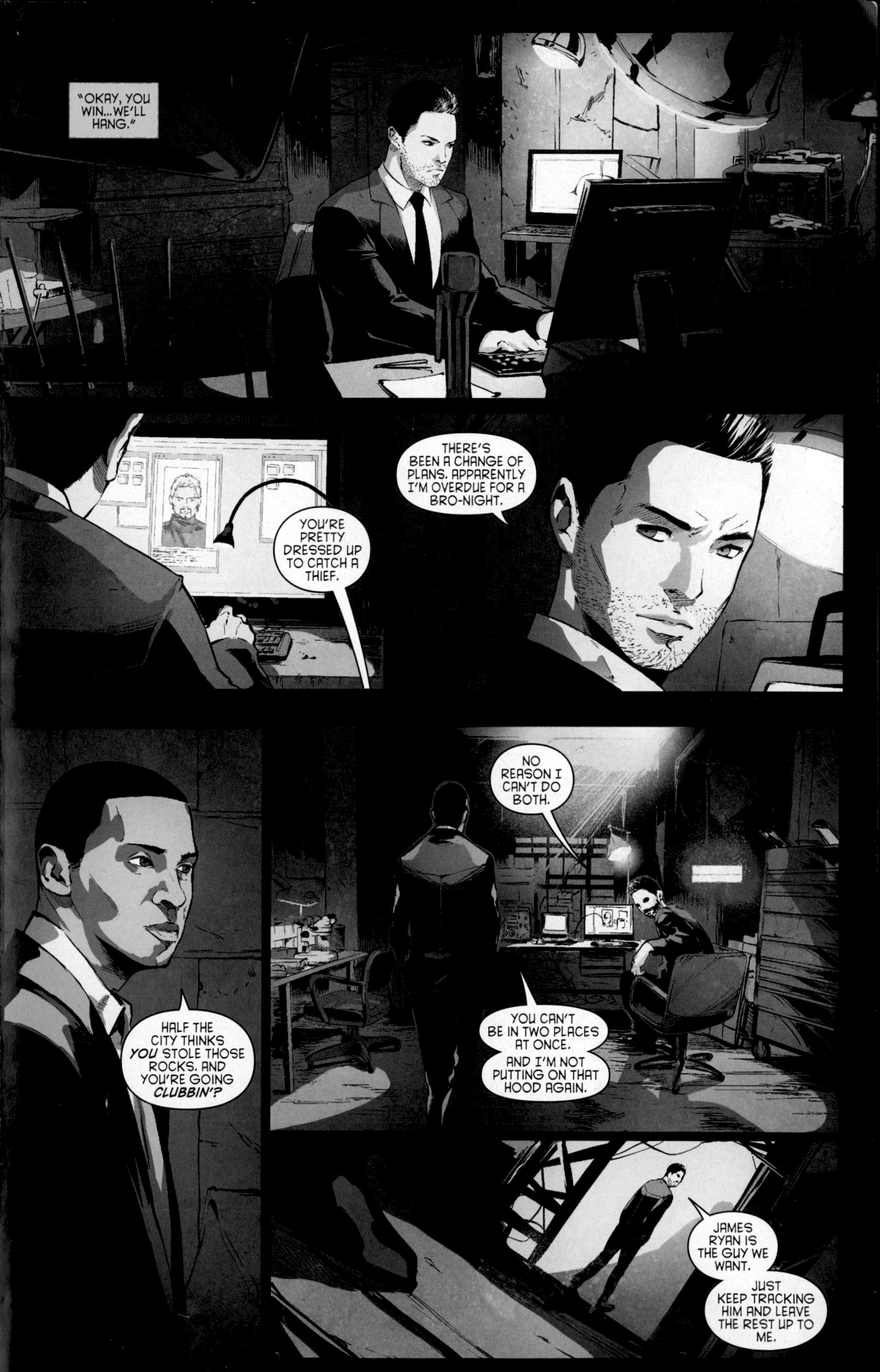
"OKAY, YOU WIN... WE'LL HANG."
THERE'S BEEN A CHANGE OF PLANS. APPARENTLY I'M OVERDUE FOR A BRO-NIGHT.
YOU'RE PRETTY DRESSED UP TO CATCH A THIEF.
NO REASON I CAN'T DO BOTH.
HALF THE CITY THINKS *YOU* STOLE THOSE ROCKS. AND YOU'RE GOING *CLUBBIN'?*
YOU CAN'T BE IN TWO PLACES AT ONCE.
AND I'M NOT PUTTING ON THAT HOOD AGAIN.
JAMES RYAN IS THE GUY WE WANT.
JUST KEEP TRACKING HIM AND LEAVE THE REST UP TO ME.

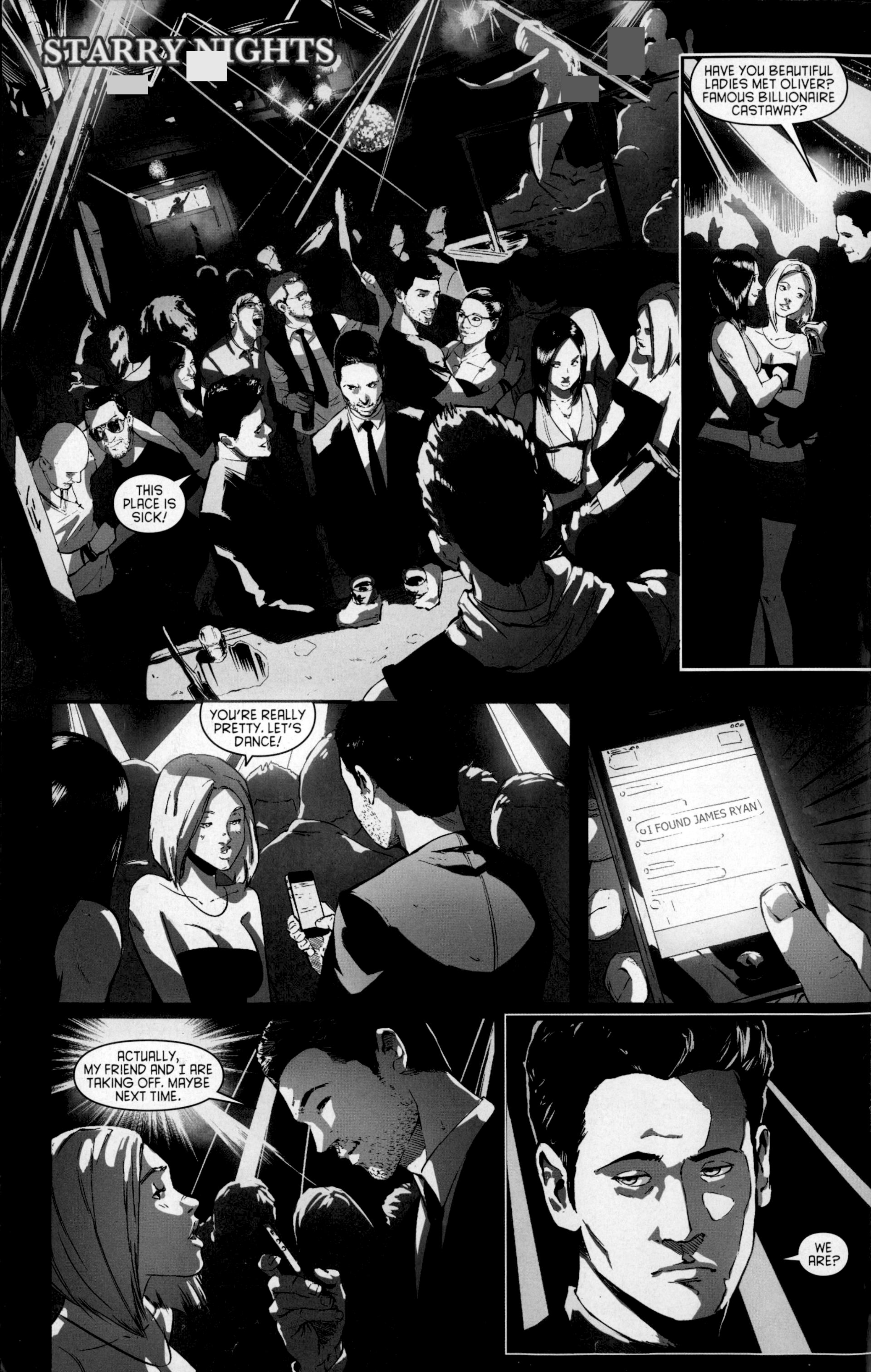
STARRY NIGHTS
HAVE YOU BEAUTIFUL LADIES MET OLIVER? FAMOUS BILLIONAIRE CASTAWAY?
THIS PLACE IS SICK!
YOU'RE REALLY PRETTY. LET'S DANCE!
I FOUND JAMES RYAN
ACTUALLY, MY FRIEND AND I ARE TAKING OFF. MAYBE NEXT TIME.
WE ARE?

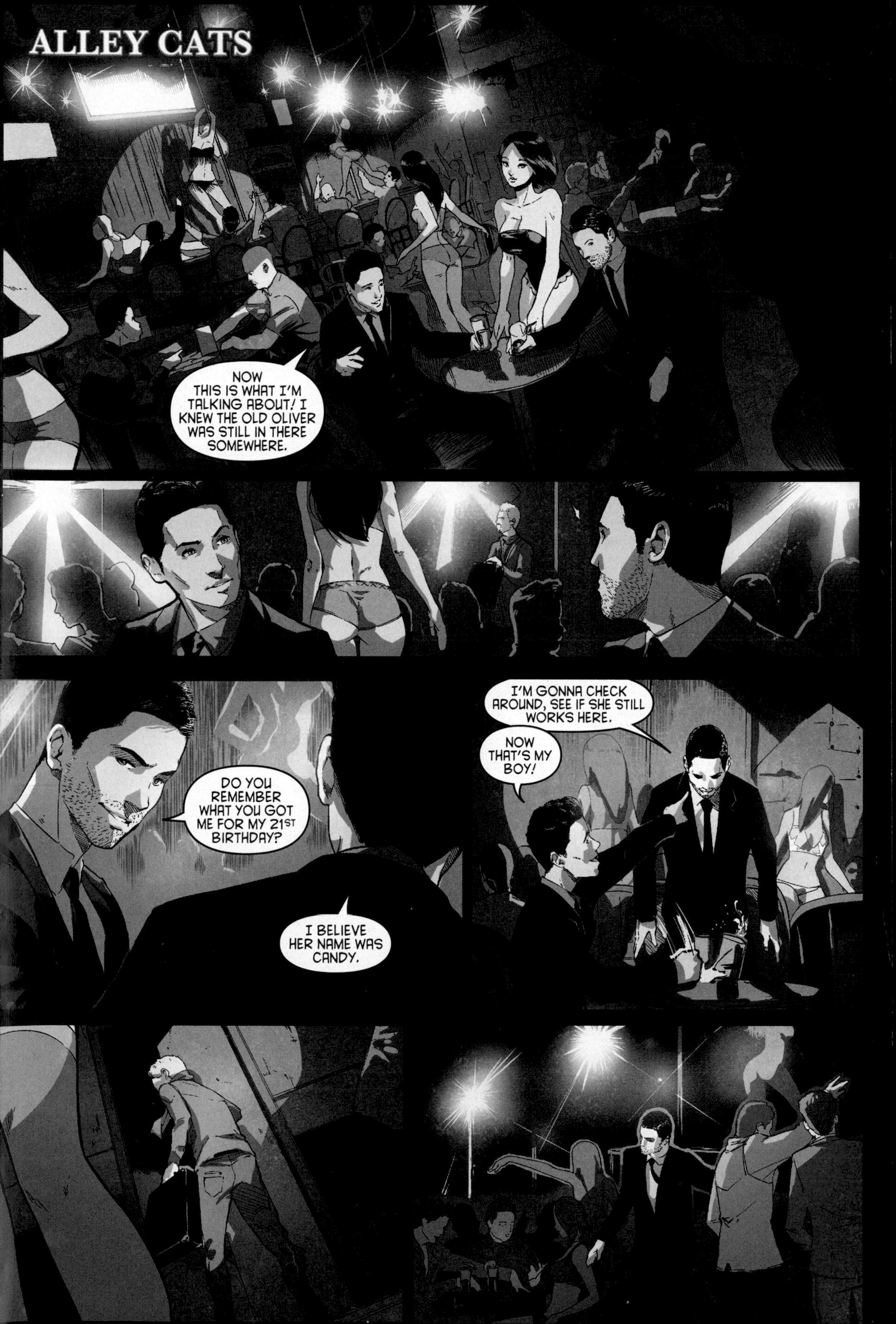
ALLEY CATS
NOW THIS IS WHAT I'M TALKING ABOUT! I KNEW THE OLD OLIVER WAS STILL IN THERE SOMEWHERE.
DO YOU REMEMBER WHAT YOU GOT ME FOR MY 21ST BIRTHDAY?
I BELIEVE HER NAME WAS CANDY.
I'M GONNA CHECK AROUND, SEE IF SHE STILL WORKS HERE.
NOW THAT'S MY BOY!

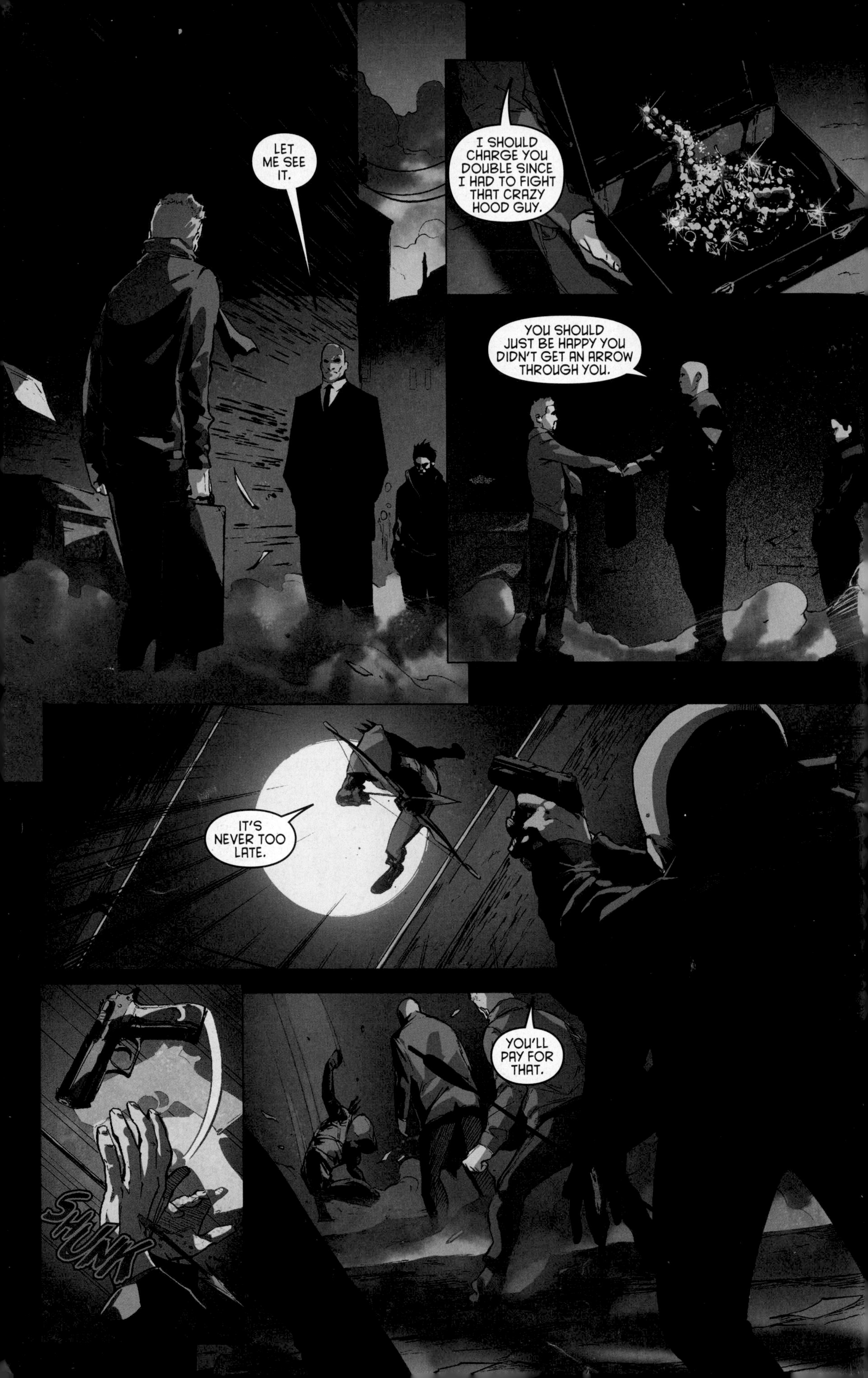
LET ME SEE IT.
I SHOULD CHARGE YOU DOUBLE SINCE I HAD TO FIGHT THAT CRAZY HOOD GUY.
YOU SHOULD JUST BE HAPPY YOU DIDN'T GET AN ARROW THROUGH YOU.
IT'S NEVER TOO LATE.
SHUNK
YOU'LL PAY FOR THAT.

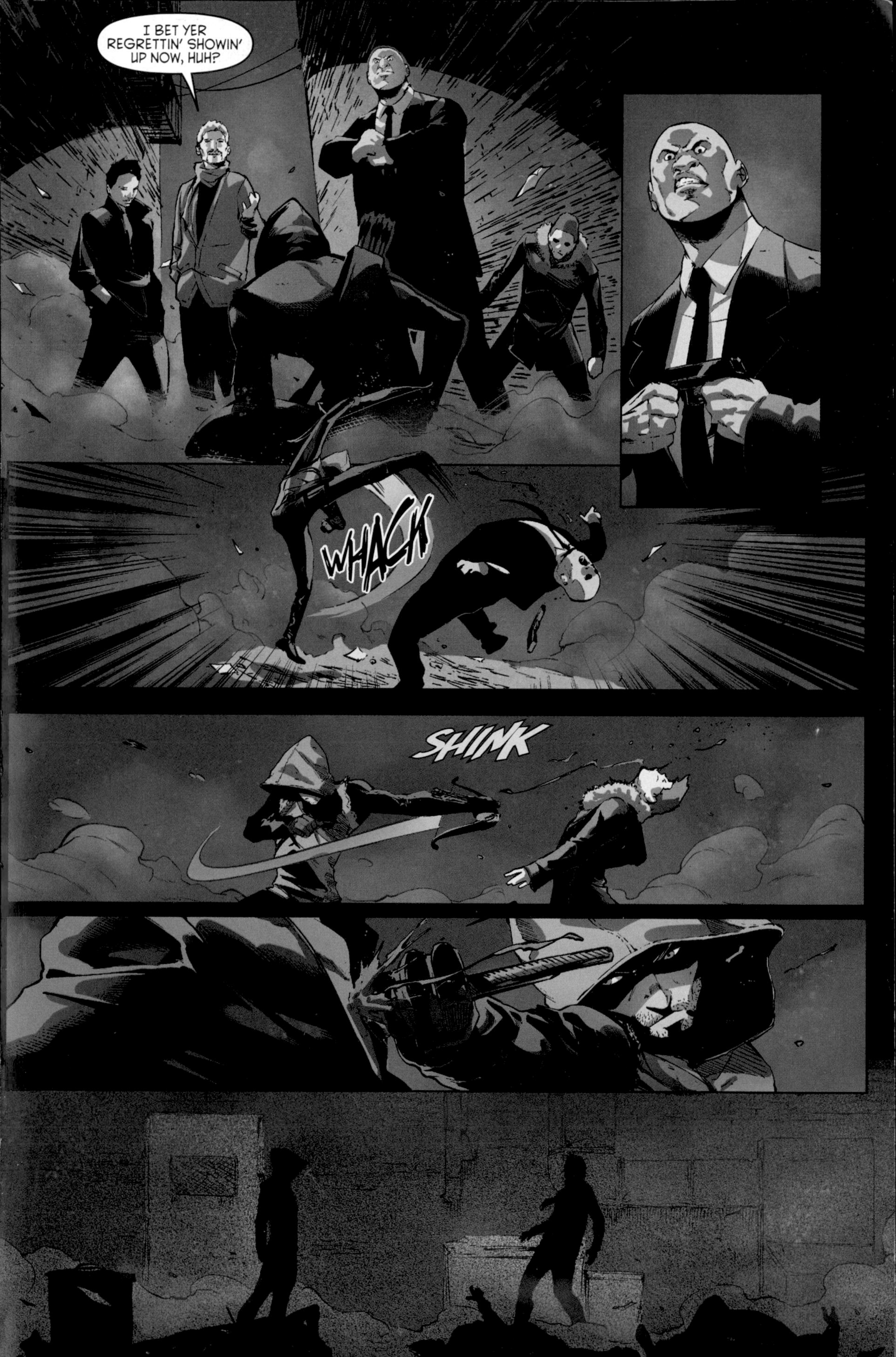
I BET YER REGRETTIN' SHOWIN' UP NOW, HUH?
WHACK
SHINK

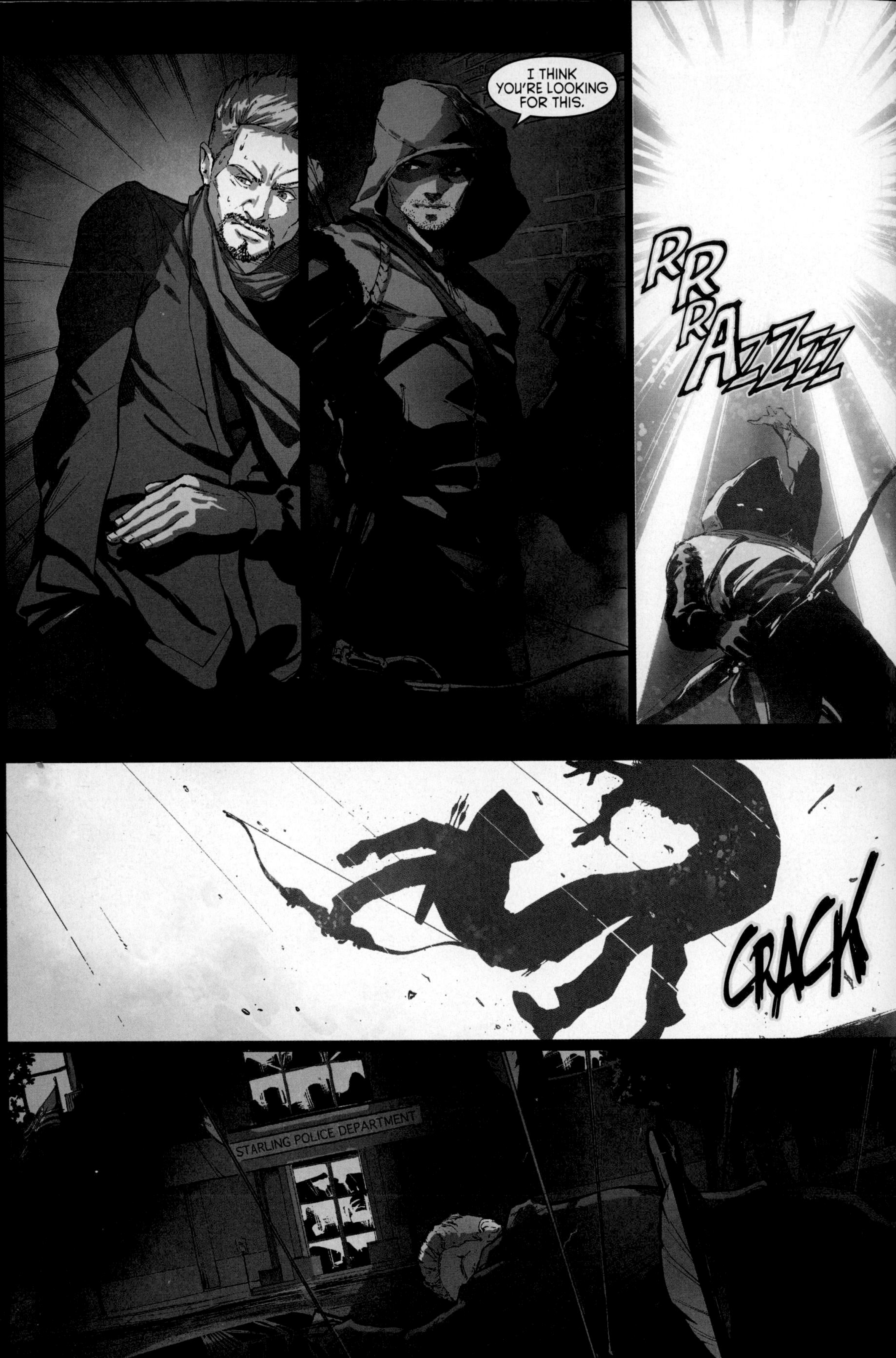
I THINK YOU'RE LOOKING FOR THIS.
RRRAZZZZ
CRACK
STARLING POLICE DEPARTMENT

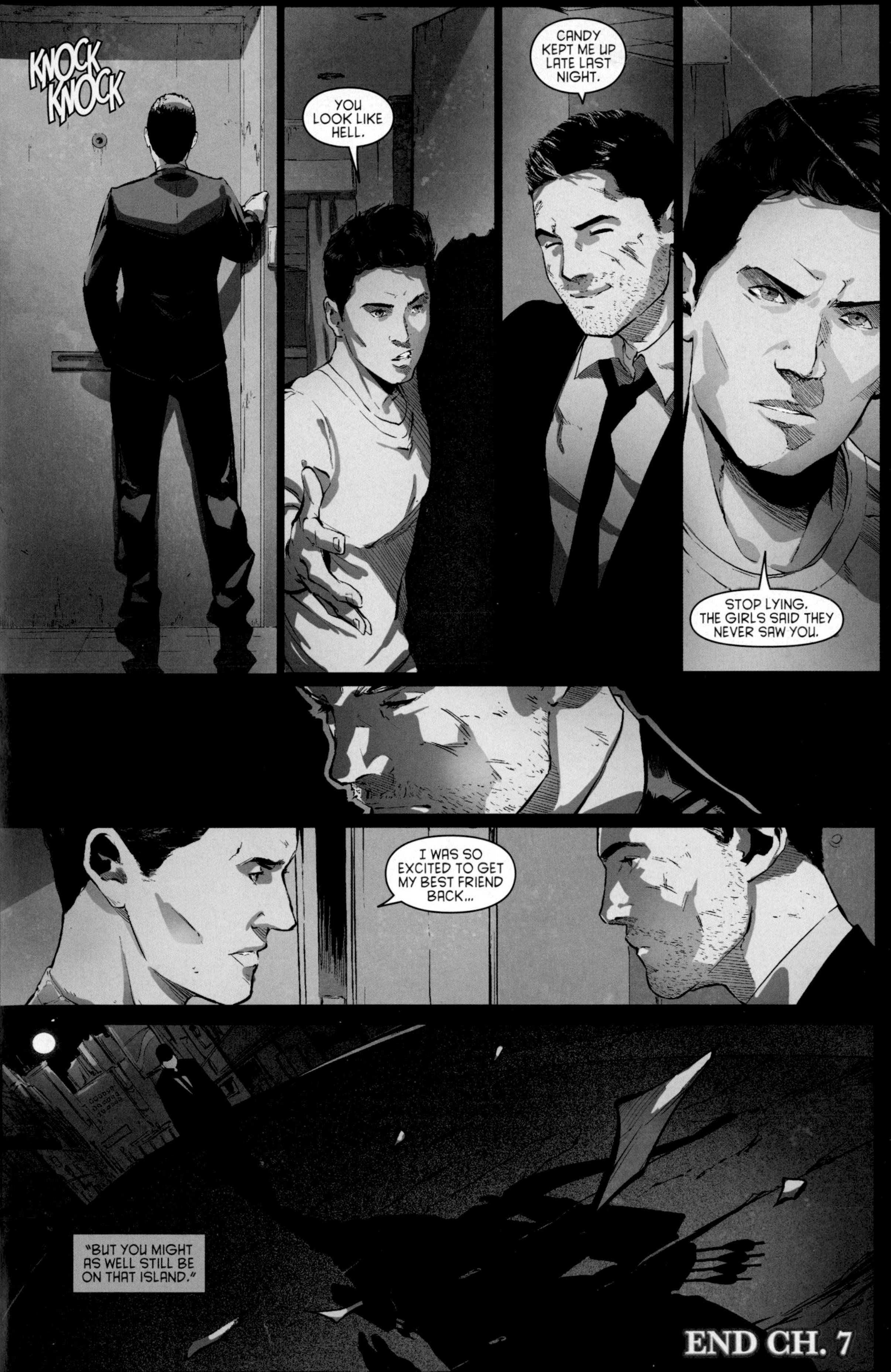
KNOCK KNOCK
YOU LOOK LIKE HELL.
CANDY KEPT ME UP LATE LAST NIGHT.
STOP LYING. THE GIRLS SAID THEY NEVER SAW YOU.
I WAS SO EXCITED TO GET MY BEST FRIEND BACK...
"BUT YOU MIGHT AS WELL STILL BE ON THAT ISLAND."
END CH. 7

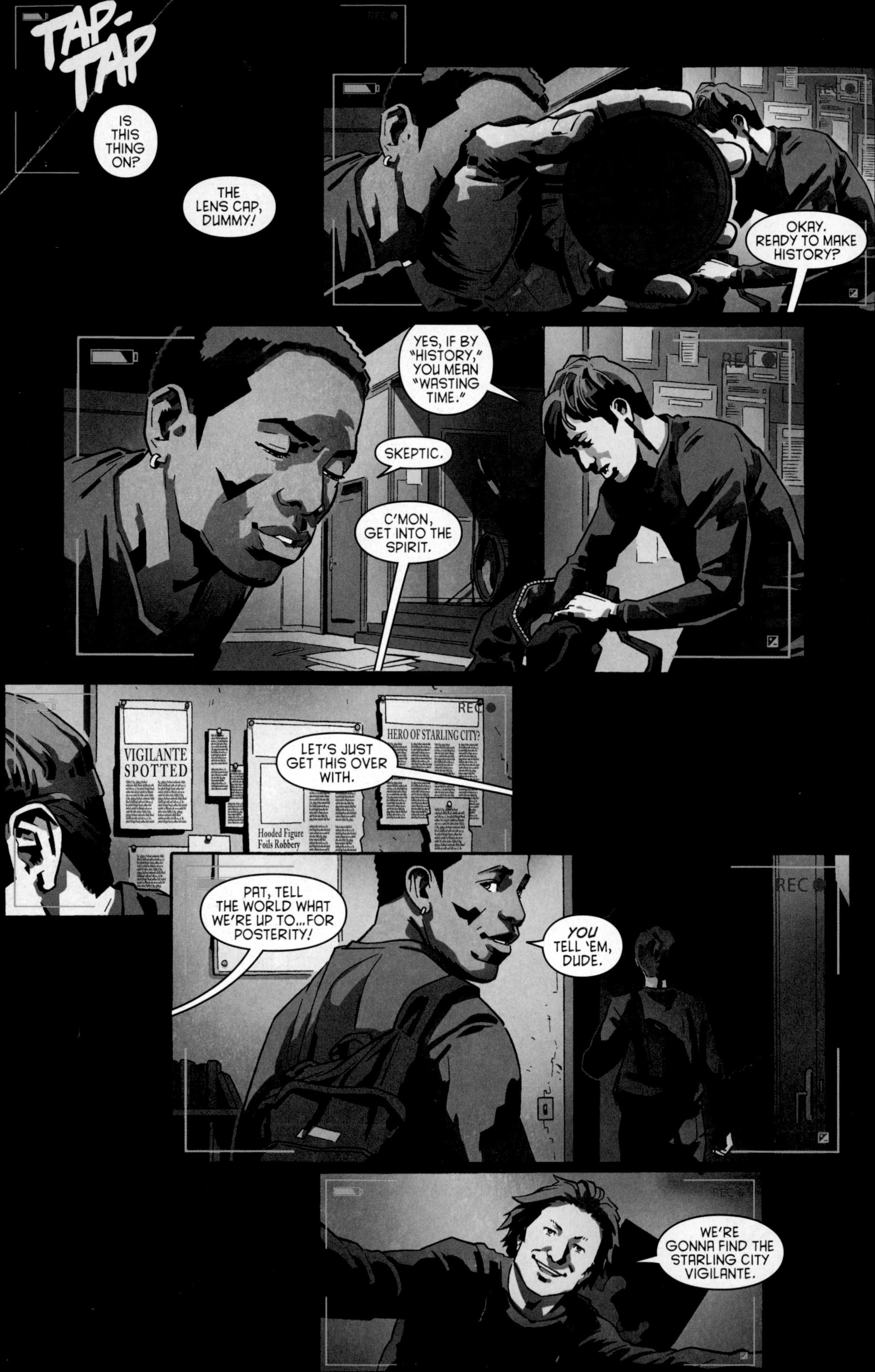
TAP-TAP
IS THIS THING ON?
THE LENS CAP, DUMMY!
OKAY. READY TO MAKE HISTORY?
YES, IF BY "HISTORY," YOU MEAN "WASTING TIME."
SKEPTIC.
C'MON, GET INTO THE SPIRIT.
VIGILANTE SPOTTED
HERO OF STARLING CITY?
Hooded Figure Foils Robbery
LET'S JUST GET THIS OVER WITH.
PAT, TELL THE WORLD WHAT WE'RE UP TO...FOR POSTERITY!
YOU TELL 'EM, DUDE.
WE'RE GONNA FIND THE STARLING CITY VIGILANTE.

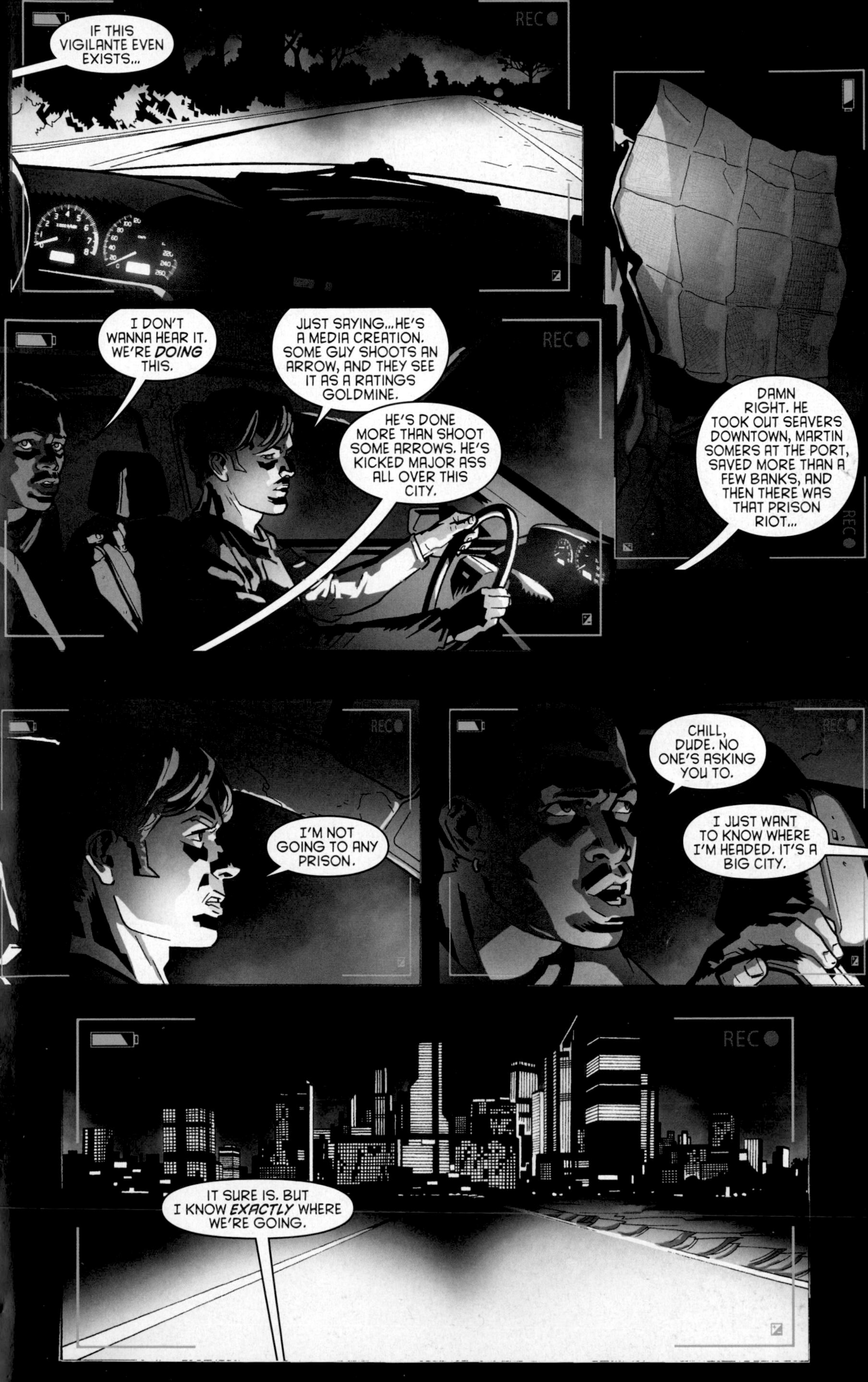
REC
IF THIS VIGILANTE EVEN EXISTS...
I DON'T WANNA HEAR IT. WE'RE *DOING* THIS.
JUST SAYING...HE'S A MEDIA CREATION. SOME GUY SHOOTS AN ARROW, AND THEY SEE IT AS A RATINGS GOLDMINE.
HE'S DONE MORE THAN SHOOT SOME ARROWS. HE'S KICKED MAJOR ASS ALL OVER THIS CITY.
DAMN RIGHT. HE TOOK OUT SEAVERS DOWNTOWN, MARTIN SOMERS AT THE PORT, SAVED MORE THAN A FEW BANKS, AND THEN THERE WAS THAT PRISON RIOT...
I'M NOT GOING TO ANY PRISON.
CHILL, DUDE. NO ONE'S ASKING YOU TO.
I JUST WANT TO KNOW WHERE I'M HEADED. IT'S A BIG CITY.
IT SURE IS. BUT I KNOW *EXACTLY* WHERE WE'RE GOING.

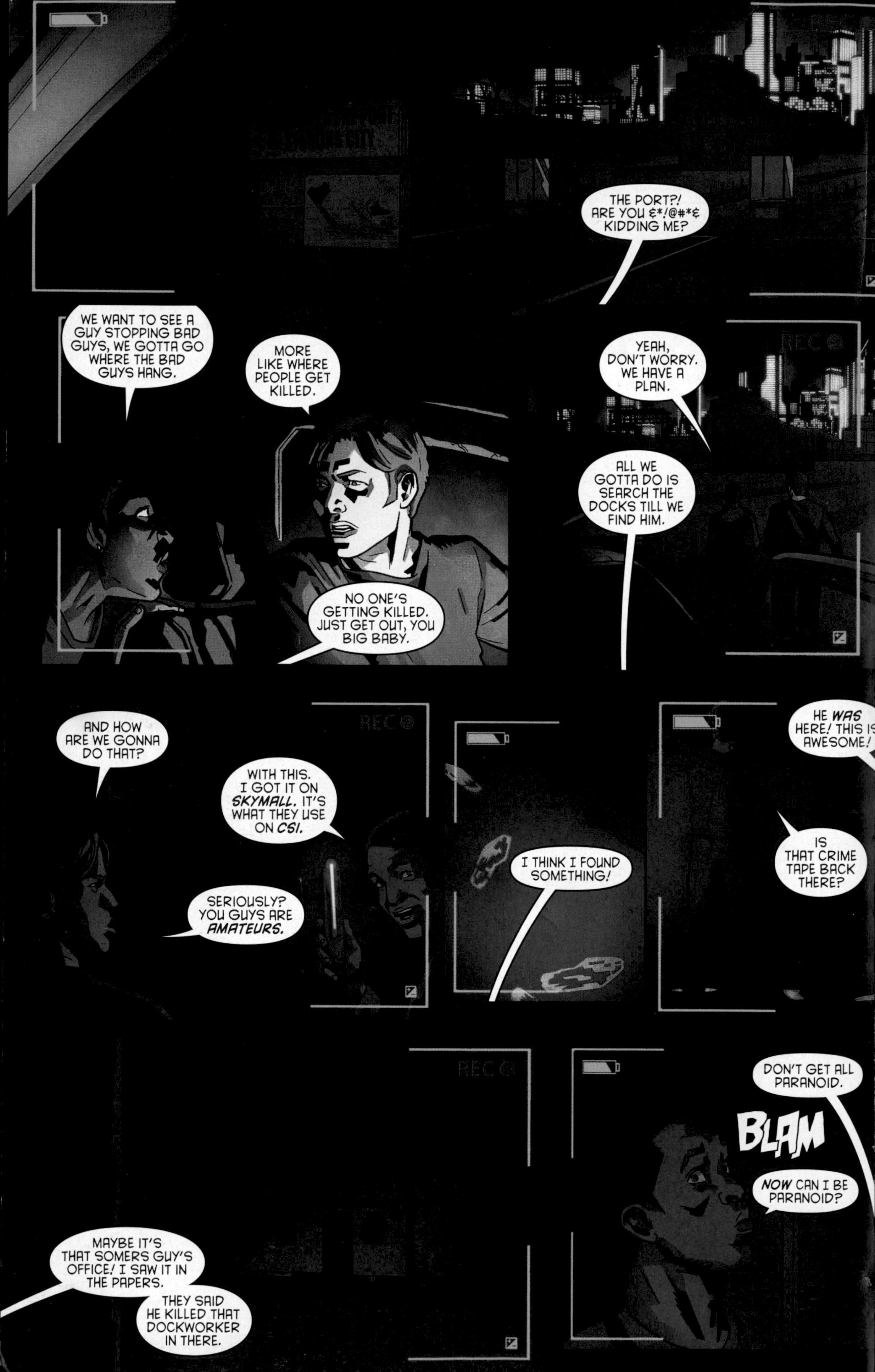
THE PORT?! ARE YOU &*!@#*& KIDDING ME?
WE WANT TO SEE A GUY STOPPING BAD GUYS, WE GOTTA GO WHERE THE BAD GUYS HANG.
MORE LIKE WHERE PEOPLE GET KILLED.
NO ONE'S GETTING KILLED. JUST GET OUT, YOU BIG BABY.
YEAH, DON'T WORRY. WE HAVE A PLAN.
ALL WE GOTTA DO IS SEARCH THE DOCKS TILL WE FIND HIM.
AND HOW ARE WE GONNA DO THAT?
WITH THIS. I GOT IT ON SKYMALL. IT'S WHAT THEY USE ON CSI.
SERIOUSLY? YOU GUYS ARE AMATEURS.
I THINK I FOUND SOMETHING!
HE WAS HERE! THIS IS AWESOME!
IS THAT CRIME TAPE BACK THERE?
MAYBE IT'S THAT SOMERS GUY'S OFFICE! I SAW IT IN THE PAPERS.
THEY SAID HE KILLED THAT DOCKWORKER IN THERE.
DON'T GET ALL PARANOID.
BLAM
NOW CAN I BE PARANOID?

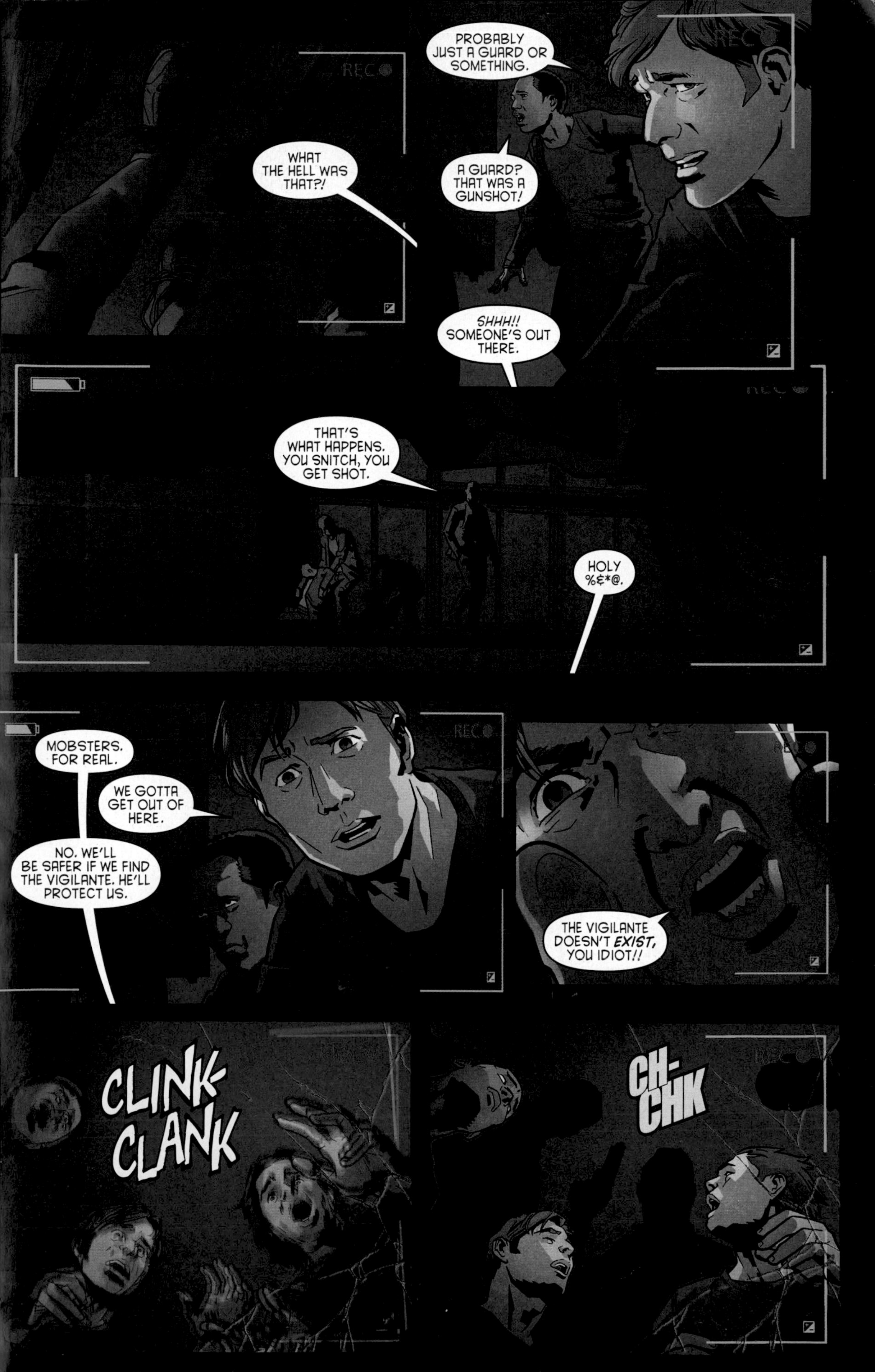
PROBABLY JUST A GUARD OR SOMETHING.
WHAT THE HELL WAS THAT?!
A GUARD? THAT WAS A GUNSHOT!
SHHH!! SOMEONE'S OUT THERE.
THAT'S WHAT HAPPENS. YOU SNITCH, YOU GET SHOT.
HOLY %&*@.
MOBSTERS. FOR REAL.
WE GOTTA GET OUT OF HERE.
NO. WE'LL BE SAFER IF WE FIND THE VIGILANTE. HE'LL PROTECT US.
THE VIGILANTE DOESN'T *EXIST,* YOU IDIOT!!
CLINK-CLANK
CH-CHK

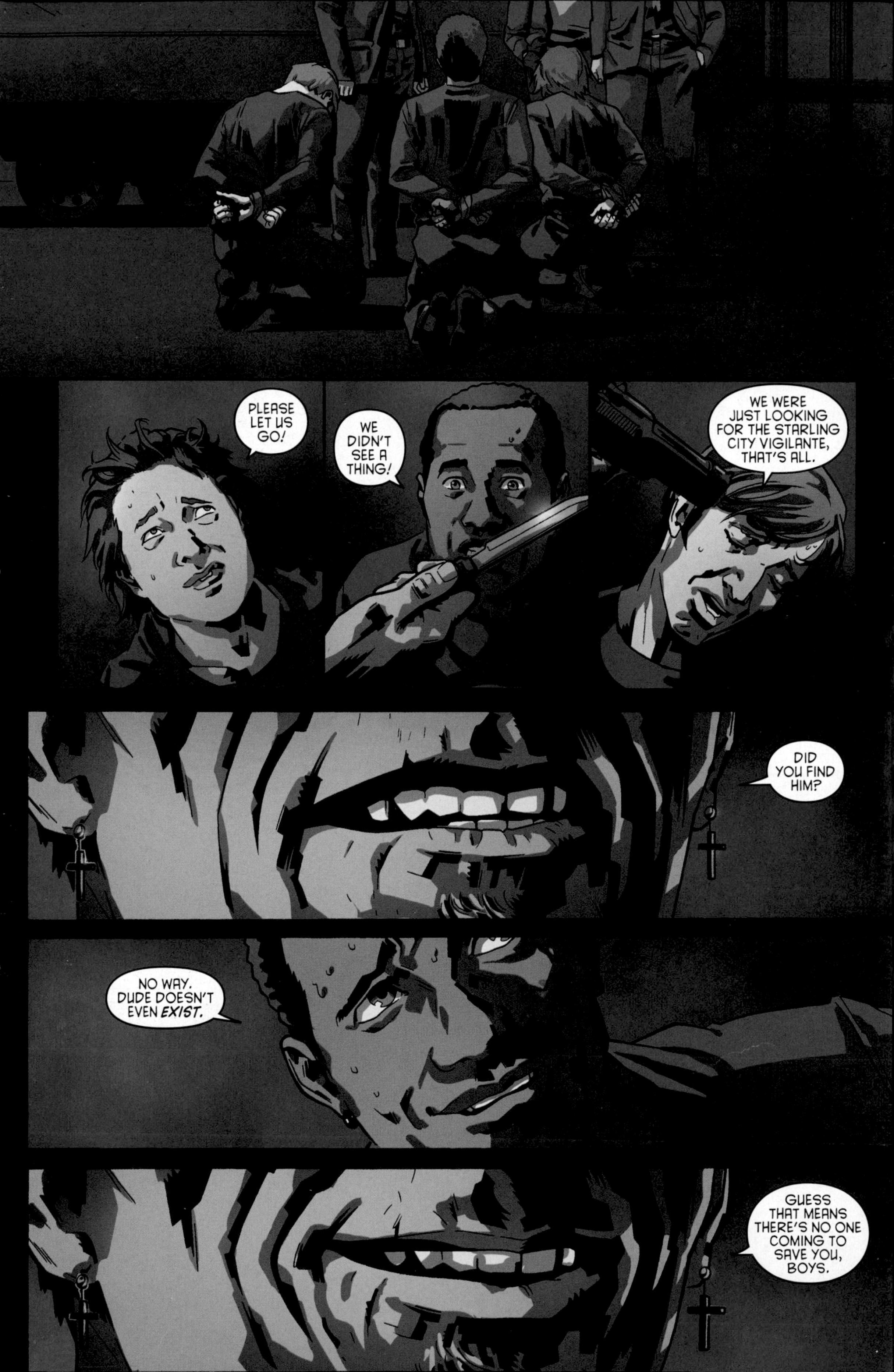
PLEASE LET US GO!
WE DIDN'T SEE A THING!
WE WERE JUST LOOKING FOR THE STARLING CITY VIGILANTE, THAT'S ALL.
DID YOU FIND HIM?
NO WAY. DUDE DOESN'T EVEN *EXIST*.
GUESS THAT MEANS THERE'S NO ONE COMING TO SAVE YOU, BOYS.

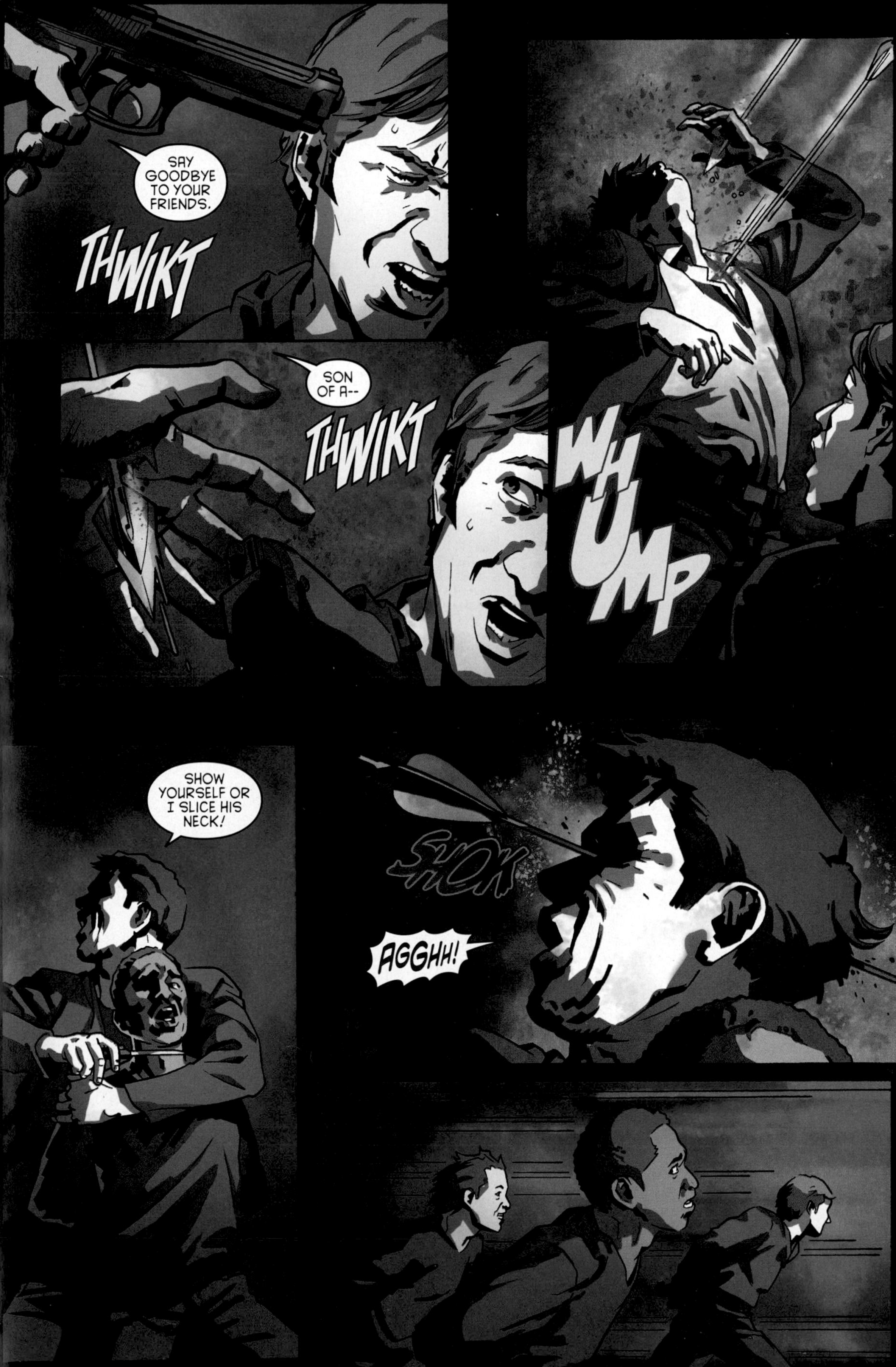
SAY GOODBYE TO YOUR FRIENDS.
THWIKT
SON OF A--
THWIKT
WHUMP
SHOW YOURSELF OR I SLICE HIS NECK!
SHOK
AGGHH!

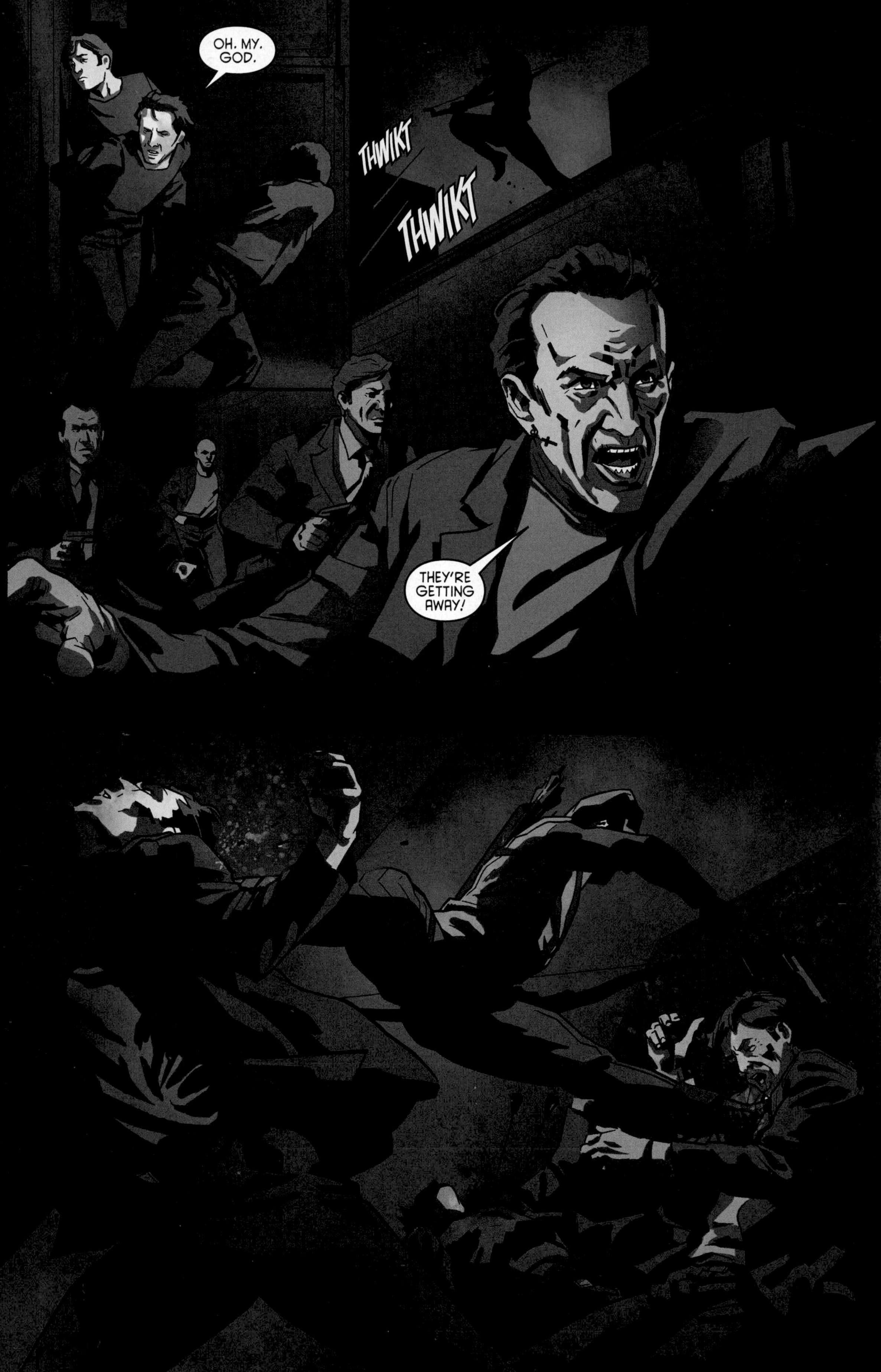
OH. MY. GOD.
THWIKT
THWIKT
THEY'RE GETTING AWAY!

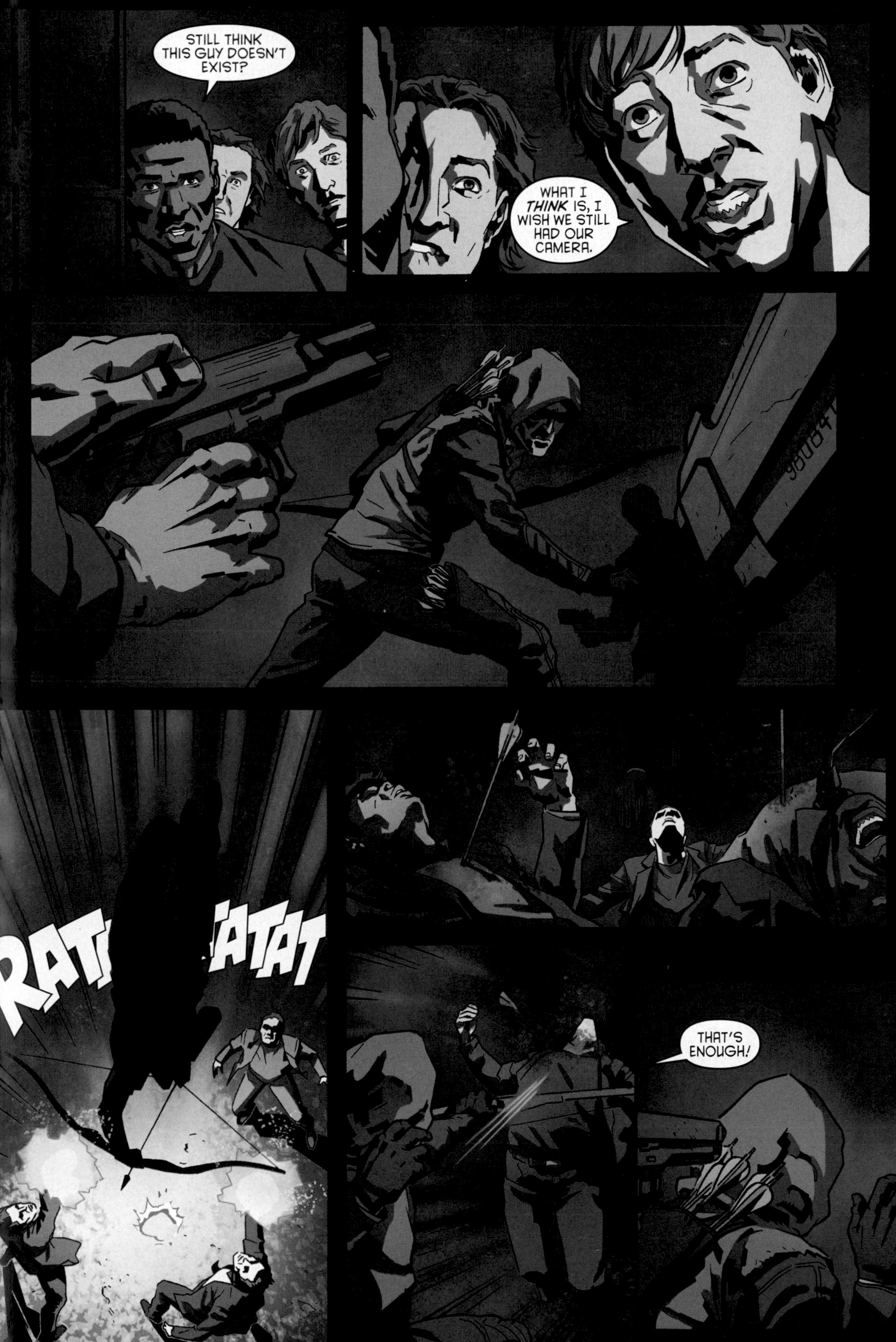
STILL THINK THIS GUY DOESN'T EXIST?
WHAT I THINK IS, I WISH WE STILL HAD OUR CAMERA.
THAT'S ENOUGH!

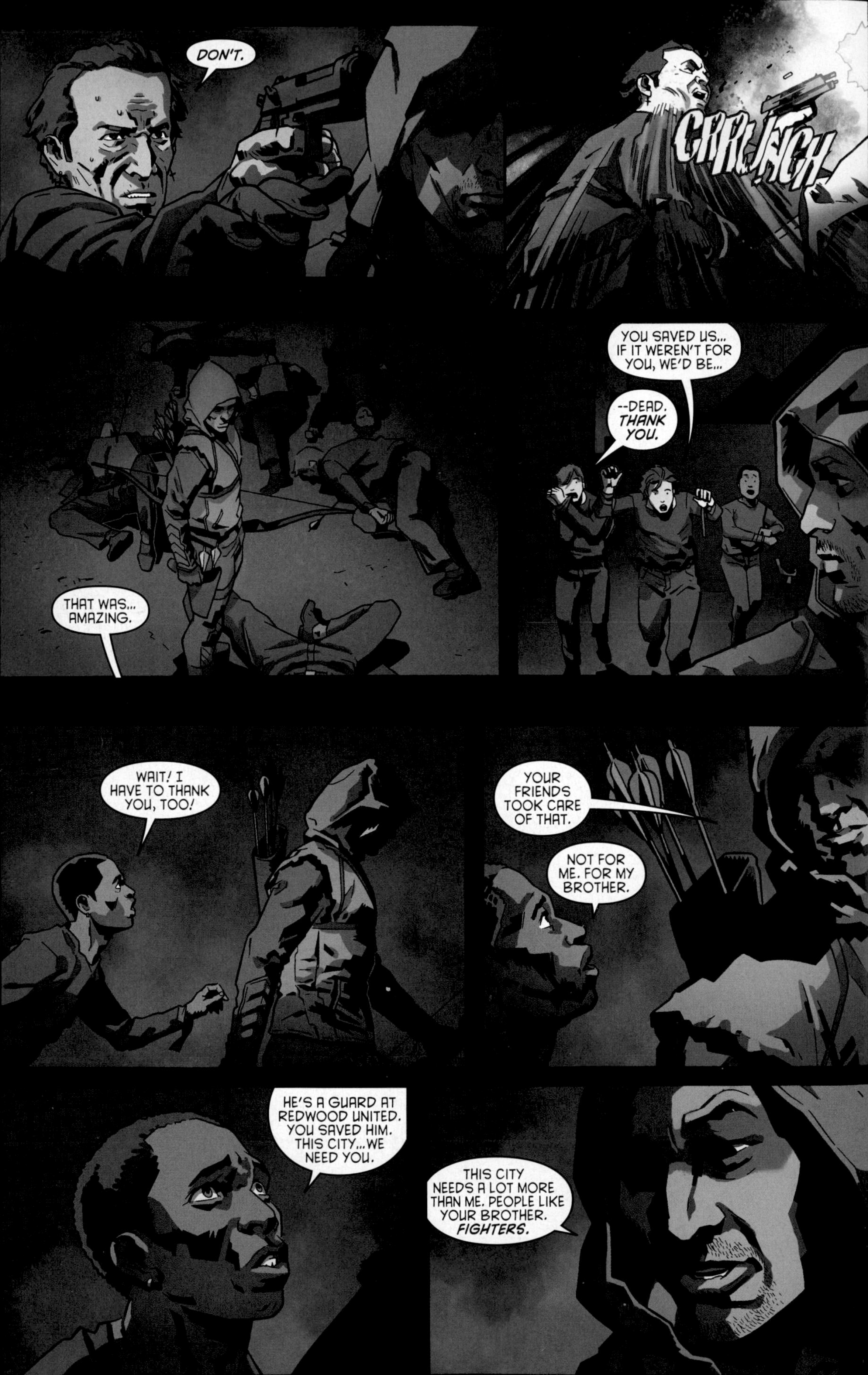
DON'T.
CRRUNCH
THAT WAS... AMAZING.
YOU SAVED US... IF IT WEREN'T FOR YOU, WE'D BE...
--DEAD. THANK YOU.
WAIT! I HAVE TO THANK YOU, TOO!
YOUR FRIENDS TOOK CARE OF THAT.
NOT FOR ME. FOR MY BROTHER.
HE'S A GUARD AT REDWOOD UNITED. YOU SAVED HIM. THIS CITY...WE NEED YOU.
THIS CITY NEEDS A LOT MORE THAN ME. PEOPLE LIKE YOUR BROTHER. FIGHTERS.

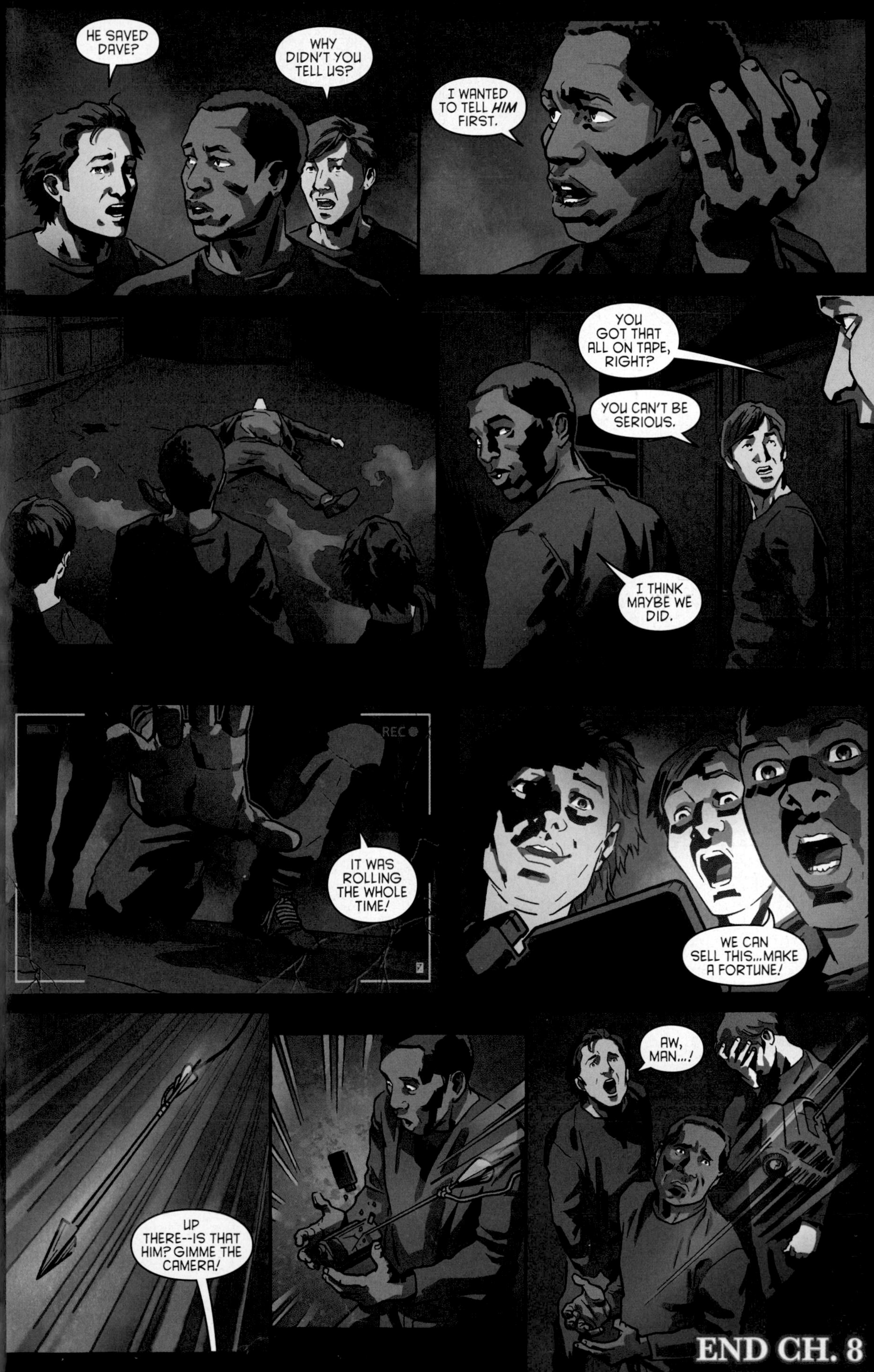
HE SAVED DAVE?
WHY DIDN'T YOU TELL US?
I WANTED TO TELL HIM FIRST.
YOU GOT THAT ALL ON TAPE, RIGHT?
YOU CAN'T BE SERIOUS.
I THINK MAYBE WE DID.
REC
IT WAS ROLLING THE WHOLE TIME!
WE CAN SELL THIS...MAKE A FORTUNE!
UP THERE--IS THAT HIM? GIMME THE CAMERA!
AW, MAN...!

END CH. 8

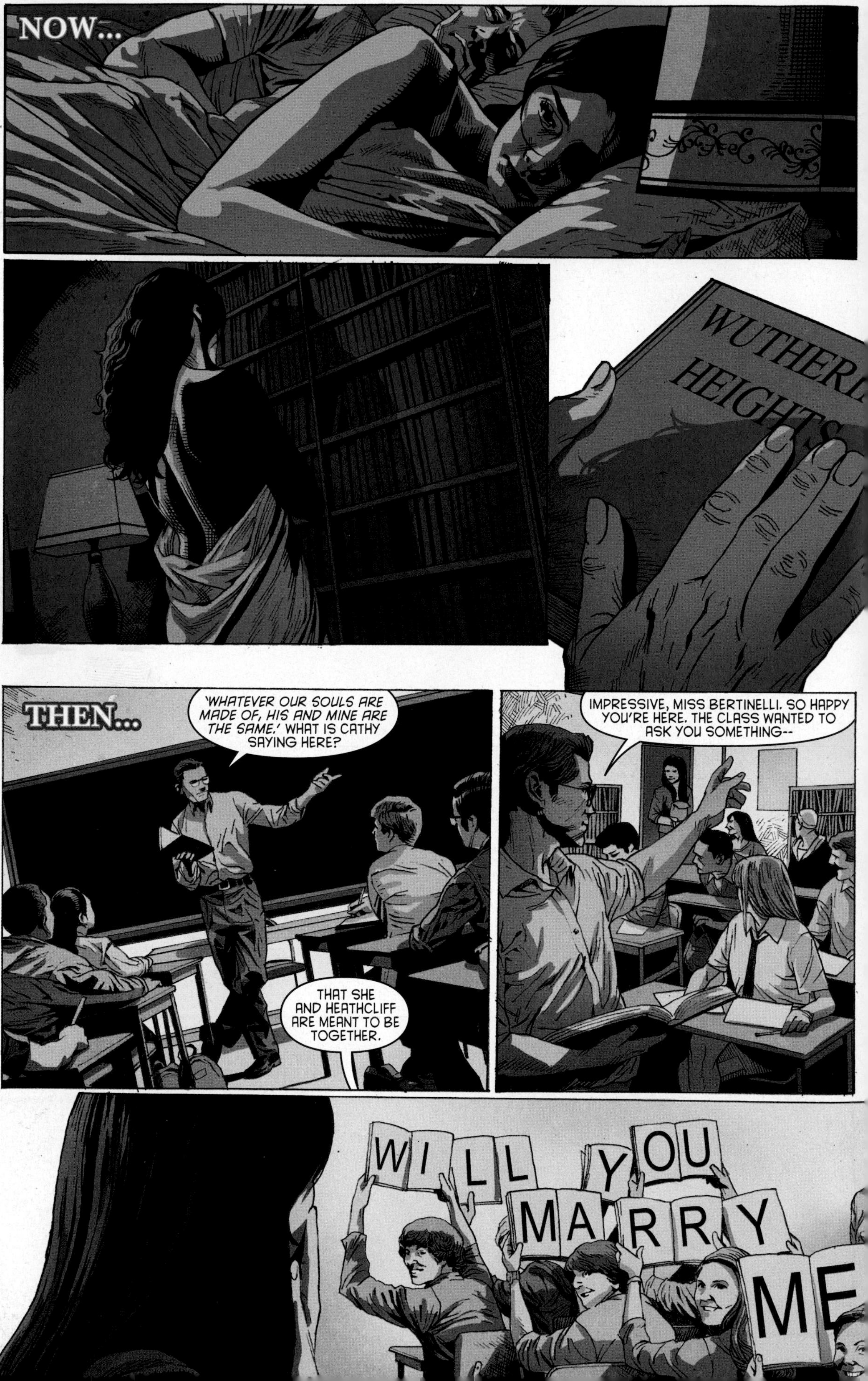
NOW...
WUTHERING HEIGHTS
THEN...
'WHATEVER OUR SOULS ARE MADE OF, HIS AND MINE ARE THE SAME.' WHAT IS CATHY SAYING HERE?
THAT SHE AND HEATHCLIFF ARE MEANT TO BE TOGETHER.
IMPRESSIVE, MISS BERTINELLI. SO HAPPY YOU'RE HERE. THE CLASS WANTED TO ASK YOU SOMETHING--
WILL YOU MARRY ME

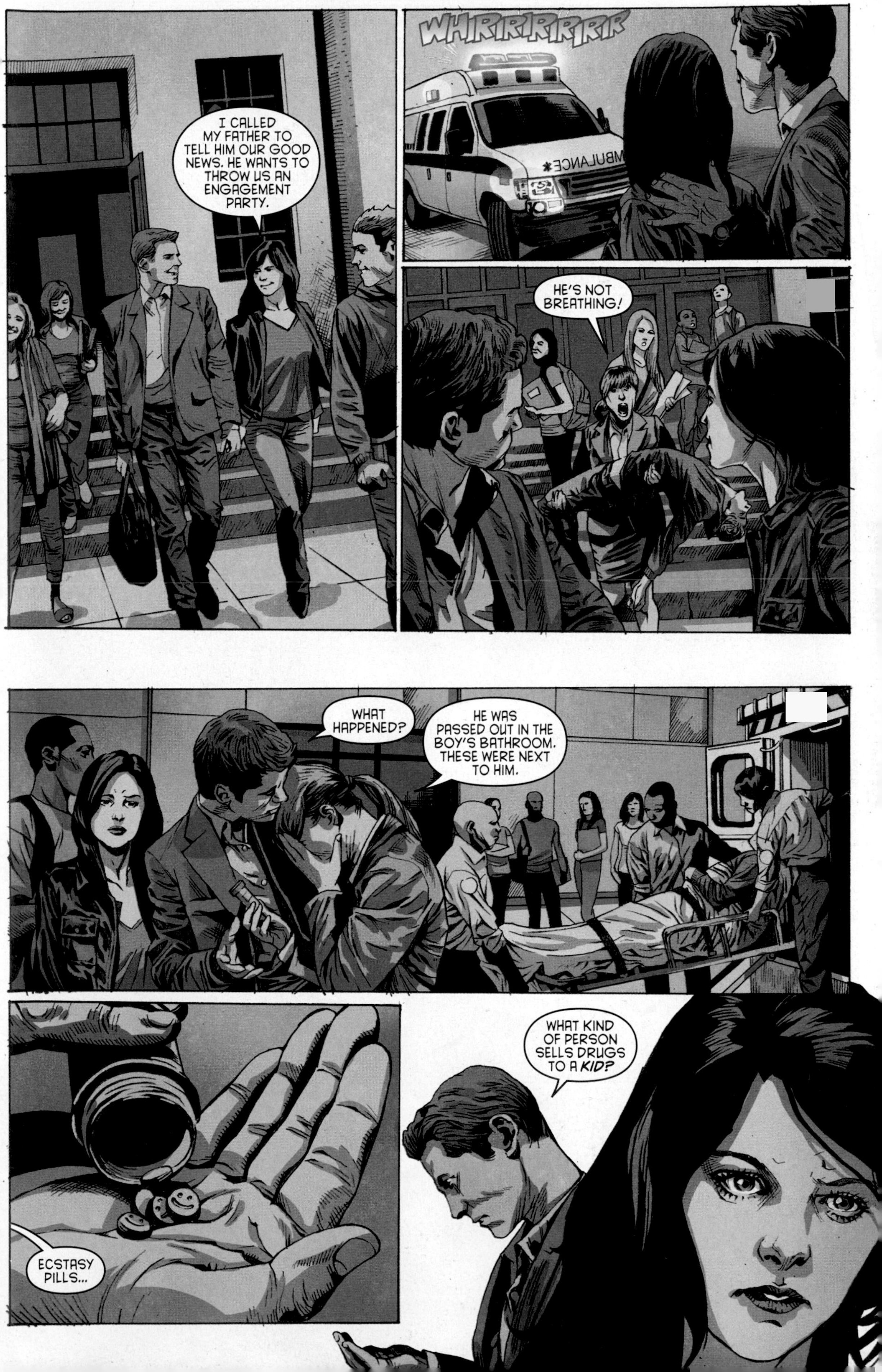
I CALLED MY FATHER TO TELL HIM OUR GOOD NEWS. HE WANTS TO THROW US AN ENGAGEMENT PARTY.
WHIRIRIRIRIRIR
AMBULANCE
HE'S NOT BREATHING!
WHAT HAPPENED?
HE WAS PASSED OUT IN THE BOY'S BATHROOM. THESE WERE NEXT TO HIM.
ECSTASY PILLS...
WHAT KIND OF PERSON SELLS DRUGS TO A *KID?*

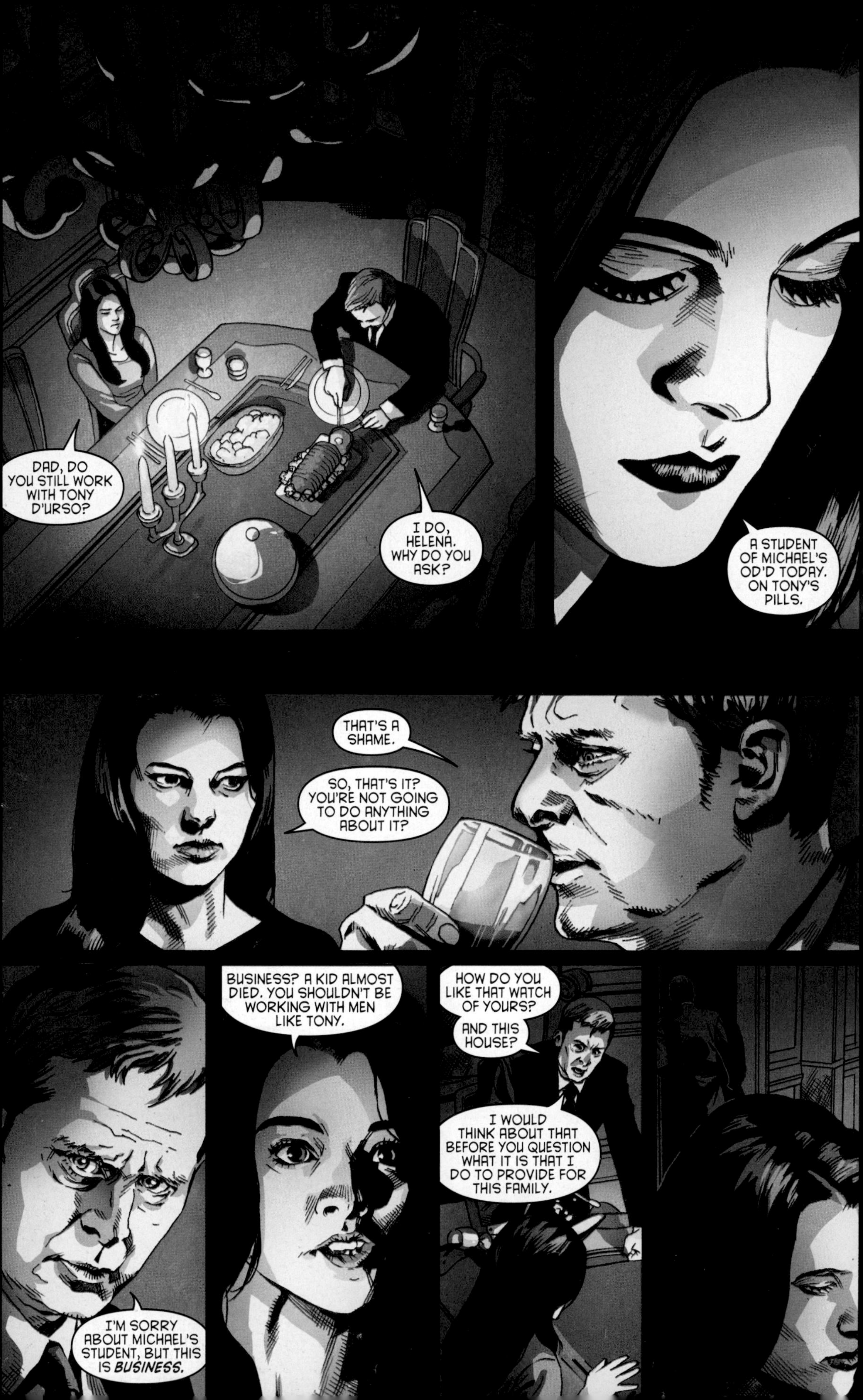
DAD, DO YOU STILL WORK WITH TONY D'URSO?
I DO, HELENA. WHY DO YOU ASK?
A STUDENT OF MICHAEL'S OD'D TODAY. ON TONY'S PILLS.
THAT'S A SHAME.
SO, THAT'S IT? YOU'RE NOT GOING TO DO ANYTHING ABOUT IT?
I'M SORRY ABOUT MICHAEL'S STUDENT, BUT THIS IS *BUSINESS.*
BUSINESS? A KID ALMOST DIED. YOU SHOULDN'T BE WORKING WITH MEN LIKE TONY.
HOW DO YOU LIKE THAT WATCH OF YOURS?
AND THIS HOUSE?
I WOULD THINK ABOUT THAT BEFORE YOU QUESTION WHAT IT IS THAT I DO TO PROVIDE FOR THIS FAMILY.

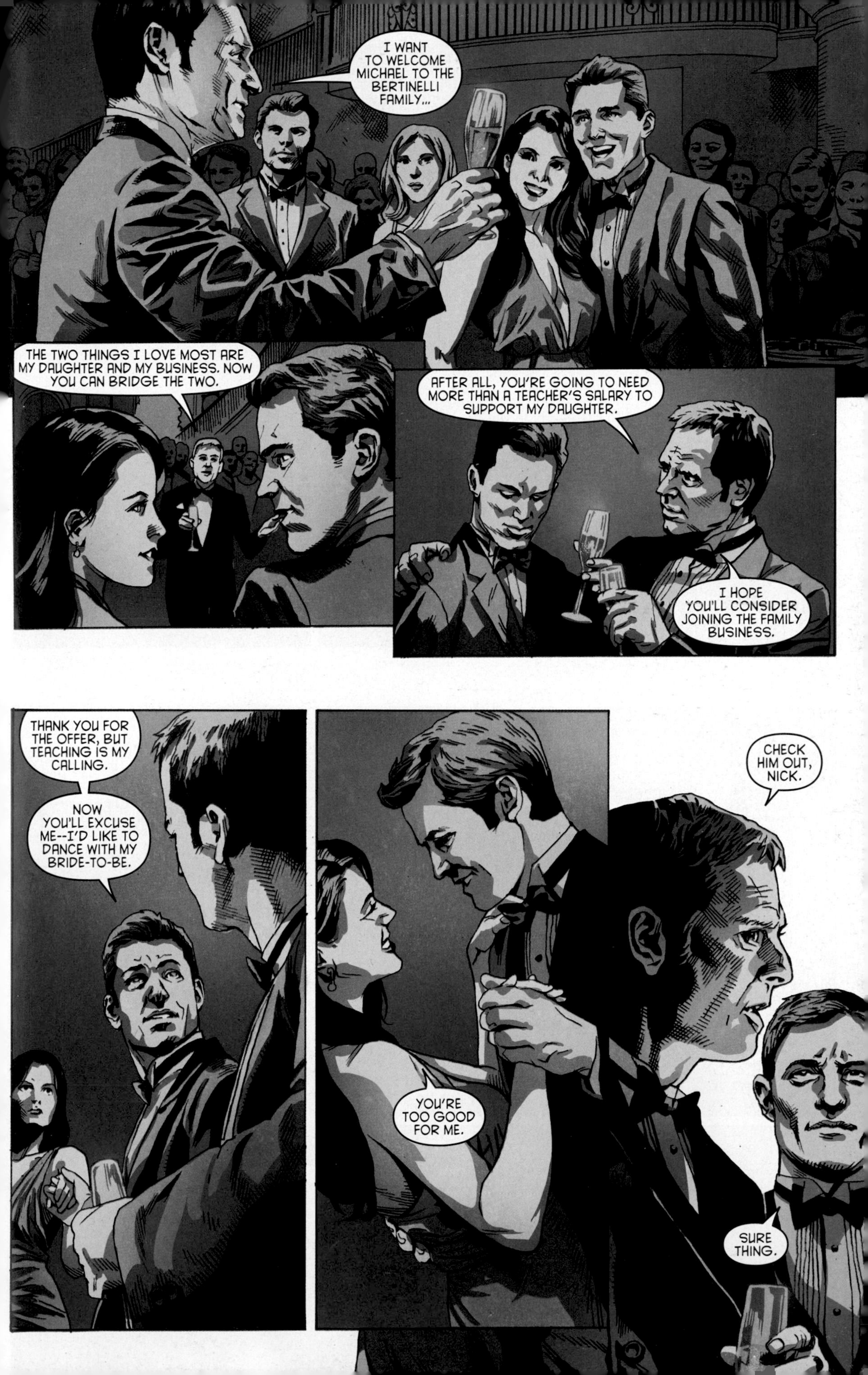
I WANT TO WELCOME MICHAEL TO THE BERTINELLI FAMILY...
THE TWO THINGS I LOVE MOST ARE MY DAUGHTER AND MY BUSINESS. NOW YOU CAN BRIDGE THE TWO.
AFTER ALL, YOU'RE GOING TO NEED MORE THAN A TEACHER'S SALARY TO SUPPORT MY DAUGHTER.
I HOPE YOU'LL CONSIDER JOINING THE FAMILY BUSINESS.
THANK YOU FOR THE OFFER, BUT TEACHING IS MY CALLING.
NOW YOU'LL EXCUSE ME--I'D LIKE TO DANCE WITH MY BRIDE-TO-BE.
CHECK HIM OUT, NICK.
YOU'RE TOO GOOD FOR ME.
SURE THING.

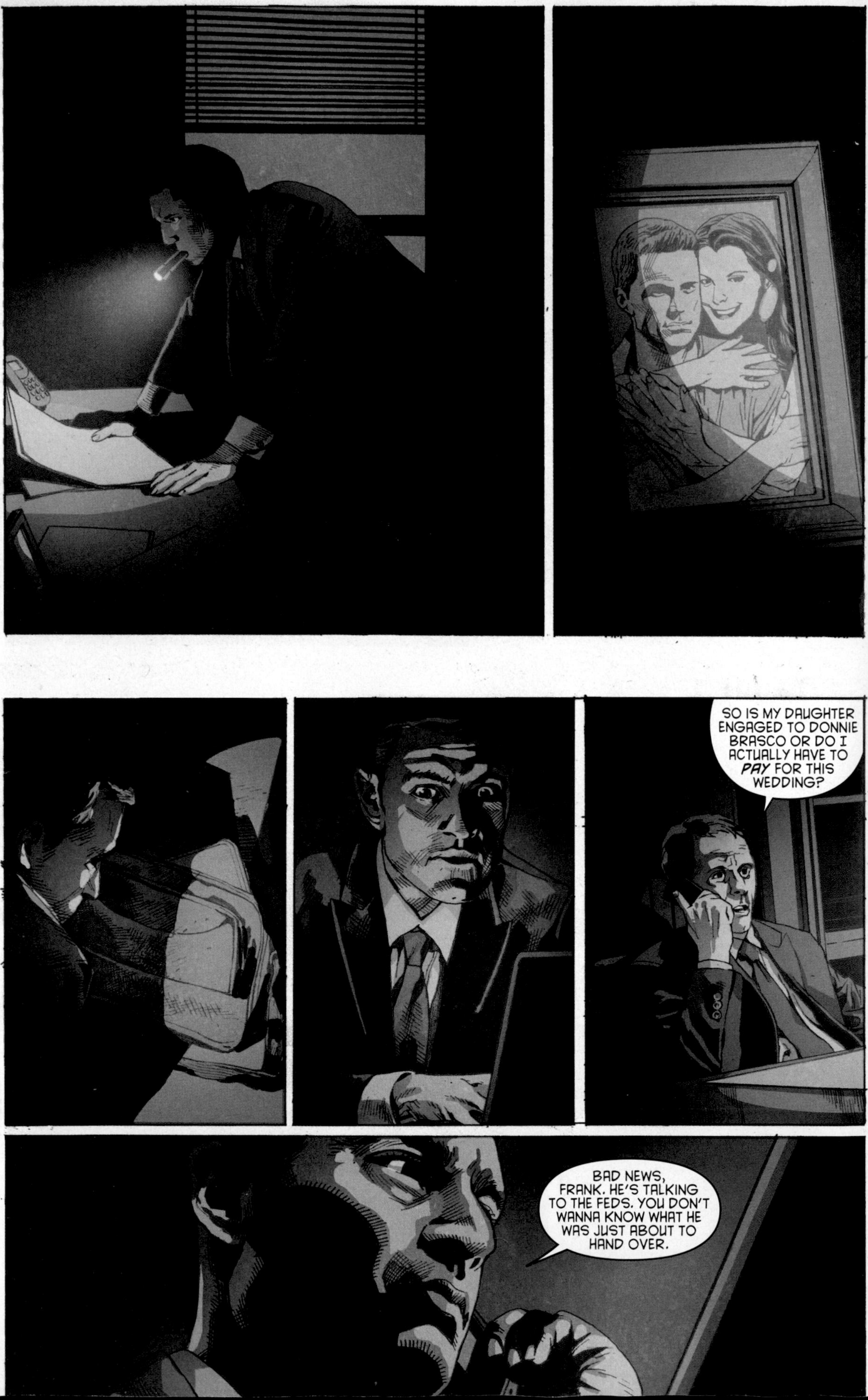
SO IS MY DAUGHTER ENGAGED TO DONNIE BRASCO OR DO I ACTUALLY HAVE TO PAY FOR THIS WEDDING?
BAD NEWS, FRANK. HE'S TALKING TO THE FEDS. YOU DON'T WANNA KNOW WHAT HE WAS JUST ABOUT TO HAND OVER.

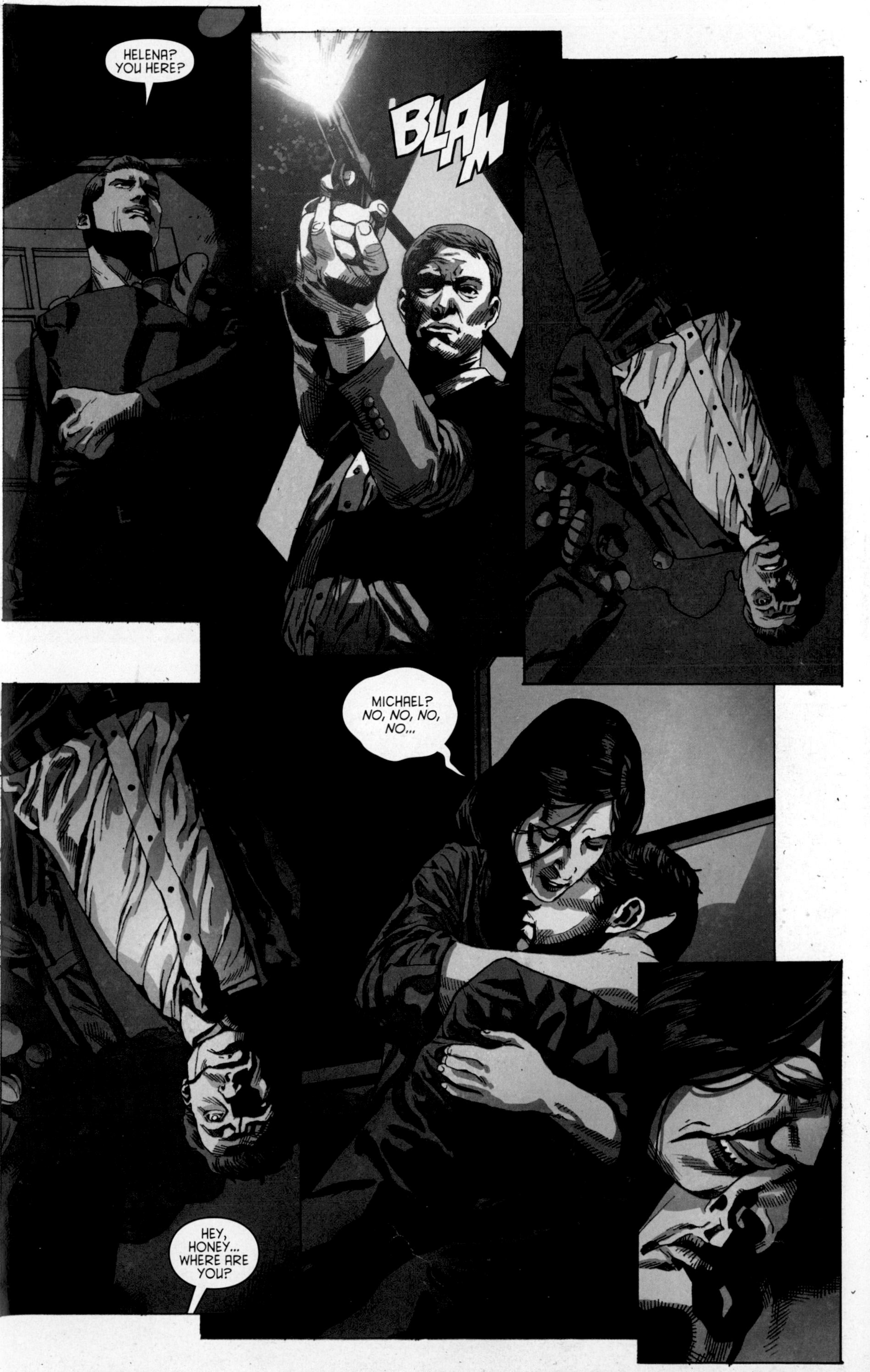
HELENA? YOU HERE?
BLAM
MICHAEL? NO, NO, NO, NO...
HEY, HONEY... WHERE ARE YOU?

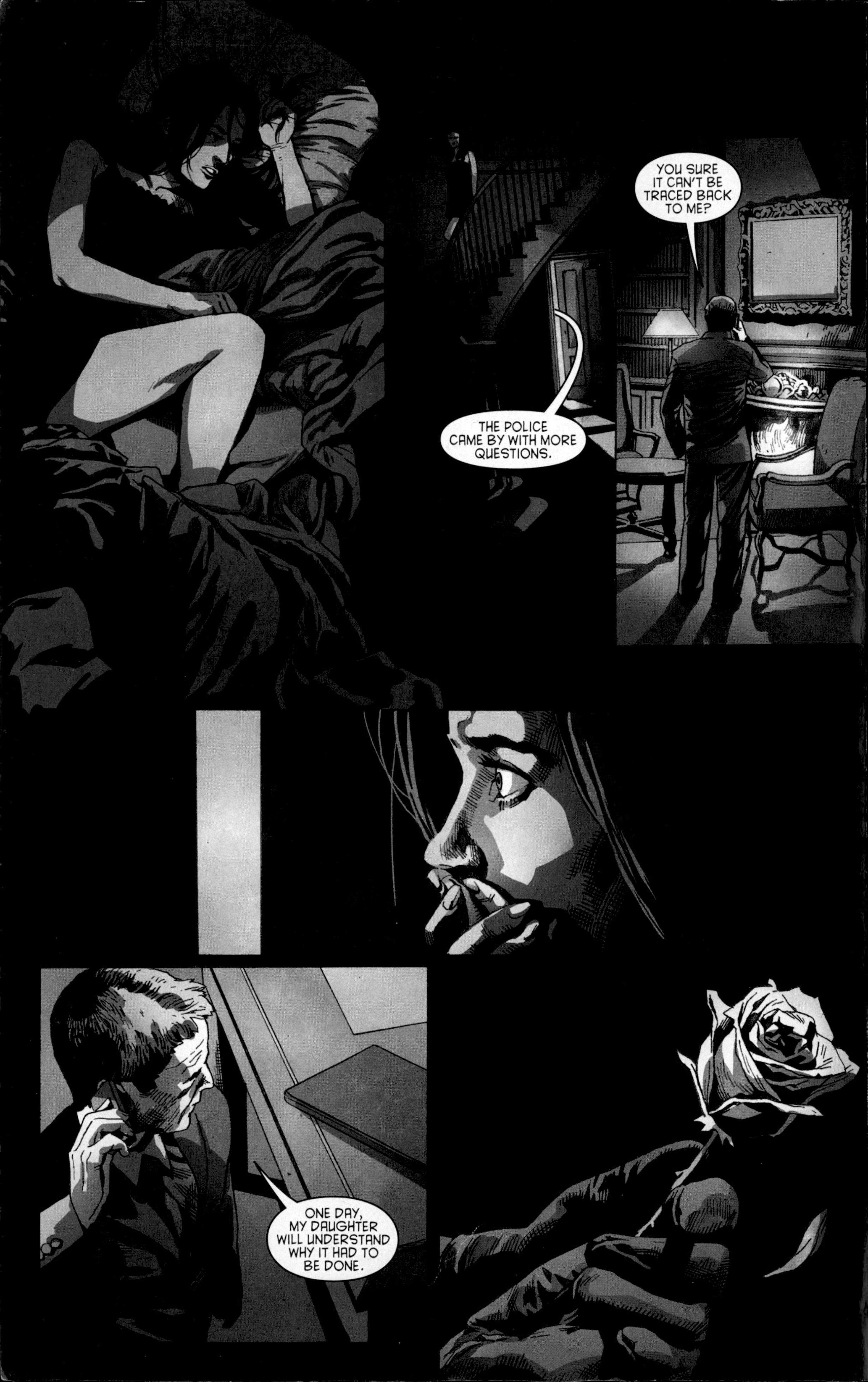
THE POLICE CAME BY WITH MORE QUESTIONS.
YOU SURE IT CAN'T BE TRACED BACK TO ME?
ONE DAY, MY DAUGHTER WILL UNDERSTAND WHY IT HAD TO BE DONE.

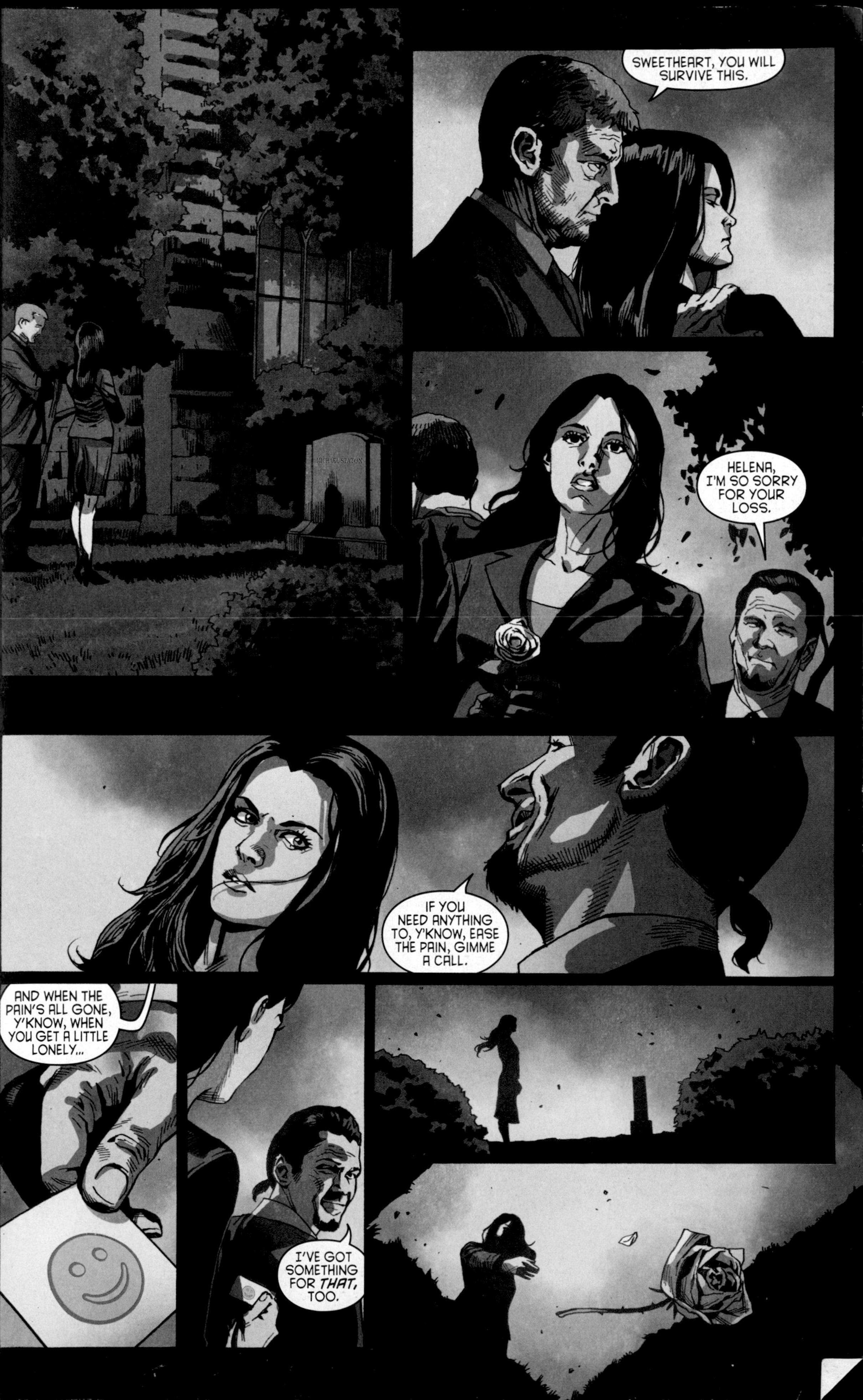
SWEETHEART, YOU WILL SURVIVE THIS.
HELENA, I'M SO SORRY FOR YOUR LOSS.
IF YOU NEED ANYTHING TO, Y'KNOW, EASE THE PAIN, GIMME A CALL.
AND WHEN THE PAIN'S ALL GONE, Y'KNOW, WHEN YOU GET A LITTLE LONELY...
I'VE GOT SOMETHING FOR *THAT,* TOO.

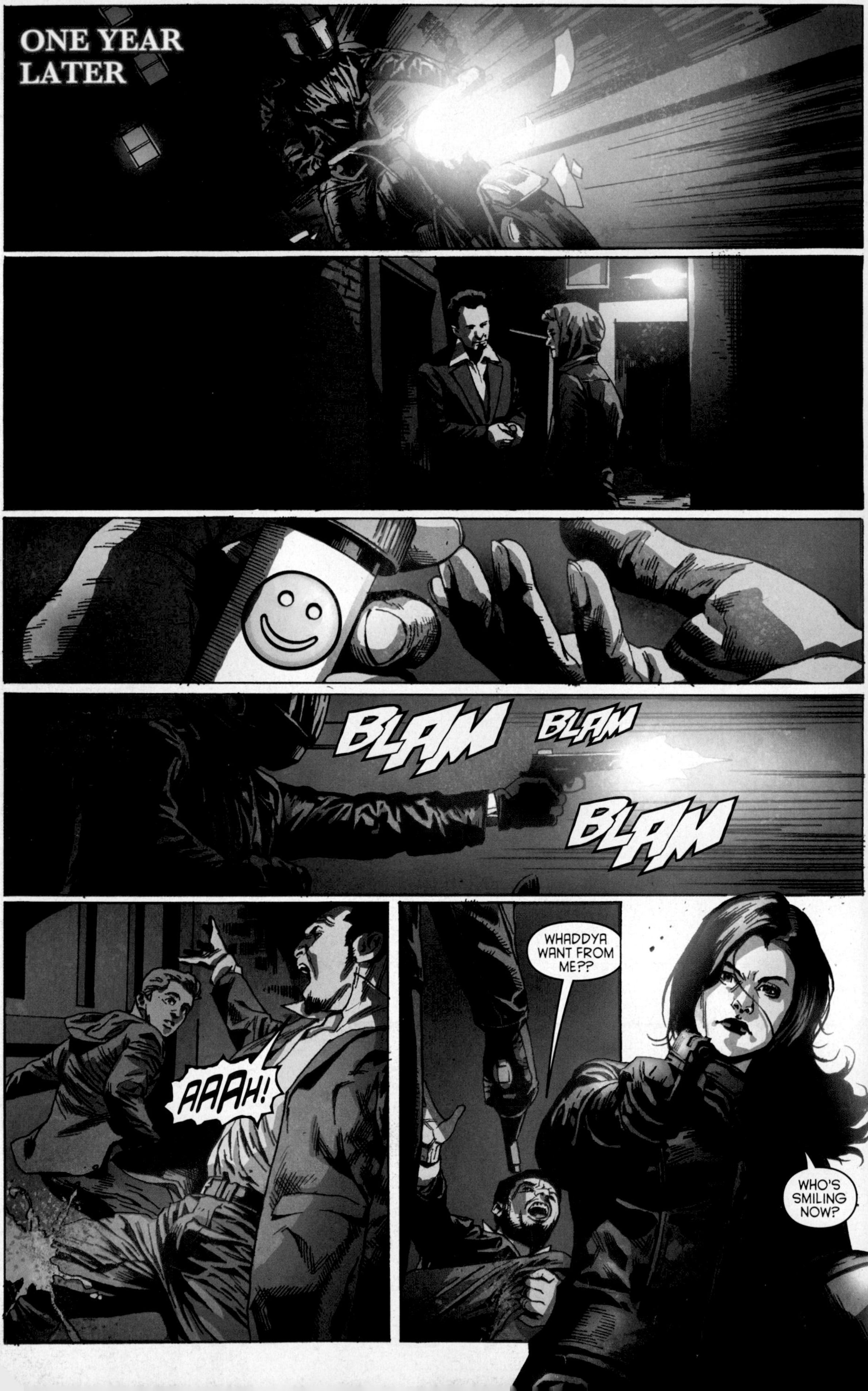
ONE YEAR LATER
BLAM
BLAM
BLAM
AAAH!
WHADDYA WANT FROM ME??
WHO'S SMILING NOW?

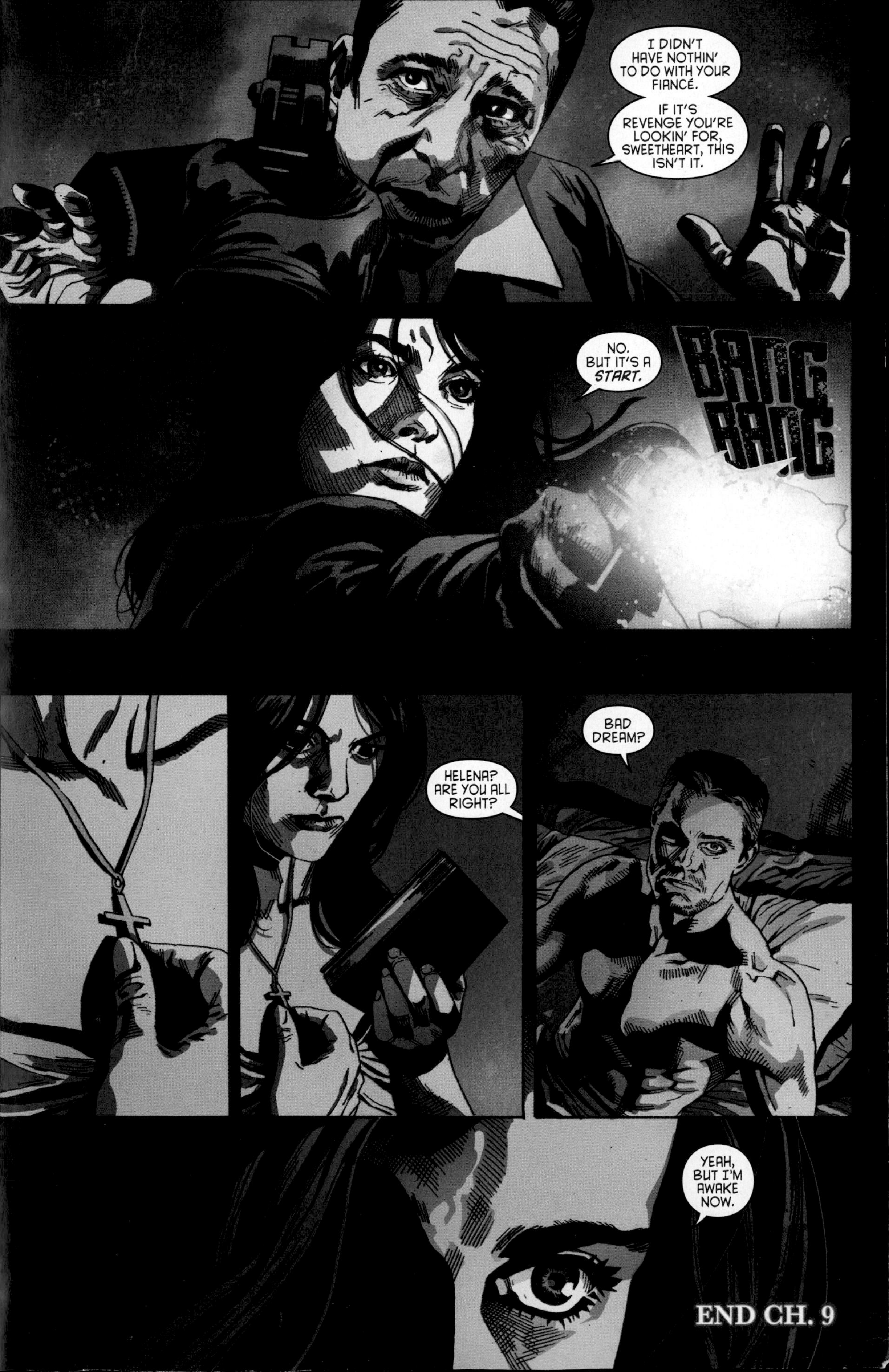
I DIDN'T HAVE NOTHIN' TO DO WITH YOUR FIANCÉ.
IF IT'S REVENGE YOU'RE LOOKIN' FOR, SWEETHEART, THIS ISN'T IT.
NO. BUT IT'S A *START.*
BANG BANG
HELENA? ARE YOU ALL RIGHT?
BAD DREAM?
YEAH, BUT I'M AWAKE NOW.
END CH. 9

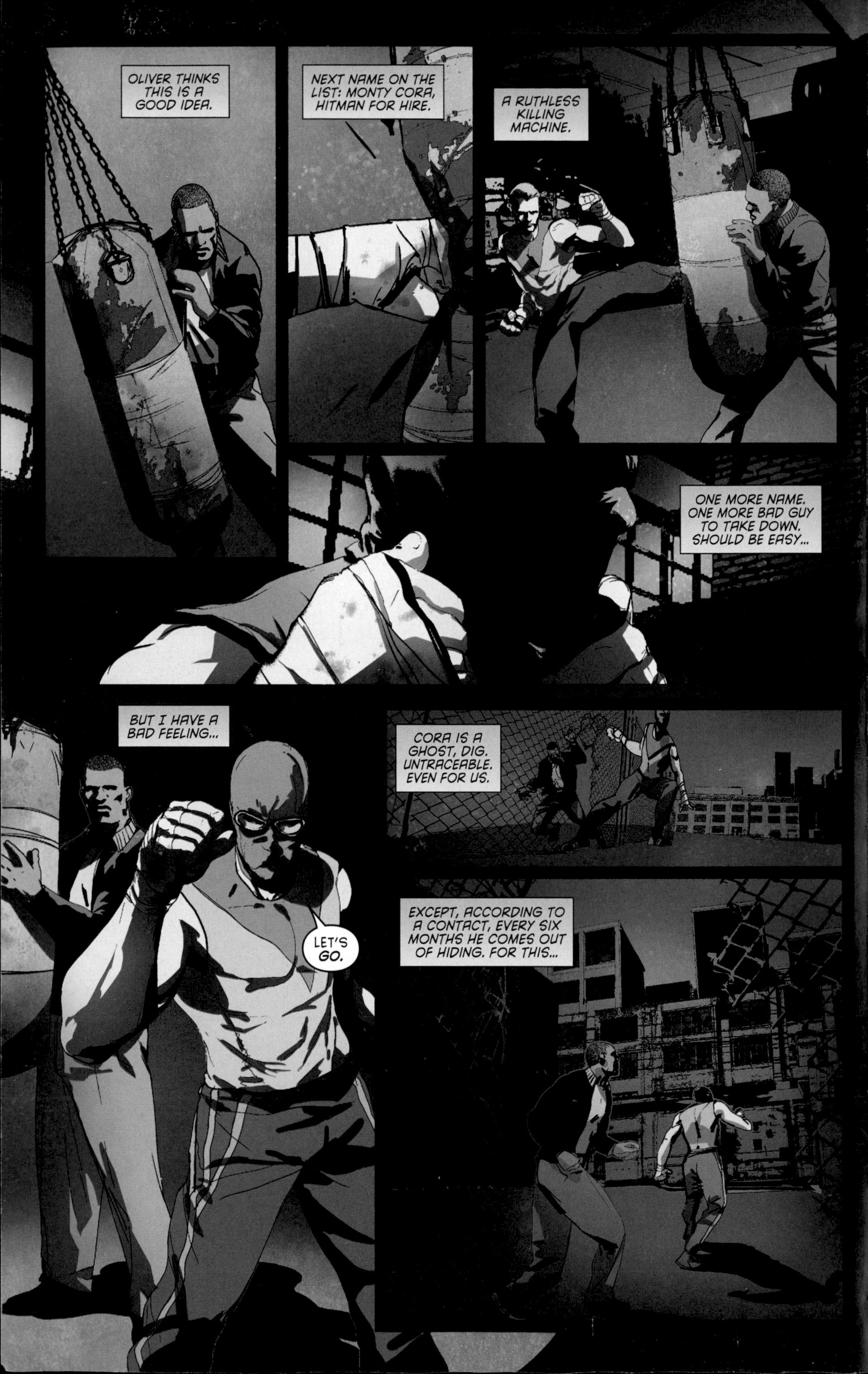
OLIVER THINKS THIS IS A GOOD IDEA.
NEXT NAME ON THE LIST: MONTY CORA, HITMAN FOR HIRE.
A RUTHLESS KILLING MACHINE.
ONE MORE NAME. ONE MORE BAD GUY TO TAKE DOWN. SHOULD BE EASY...
BUT I HAVE A BAD FEELING...
LET'S GO.
CORA IS A GHOST, DIG. UNTRACEABLE. EVEN FOR US.
EXCEPT, ACCORDING TO A CONTACT, EVERY SIX MONTHS HE COMES OUT OF HIDING. FOR THIS...

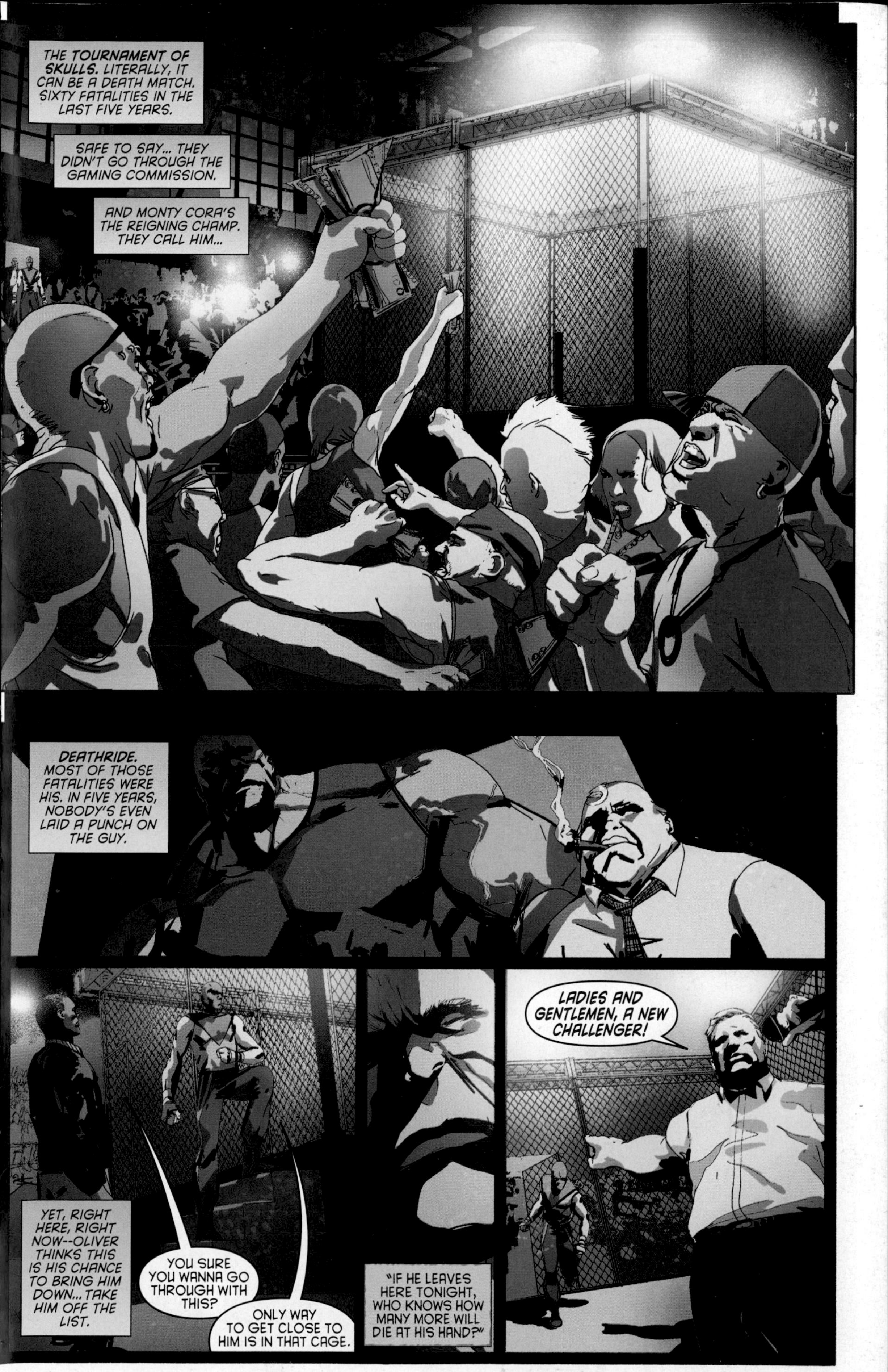
THE TOURNAMENT OF SKULLS. LITERALLY, IT CAN BE A DEATH MATCH. SIXTY FATALITIES IN THE LAST FIVE YEARS.
SAFE TO SAY... THEY DIDN'T GO THROUGH THE GAMING COMMISSION.
AND MONTY CORA'S THE REIGNING CHAMP. THEY CALL HIM...
DEATHRIDE. MOST OF THOSE FATALITIES WERE HIS. IN FIVE YEARS, NOBODY'S EVEN LAID A PUNCH ON THE GUY.
YET, RIGHT HERE, RIGHT NOW--OLIVER THINKS THIS IS HIS CHANCE TO BRING HIM DOWN...TAKE HIM OFF THE LIST.
YOU SURE YOU WANNA GO THROUGH WITH THIS?
ONLY WAY TO GET CLOSE TO HIM IS IN THAT CAGE.
"IF HE LEAVES HERE TONIGHT, WHO KNOWS HOW MANY MORE WILL DIE AT HIS HAND?"
LADIES AND GENTLEMEN, A NEW CHALLENGER!

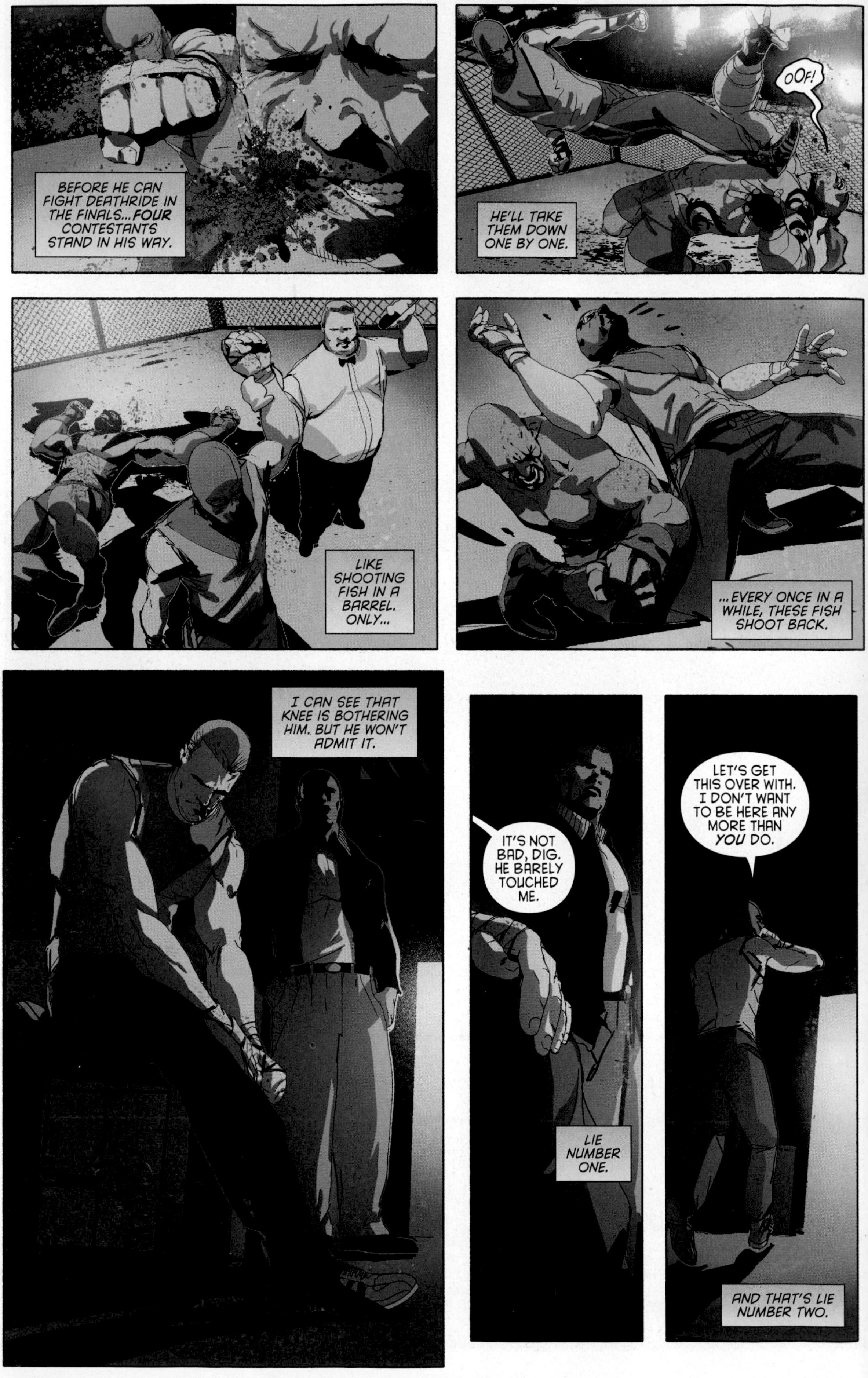
BEFORE HE CAN FIGHT DEATHRIDE IN THE FINALS... FOUR CONTESTANTS STAND IN HIS WAY.
HE'LL TAKE THEM DOWN ONE BY ONE.
OOF!
LIKE SHOOTING FISH IN A BARREL. ONLY...
...EVERY ONCE IN A WHILE, THESE FISH SHOOT BACK.
I CAN SEE THAT KNEE IS BOTHERING HIM. BUT HE WON'T ADMIT IT.
IT'S NOT BAD, DIG. HE BARELY TOUCHED ME.
LIE NUMBER ONE.
LET'S GET THIS OVER WITH. I DON'T WANT TO BE HERE ANY MORE THAN YOU DO.
AND THAT'S LIE NUMBER TWO.

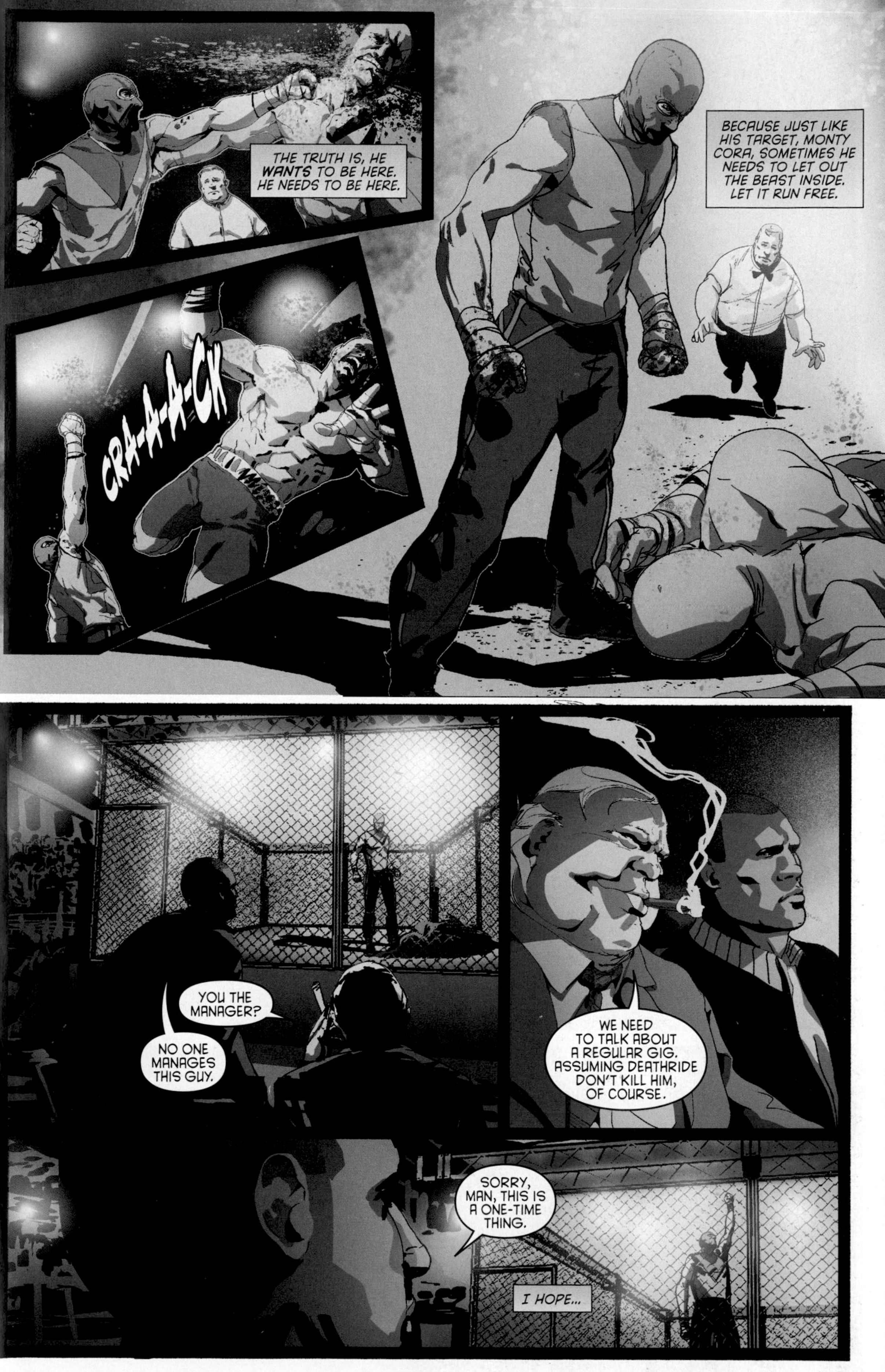

THE TRUTH IS, HE WANTS TO BE HERE. HE NEEDS TO BE HERE.
CRA-A-A-CK
BECAUSE JUST LIKE HIS TARGET, MONTY CORA, SOMETIMES HE NEEDS TO LET OUT THE BEAST INSIDE. LET IT RUN FREE.
YOU THE MANAGER?
NO ONE MANAGES THIS GUY.
WE NEED TO TALK ABOUT A REGULAR GIG. ASSUMING DEATHRIDE DON'T KILL HIM, OF COURSE.
SORRY, MAN, THIS IS A ONE-TIME THING.
I HOPE...

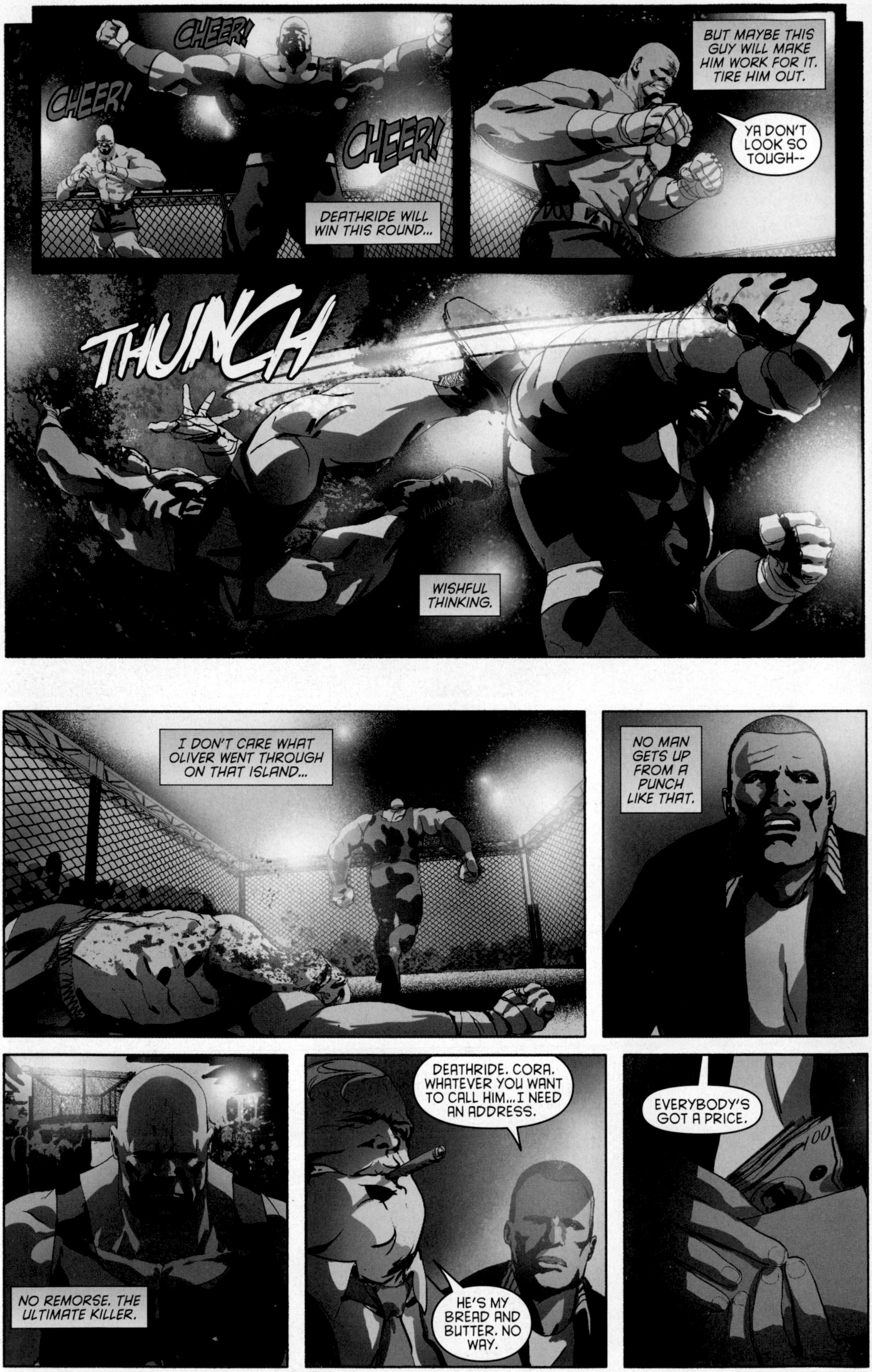
CHEER!
CHEER!
CHEER!
DEATHRIDE WILL WIN THIS ROUND...
BUT MAYBE THIS GUY WILL MAKE HIM WORK FOR IT. TIRE HIM OUT.
YA DON'T LOOK SO TOUGH--
THUNCH
WISHFUL THINKING.
I DON'T CARE WHAT OLIVER WENT THROUGH ON THAT ISLAND...
NO MAN GETS UP FROM A PUNCH LIKE THAT.
NO REMORSE. THE ULTIMATE KILLER.
DEATHRIDE. CORA. WHATEVER YOU WANT TO CALL HIM...I NEED AN ADDRESS.
HE'S MY BREAD AND BUTTER. NO WAY.
EVERYBODY'S GOT A PRICE.

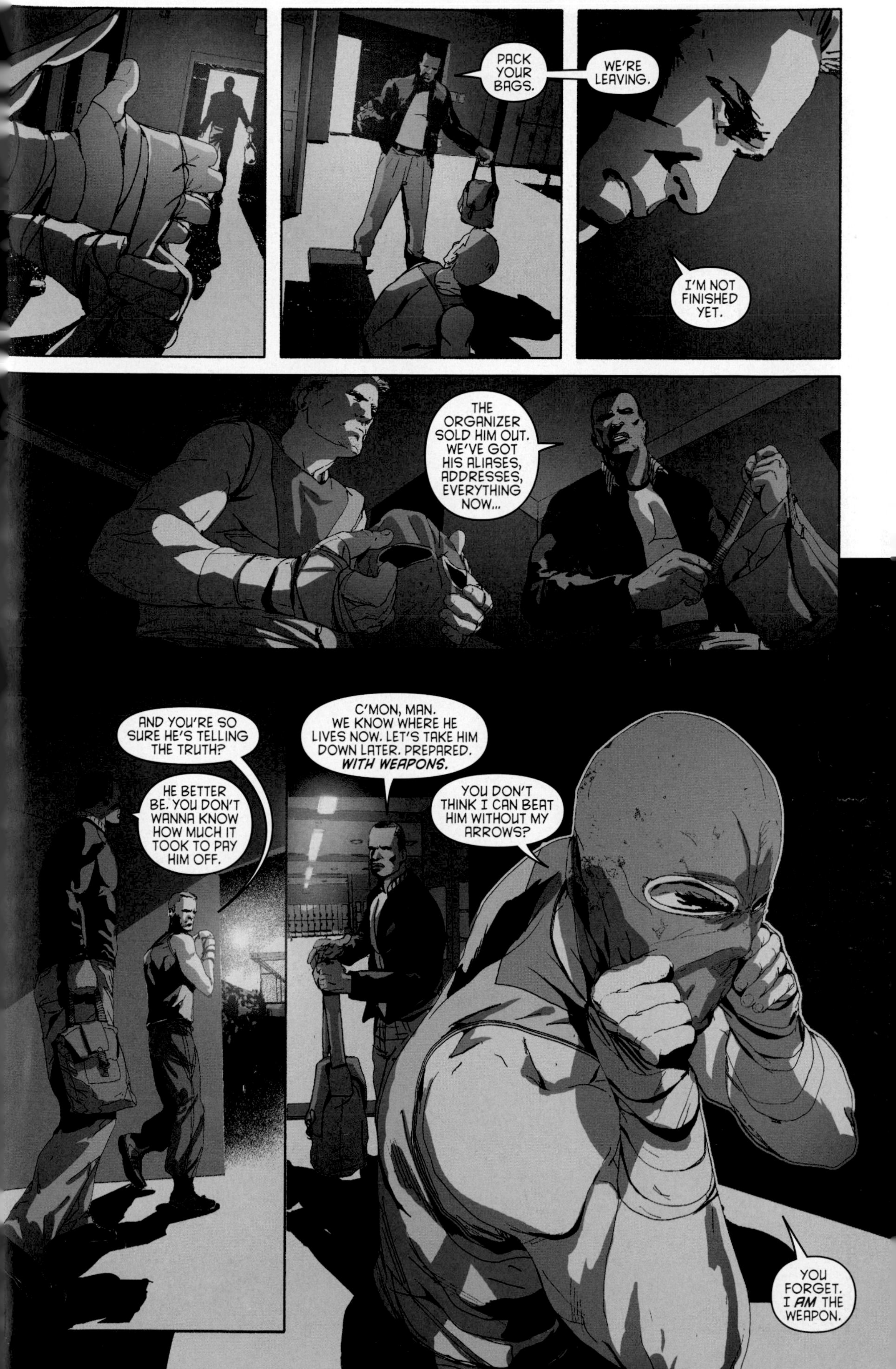
PACK YOUR BAGS.
WE'RE LEAVING.
I'M NOT FINISHED YET.
THE ORGANIZER SOLD HIM OUT. WE'VE GOT HIS ALIASES, ADDRESSES, EVERYTHING NOW...
AND YOU'RE SO SURE HE'S TELLING THE TRUTH?
HE BETTER BE. YOU DON'T WANNA KNOW HOW MUCH IT TOOK TO PAY HIM OFF.
C'MON, MAN. WE KNOW WHERE HE LIVES NOW. LET'S TAKE HIM DOWN LATER. PREPARED. WITH WEAPONS.
YOU DON'T THINK I CAN BEAT HIM WITHOUT MY ARROWS?
YOU FORGET. I AM THE WEAPON.

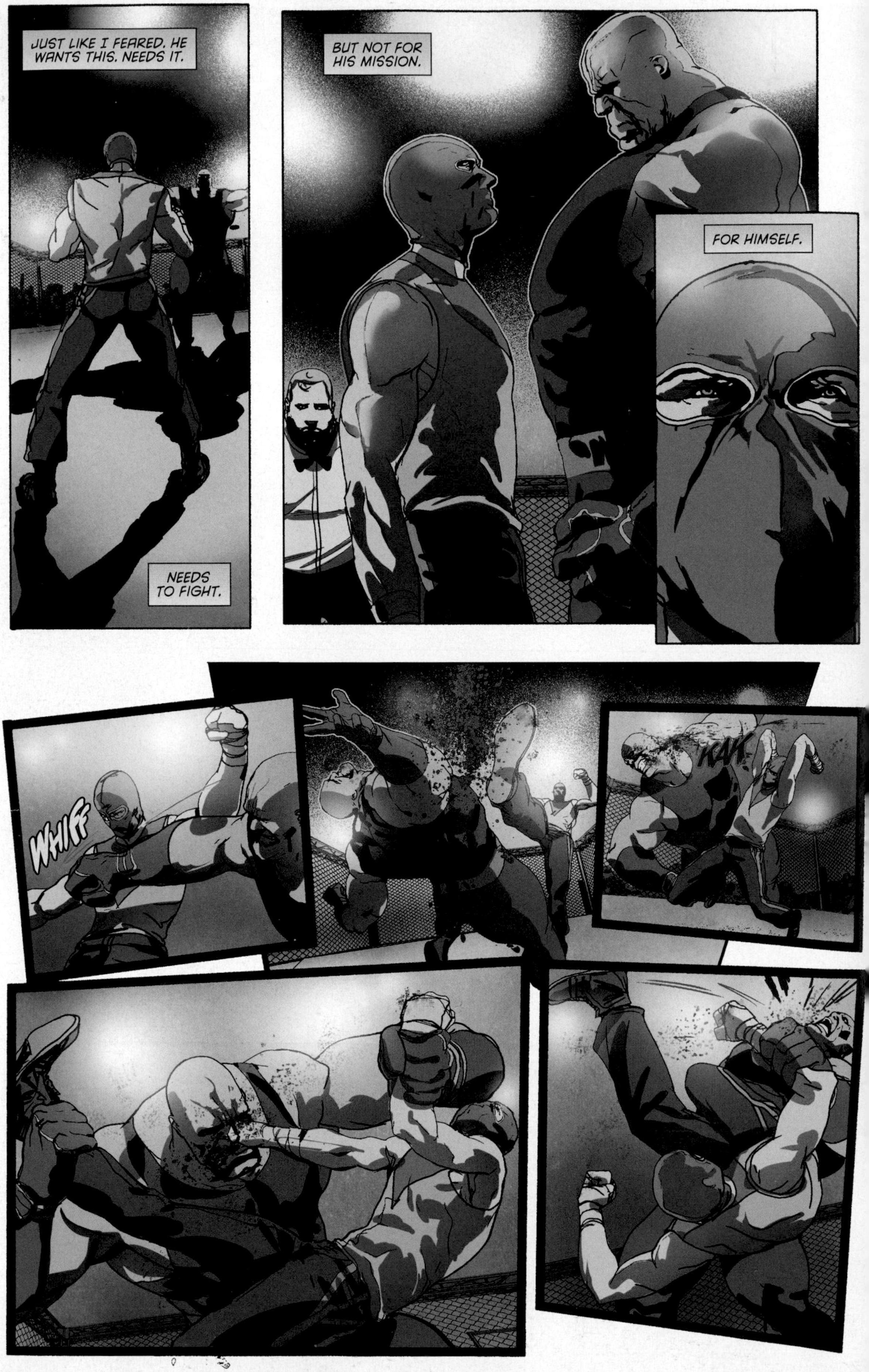
JUST LIKE I FEARED. HE WANTS THIS. NEEDS IT.
NEEDS TO FIGHT.
BUT NOT FOR HIS MISSION.
FOR HIMSELF.
WHIFF
KAK

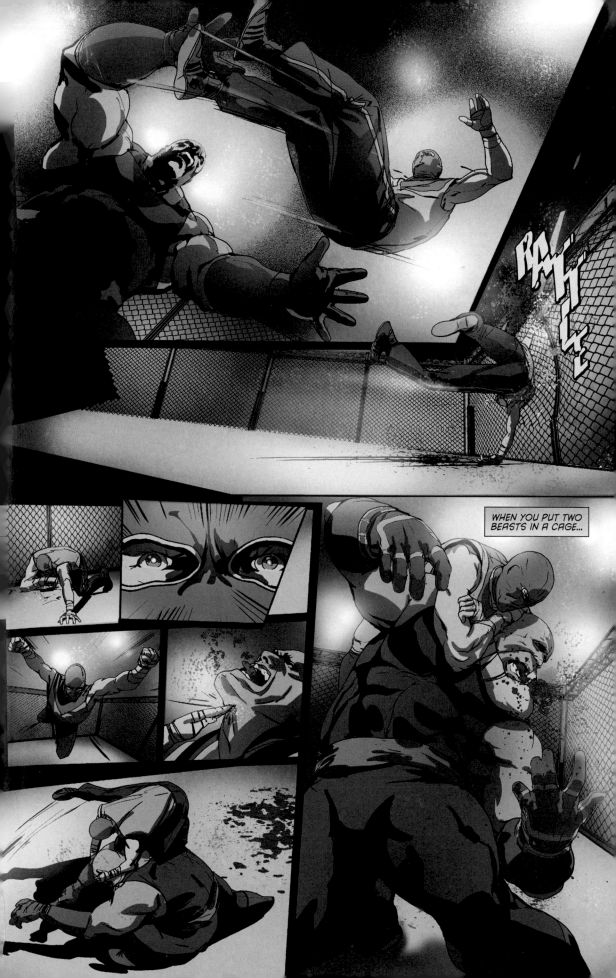

WHEN YOU PUT TWO BEASTS IN A CAGE...

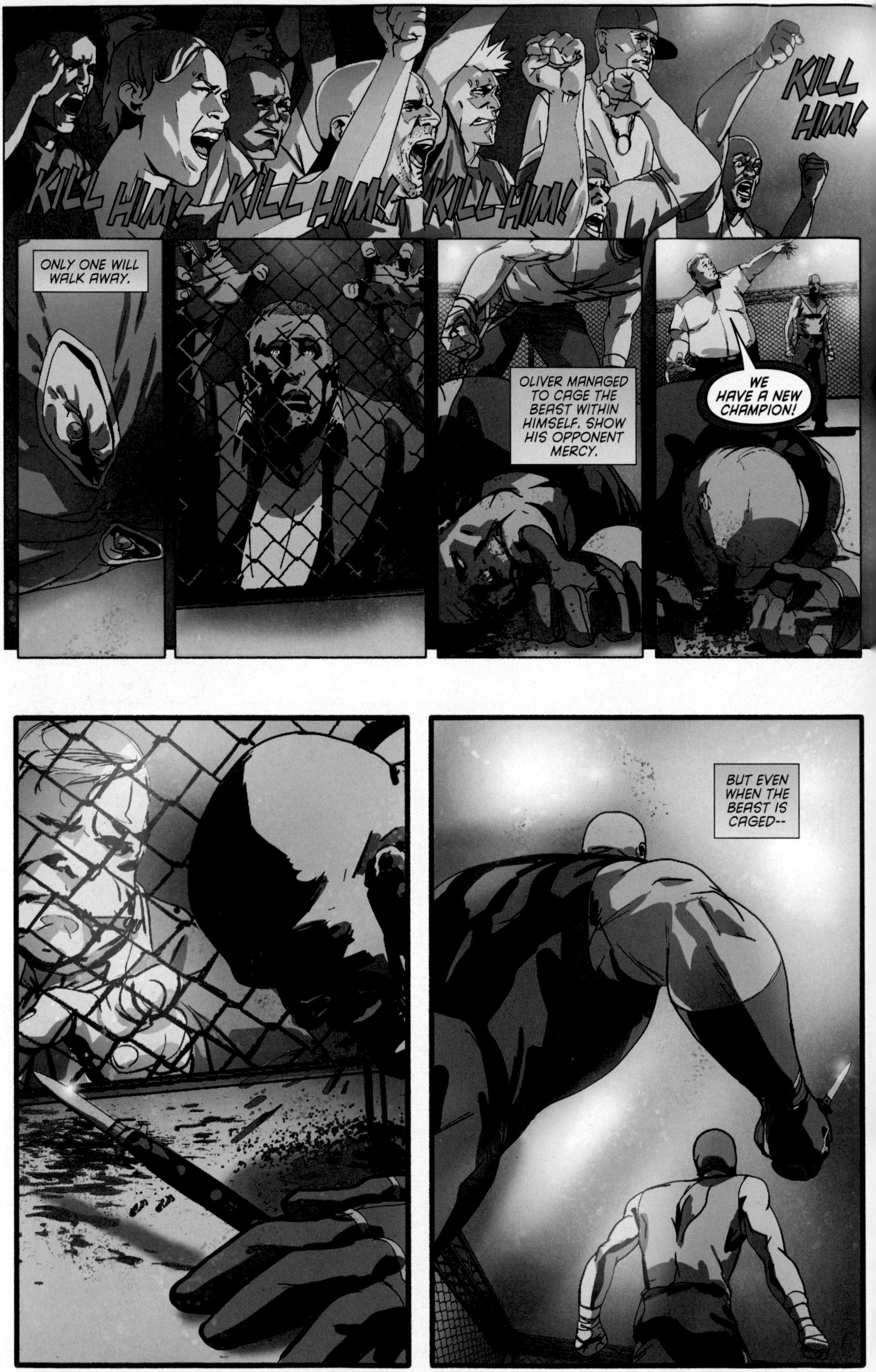
KILL HIM!
KILL HIM! KILL HIM! KILL HIM!
ONLY ONE WILL WALK AWAY.
OLIVER MANAGED TO CAGE THE BEAST WITHIN HIMSELF. SHOW HIS OPPONENT MERCY.
WE HAVE A NEW CHAMPION!
BUT EVEN WHEN THE BEAST IS CAGED--

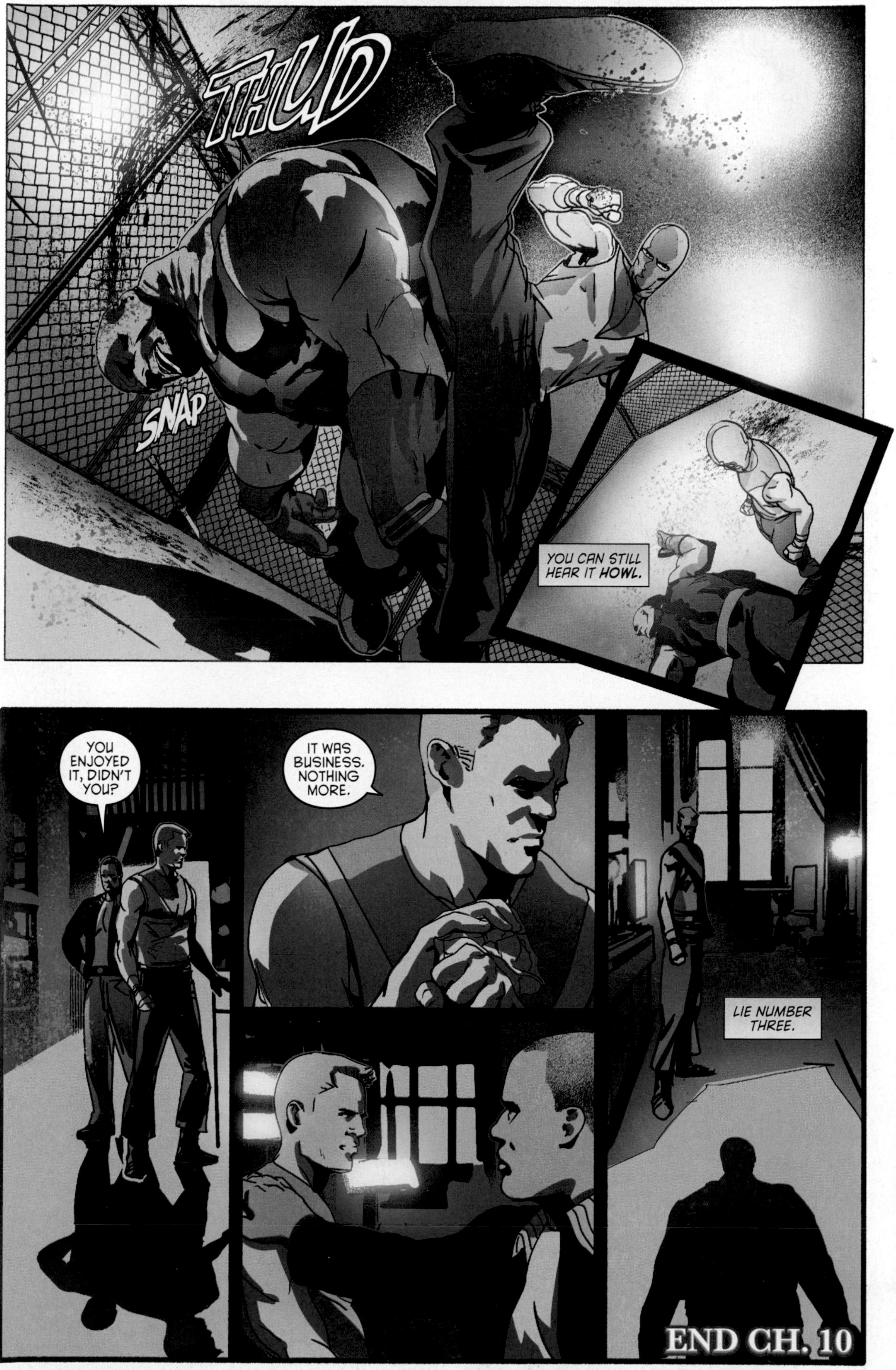
THUD
SNAP
YOU CAN STILL HEAR IT HOWL.
YOU ENJOYED IT, DIDN'T YOU?
IT WAS BUSINESS. NOTHING MORE.
LIE NUMBER THREE.
END CH. 10

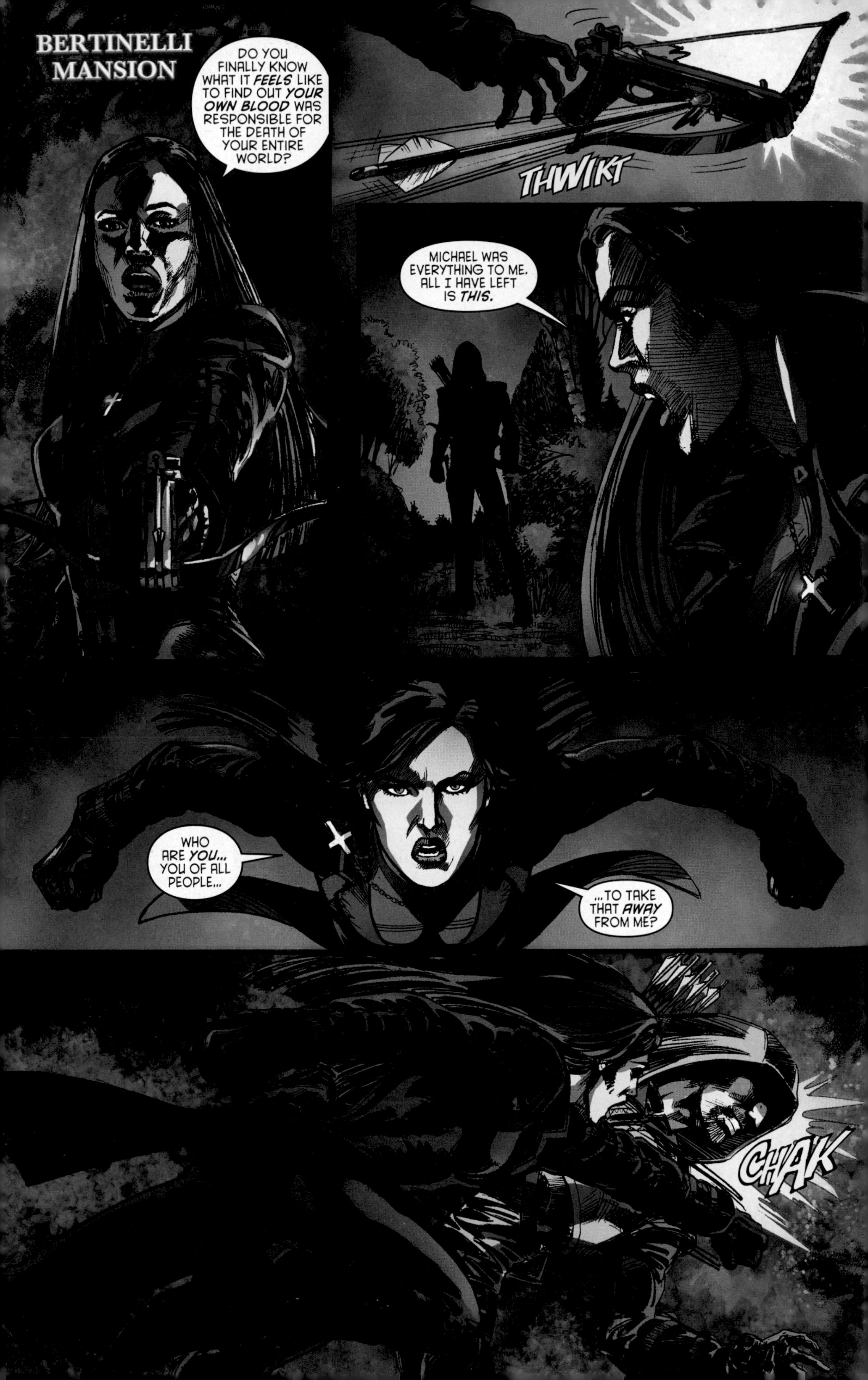
BERTINELLI MANSION
DO YOU FINALLY KNOW WHAT IT FEELS LIKE TO FIND OUT YOUR OWN BLOOD WAS RESPONSIBLE FOR THE DEATH OF YOUR ENTIRE WORLD?
THWIKT
MICHAEL WAS EVERYTHING TO ME. ALL I HAVE LEFT IS THIS.
WHO ARE YOU... YOU OF ALL PEOPLE...
...TO TAKE THAT AWAY FROM ME?
CHAK

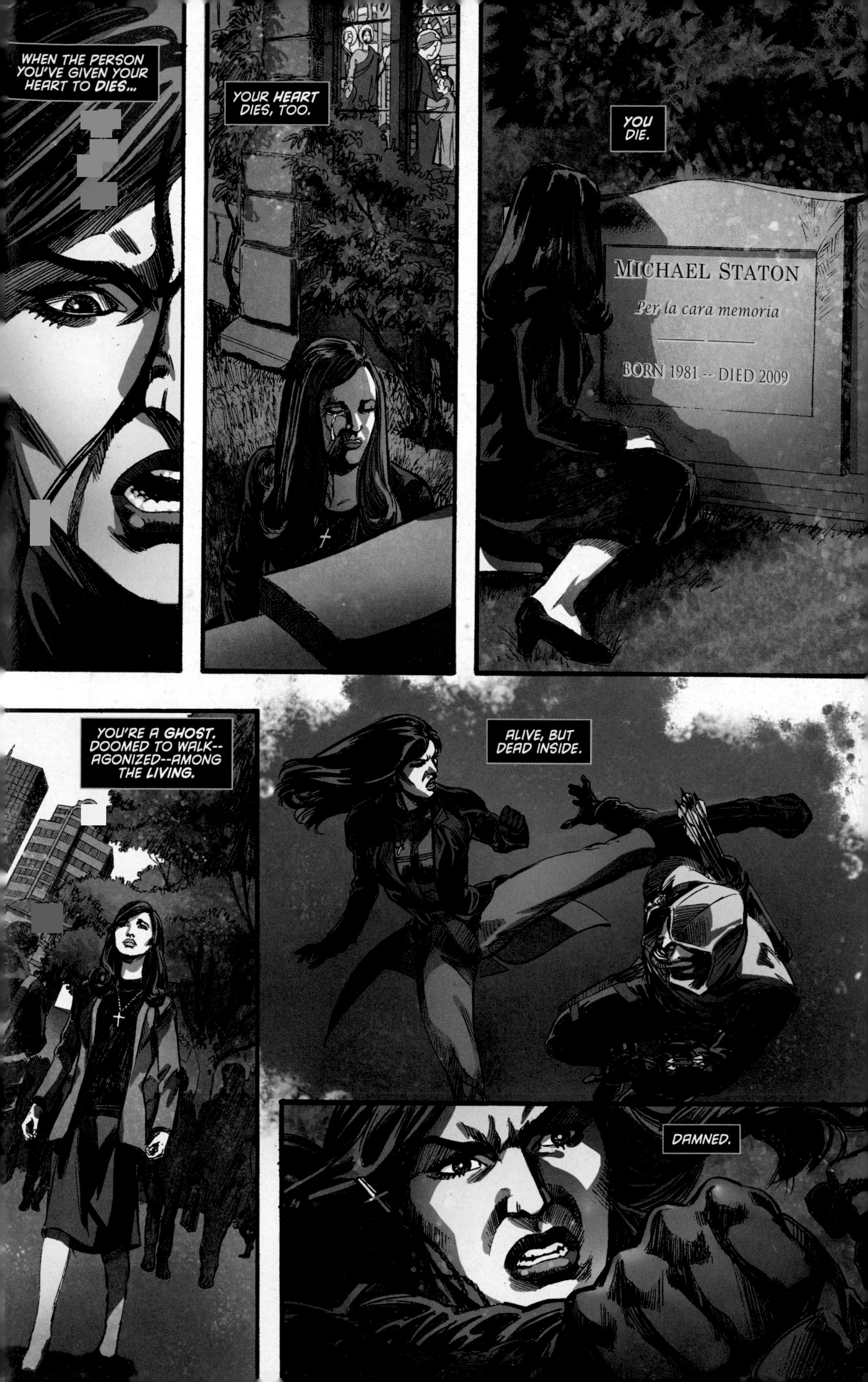

WHEN THE PERSON YOU'VE GIVEN YOUR HEART TO DIES...
YOUR HEART DIES, TOO.
YOU DIE.
MICHAEL STATON
Per la cara memoria
BORN 1981 -- DIED 2009
YOU'RE A GHOST. DOOMED TO WALK--AGONIZED--AMONG THE LIVING.
ALIVE, BUT DEAD INSIDE.
DAMNED.

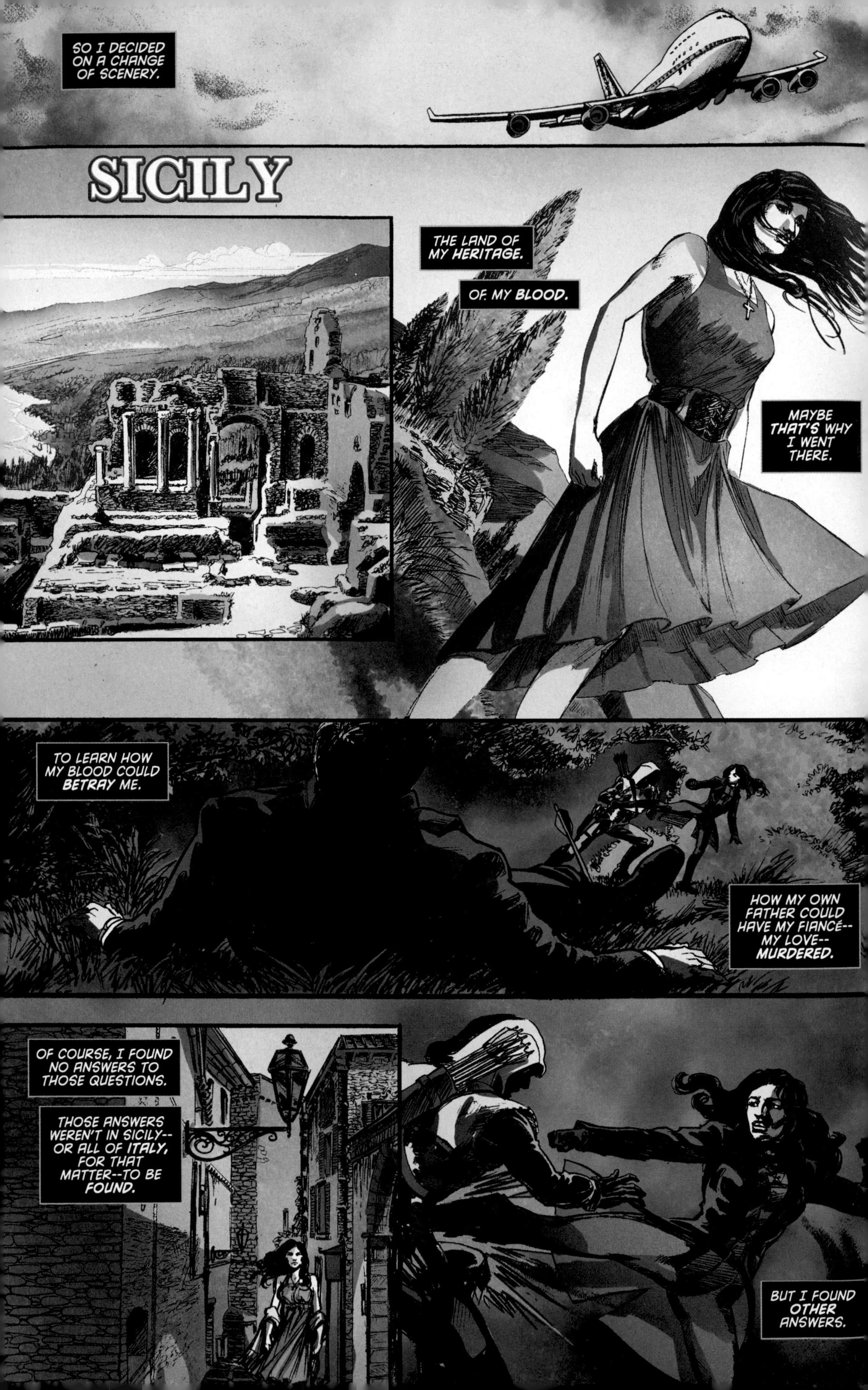
SO I DECIDED ON A CHANGE OF SCENERY.
SICILY
THE LAND OF MY HERITAGE.
OF. MY BLOOD.
MAYBE THAT'S WHY I WENT THERE.
TO LEARN HOW MY BLOOD COULD BETRAY ME.
HOW MY OWN FATHER COULD HAVE MY FIANCÉ-- MY LOVE-- MURDERED.
OF COURSE, I FOUND NO ANSWERS TO THOSE QUESTIONS.
THOSE ANSWERS WEREN'T IN SICILY-- OR ALL OF ITALY, FOR THAT MATTER--TO BE FOUND.
BUT I FOUND OTHER ANSWERS.

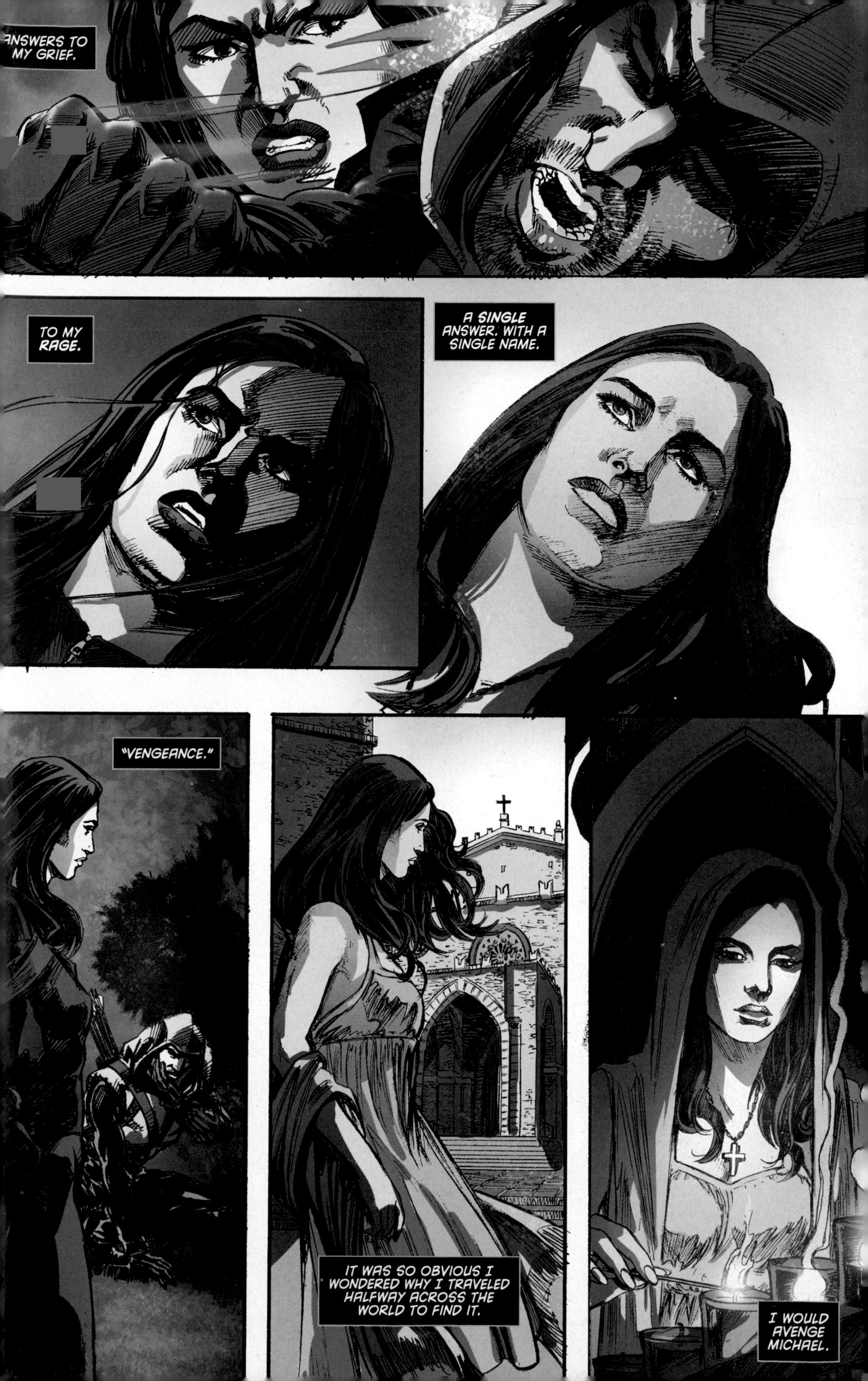
ANSWERS TO MY GRIEF.
TO MY RAGE.
A SINGLE ANSWER. WITH A SINGLE NAME.
"VENGEANCE."
IT WAS SO OBVIOUS I WONDERED WHY I TRAVELED HALFWAY ACROSS THE WORLD TO FIND IT.
I WOULD AVENGE MICHAEL.

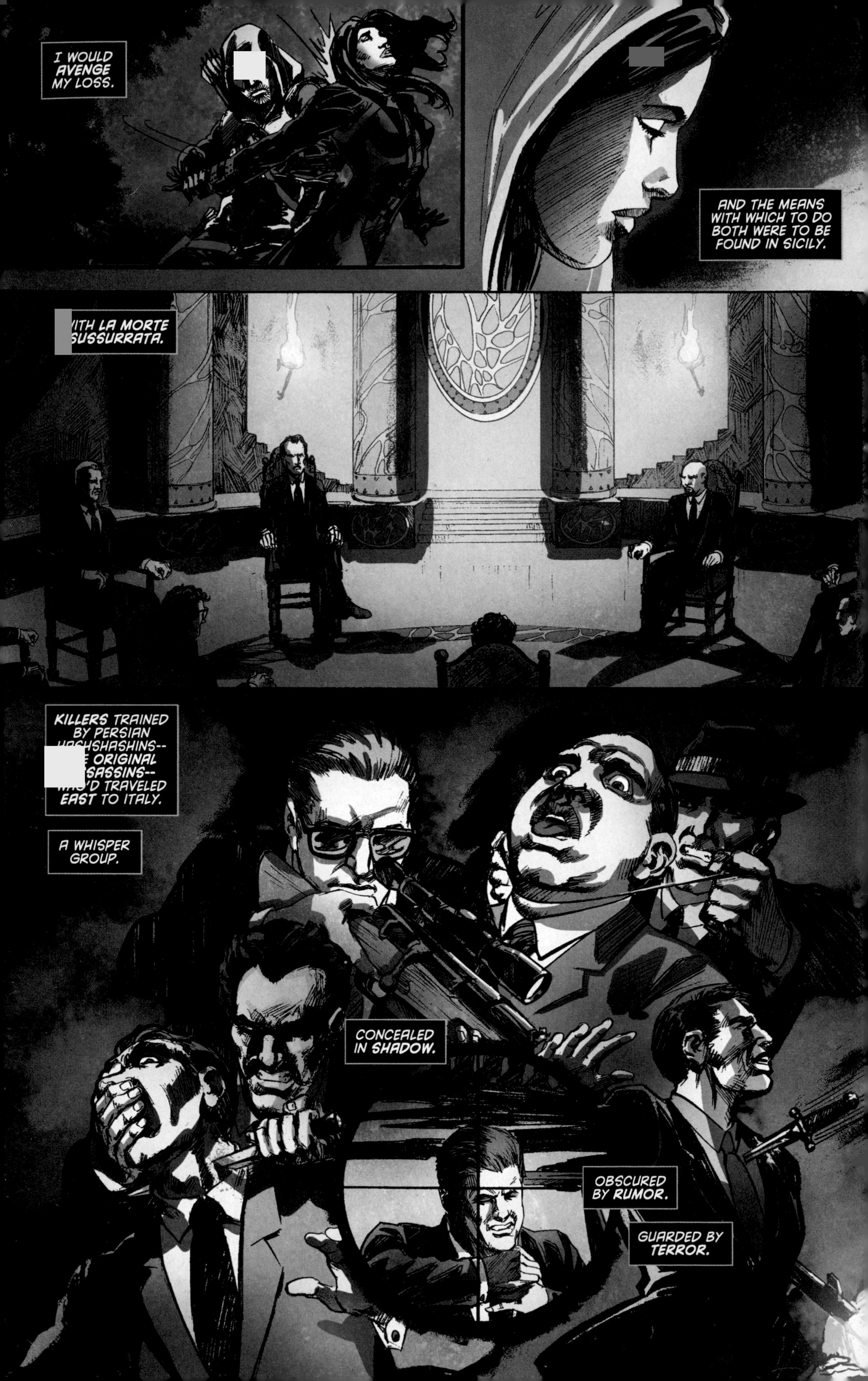
I WOULD AVENGE MY LOSS.
AND THE MEANS WITH WHICH TO DO BOTH WERE TO BE FOUND IN SICILY.
WITH LA MORTE SUSSURRATA.
KILLERS TRAINED BY PERSIAN HASHSHASHINS-- THE ORIGINAL ASSASSINS-- WHO'D TRAVELED EAST TO ITALY.
A WHISPER GROUP.
CONCEALED IN SHADOW.
OBSCURED BY RUMOR.
GUARDED BY TERROR.

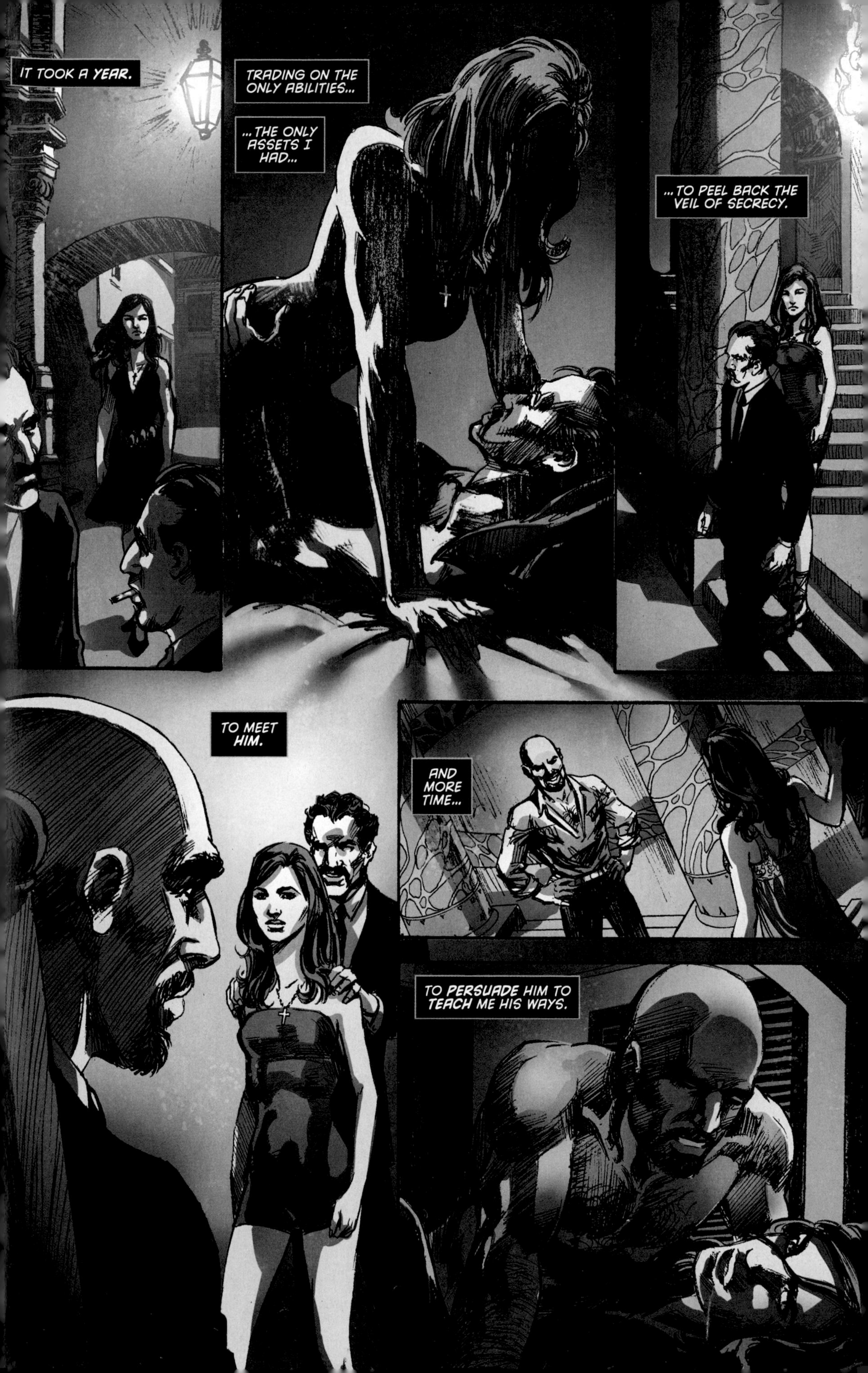
IT TOOK A YEAR.
TRADING ON THE ONLY ABILITIES...
...THE ONLY ASSETS I HAD...
...TO PEEL BACK THE VEIL OF SECRECY.
TO MEET HIM.
AND MORE TIME...
TO PERSUADE HIM TO TEACH ME HIS WAYS.

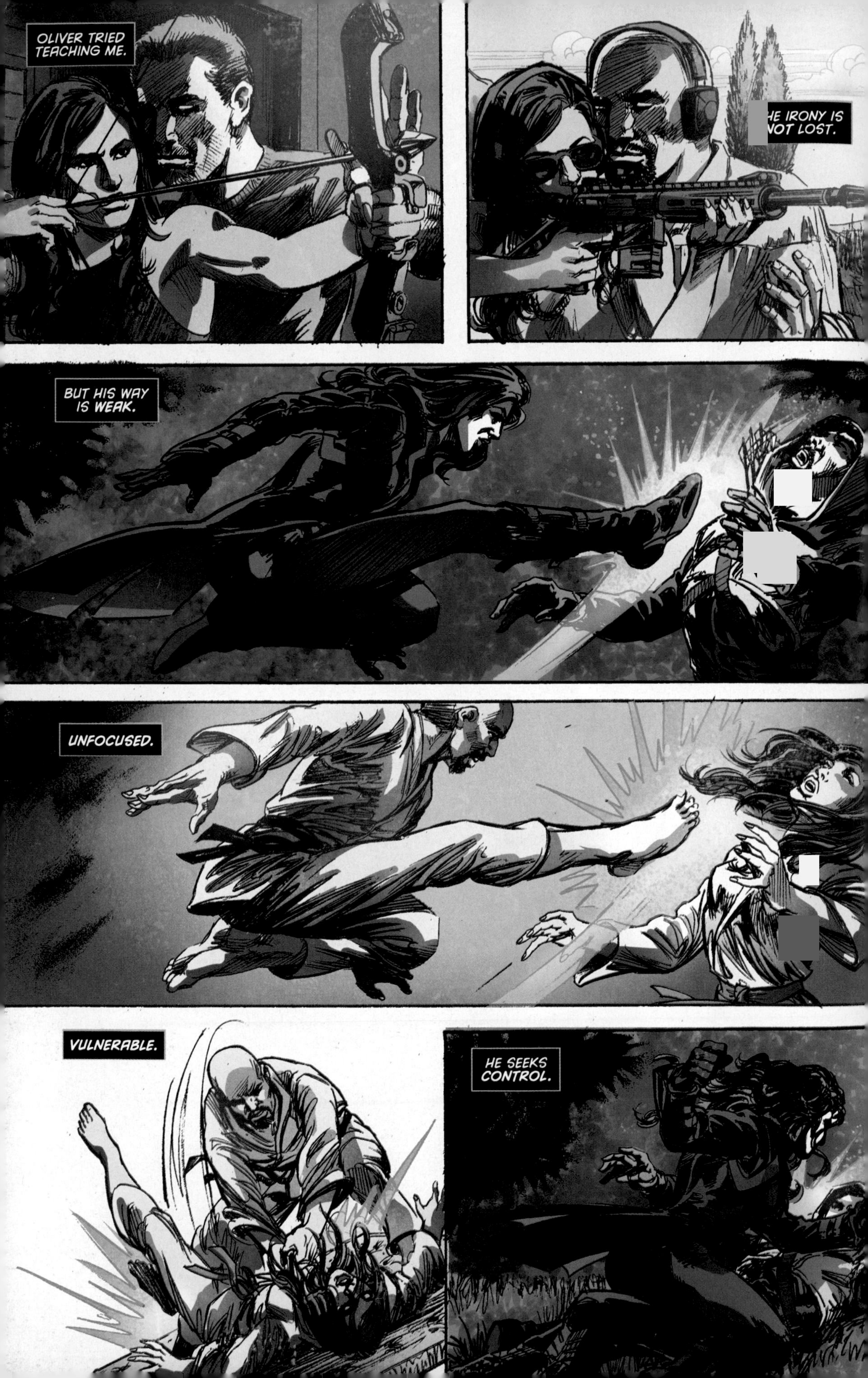
OLIVER TRIED TEACHING ME.
HE IRONY IS NOT LOST.
BUT HIS WAY IS WEAK.
UNFOCUSED.
VULNERABLE.
HE SEEKS CONTROL.

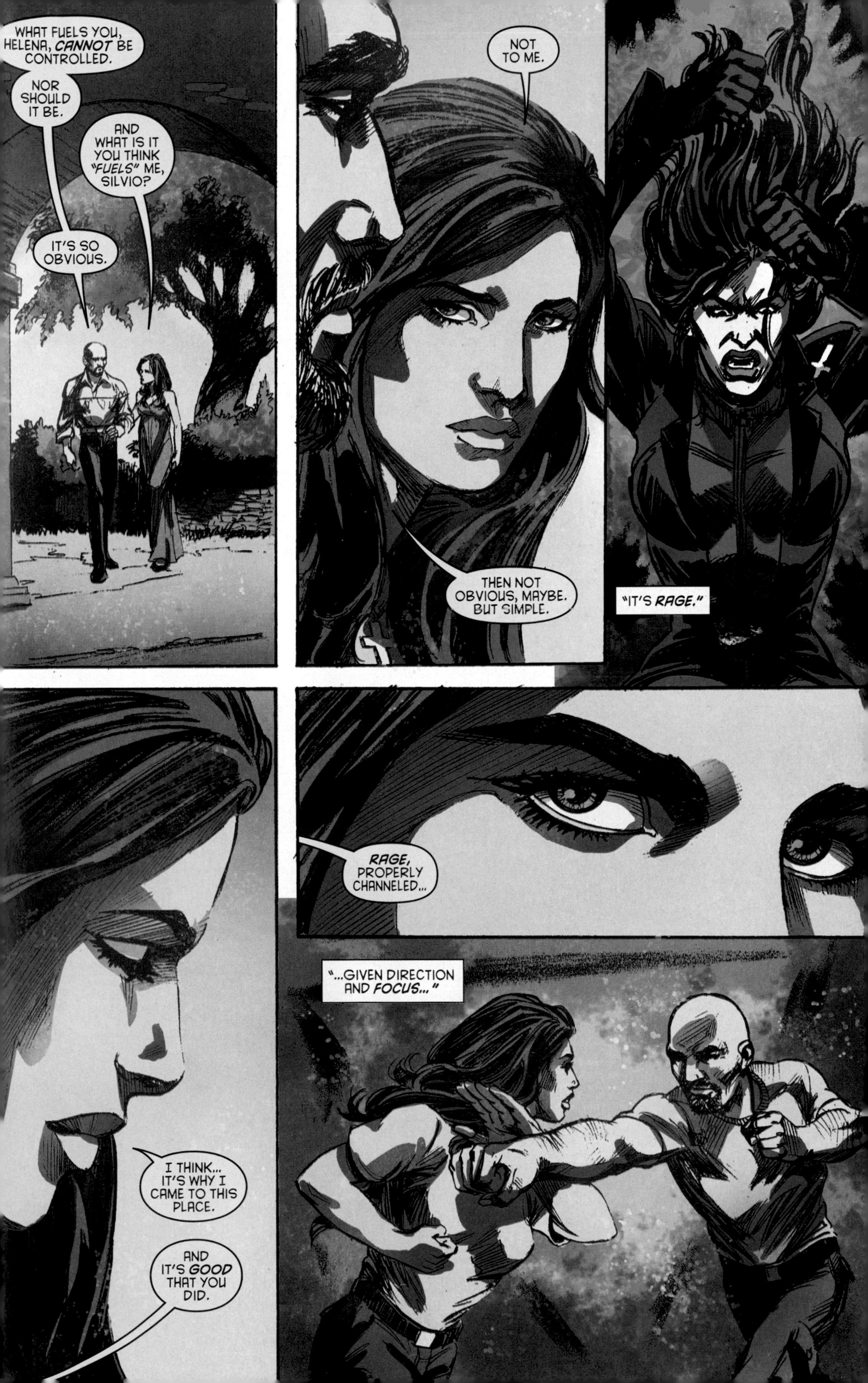

WHAT FUELS YOU, HELENA, *CANNOT* BE CONTROLLED.
NOR SHOULD IT BE.
AND WHAT IS IT YOU THINK *"FUELS"* ME, SILVIO?
IT'S SO OBVIOUS.
NOT TO ME.
THEN NOT OBVIOUS, MAYBE. BUT SIMPLE.
"IT'S *RAGE."*
RAGE, PROPERLY CHANNELED...
"...GIVEN DIRECTION AND *FOCUS..."*
I THINK... IT'S WHY I CAME TO THIS PLACE.
AND IT'S *GOOD* THAT YOU DID.

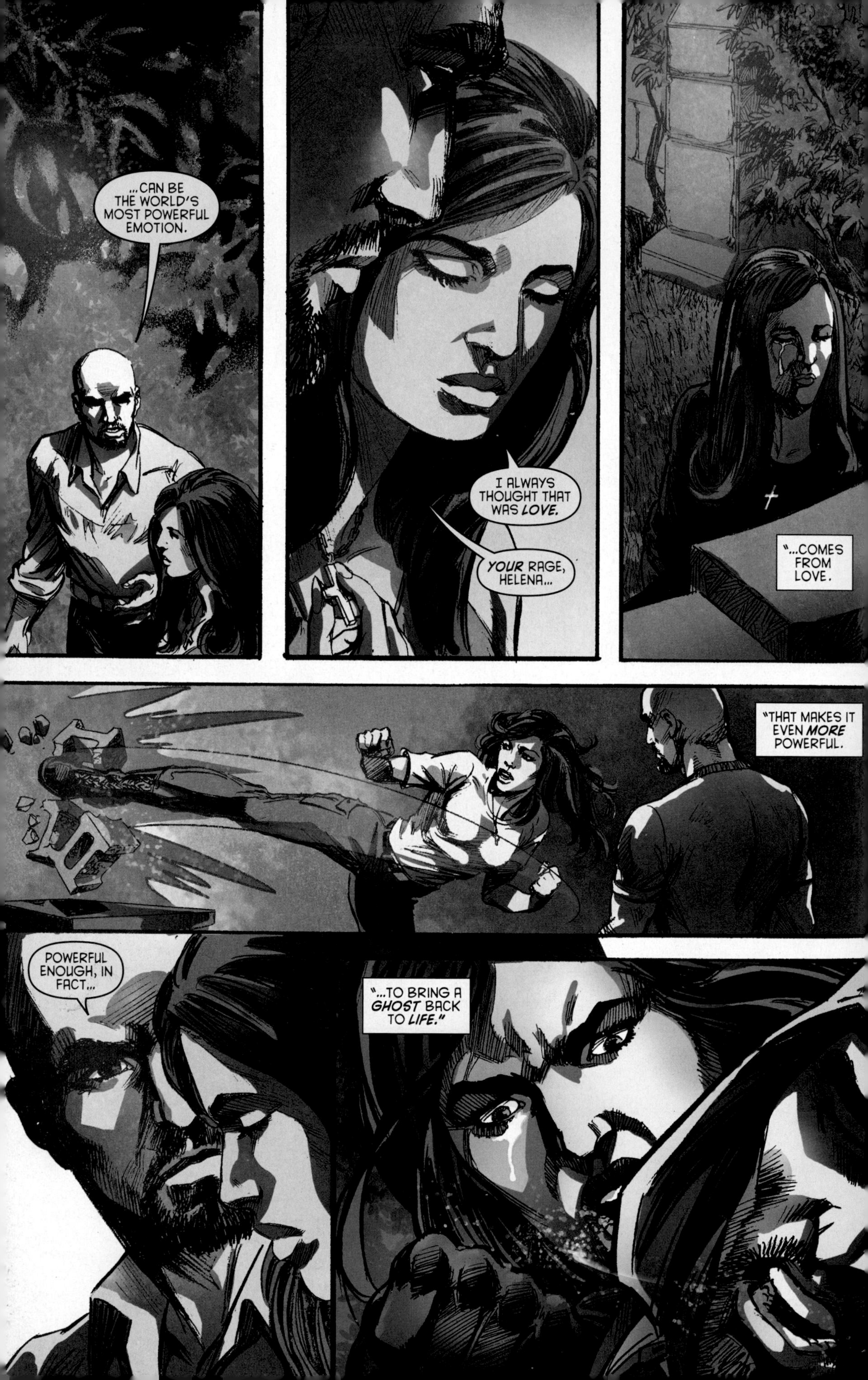
...CAN BE THE WORLD'S MOST POWERFUL EMOTION.
I ALWAYS THOUGHT THAT WAS *LOVE.*
YOUR RAGE, HELENA...
"...COMES FROM LOVE.
"THAT MAKES IT EVEN *MORE* POWERFUL.
POWERFUL ENOUGH, IN FACT...
"...TO BRING A *GHOST* BACK TO *LIFE.*"

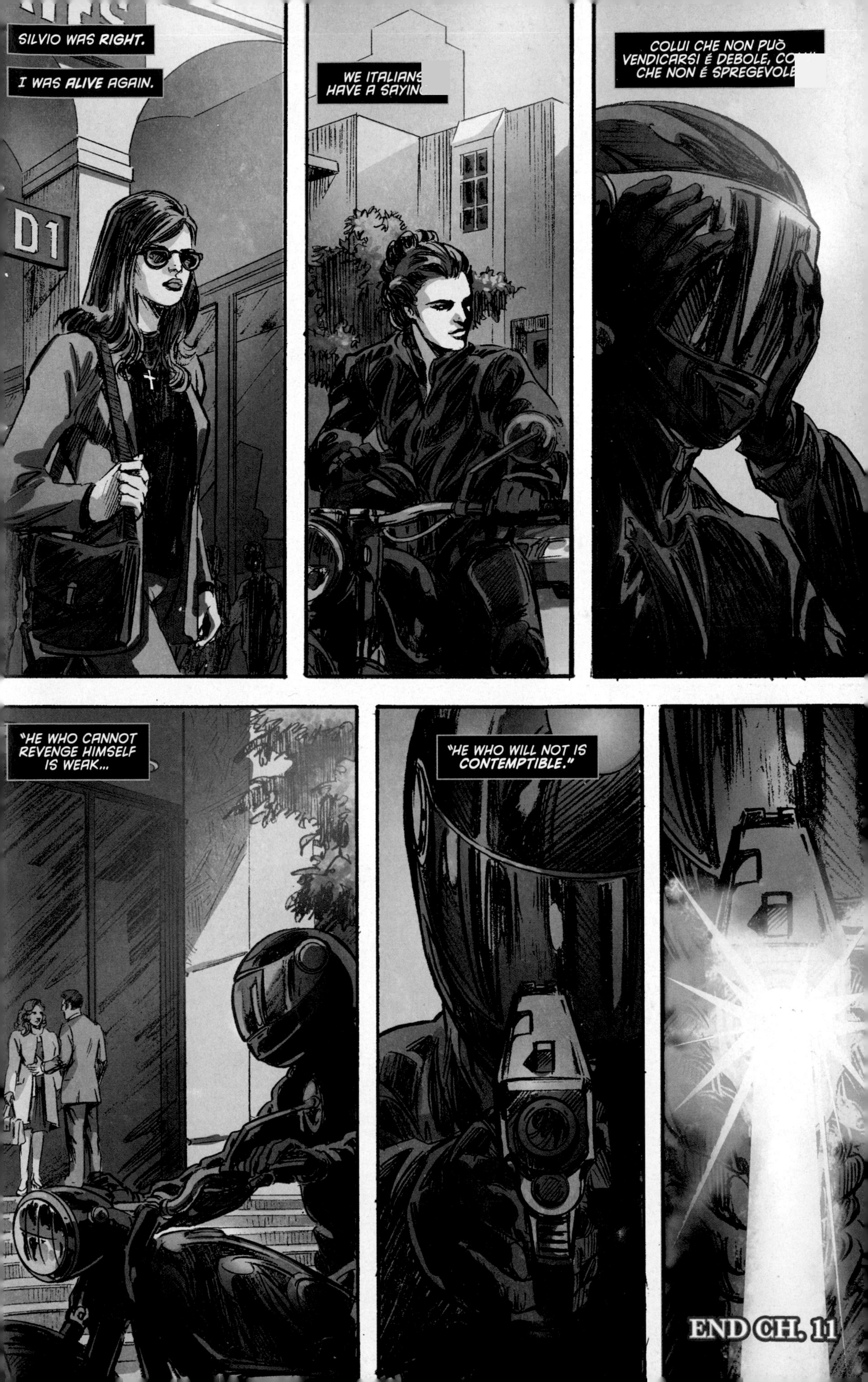
SILVIO WAS RIGHT.
I WAS ALIVE AGAIN.
WE ITALIANS HAVE A SAYIN
COLUI CHE NON PUÒ VENDICARSI É DEBOLE, CO CHE NON É SPREGEVOLE
"HE WHO CANNOT REVENGE HIMSELF IS WEAK...
"HE WHO WILL NOT IS CONTEMPTIBLE."
END CH. 11

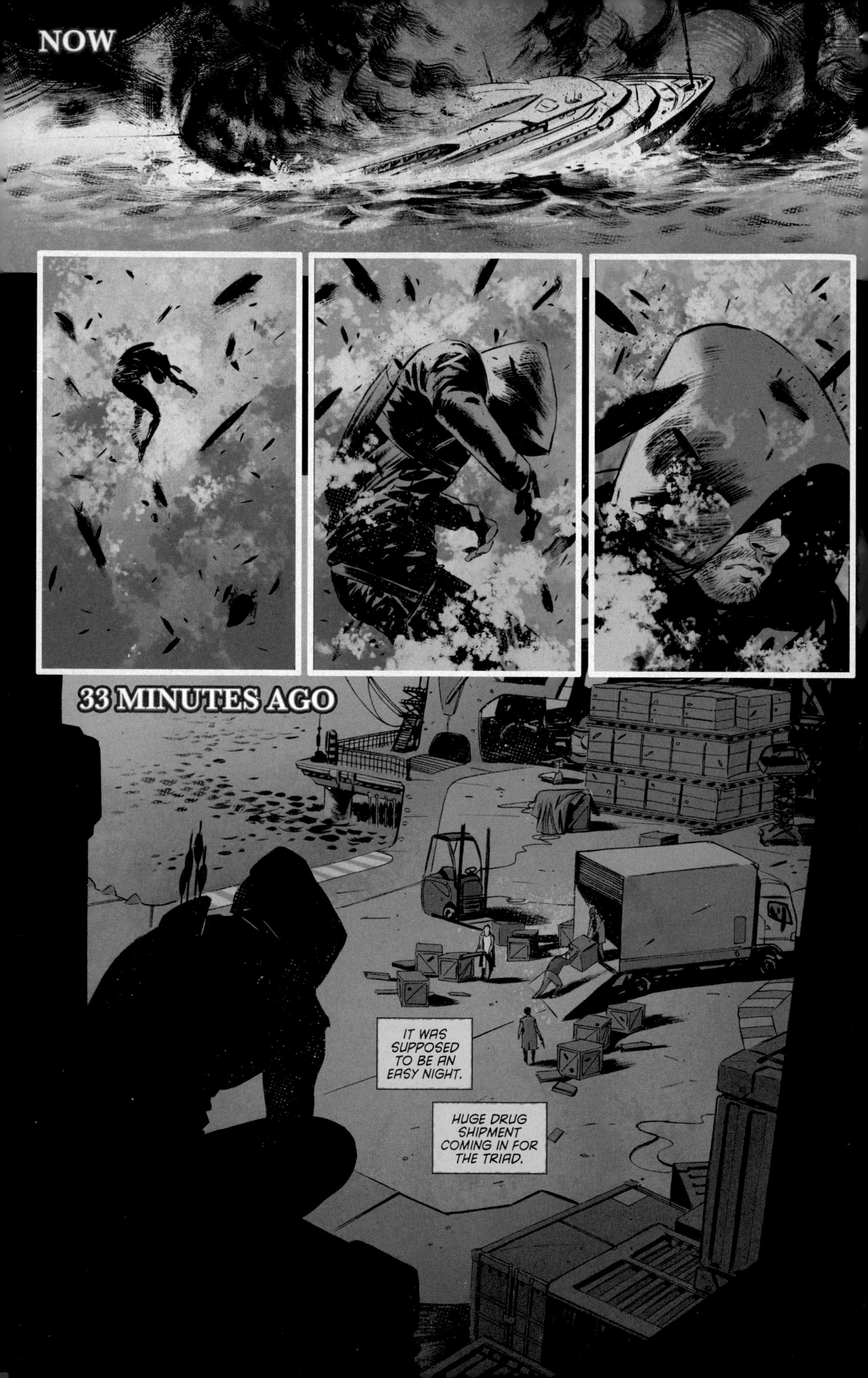
NOW
33 MINUTES AGO
IT WAS SUPPOSED TO BE AN EASY NIGHT.
HUGE DRUG SHIPMENT COMING IN FOR THE TRIAD.

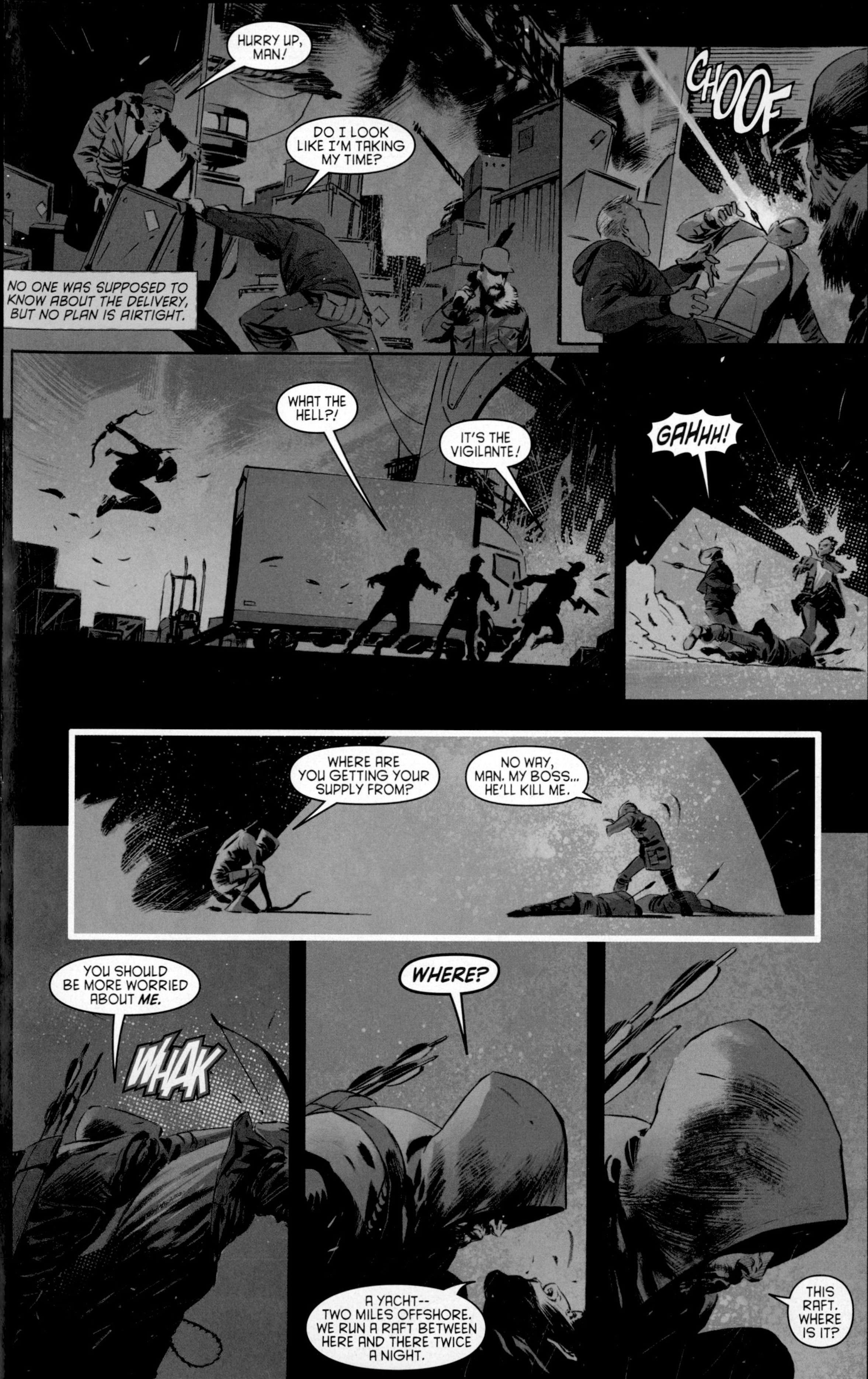
HURRY UP, MAN!
DO I LOOK LIKE I'M TAKING MY TIME?
NO ONE WAS SUPPOSED TO KNOW ABOUT THE DELIVERY, BUT NO PLAN IS AIRTIGHT.
CHOOF
WHAT THE HELL?!
IT'S THE VIGILANTE!
GAHHH!
WHERE ARE YOU GETTING YOUR SUPPLY FROM?
NO WAY, MAN. MY BOSS... HE'LL KILL ME.
YOU SHOULD BE MORE WORRIED ABOUT ME.
WHAK
WHERE?
A YACHT-- TWO MILES OFFSHORE. WE RUN A RAFT BETWEEN HERE AND THERE TWICE A NIGHT.
THIS RAFT. WHERE IS IT?

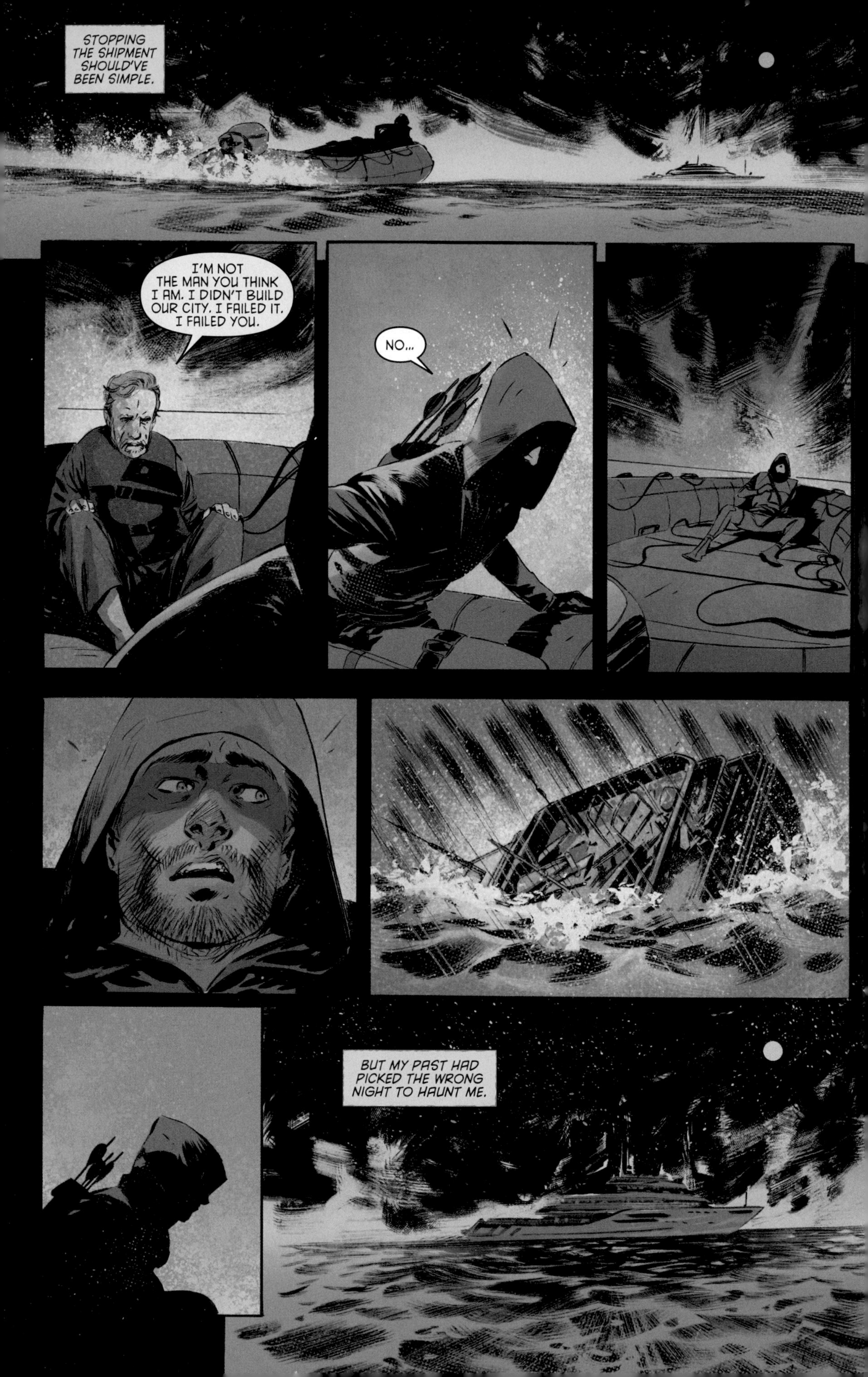
STOPPING THE SHIPMENT SHOULD'VE BEEN SIMPLE.
I'M NOT THE MAN YOU THINK I AM. I DIDN'T BUILD OUR CITY. I FAILED IT. I FAILED YOU.
NO...
BUT MY PAST HAD PICKED THE WRONG NIGHT TO HAUNT ME.

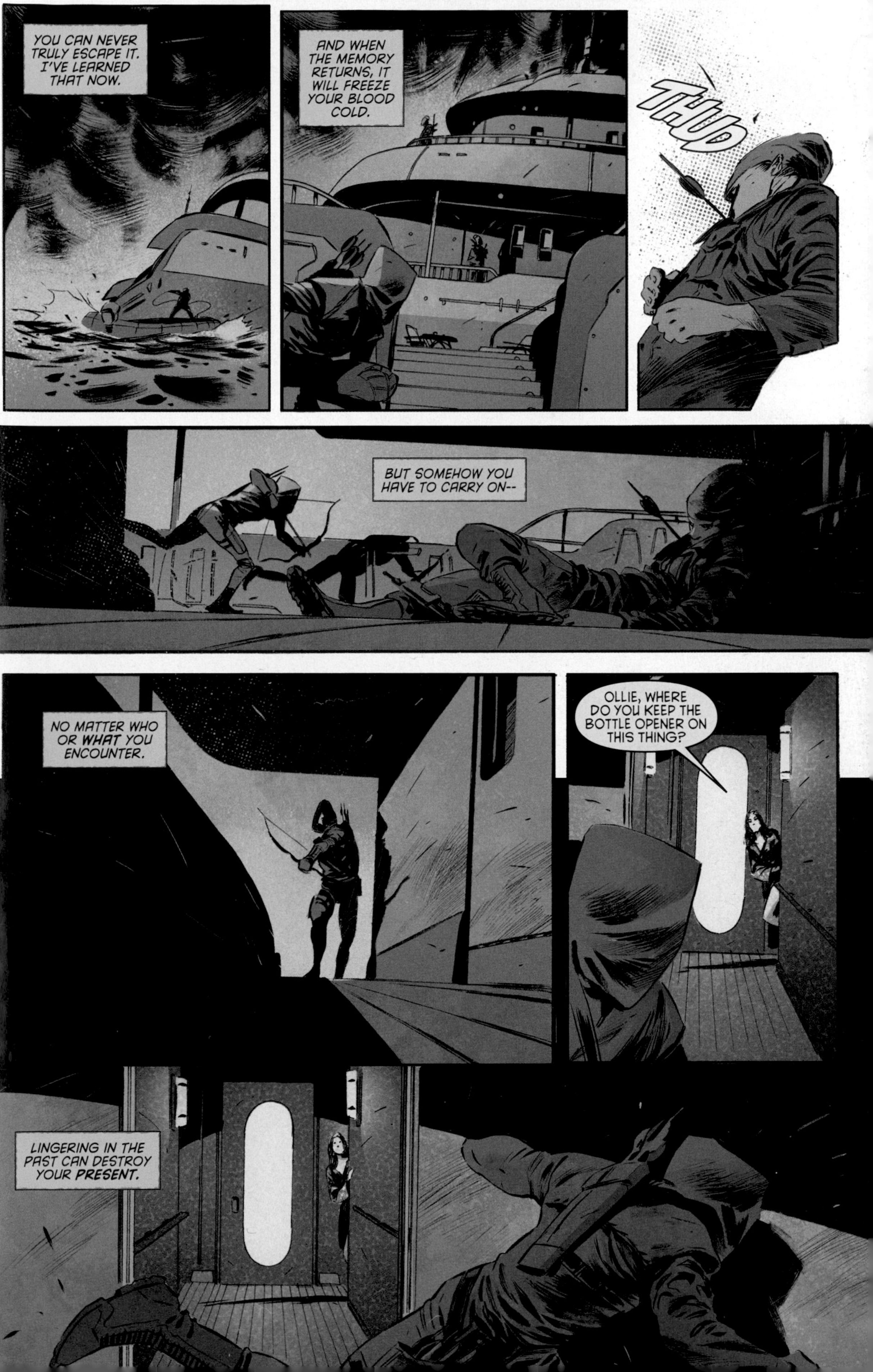
YOU CAN NEVER TRULY ESCAPE IT. I'VE LEARNED THAT NOW.
AND WHEN THE MEMORY RETURNS, IT WILL FREEZE YOUR BLOOD COLD.
THUD
BUT SOMEHOW YOU HAVE TO CARRY ON--
NO MATTER WHO OR WHAT YOU ENCOUNTER.
OLLIE, WHERE DO YOU KEEP THE BOTTLE OPENER ON THIS THING?
LINGERING IN THE PAST CAN DESTROY YOUR PRESENT.

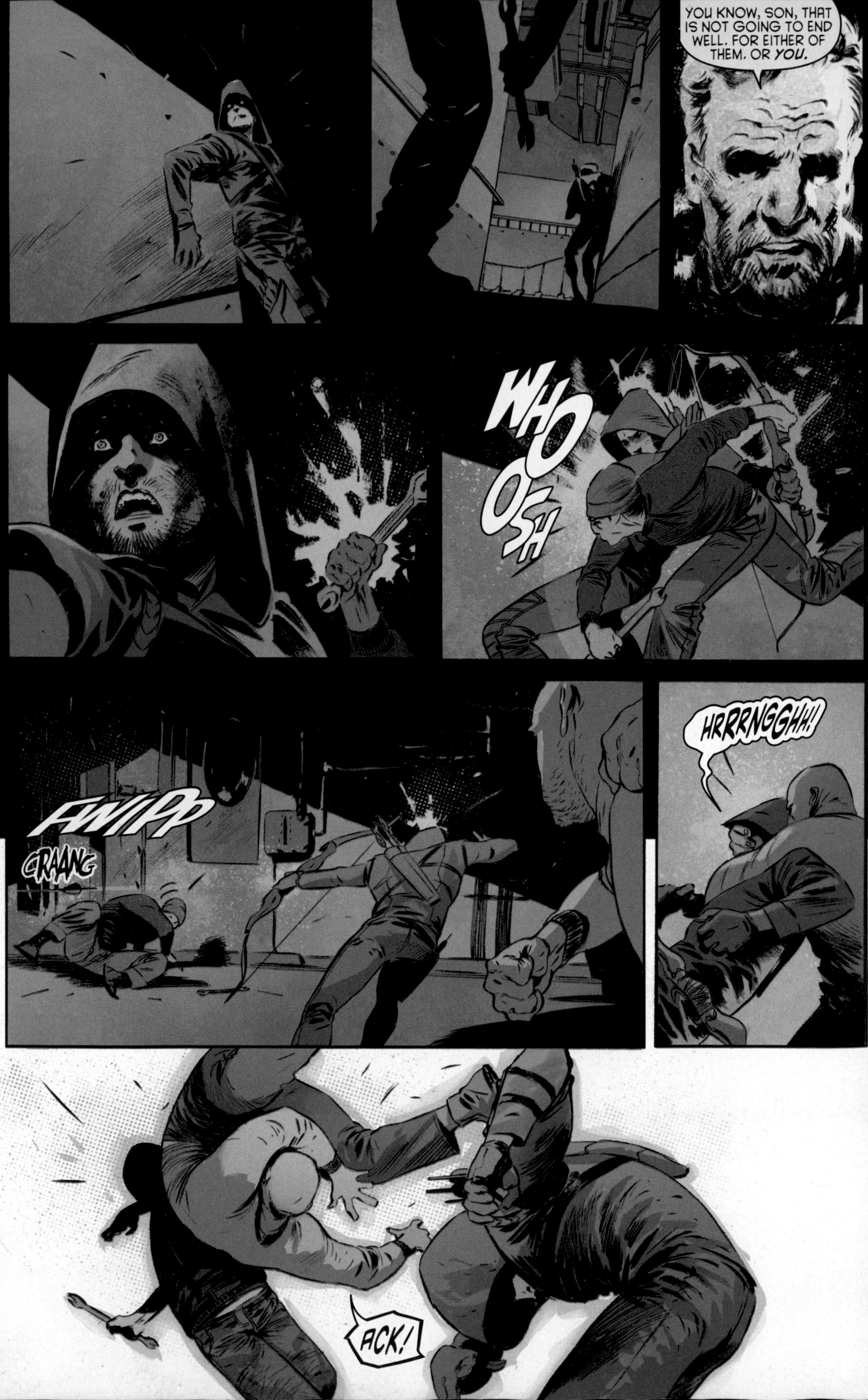

YOU KNOW, SON, THAT IS NOT GOING TO END WELL. FOR EITHER OF THEM. OR *YOU*.
WHOOOSH
FWIPP
CRAANG
HRRRNGGHH!
ACK!

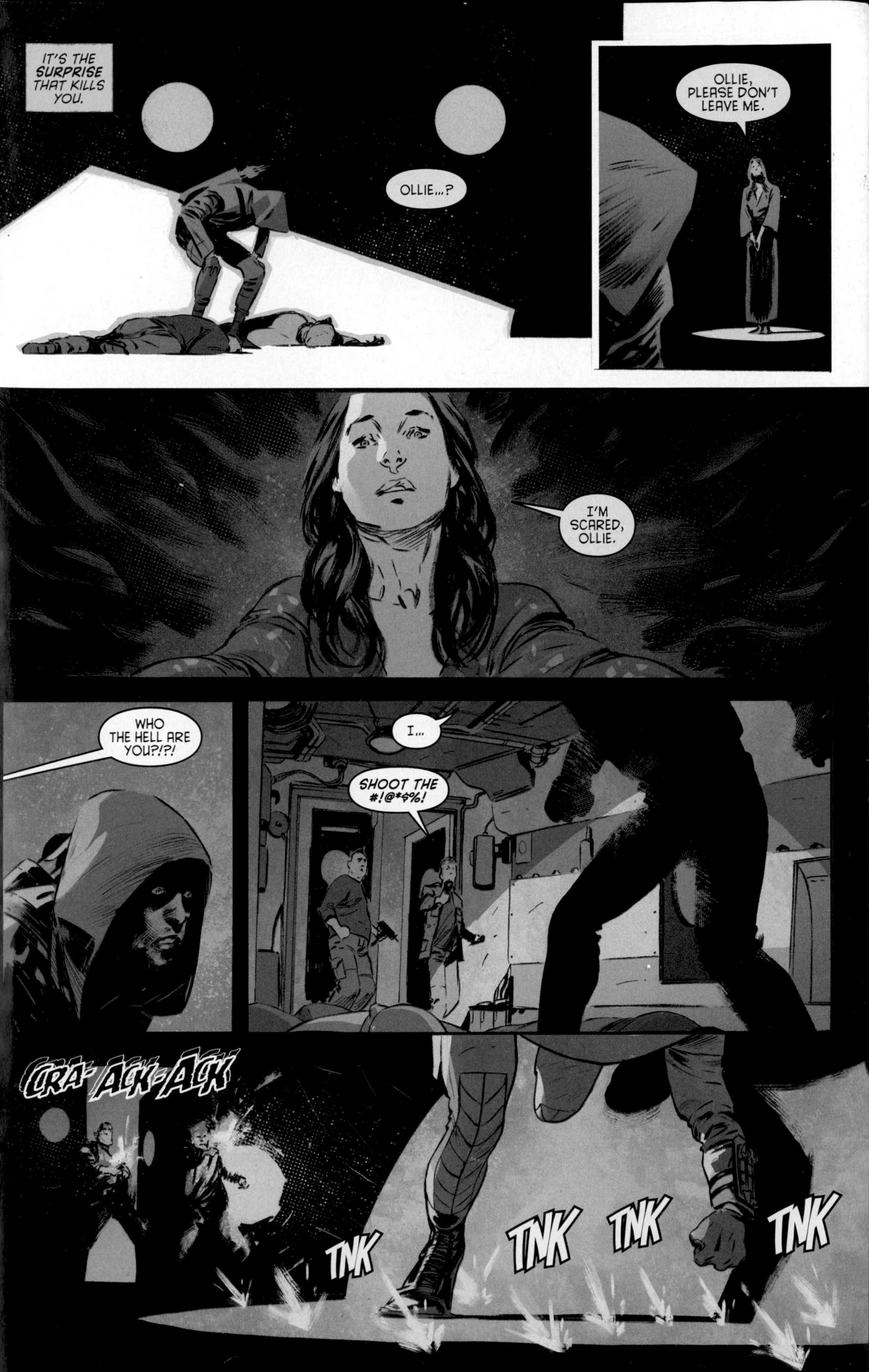

IT'S THE SURPRISE THAT KILLS YOU.
OLLIE...?
OLLIE, PLEASE DON'T LEAVE ME.
I'M SCARED, OLLIE.
WHO THE HELL ARE YOU?!?!
I...
SHOOT THE #!@*$%!
CRA-ACK-ACK
TNK
TNK
TNK
TNK

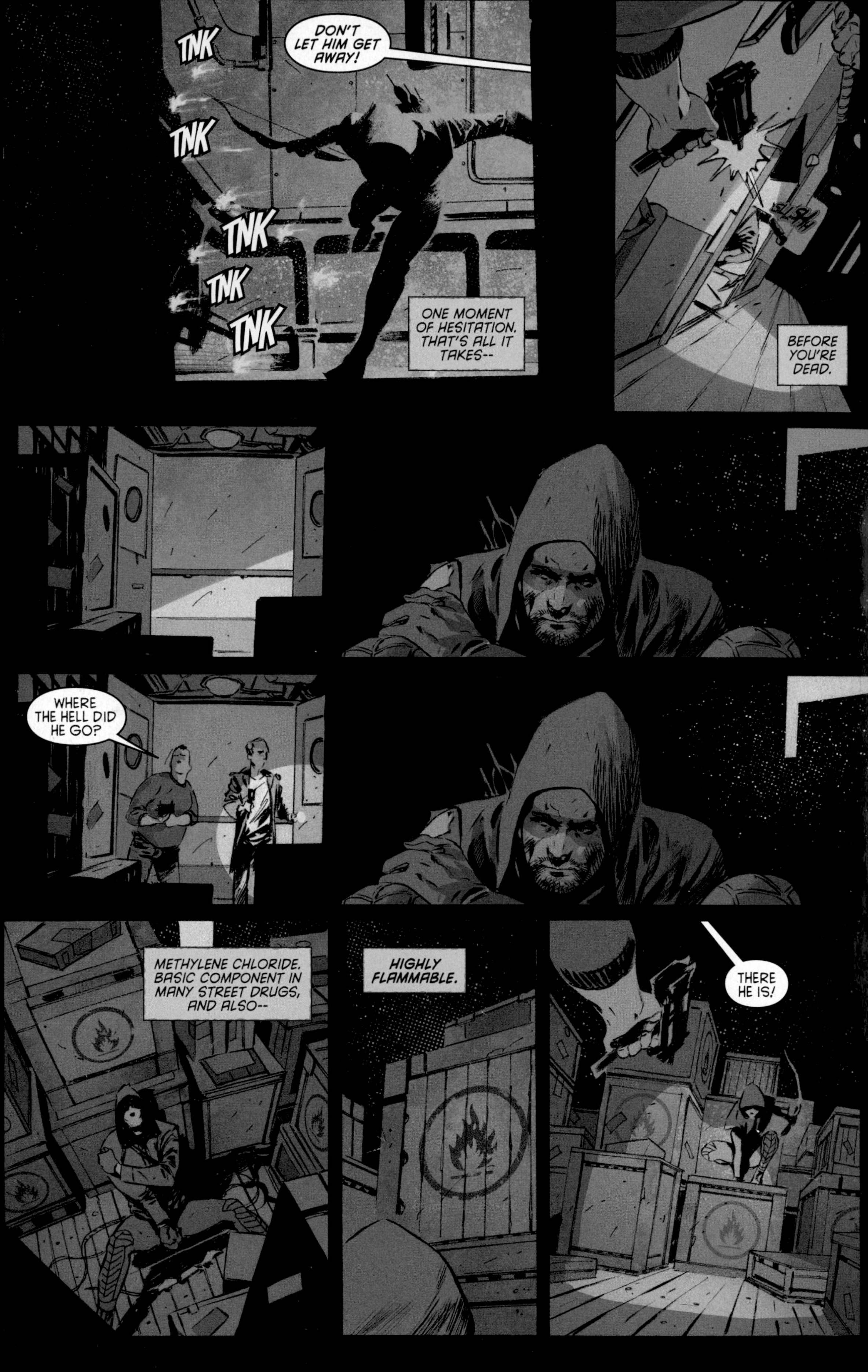
TNK
DON'T LET HIM GET AWAY!
TNK
TNK
TNK
TNK
ONE MOMENT OF HESITATION. THAT'S ALL IT TAKES--
BEFORE YOU'RE DEAD.
WHERE THE HELL DID HE GO?
METHYLENE CHLORIDE. BASIC COMPONENT IN MANY STREET DRUGS, AND ALSO--
HIGHLY FLAMMABLE.
THERE HE IS!

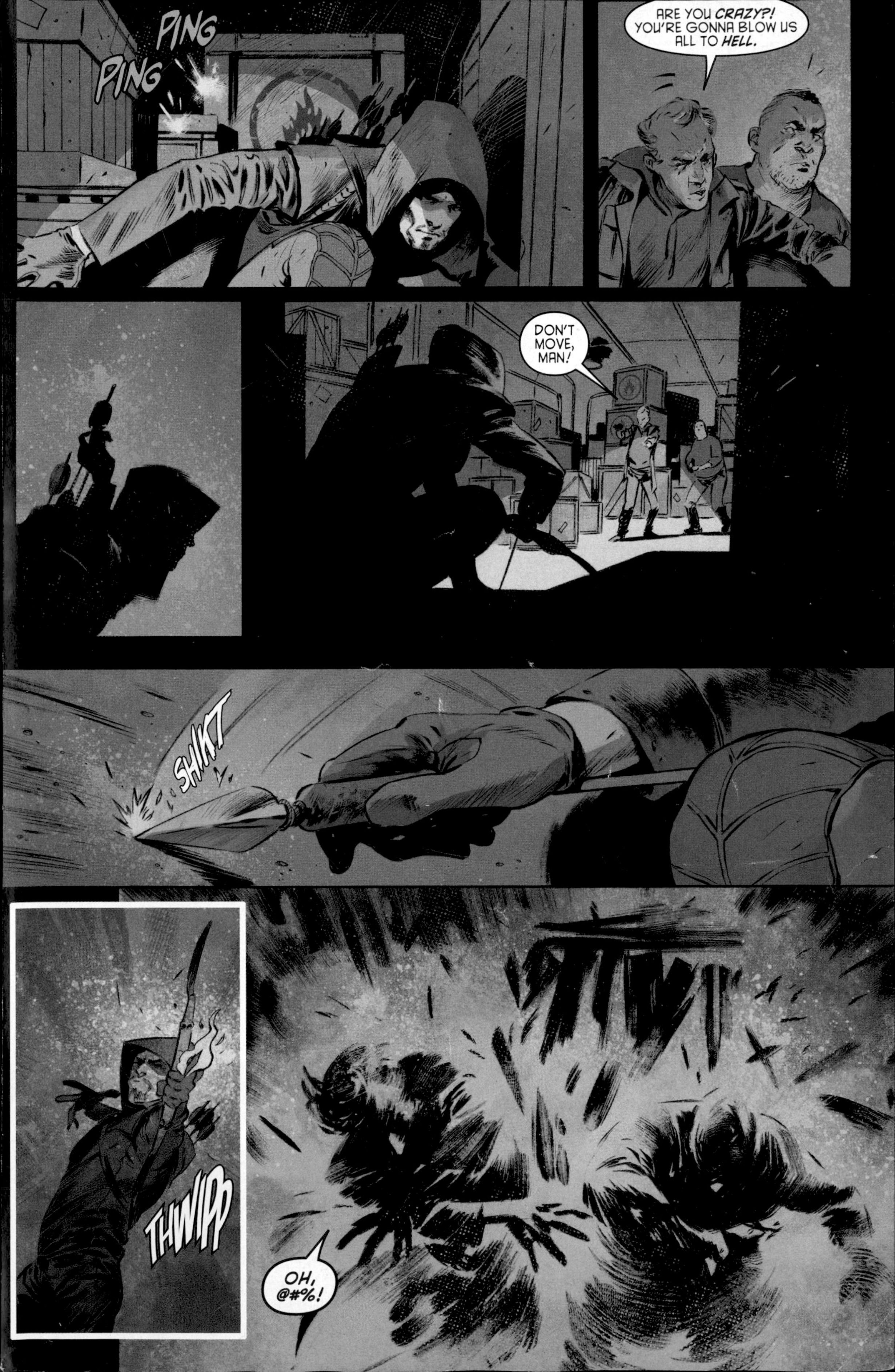
PING
PING
ARE YOU CRAZY?! YOU'RE GONNA BLOW US ALL TO HELL.
DON'T MOVE, MAN!
SHIKT
THWIPP
OH, @#%!

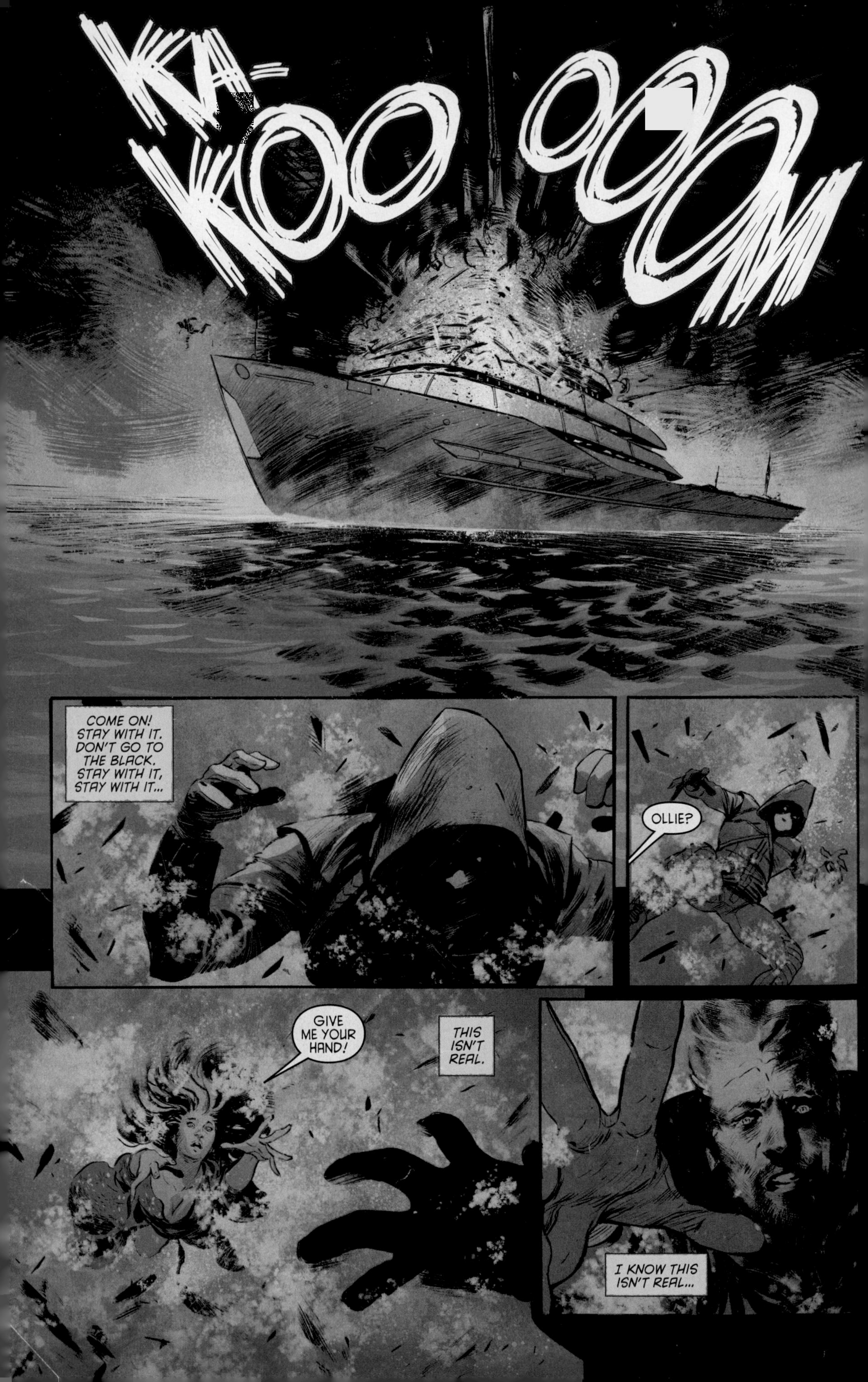
KA-KOOOOOOM
COME ON! STAY WITH IT. DON'T GO TO THE BLACK. STAY WITH IT, STAY WITH IT...
OLLIE?
GIVE ME YOUR HAND!
THIS ISN'T REAL.
I KNOW THIS ISN'T REAL...

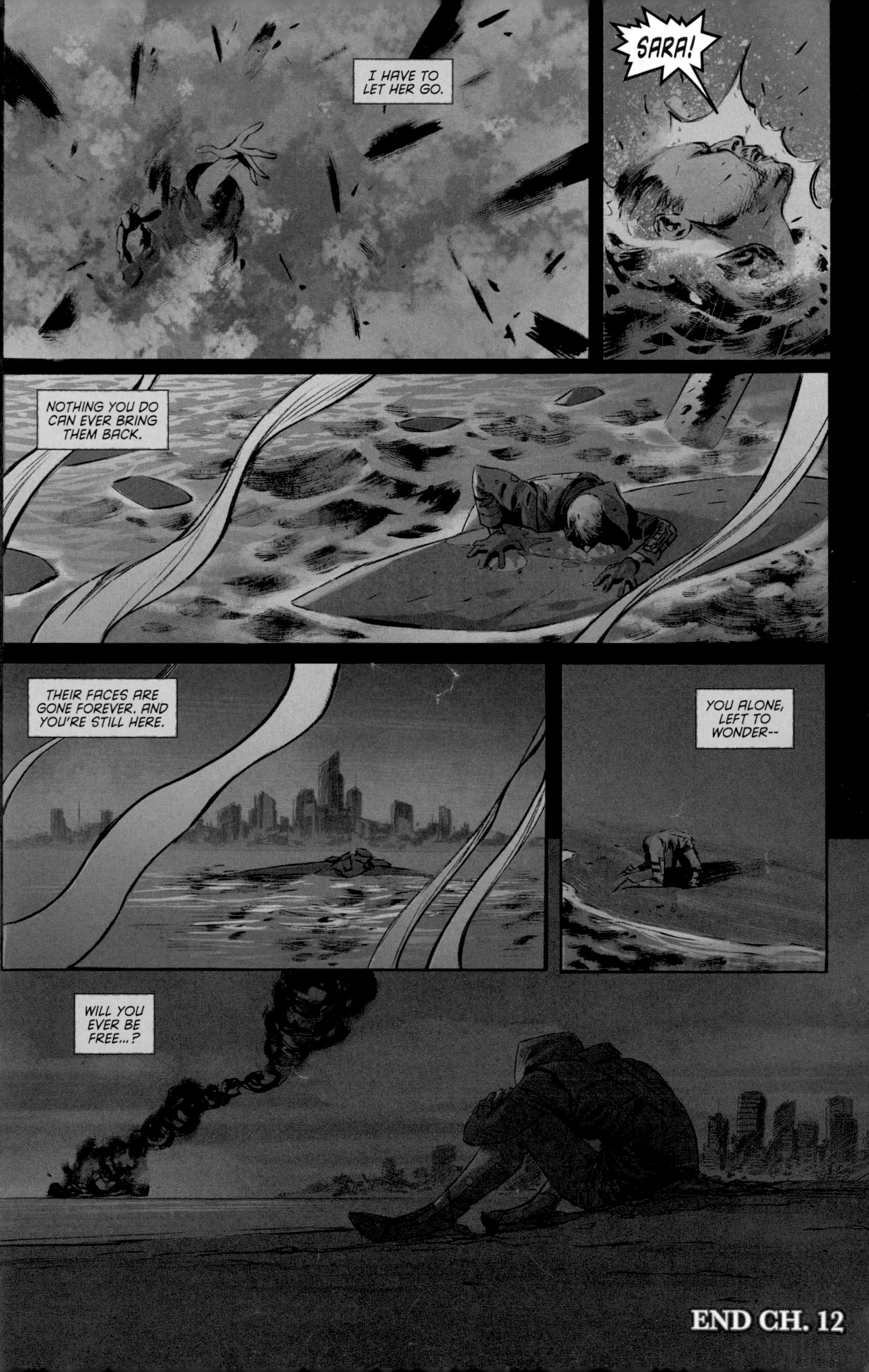
I HAVE TO LET HER GO.
SARA!
NOTHING YOU DO CAN EVER BRING THEM BACK.
THEIR FACES ARE GONE FOREVER. AND YOU'RE STILL HERE.
YOU ALONE, LEFT TO WONDER--
WILL YOU EVER BE FREE...?
END CH. 12

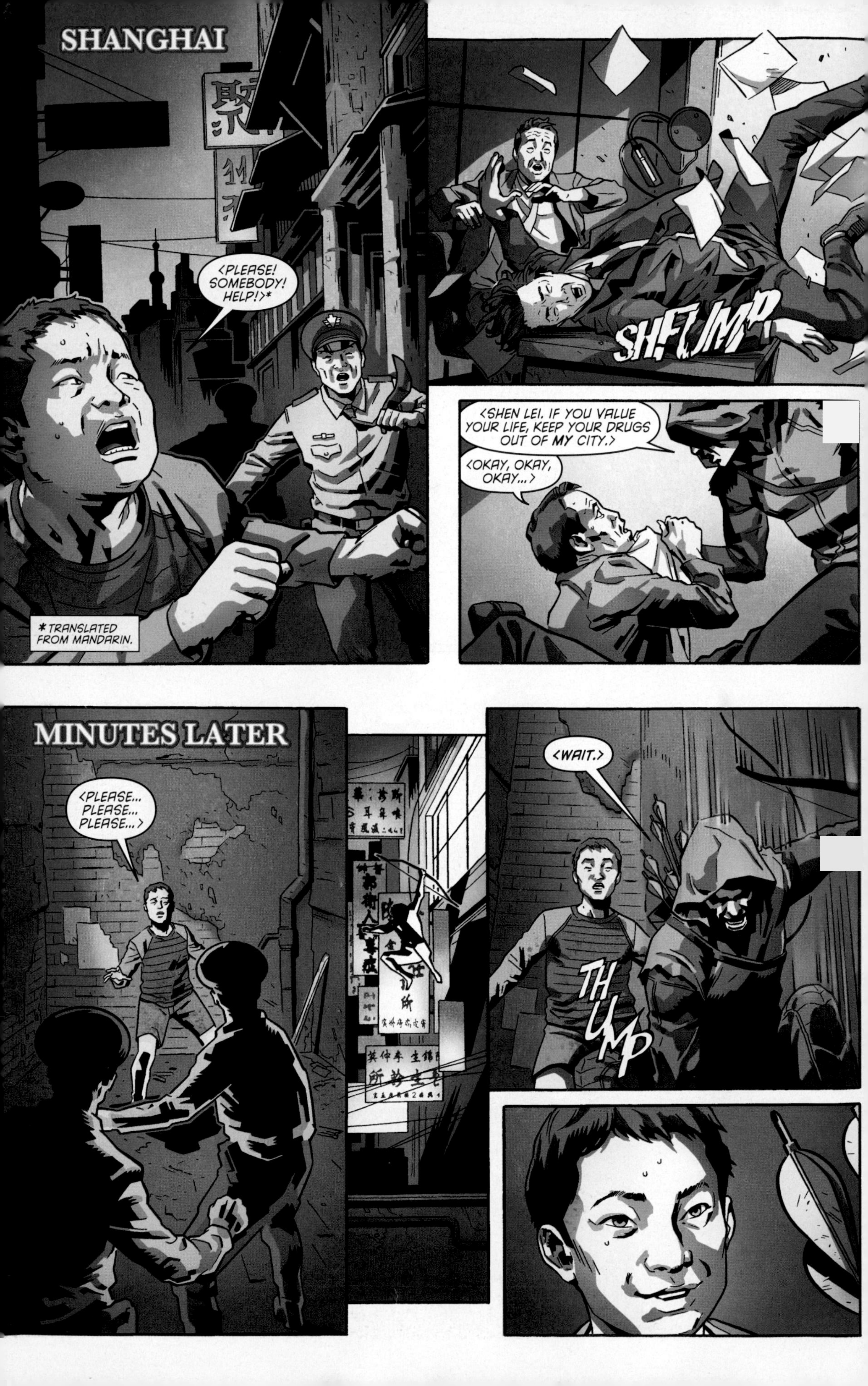
SHANGHAI
<PLEASE! SOMEBODY! HELP!>*
*TRANSLATED FROM MANDARIN.
SHFUMP
<SHEN LEI. IF YOU VALUE YOUR LIFE, KEEP YOUR DRUGS OUT OF MY CITY.>
<OKAY, OKAY, OKAY...>
MINUTES LATER
<PLEASE... PLEASE... PLEASE...>
<WAIT.>
THUMP

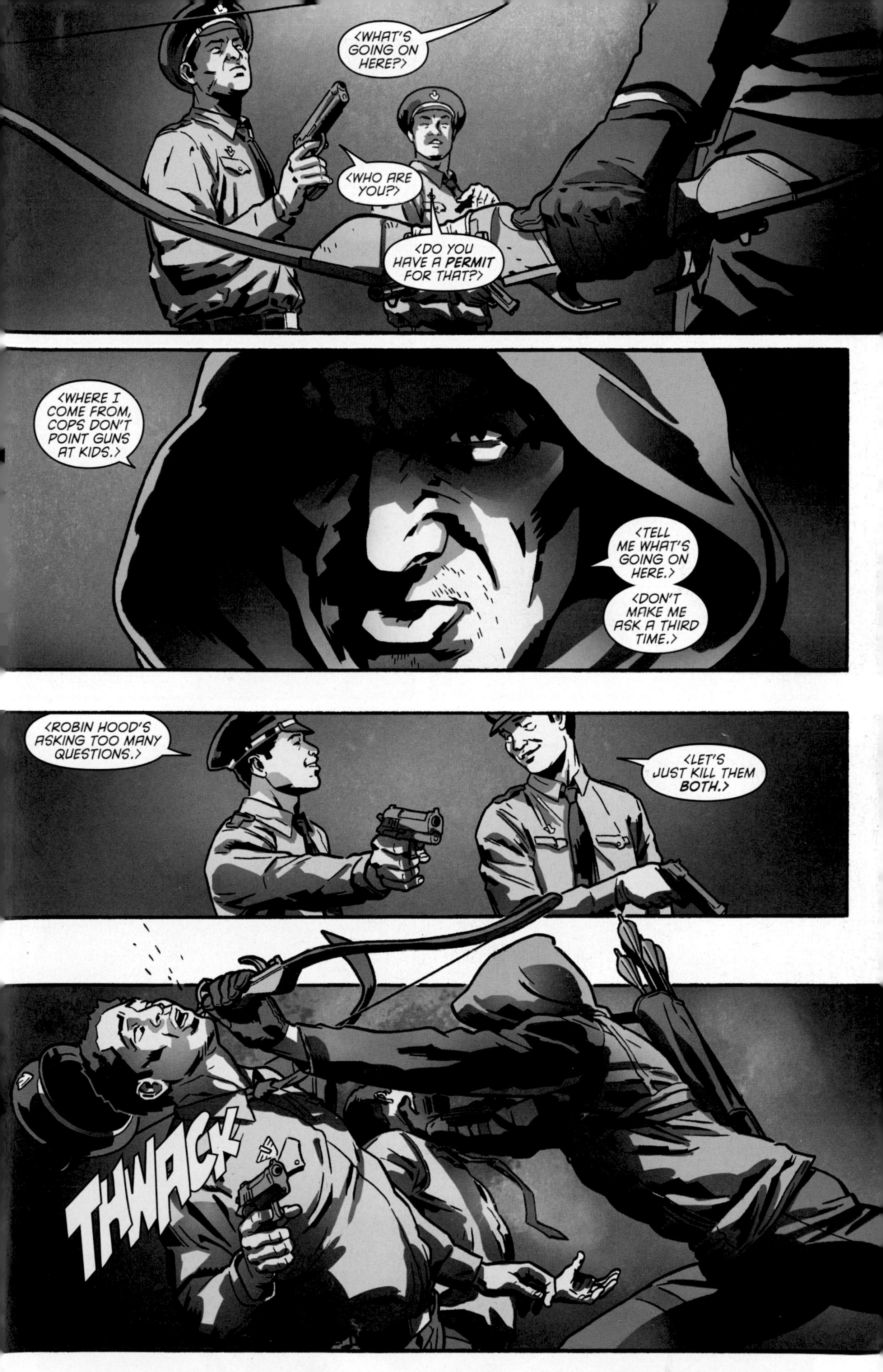
<WHAT'S GOING ON HERE?>
<WHO ARE YOU?>
<DO YOU HAVE A **PERMIT** FOR THAT?>
<WHERE I COME FROM, COPS DON'T POINT GUNS AT KIDS.>
<TELL ME WHAT'S GOING ON HERE.>
<DON'T MAKE ME ASK A THIRD TIME.>
<ROBIN HOOD'S ASKING TOO MANY QUESTIONS.>
<LET'S JUST KILL THEM **BOTH**.>
THWACK

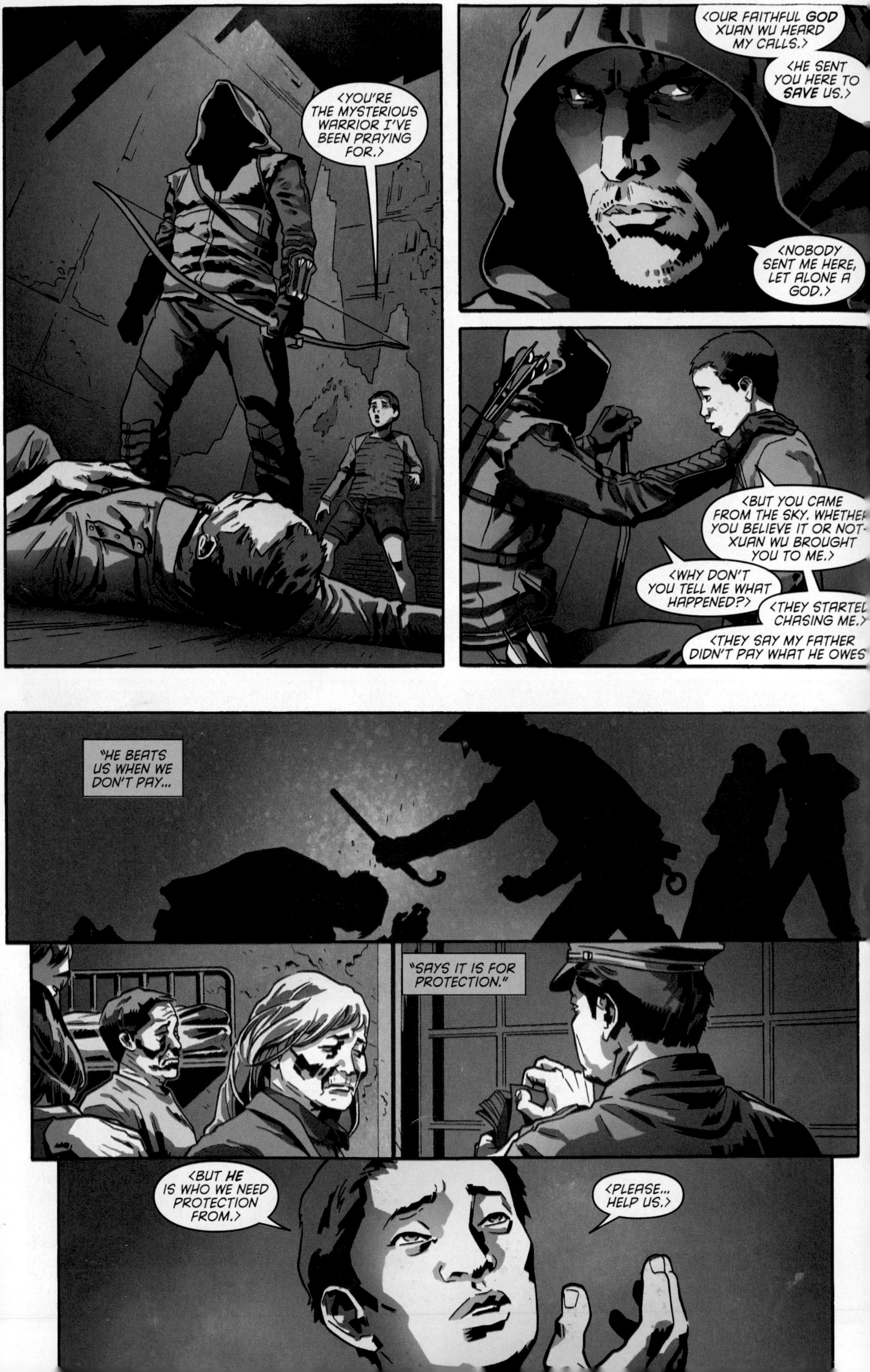

<YOU'RE THE MYSTERIOUS WARRIOR I'VE BEEN PRAYING FOR.>
<OUR FAITHFUL GOD XUAN WU HEARD MY CALLS.>
<HE SENT YOU HERE TO SAVE US.>
<NOBODY SENT ME HERE, LET ALONE A GOD.>
<BUT YOU CAME FROM THE SKY. WHETHER YOU BELIEVE IT OR NOT-XUAN WU BROUGHT YOU TO ME.>
<WHY DON'T YOU TELL ME WHAT HAPPENED?>
<THEY STARTED CHASING ME.>
<THEY SAY MY FATHER DIDN'T PAY WHAT HE OWES
"HE BEATS US WHEN WE DON'T PAY...
"SAYS IT IS FOR PROTECTION."
<BUT HE IS WHO WE NEED PROTECTION FROM.>
<PLEASE... HELP US.>

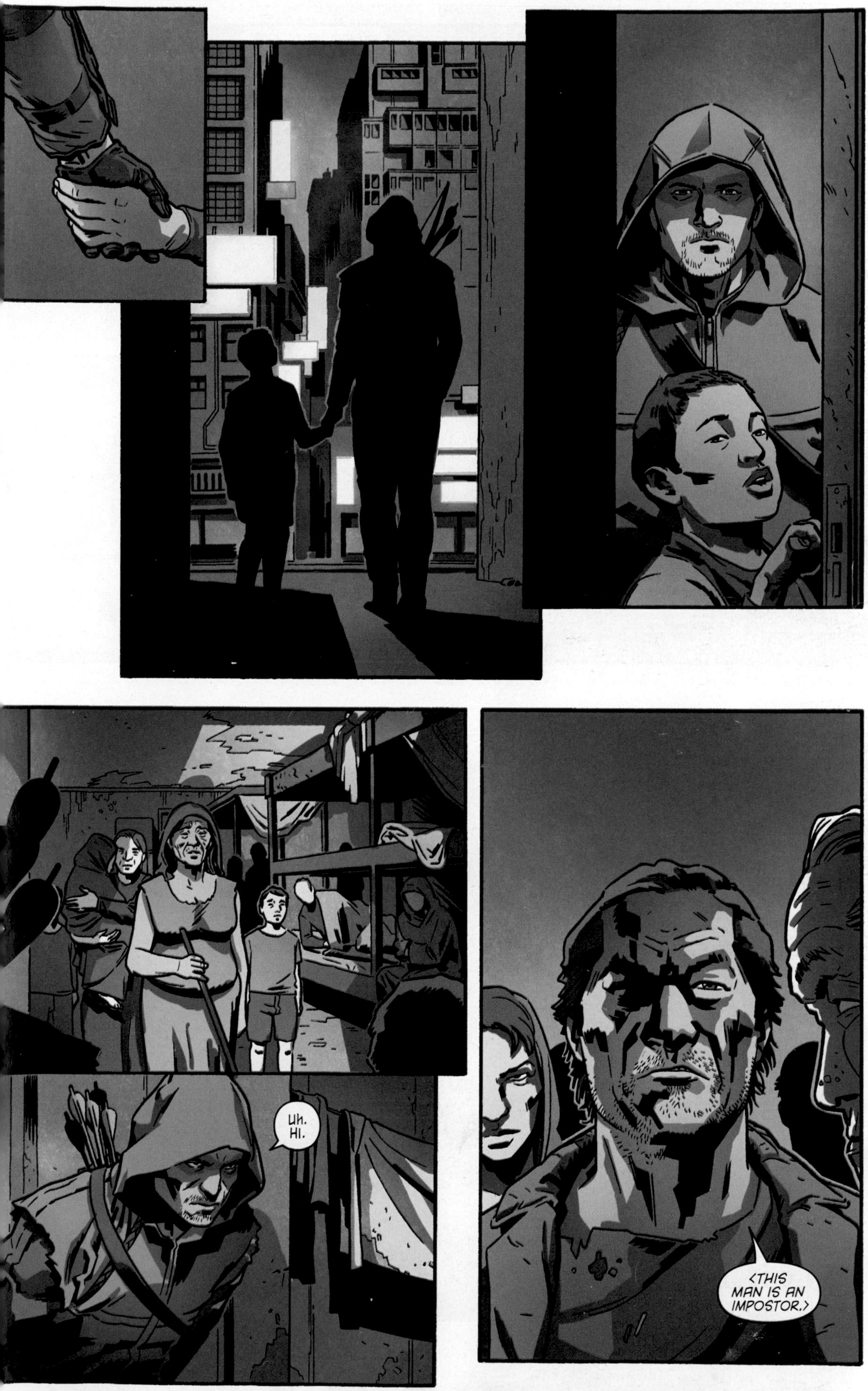
UH.
HI.
<THIS MAN IS AN IMPOSTOR.>

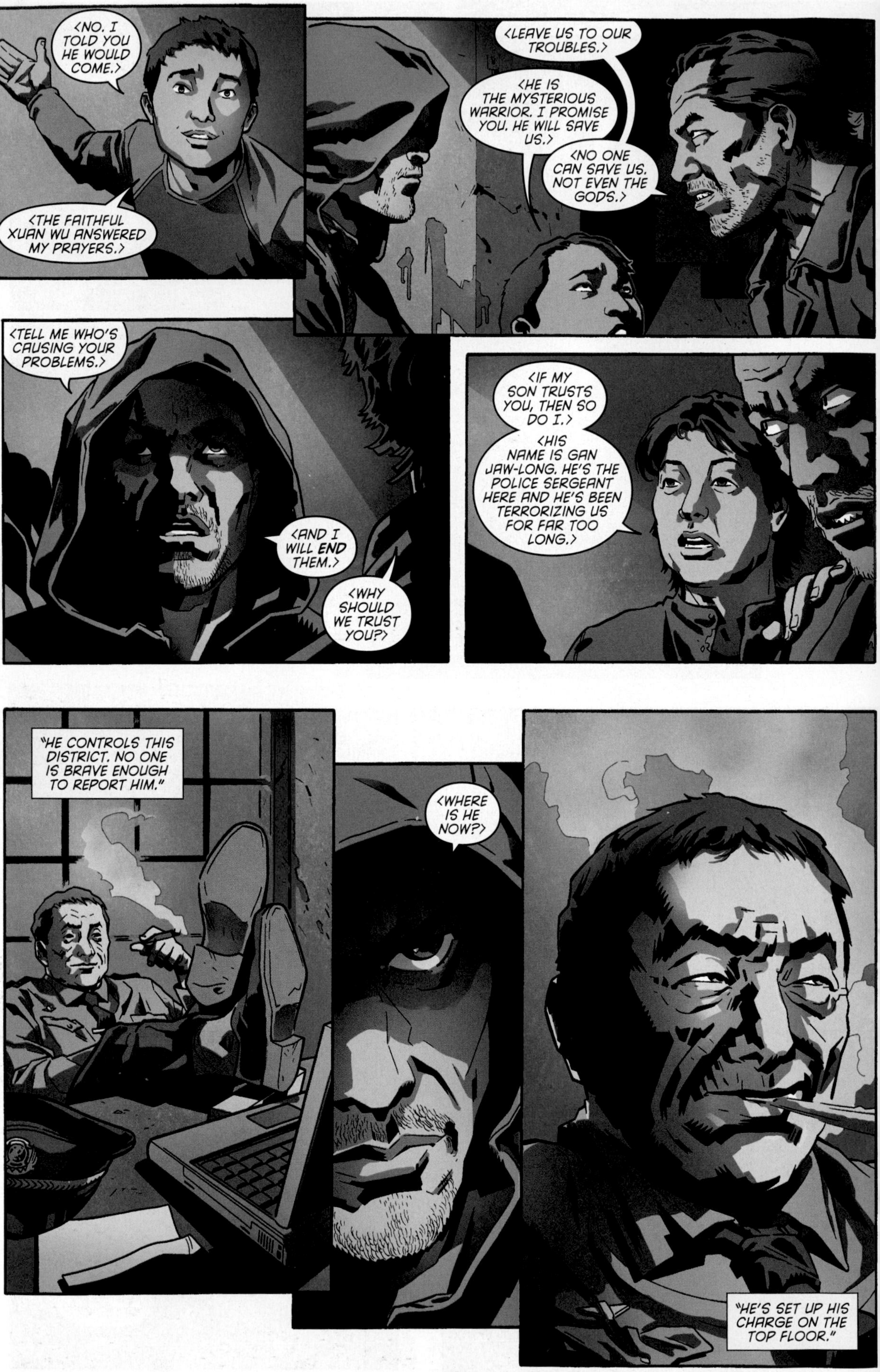
<NO. I TOLD YOU HE WOULD COME.>
<THE FAITHFUL XUAN WU ANSWERED MY PRAYERS.>
<LEAVE US TO OUR TROUBLES.>
<HE IS THE MYSTERIOUS WARRIOR. I PROMISE YOU. HE WILL SAVE US.>
<NO ONE CAN SAVE US. NOT EVEN THE GODS.>
<TELL ME WHO'S CAUSING YOUR PROBLEMS.>
<AND I WILL **END** THEM.>
<WHY SHOULD WE TRUST YOU?>
<IF MY SON TRUSTS YOU, THEN SO DO I.>
<HIS NAME IS GAN JAW-LONG. HE'S THE POLICE SERGEANT HERE AND HE'S BEEN TERRORIZING US FOR FAR TOO LONG.>
"HE CONTROLS THIS DISTRICT. NO ONE IS BRAVE ENOUGH TO REPORT HIM."
<WHERE IS HE NOW?>
"HE'S SET UP HIS CHARGE ON THE TOP FLOOR."

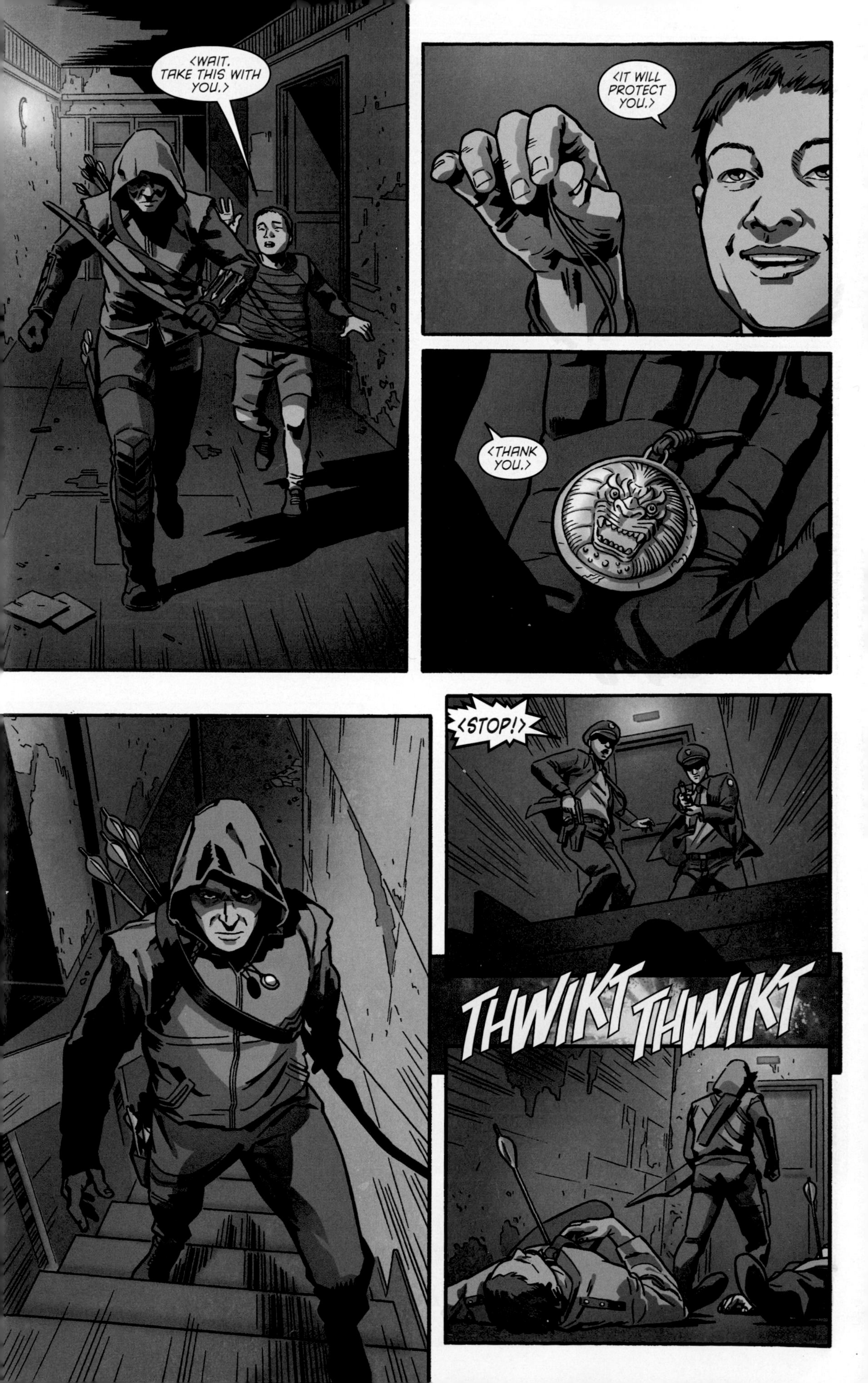
<WAIT. TAKE THIS WITH YOU.>
<IT WILL PROTECT YOU.>
<THANK YOU.>
<STOP!>
THWIKT THWIKT

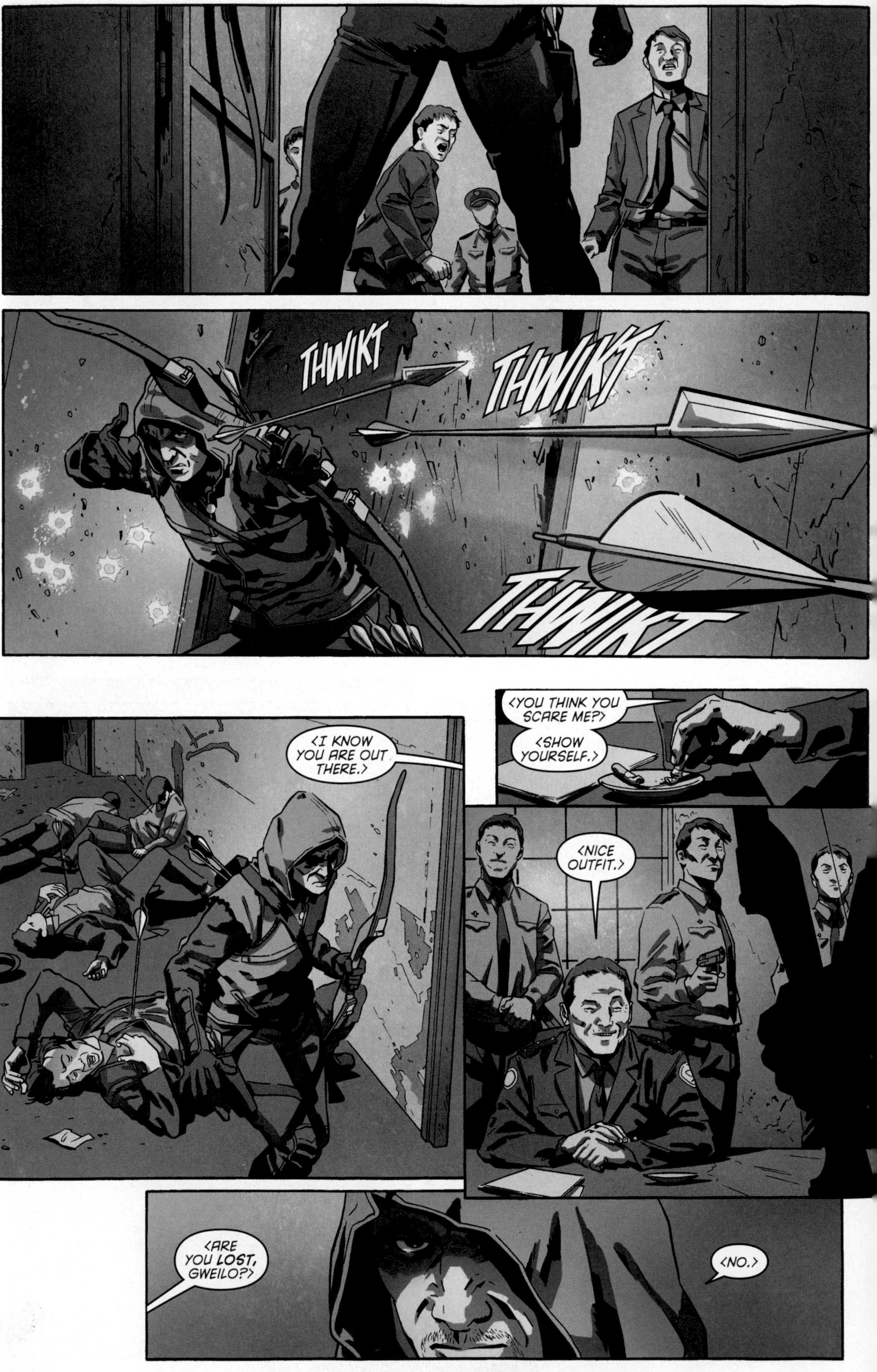
THWIKT
THWIKT
THWIKT
<I KNOW YOU ARE OUT THERE.>
<YOU THINK YOU SCARE ME?>
<SHOW YOURSELF.>
<NICE OUTFIT.>
<ARE YOU LOST, GWEILO?>
<NO.>

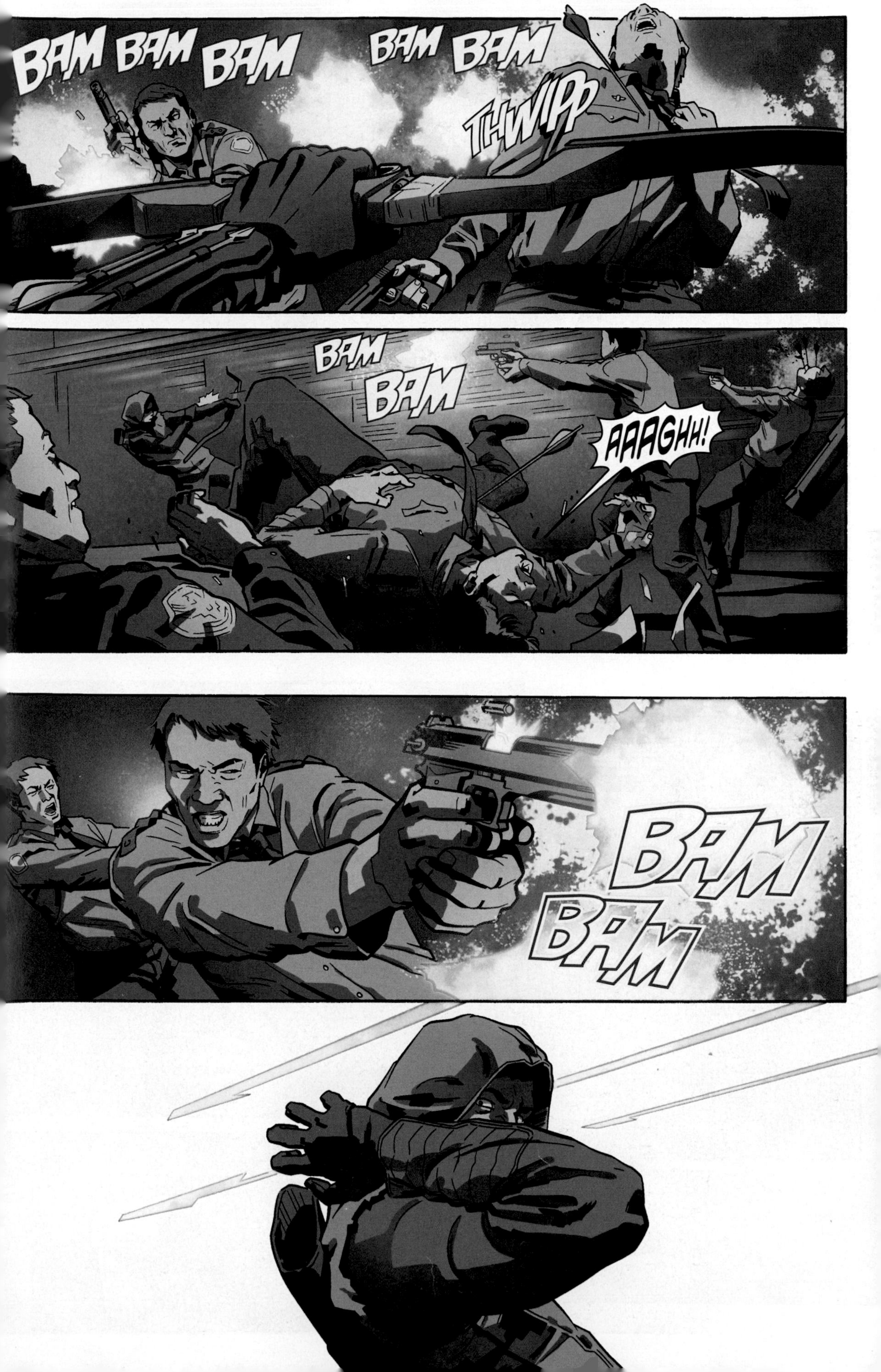
BAM BAM BAM
BAM BAM
THWIPP
BAM
BAM
AAAGHH!
BAM
BAM

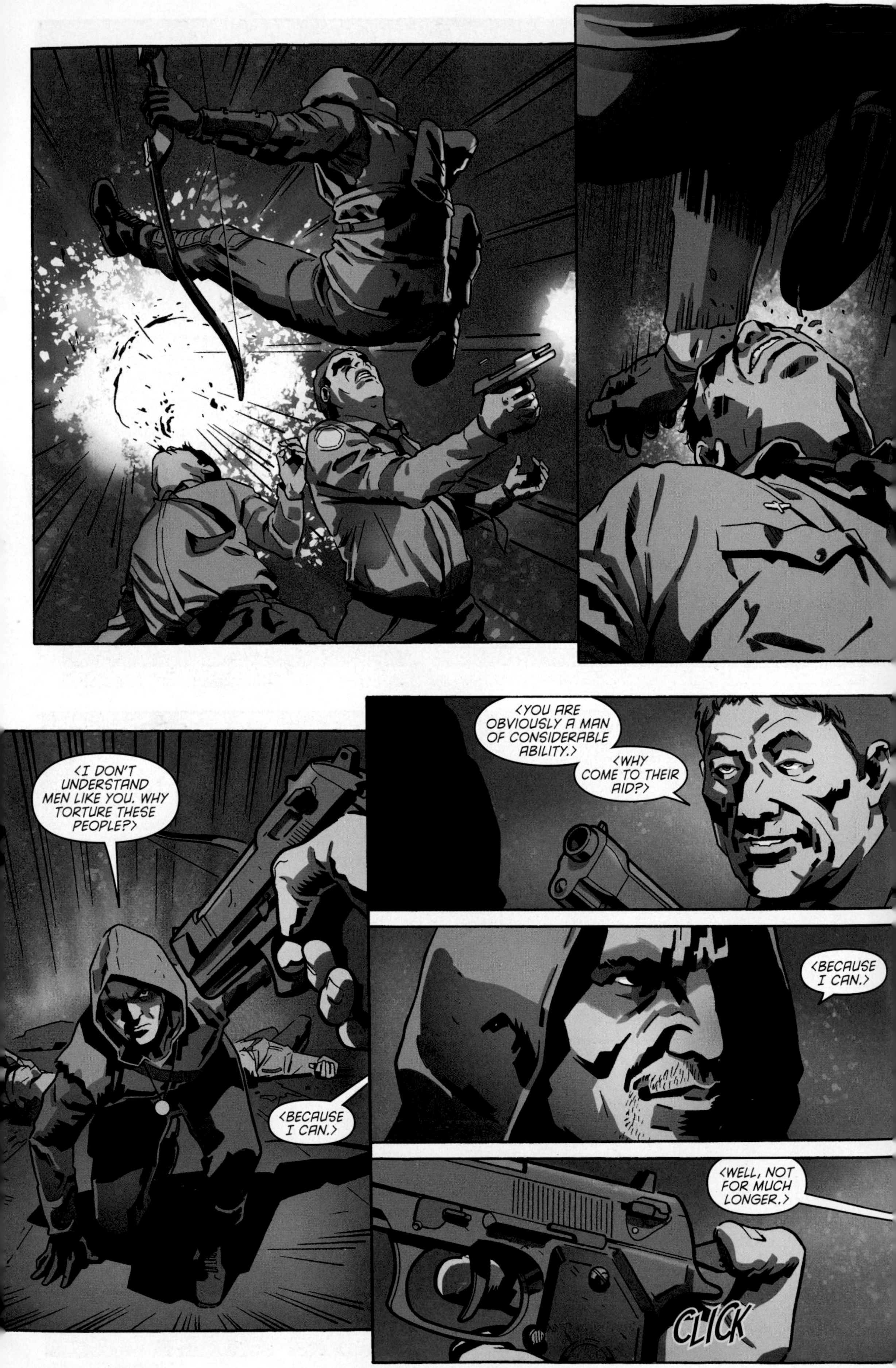

<I DON'T UNDERSTAND MEN LIKE YOU. WHY TORTURE THESE PEOPLE?>
<BECAUSE I CAN.>
<YOU ARE OBVIOUSLY A MAN OF CONSIDERABLE ABILITY.>
<WHY COME TO THEIR AID?>
<BECAUSE I CAN.>
<WELL, NOT FOR MUCH LONGER.>
CLICK

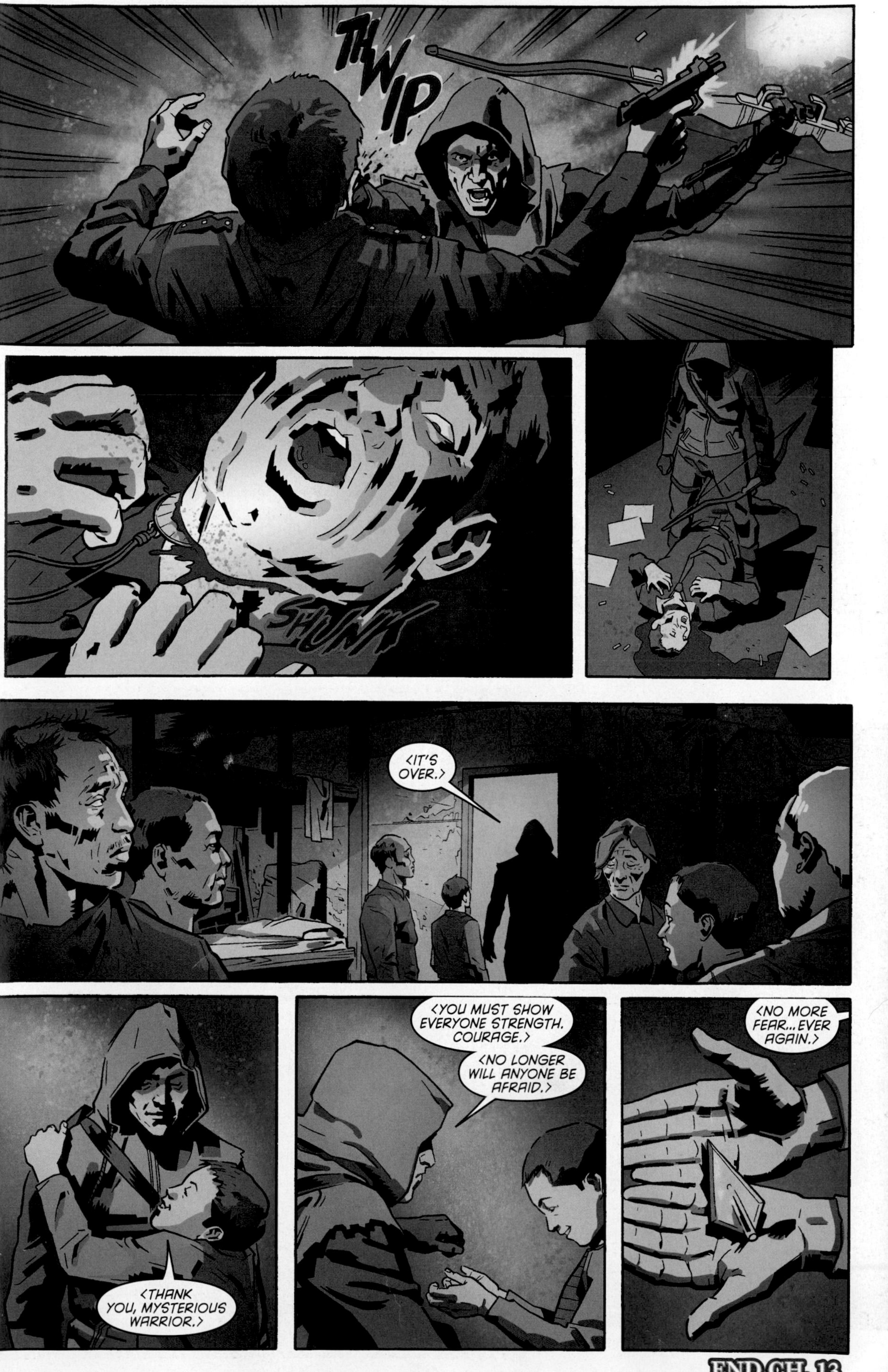
THWIP
SHUNK
<IT'S OVER.>
<THANK YOU, MYSTERIOUS WARRIOR.>
<YOU MUST SHOW EVERYONE STRENGTH. COURAGE.>
<NO LONGER WILL ANYONE BE AFRAID.>
<NO MORE FEAR... EVER AGAIN.>

END CH. 13

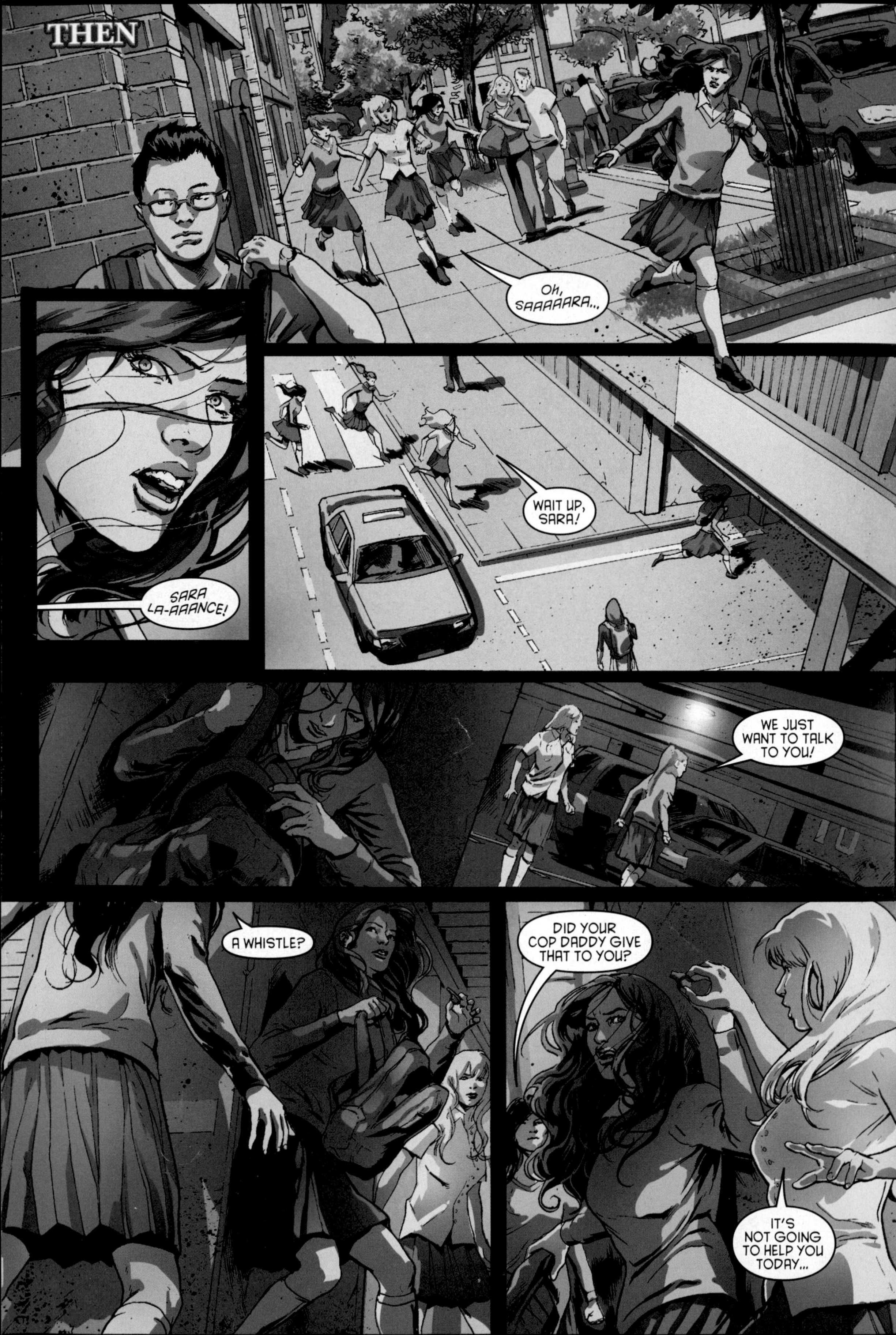
THEN
OH, SAAAAARA...
SARA LA-AAANCE!
WAIT UP, SARA!
WE JUST WANT TO TALK TO YOU!
A WHISTLE?
DID YOUR COP DADDY GIVE THAT TO YOU?
IT'S NOT GOING TO HELP YOU TODAY...

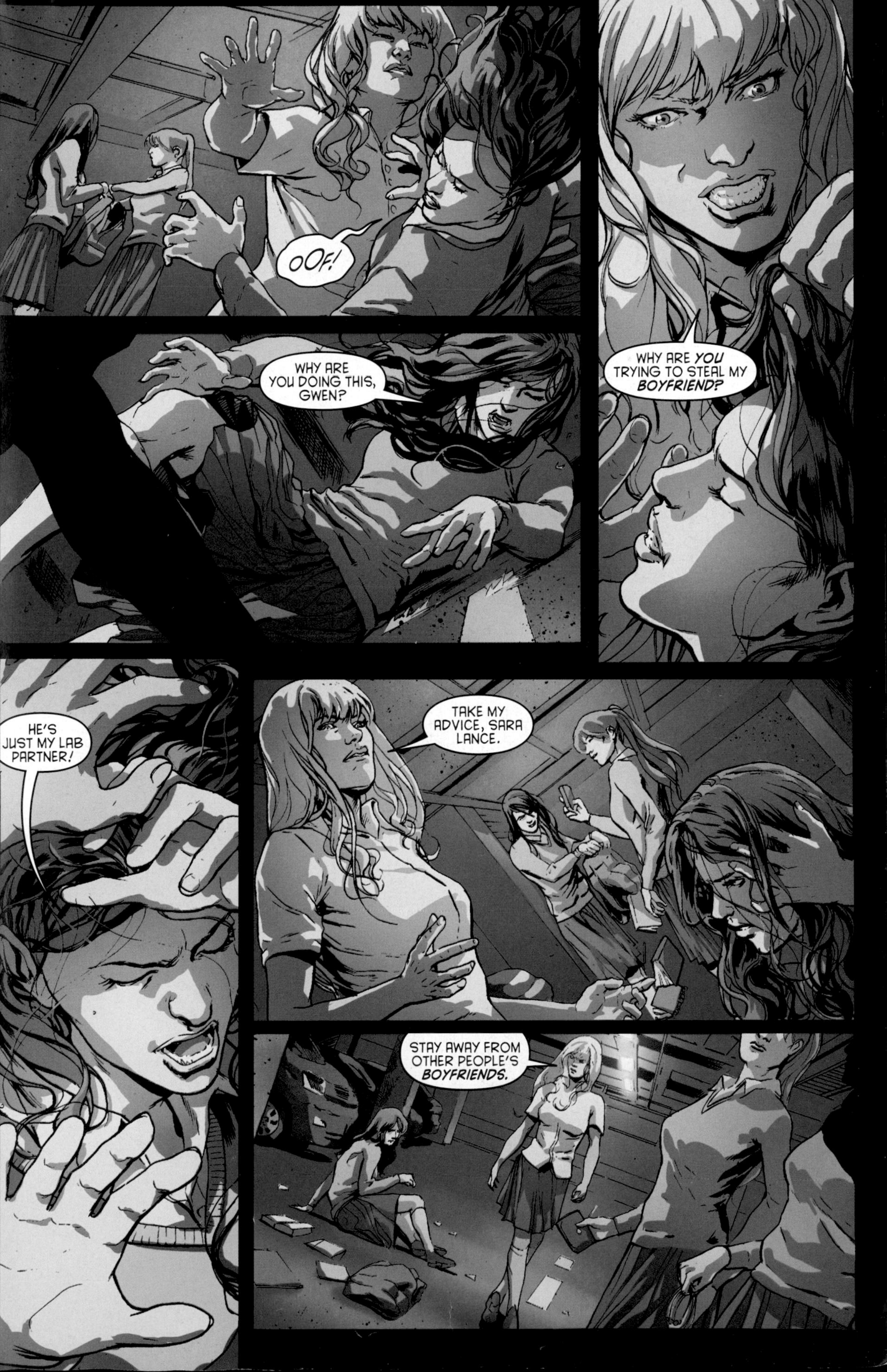
OOF!
WHY ARE YOU DOING THIS, GWEN?
WHY ARE *YOU* TRYING TO STEAL MY *BOYFRIEND?*
HE'S JUST MY LAB PARTNER!
TAKE MY ADVICE, SARA LANCE.
STAY AWAY FROM OTHER PEOPLE'S *BOYFRIENDS.*

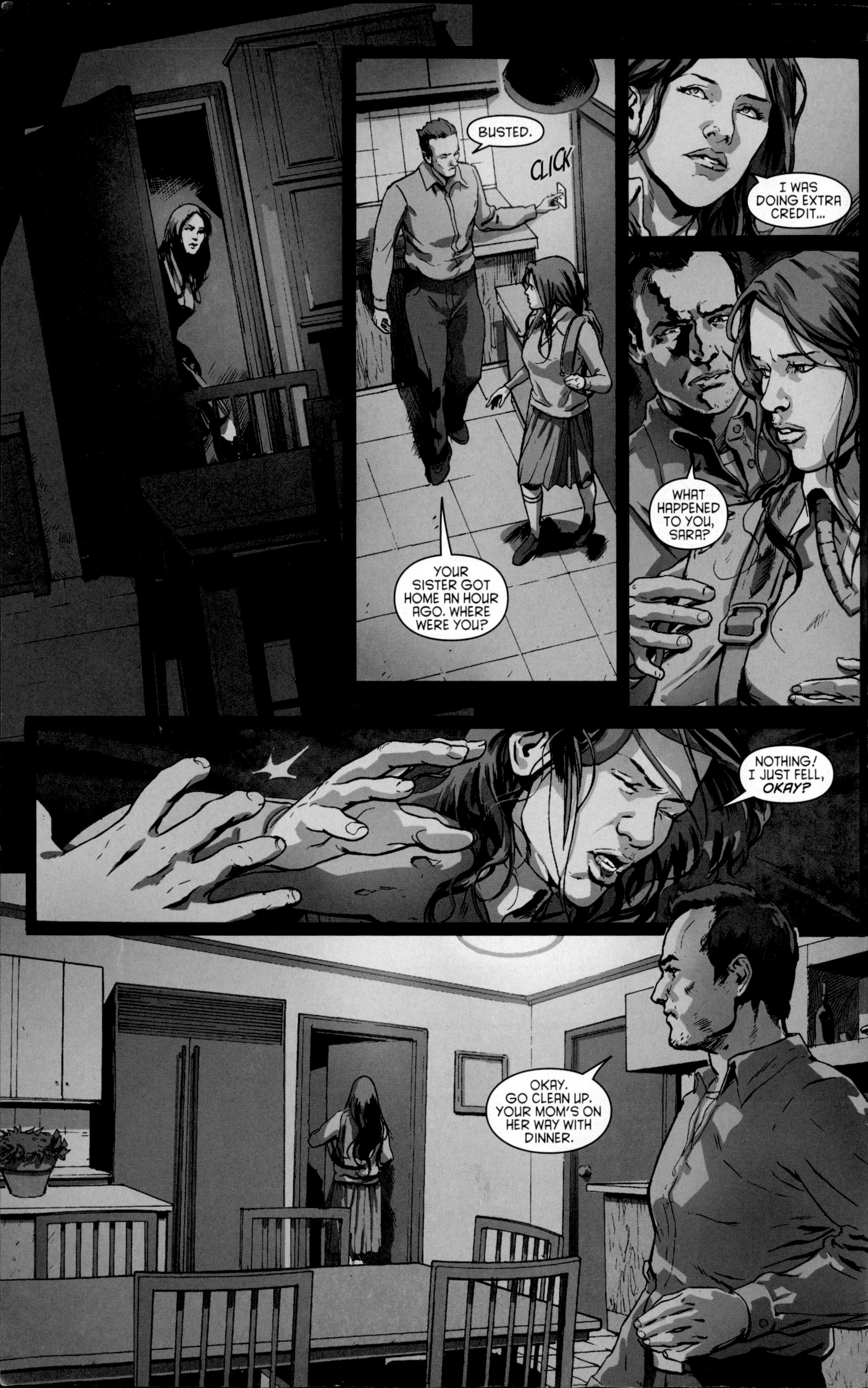
BUSTED.
CLICK
YOUR SISTER GOT HOME AN HOUR AGO. WHERE WERE YOU?
I WAS DOING EXTRA CREDIT...
WHAT HAPPENED TO YOU, SARA?
NOTHING! I JUST FELL, OKAY?
OKAY. GO CLEAN UP. YOUR MOM'S ON HER WAY WITH DINNER.

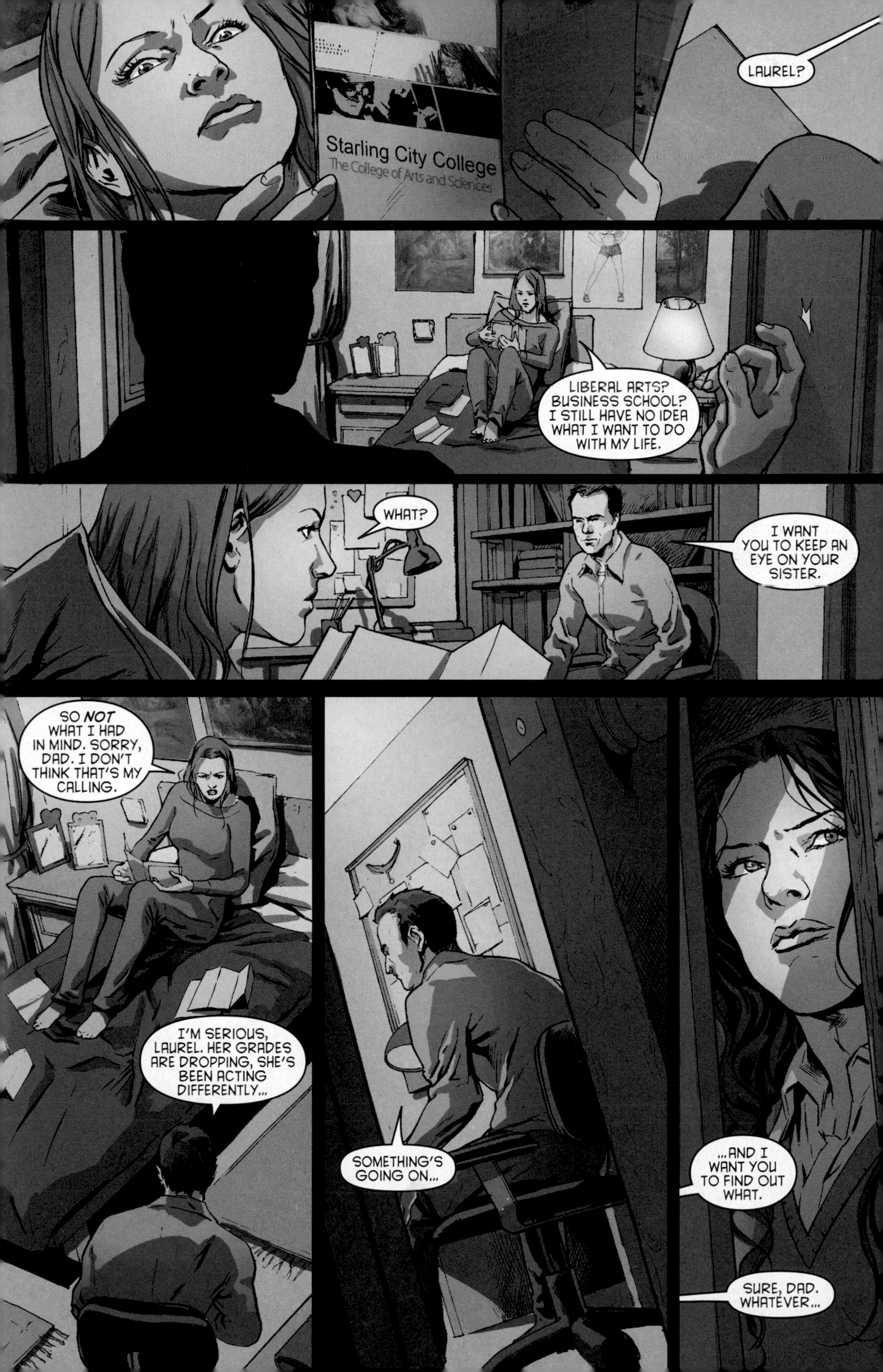
Starling City College
The College of Arts and Sciences
LAUREL?
LIBERAL ARTS? BUSINESS SCHOOL? I STILL HAVE NO IDEA WHAT I WANT TO DO WITH MY LIFE.
WHAT?
I WANT YOU TO KEEP AN EYE ON YOUR SISTER.
SO *NOT* WHAT I HAD IN MIND. SORRY, DAD. I DON'T THINK THAT'S MY CALLING.
I'M SERIOUS, LAUREL. HER GRADES ARE DROPPING, SHE'S BEEN ACTING DIFFERENTLY...
SOMETHING'S GOING ON...
...AND I WANT YOU TO FIND OUT WHAT.
SURE, DAD. WHATEVER...

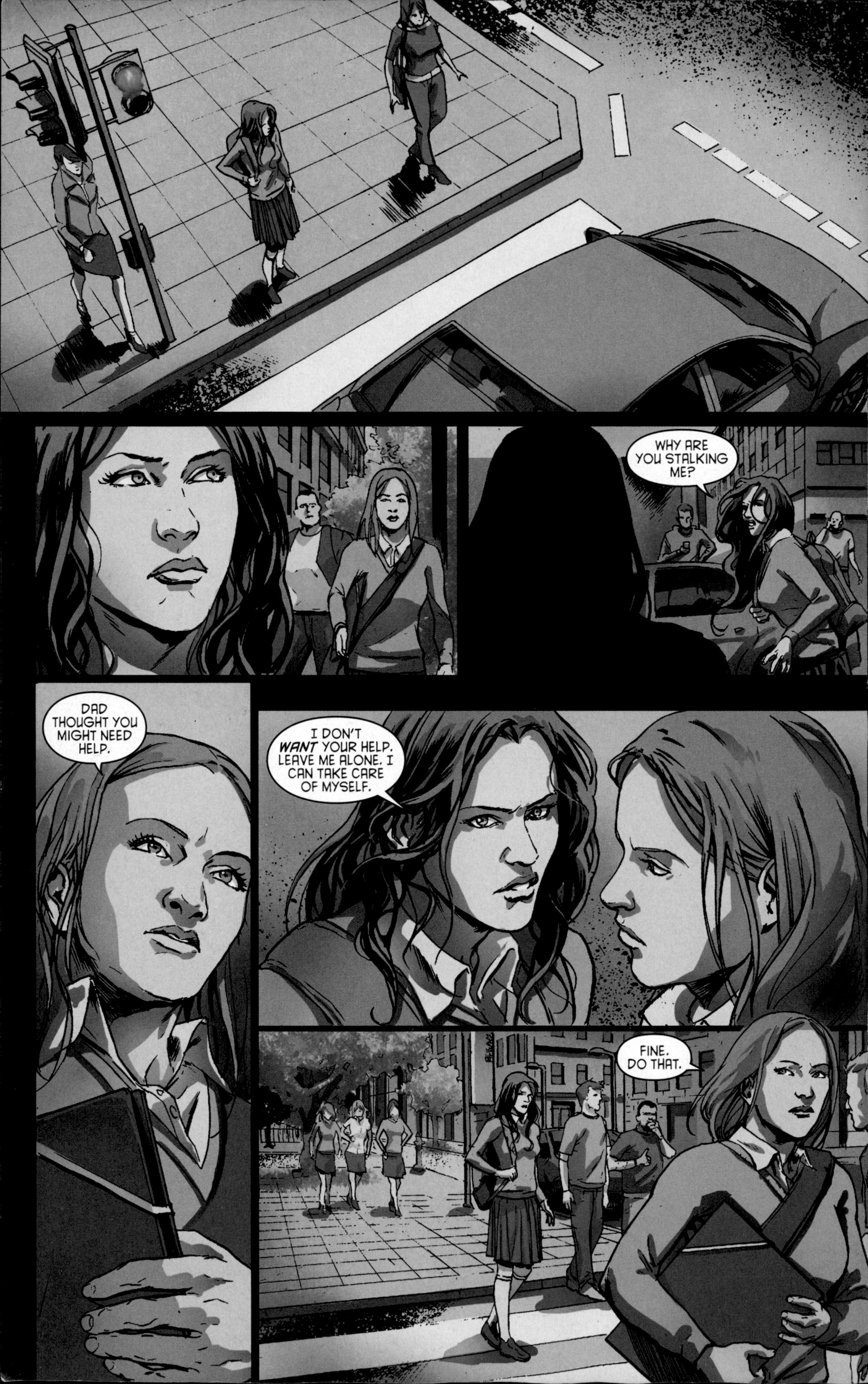
WHY ARE YOU STALKING ME?
DAD THOUGHT YOU MIGHT NEED HELP.
I DON'T *WANT* YOUR HELP. LEAVE ME ALONE. I CAN TAKE CARE OF MYSELF.
FINE. DO THAT.

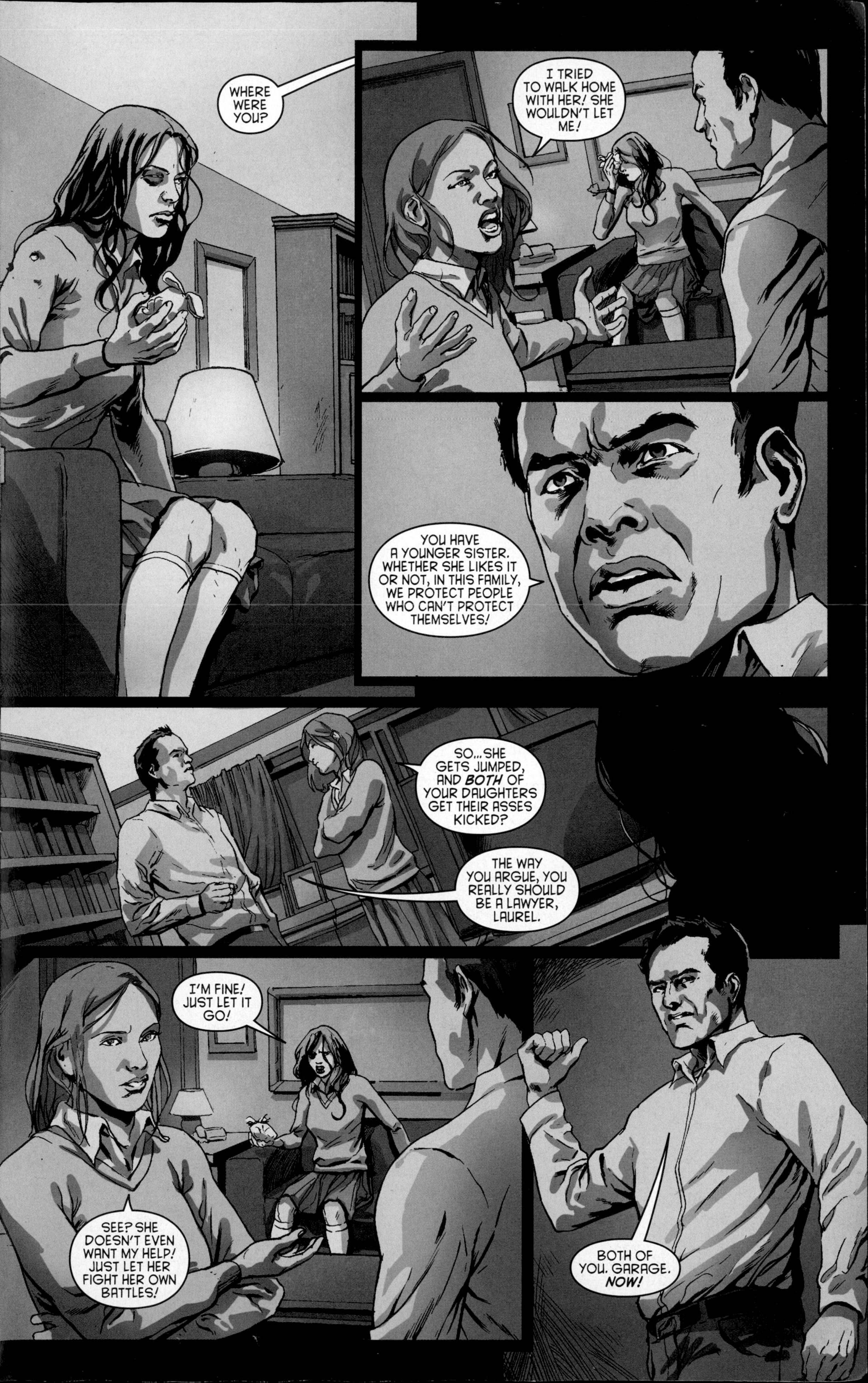

WHERE WERE YOU?
I TRIED TO WALK HOME WITH HER! SHE WOULDN'T LET ME!
YOU HAVE A YOUNGER SISTER. WHETHER SHE LIKES IT OR NOT, IN THIS FAMILY, WE PROTECT PEOPLE WHO CAN'T PROTECT THEMSELVES!
SO... SHE GETS JUMPED, AND **BOTH** OF YOUR DAUGHTERS GET THEIR ASSES KICKED?
THE WAY YOU ARGUE, YOU REALLY SHOULD BE A LAWYER, LAUREL.
I'M FINE! JUST LET IT GO!
SEE? SHE DOESN'T EVEN WANT MY HELP! JUST LET HER FIGHT HER OWN BATTLES!
BOTH OF YOU. GARAGE. ***NOW!***

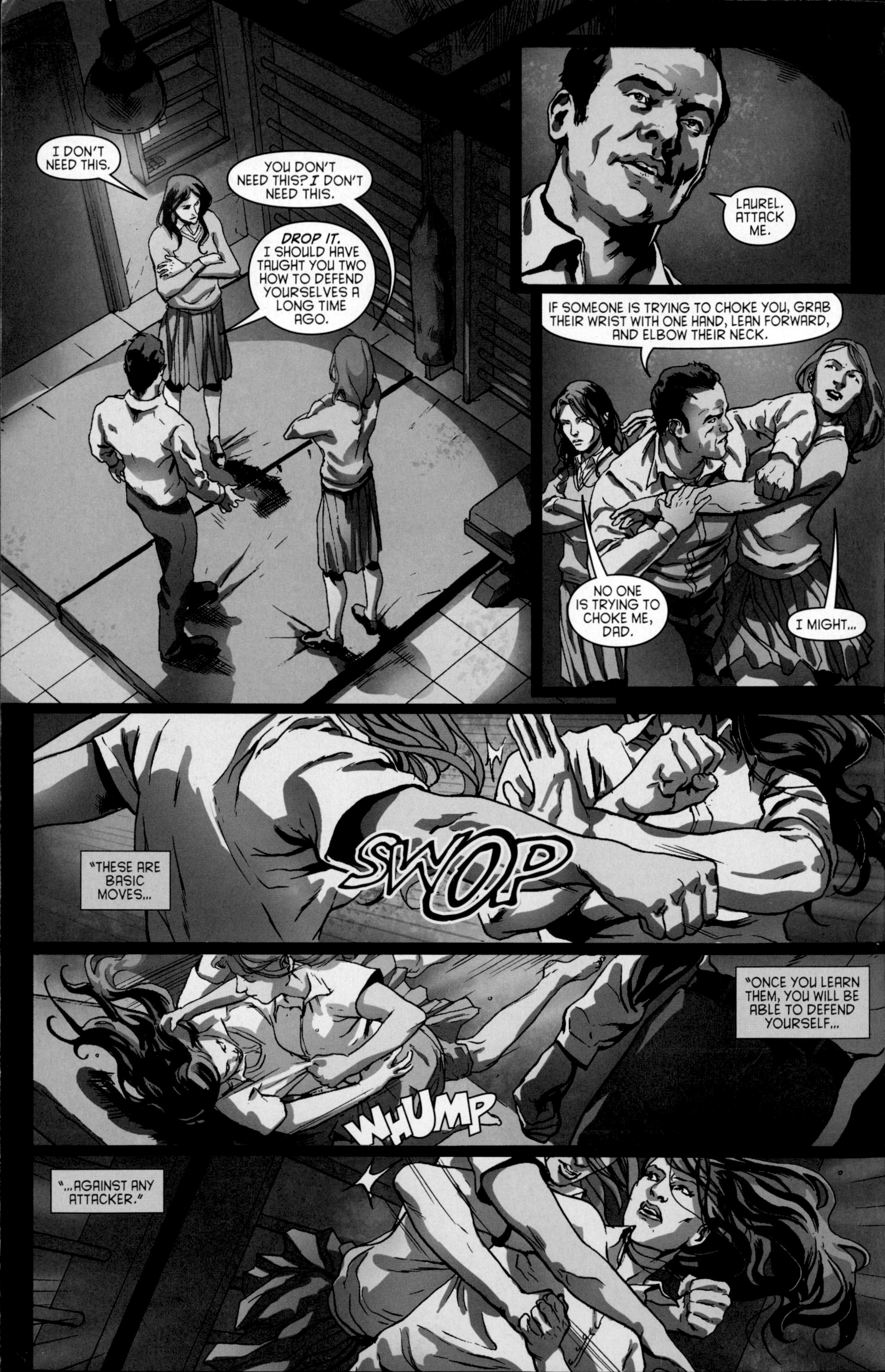

I DON'T NEED THIS.
YOU DON'T NEED THIS? I DON'T NEED THIS.
DROP IT. I SHOULD HAVE TAUGHT YOU TWO HOW TO DEFEND YOURSELVES A LONG TIME AGO.
LAUREL. ATTACK ME.
IF SOMEONE IS TRYING TO CHOKE YOU, GRAB THEIR WRIST WITH ONE HAND, LEAN FORWARD, AND ELBOW THEIR NECK.
NO ONE IS TRYING TO CHOKE ME, DAD.
I MIGHT...
"THESE ARE BASIC MOVES...
SWOP
"ONCE YOU LEARN THEM, YOU WILL BE ABLE TO DEFEND YOURSELF...
WHUMP
"...AGAINST ANY ATTACKER."

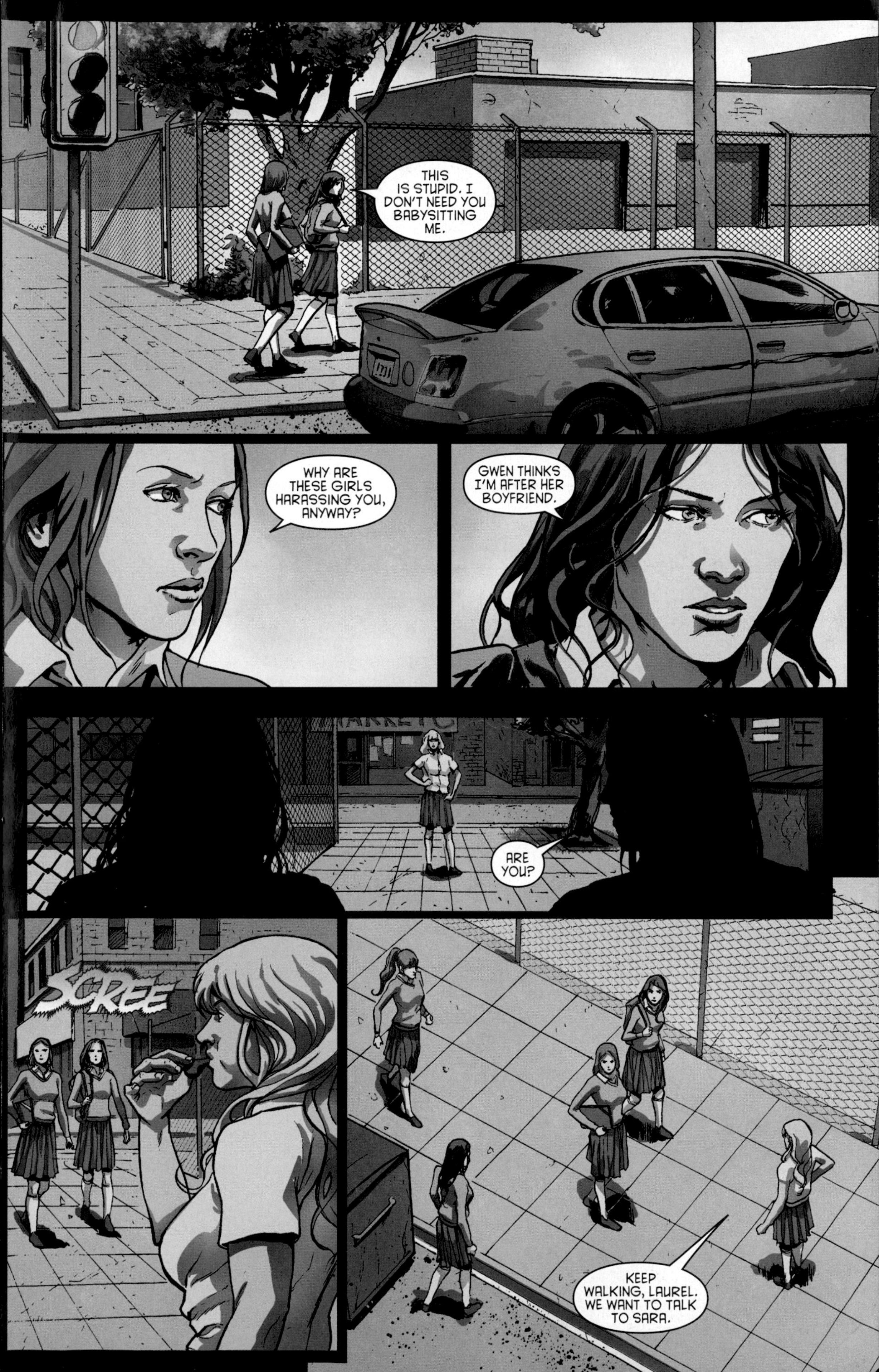
THIS IS STUPID. I DON'T NEED YOU BABYSITTING ME.
WHY ARE THESE GIRLS HARASSING YOU, ANYWAY?
GWEN THINKS I'M AFTER HER BOYFRIEND.
ARE YOU?
SCREE
KEEP WALKING, LAUREL. WE WANT TO TALK TO SARA.

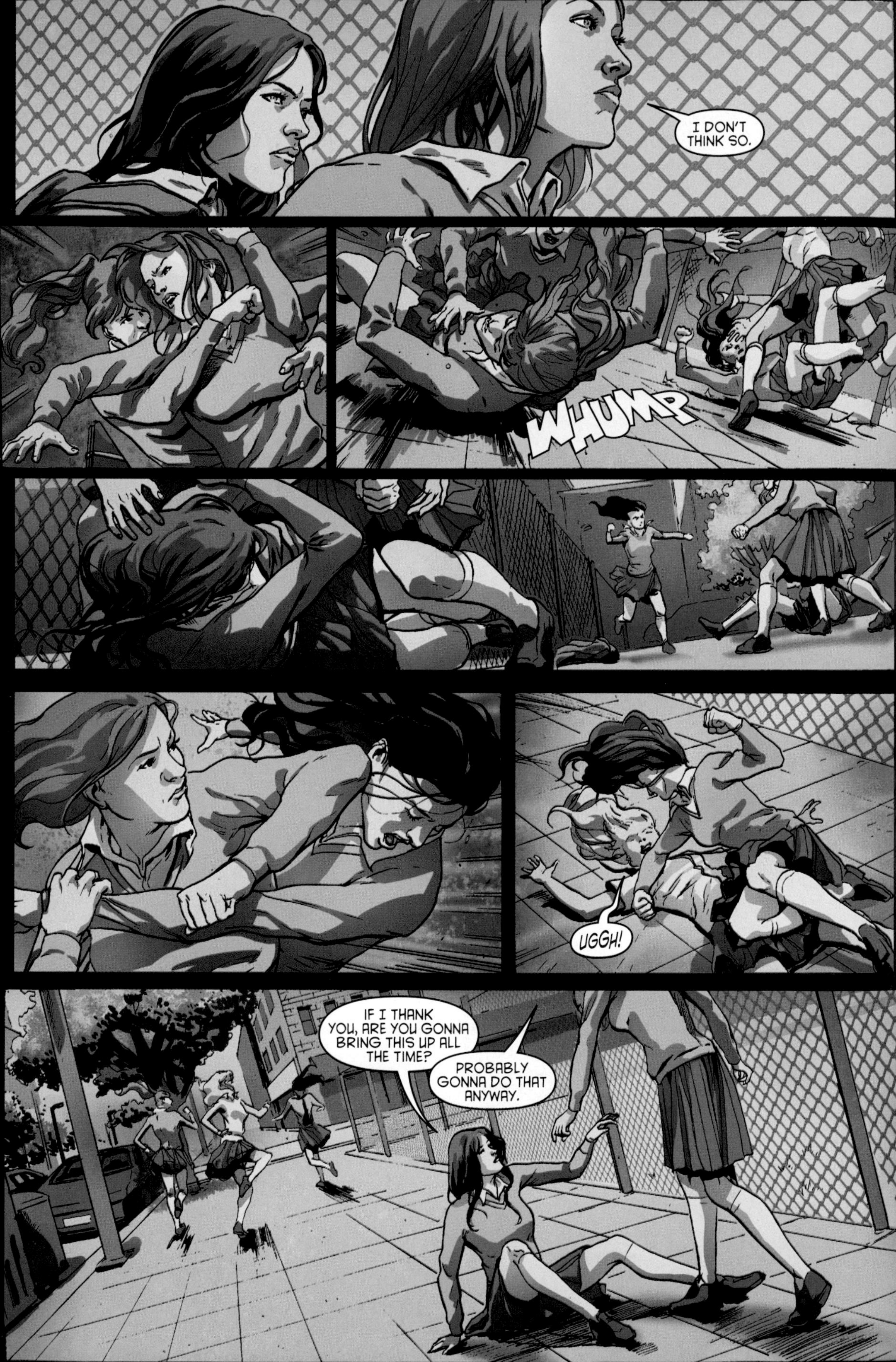
I DON'T THINK SO.
WHUMP
UGGH!
IF I THANK YOU, ARE YOU GONNA BRING THIS UP ALL THE TIME?
PROBABLY GONNA DO THAT ANYWAY.

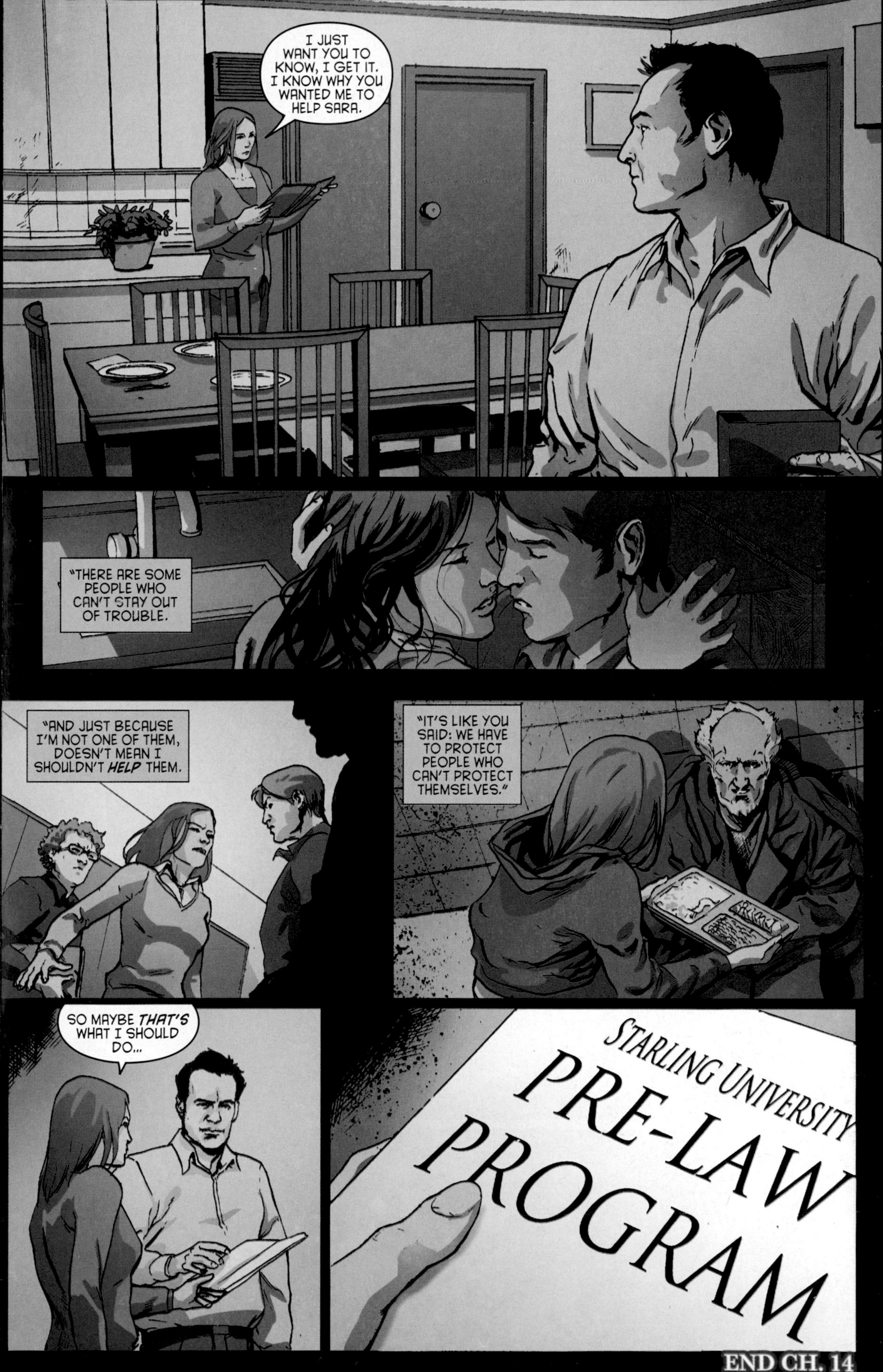
I JUST WANT YOU TO KNOW, I GET IT. I KNOW WHY YOU WANTED ME TO HELP SARA.
"THERE ARE SOME PEOPLE WHO CAN'T STAY OUT OF TROUBLE.
"AND JUST BECAUSE I'M NOT ONE OF THEM, DOESN'T MEAN I SHOULDN'T *HELP* THEM.
"IT'S LIKE YOU SAID: WE HAVE TO PROTECT PEOPLE WHO CAN'T PROTECT THEMSELVES."
SO MAYBE *THAT'S* WHAT I SHOULD DO...
STARLING UNIVERSITY
PRE-LAW PROGRAM
END CH. 14

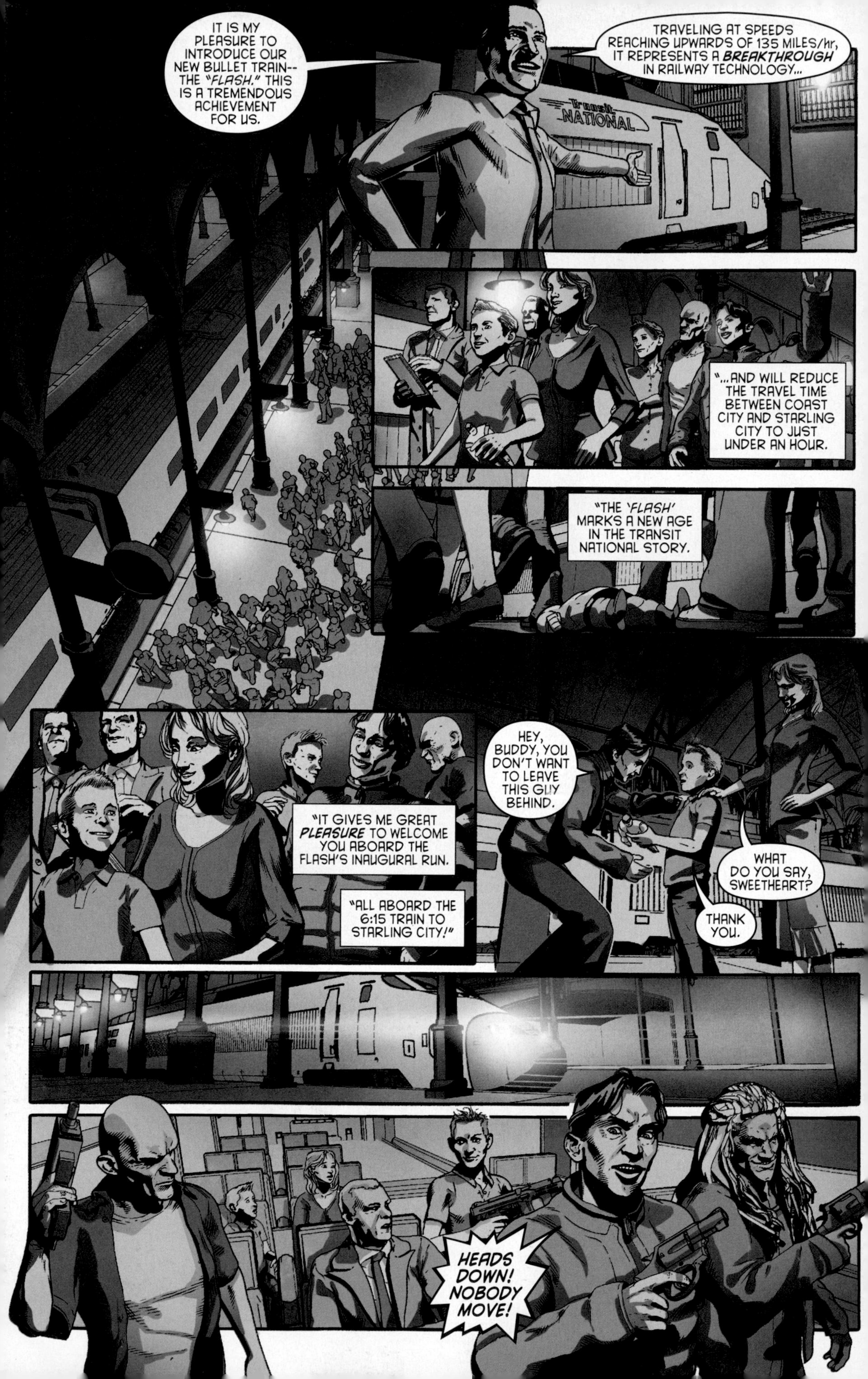
IT IS MY PLEASURE TO INTRODUCE OUR NEW BULLET TRAIN-- THE "FLASH." THIS IS A TREMENDOUS ACHIEVEMENT FOR US.
TRAVELING AT SPEEDS REACHING UPWARDS OF 135 MILES/hr, IT REPRESENTS A BREAKTHROUGH IN RAILWAY TECHNOLOGY...
Transit NATIONAL
"...AND WILL REDUCE THE TRAVEL TIME BETWEEN COAST CITY AND STARLING CITY TO JUST UNDER AN HOUR.
"THE 'FLASH' MARKS A NEW AGE IN THE TRANSIT NATIONAL STORY.
"IT GIVES ME GREAT PLEASURE TO WELCOME YOU ABOARD THE FLASH'S INAUGURAL RUN.
"ALL ABOARD THE 6:15 TRAIN TO STARLING CITY!"
HEY, BUDDY, YOU DON'T WANT TO LEAVE THIS GUY BEHIND.
WHAT DO YOU SAY, SWEETHEART?
THANK YOU.
HEADS DOWN! NOBODY MOVE!

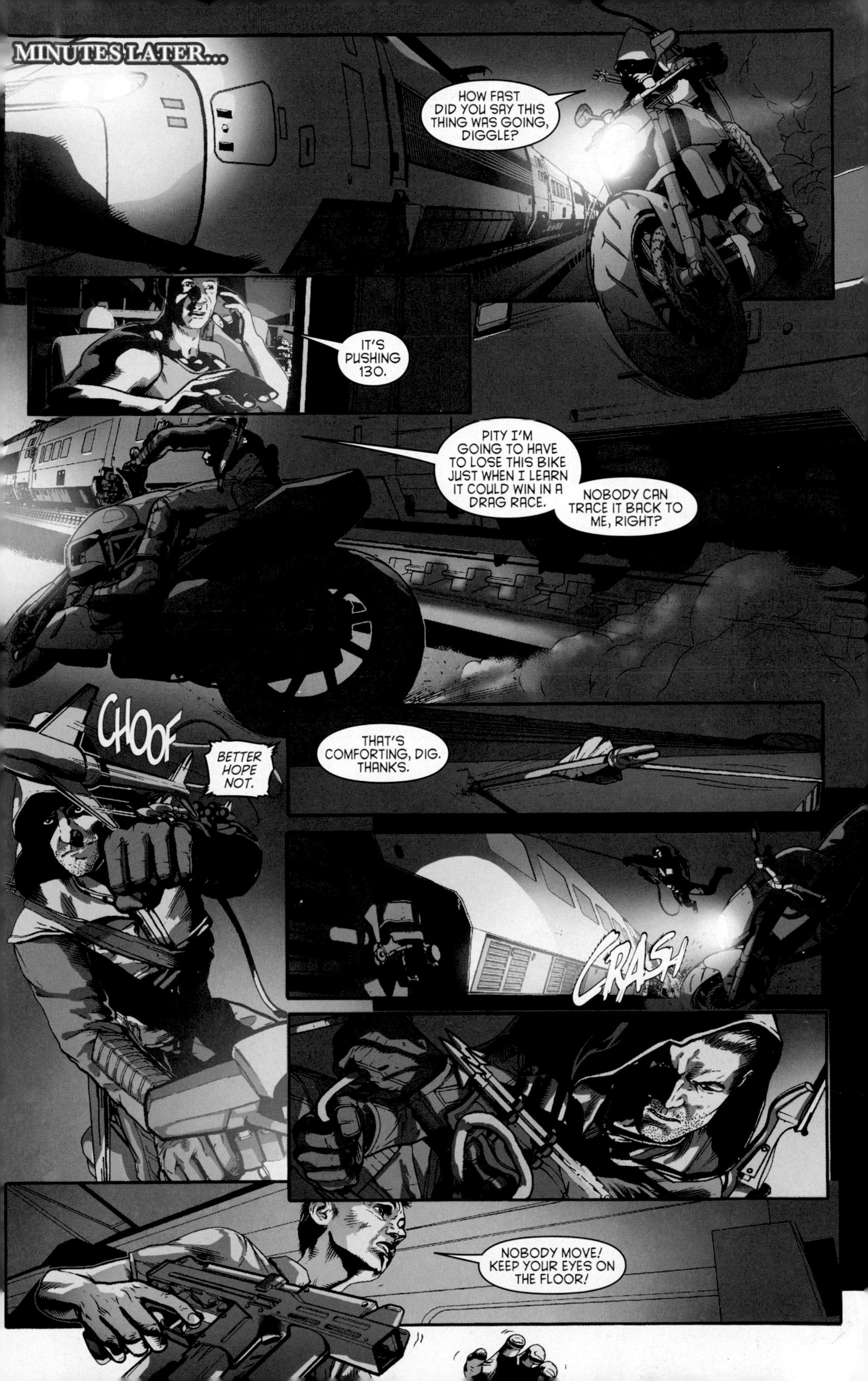
MINUTES LATER...
HOW FAST DID YOU SAY THIS THING WAS GOING, DIGGLE?
IT'S PUSHING 130.
PITY I'M GOING TO HAVE TO LOSE THIS BIKE JUST WHEN I LEARN IT COULD WIN IN A DRAG RACE.
NOBODY CAN TRACE IT BACK TO ME, RIGHT?
CHOOF
BETTER HOPE NOT.
THAT'S COMFORTING, DIG. THANKS.
CRASH
NOBODY MOVE! KEEP YOUR EYES ON THE FLOOR!

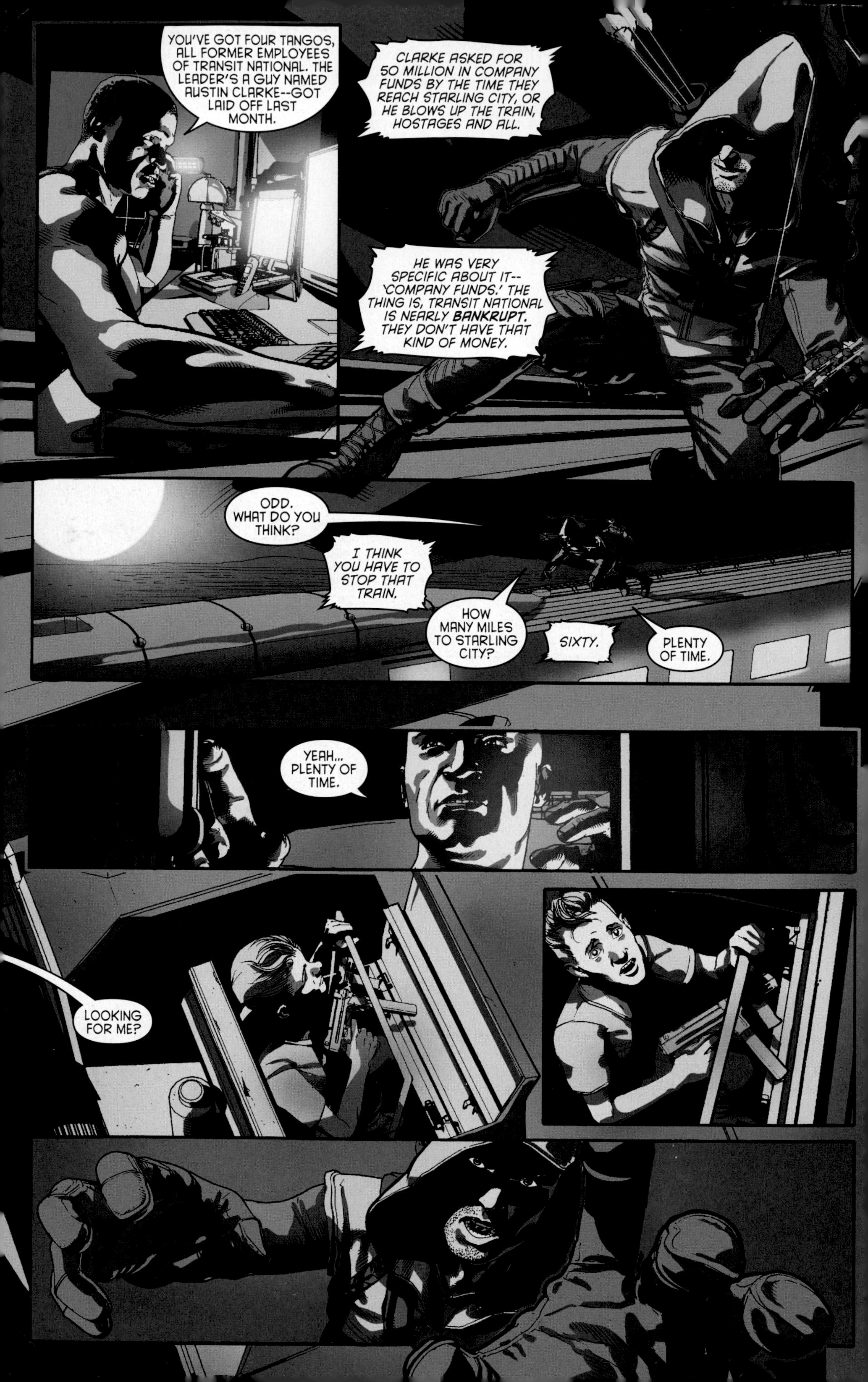
YOU'VE GOT FOUR TANGOS, ALL FORMER EMPLOYEES OF TRANSIT NATIONAL. THE LEADER'S A GUY NAMED AUSTIN CLARKE--GOT LAID OFF LAST MONTH.
CLARKE ASKED FOR 50 MILLION IN COMPANY FUNDS BY THE TIME THEY REACH STARLING CITY, OR HE BLOWS UP THE TRAIN, HOSTAGES AND ALL.
HE WAS VERY SPECIFIC ABOUT IT--'COMPANY FUNDS.' THE THING IS, TRANSIT NATIONAL IS NEARLY **BANKRUPT.** THEY DON'T HAVE THAT KIND OF MONEY.
ODD. WHAT DO YOU THINK?
I THINK YOU HAVE TO STOP THAT TRAIN.
HOW MANY MILES TO STARLING CITY?
SIXTY.
PLENTY OF TIME.
YEAH... PLENTY OF TIME.
LOOKING FOR ME?

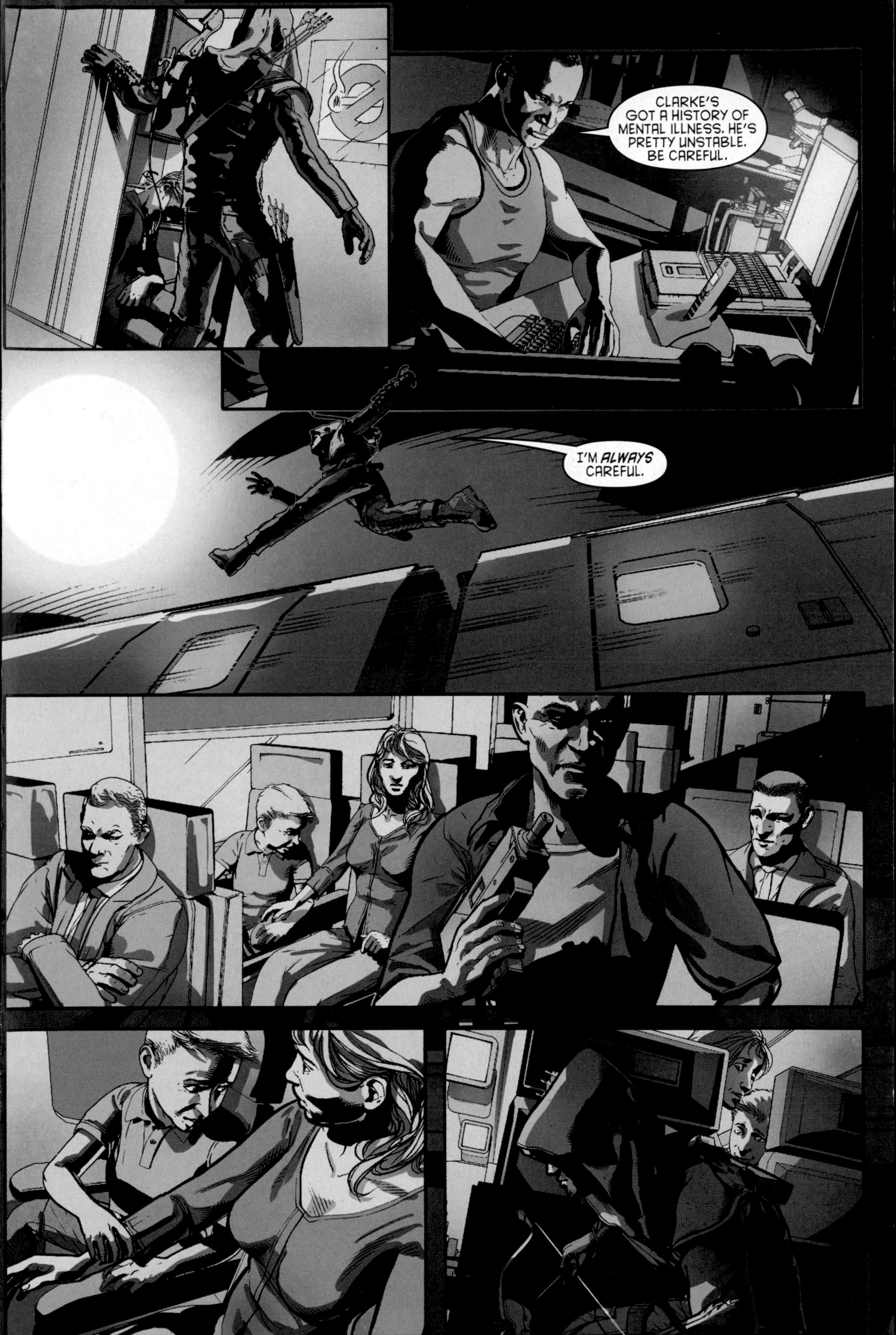
CLARKE'S GOT A HISTORY OF MENTAL ILLNESS. HE'S PRETTY UNSTABLE. BE CAREFUL.
I'M ALWAYS CAREFUL.

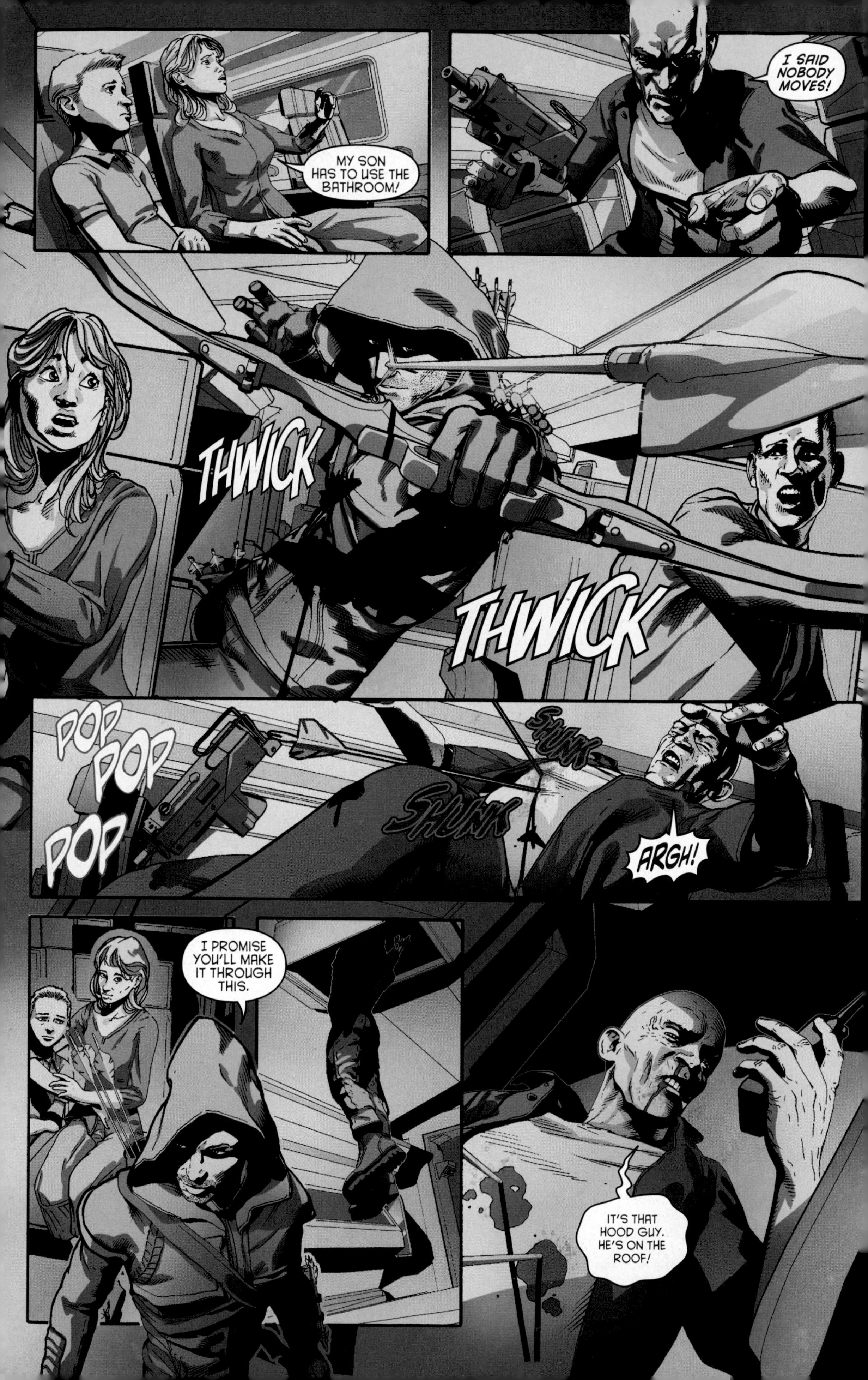
MY SON HAS TO USE THE BATHROOM!
I SAID NOBODY MOVES!
THWICK
THWICK
POP
POP
POP
SHUNK
SHUNK
ARGH!
I PROMISE YOU'LL MAKE IT THROUGH THIS.
IT'S THAT HOOD GUY. HE'S ON THE ROOF!

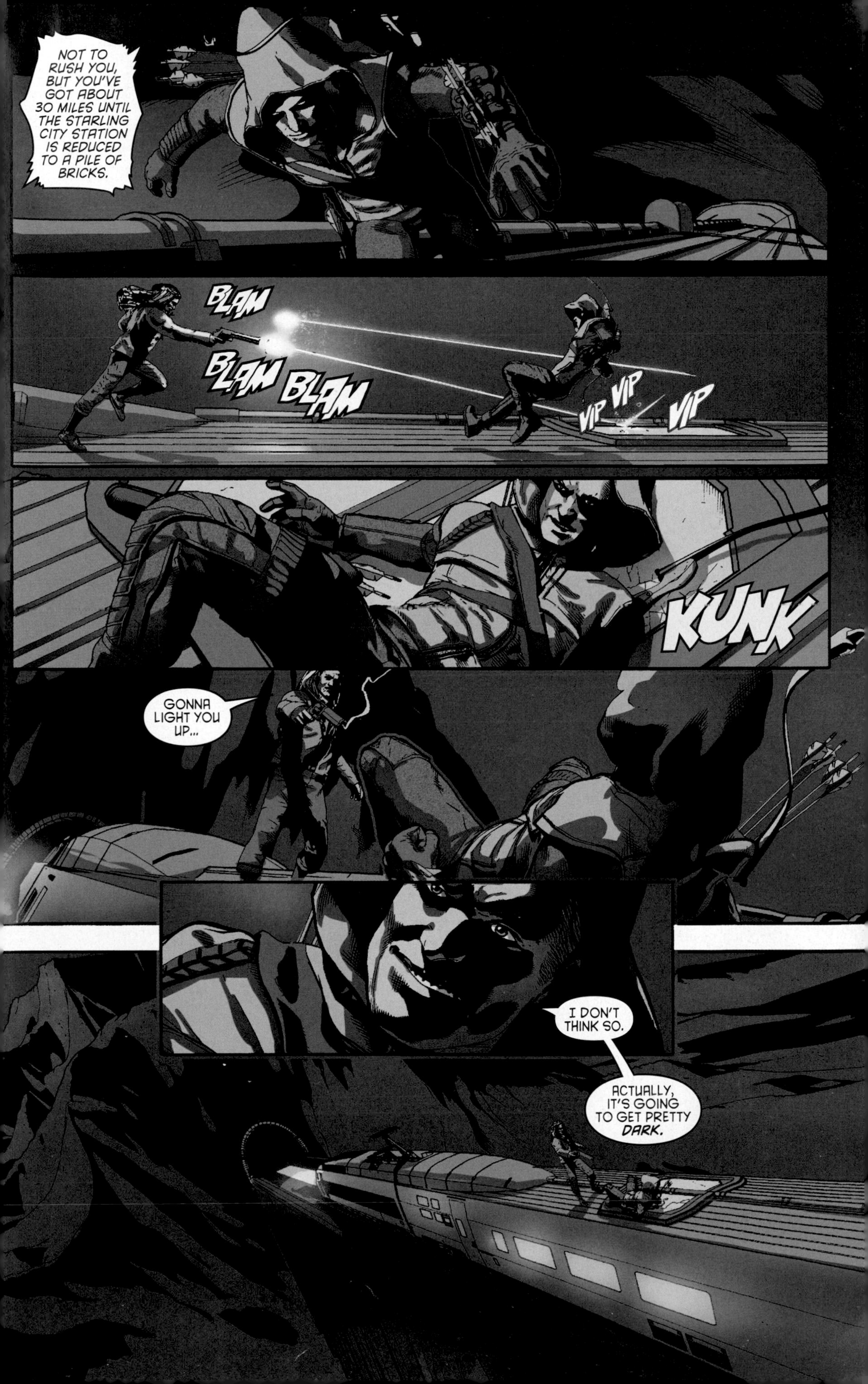
NOT TO RUSH YOU, BUT YOU'VE GOT ABOUT 30 MILES UNTIL THE STARLING CITY STATION IS REDUCED TO A PILE OF BRICKS.
BLAM
BLAM BLAM
VIP VIP
VIP
KUNK
GONNA LIGHT YOU UP...
I DON'T THINK SO.
ACTUALLY, IT'S GOING TO GET PRETTY *DARK.*

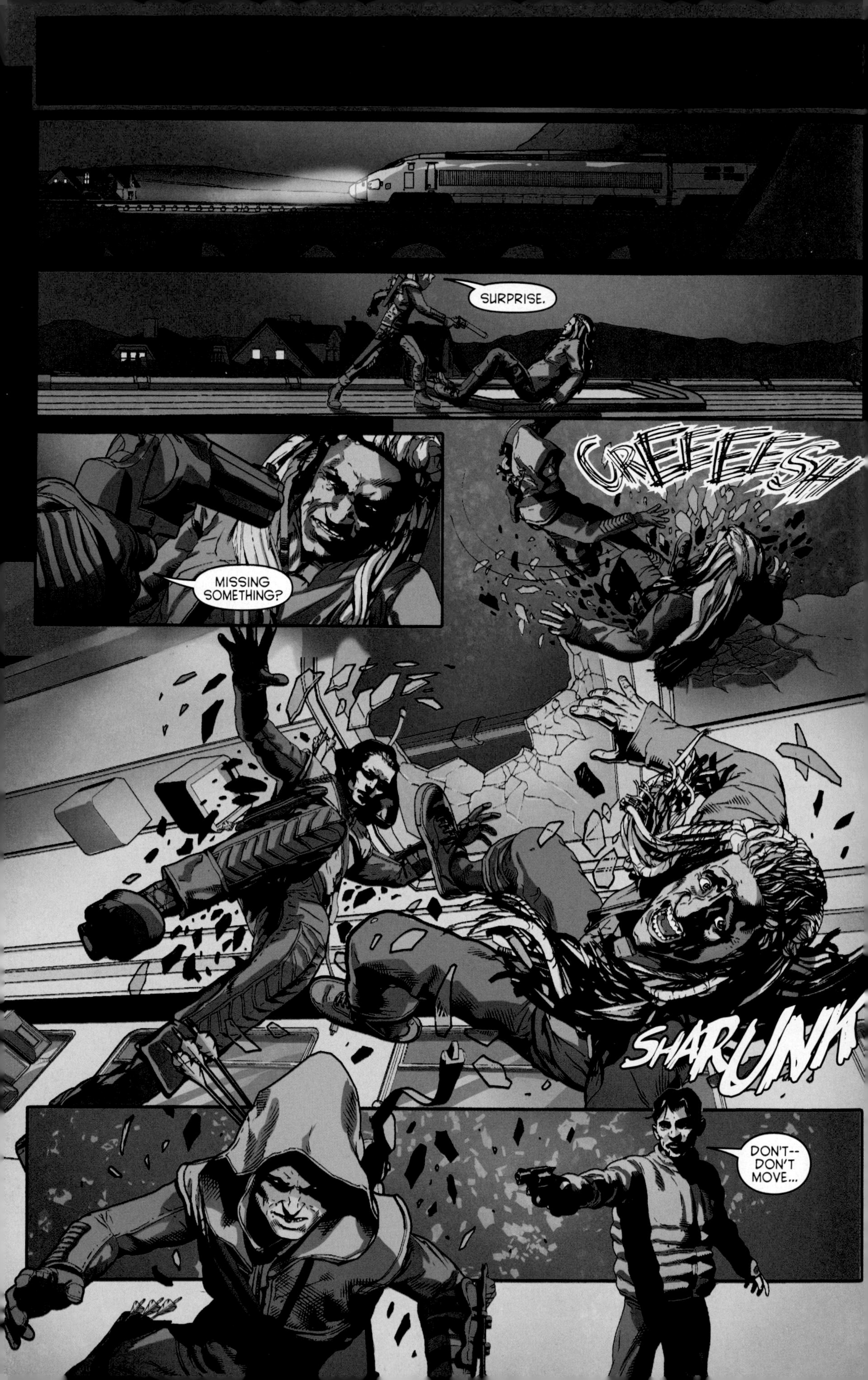
SURPRISE.
MISSING SOMETHING?
GREEEESH
SHARUNK
DON'T-- DON'T MOVE...

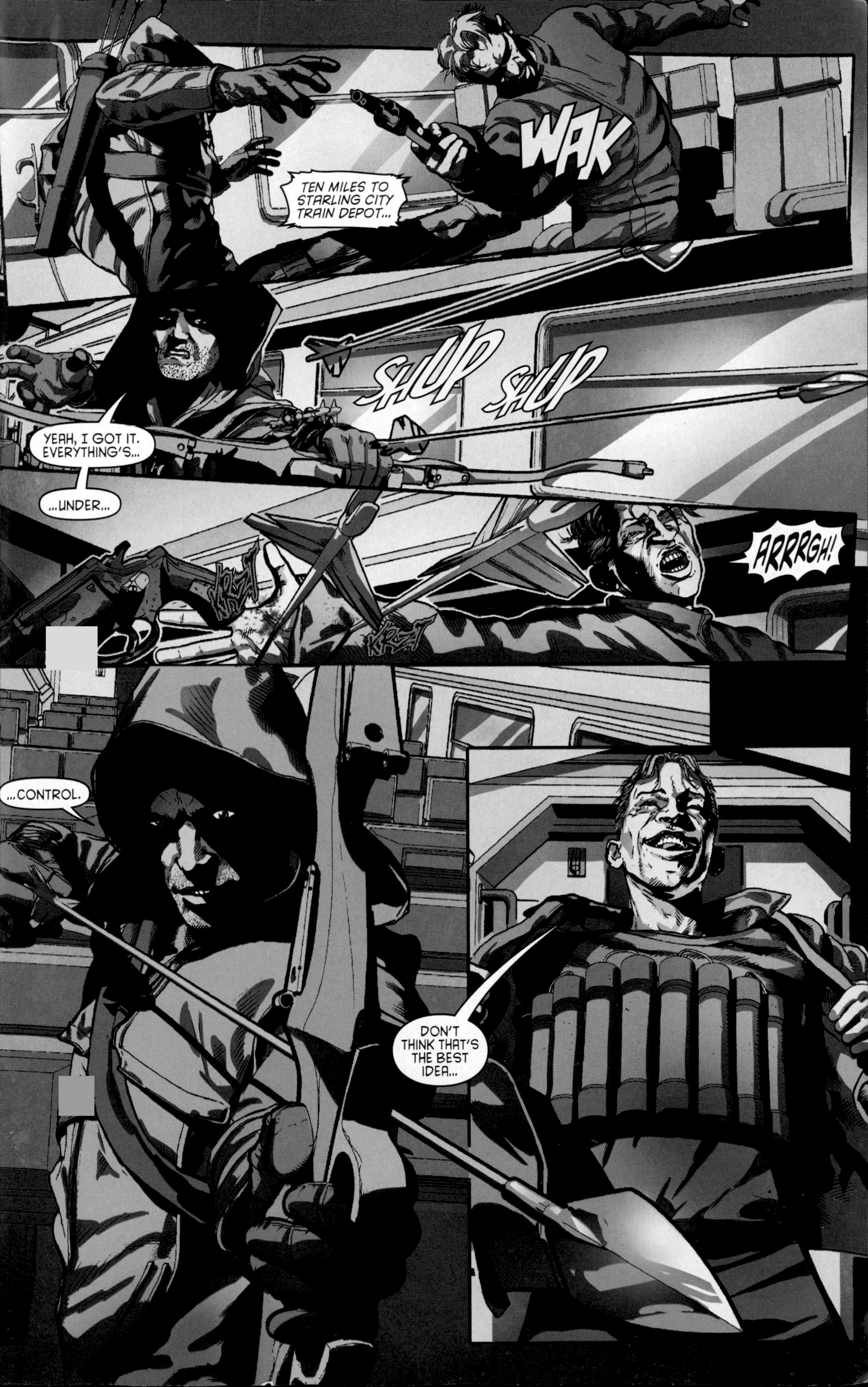
WAK
TEN MILES TO STARLING CITY TRAIN DEPOT...
YEAH, I GOT IT. EVERYTHING'S...
SHUP
SHUP
...UNDER...
ARRRGH!
...CONTROL.
DON'T THINK THAT'S THE BEST IDEA...

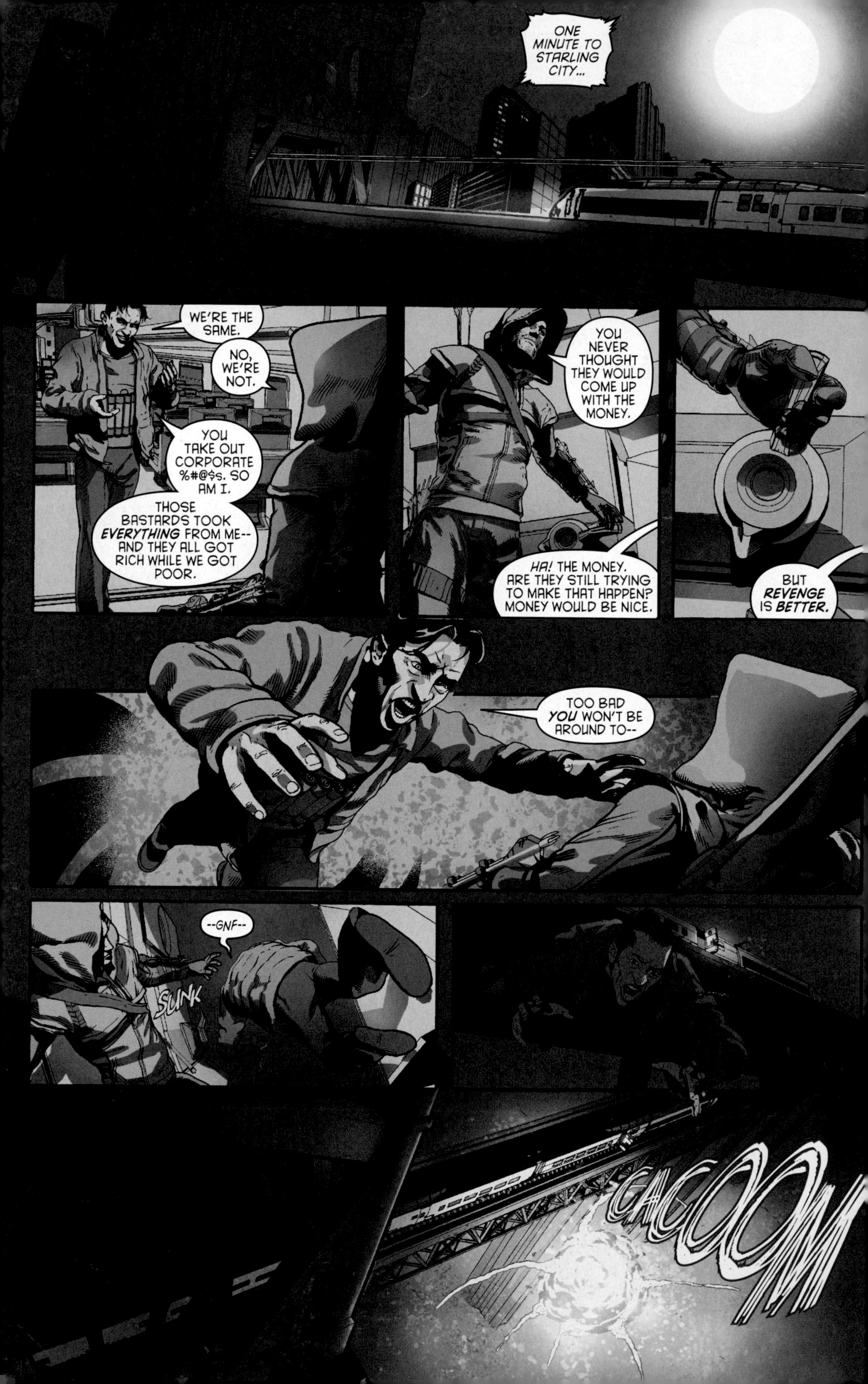
ONE MINUTE TO STARLING CITY...
WE'RE THE SAME.
NO, WE'RE NOT.
YOU TAKE OUT CORPORATE %#@$s. SO AM I.
THOSE BASTARDS TOOK EVERYTHING FROM ME--AND THEY ALL GOT RICH WHILE WE GOT POOR.
YOU NEVER THOUGHT THEY WOULD COME UP WITH THE MONEY.
HA! THE MONEY. ARE THEY STILL TRYING TO MAKE THAT HAPPEN? MONEY WOULD BE NICE.
BUT REVENGE IS BETTER.
TOO BAD YOU WON'T BE AROUND TO--
--GNF--
SUNK
CACOOM

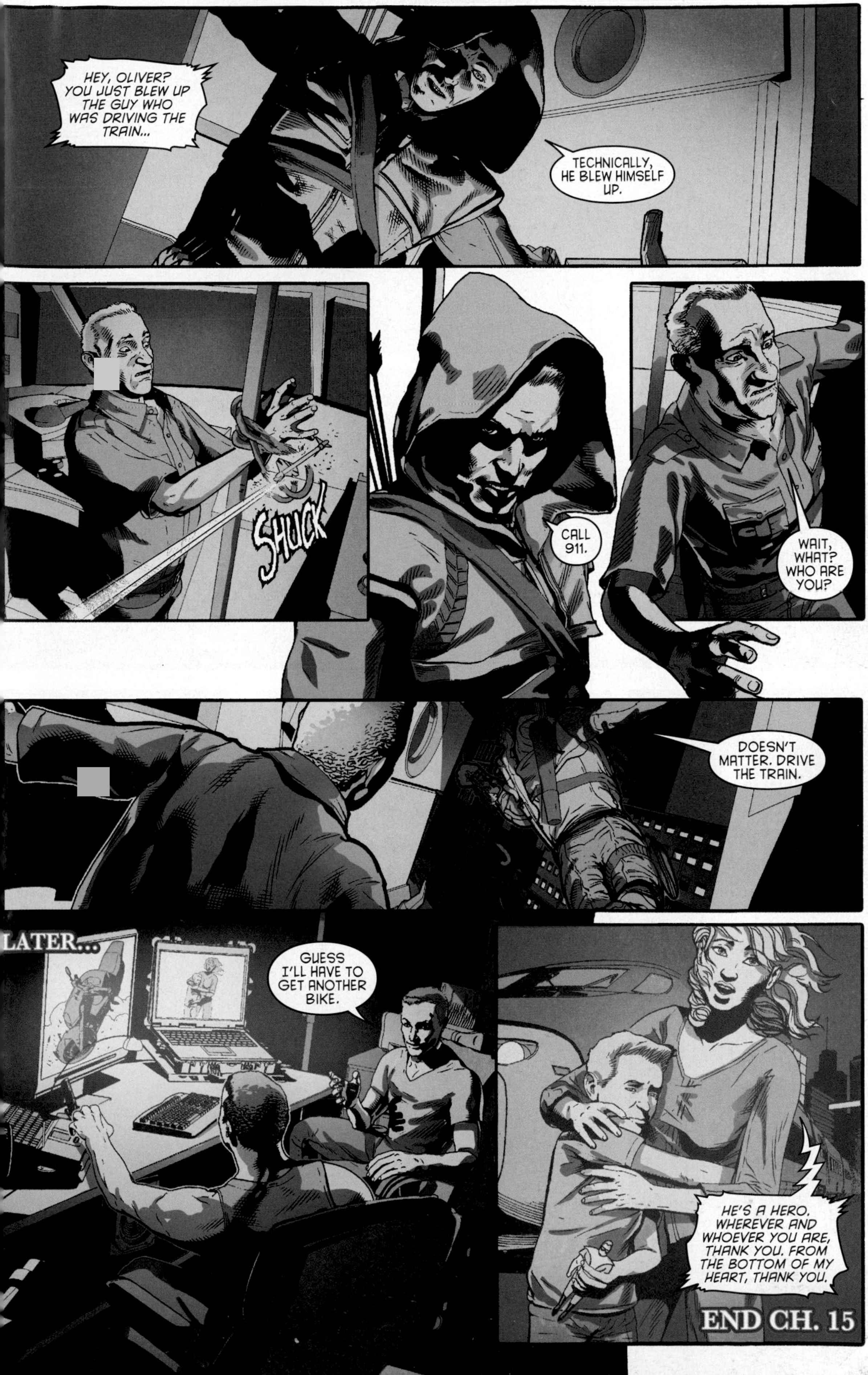
HEY, OLIVER? YOU JUST BLEW UP THE GUY WHO WAS DRIVING THE TRAIN...
TECHNICALLY, HE BLEW HIMSELF UP.
SHUCK
CALL 911.
WAIT, WHAT? WHO ARE YOU?
DOESN'T MATTER. DRIVE THE TRAIN.
LATER...
GUESS I'LL HAVE TO GET ANOTHER BIKE.
HE'S A HERO. WHEREVER AND WHOEVER YOU ARE, THANK YOU. FROM THE BOTTOM OF MY HEART, THANK YOU.
END CH. 15

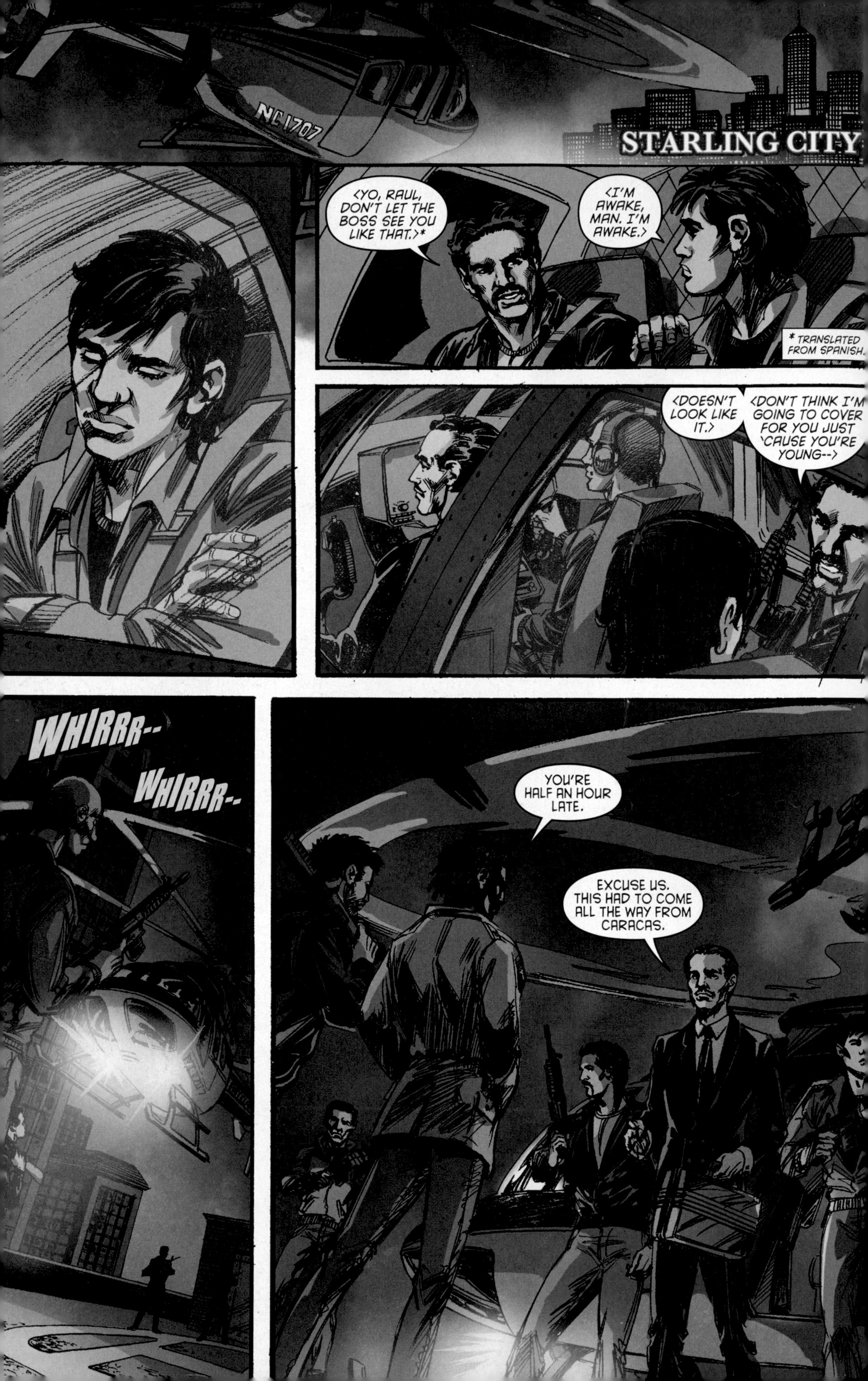

STARLING CITY
NC1707
<YO, RAUL, DON'T LET THE BOSS SEE YOU LIKE THAT.>*
<I'M AWAKE, MAN. I'M AWAKE.>
* TRANSLATED FROM SPANISH.
<DOESN'T LOOK LIKE IT.>
<DON'T THINK I'M GOING TO COVER FOR YOU JUST 'CAUSE YOU'RE YOUNG-->
WHIRRR--
WHIRRR--
YOU'RE HALF AN HOUR LATE.
EXCUSE US. THIS HAD TO COME ALL THE WAY FROM CARACAS.

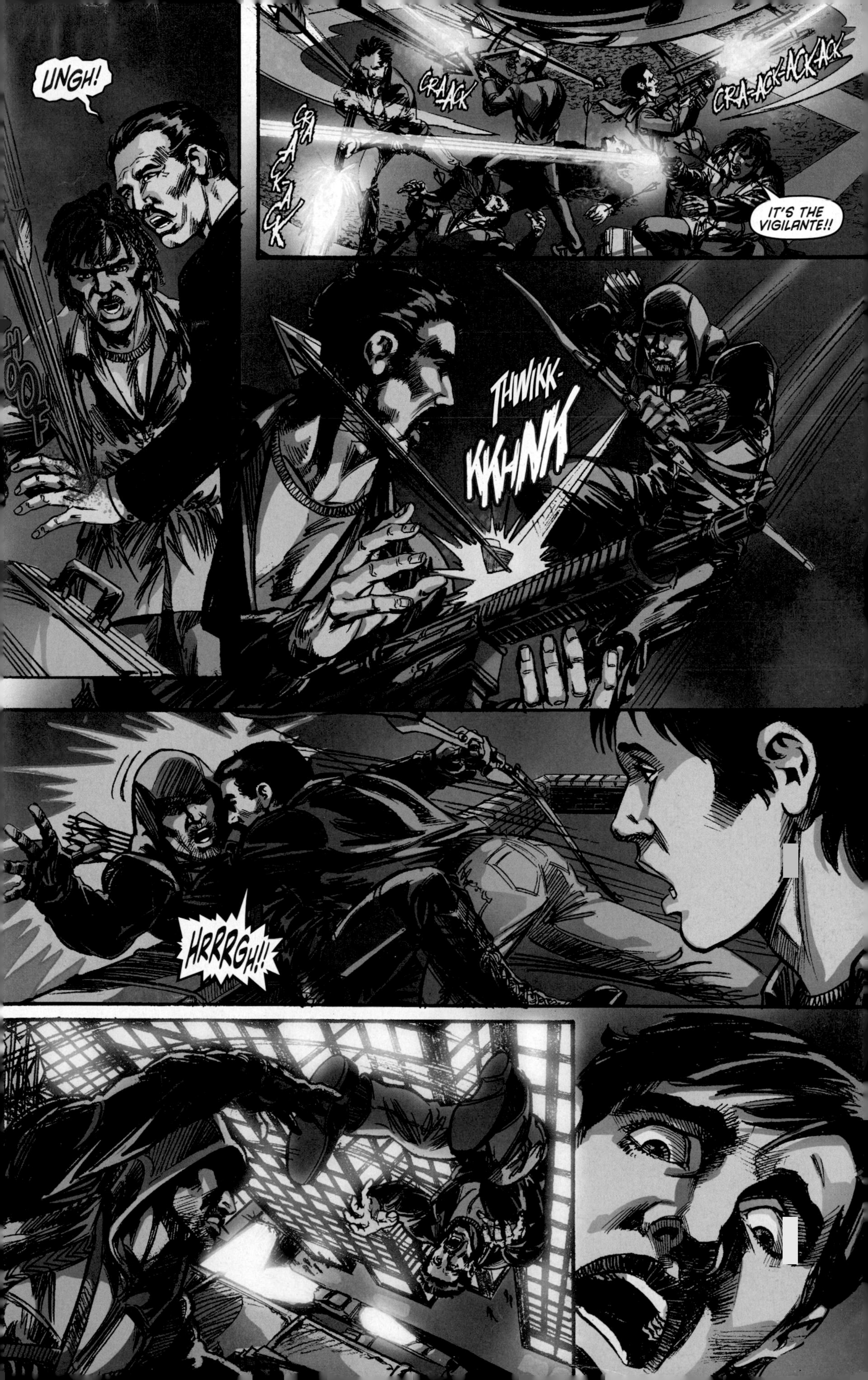
UNGH!
TOOF
CRA
A
C
K
A
C
K
CRA-ACK
CRA-ACK-ACK-ACK
IT'S THE VIGILANTE!!
THWIKK-
KKHNK
HRRRGH!!

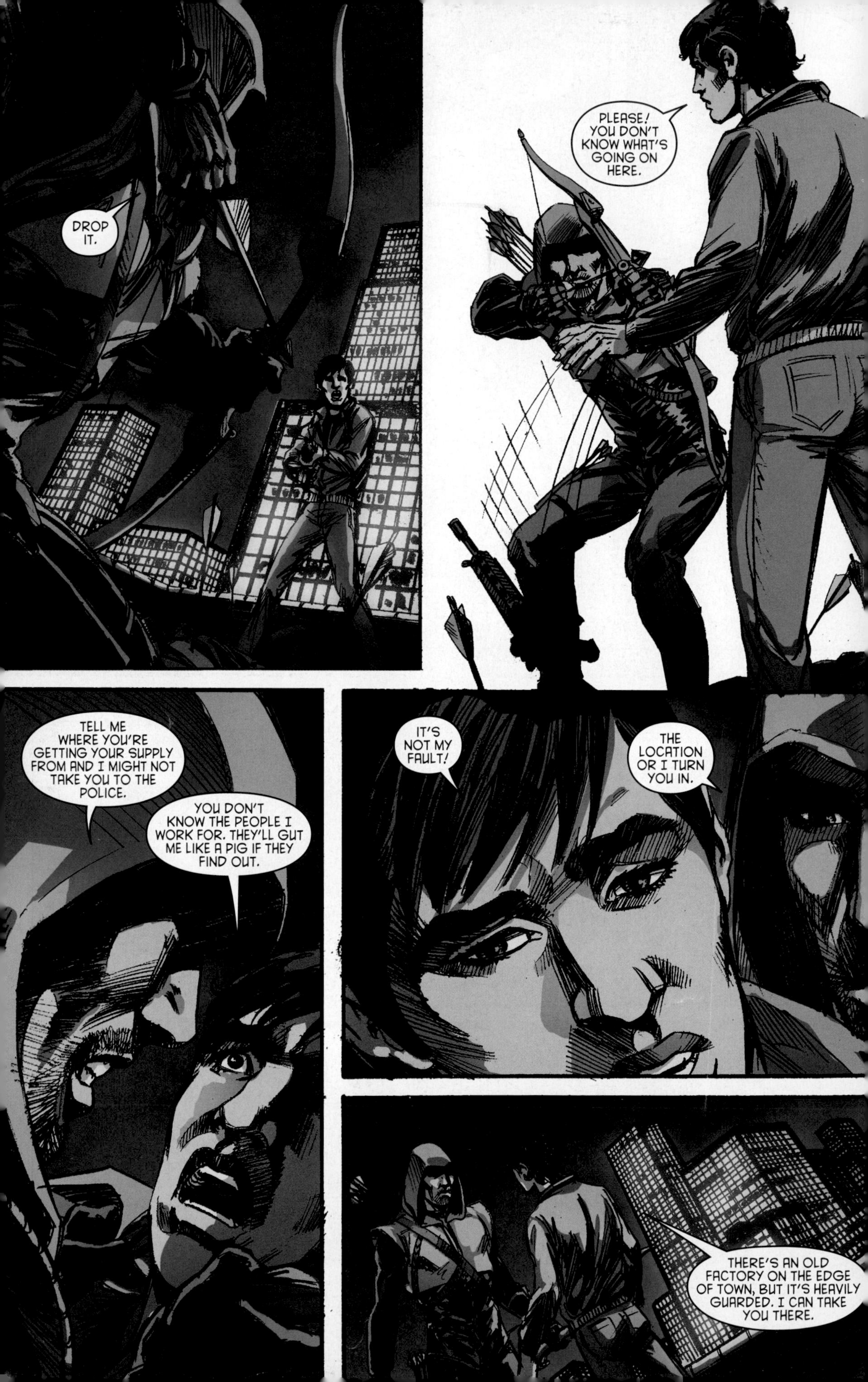
DROP IT.
PLEASE! YOU DON'T KNOW WHAT'S GOING ON HERE.
TELL ME WHERE YOU'RE GETTING YOUR SUPPLY FROM AND I MIGHT NOT TAKE YOU TO THE POLICE.
YOU DON'T KNOW THE PEOPLE I WORK FOR. THEY'LL GUT ME LIKE A PIG IF THEY FIND OUT.
IT'S NOT MY FAULT!
THE LOCATION OR I TURN YOU IN.
THERE'S AN OLD FACTORY ON THE EDGE OF TOWN, BUT IT'S HEAVILY GUARDED. I CAN TAKE YOU THERE.

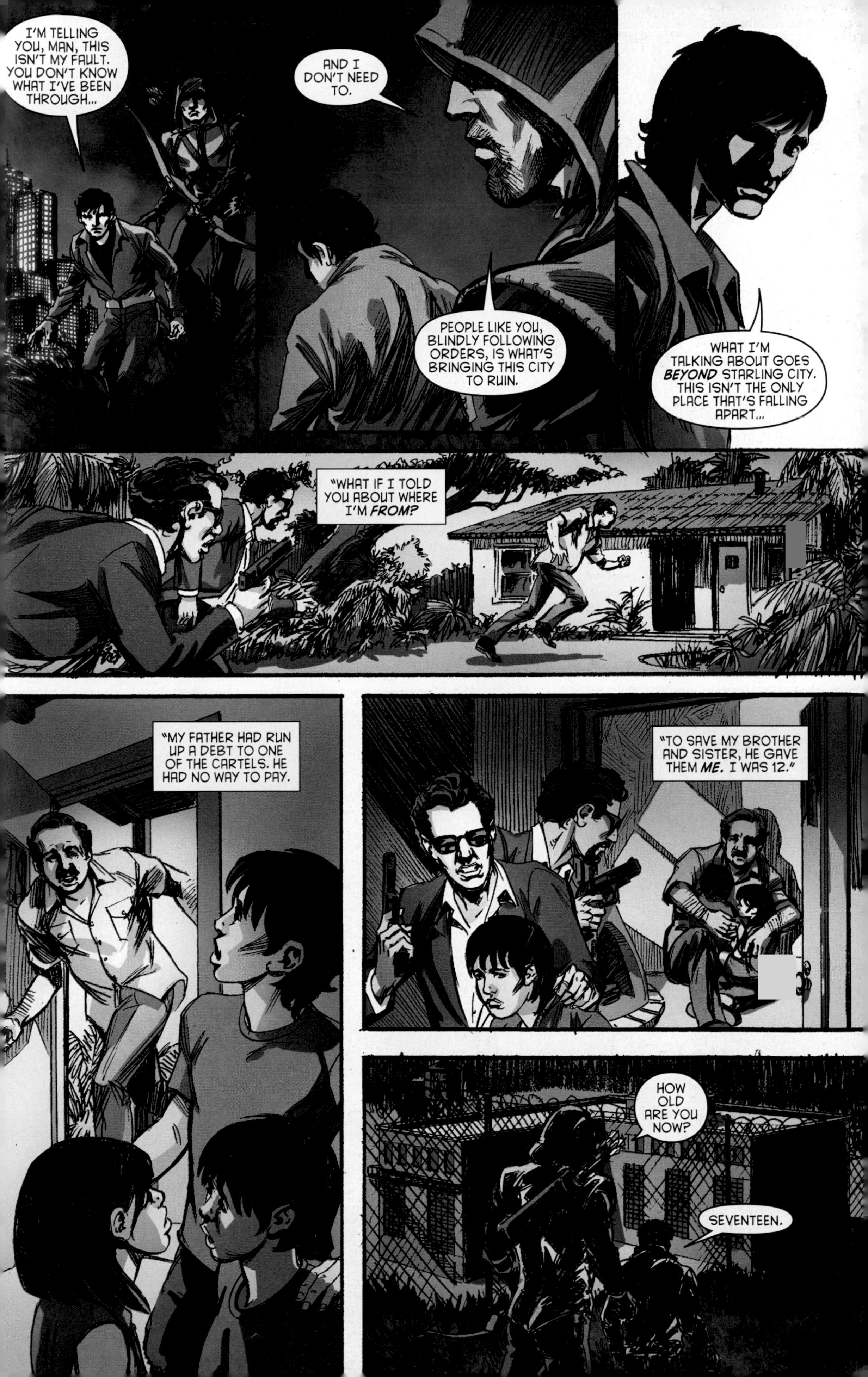
I'M TELLING YOU, MAN, THIS ISN'T MY FAULT. YOU DON'T KNOW WHAT I'VE BEEN THROUGH...
AND I DON'T NEED TO.
PEOPLE LIKE YOU, BLINDLY FOLLOWING ORDERS, IS WHAT'S BRINGING THIS CITY TO RUIN.
WHAT I'M TALKING ABOUT GOES *BEYOND* STARLING CITY. THIS ISN'T THE ONLY PLACE THAT'S FALLING APART...
"WHAT IF I TOLD YOU ABOUT WHERE I'M *FROM?*
"MY FATHER HAD RUN UP A DEBT TO ONE OF THE CARTELS. HE HAD NO WAY TO PAY.
"TO SAVE MY BROTHER AND SISTER, HE GAVE THEM *ME.* I WAS 12."
HOW OLD ARE YOU NOW?
SEVENTEEN.

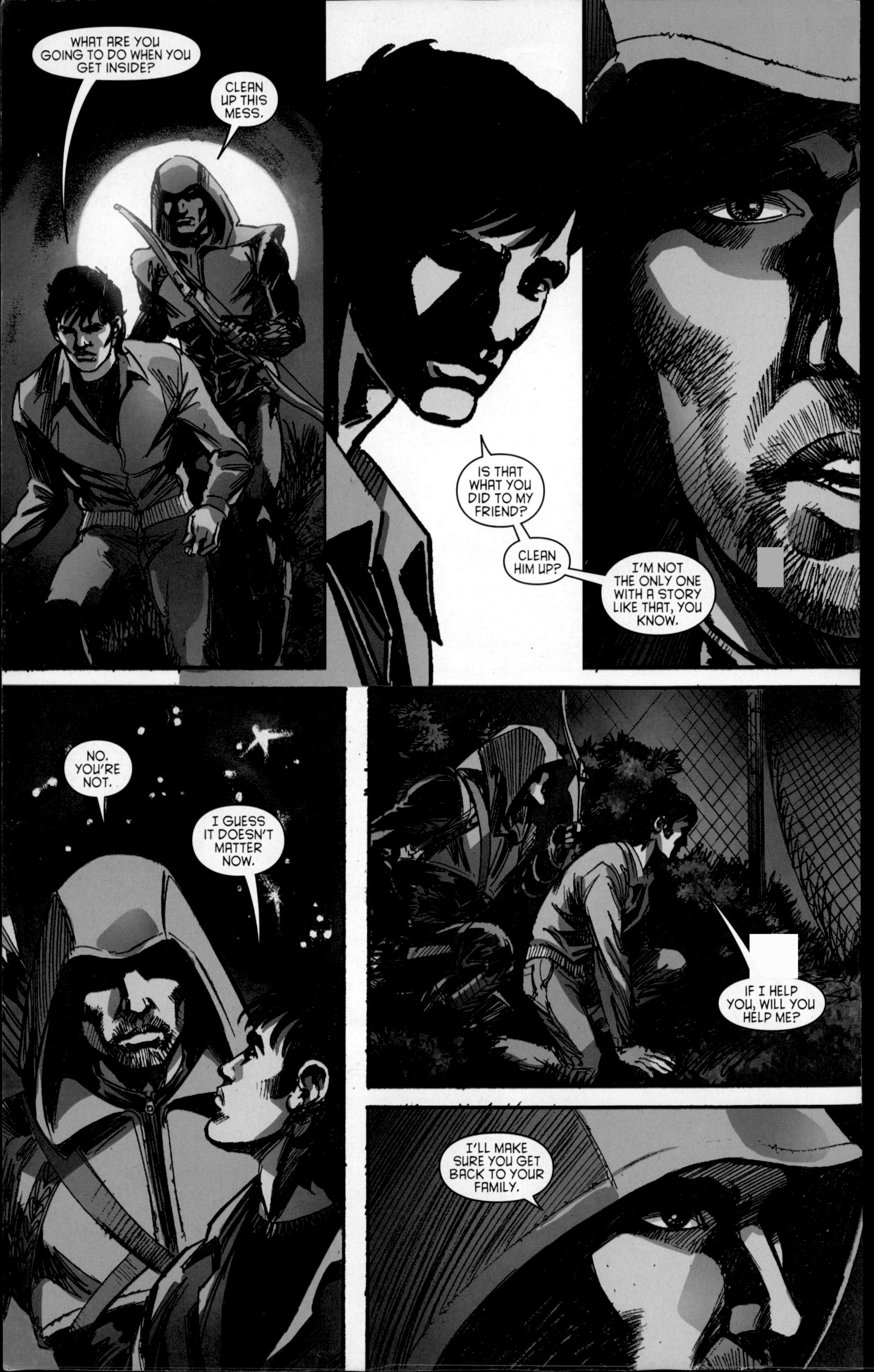
WHAT ARE YOU GOING TO DO WHEN YOU GET INSIDE?
CLEAN UP THIS MESS.
IS THAT WHAT YOU DID TO MY FRIEND?
CLEAN HIM UP?
I'M NOT THE ONLY ONE WITH A STORY LIKE THAT, YOU KNOW.
NO. YOU'RE NOT.
I GUESS IT DOESN'T MATTER NOW.
IF I HELP YOU, WILL YOU HELP ME?
I'LL MAKE SURE YOU GET BACK TO YOUR FAMILY.

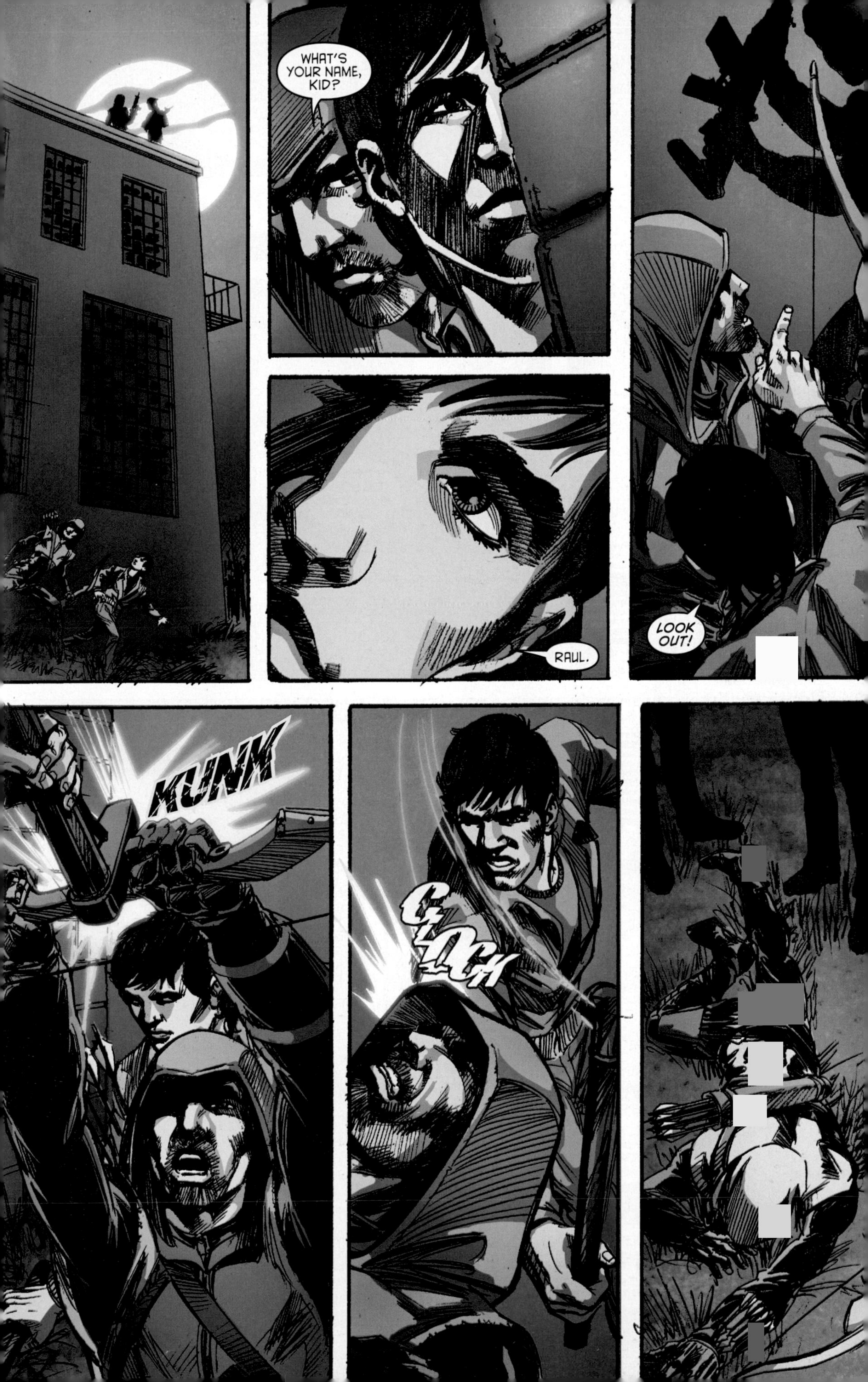
WHAT'S YOUR NAME, KID?
RAUL.
LOOK OUT!
KUNK

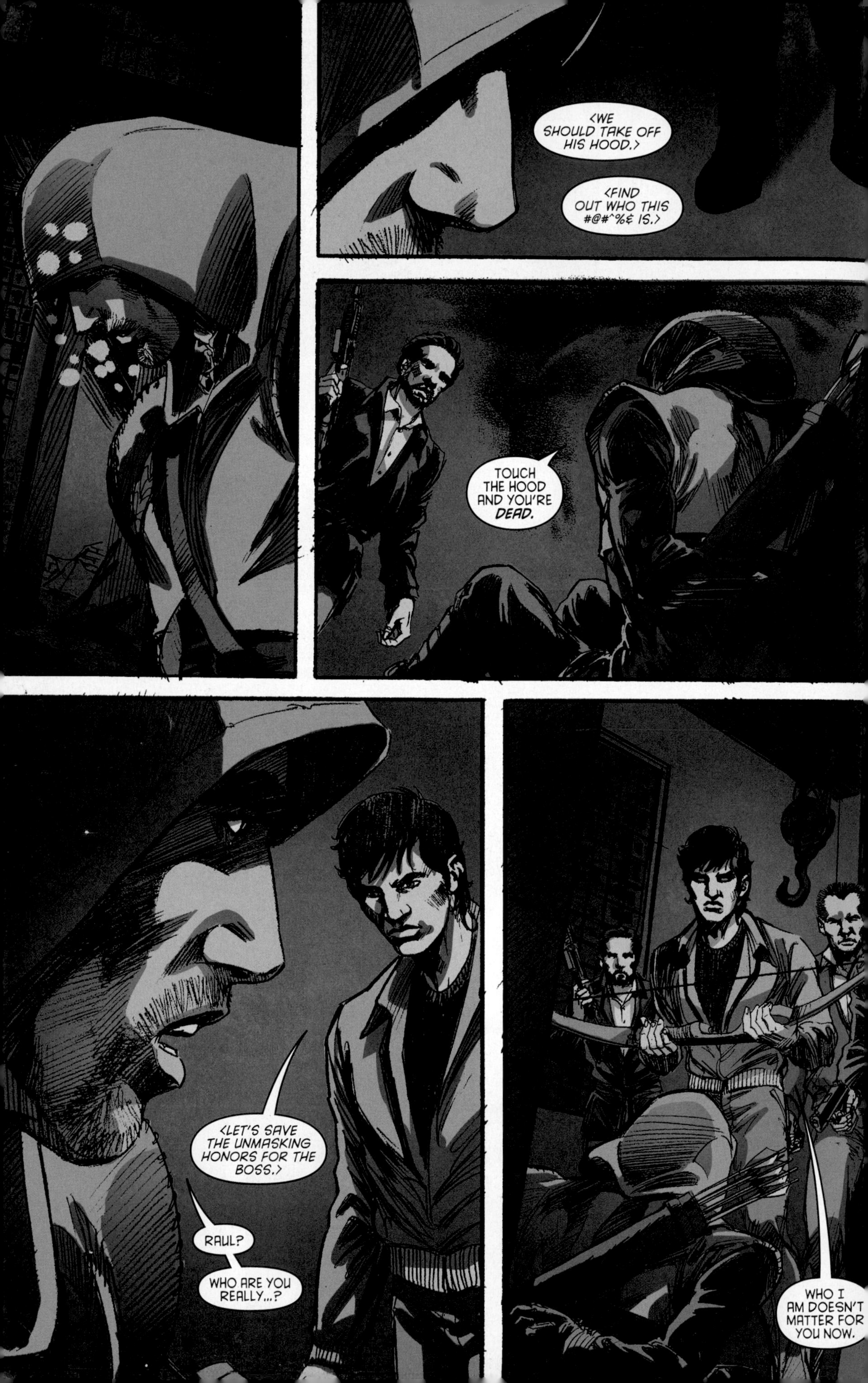
<WE SHOULD TAKE OFF HIS HOOD.>
<FIND OUT WHO THIS #@#^%& IS.>
TOUCH THE HOOD AND YOU'RE *DEAD.*
<LET'S SAVE THE UNMASKING HONORS FOR THE BOSS.>
RAUL?
WHO ARE YOU REALLY...?
WHO I AM DOESN'T MATTER FOR YOU NOW.

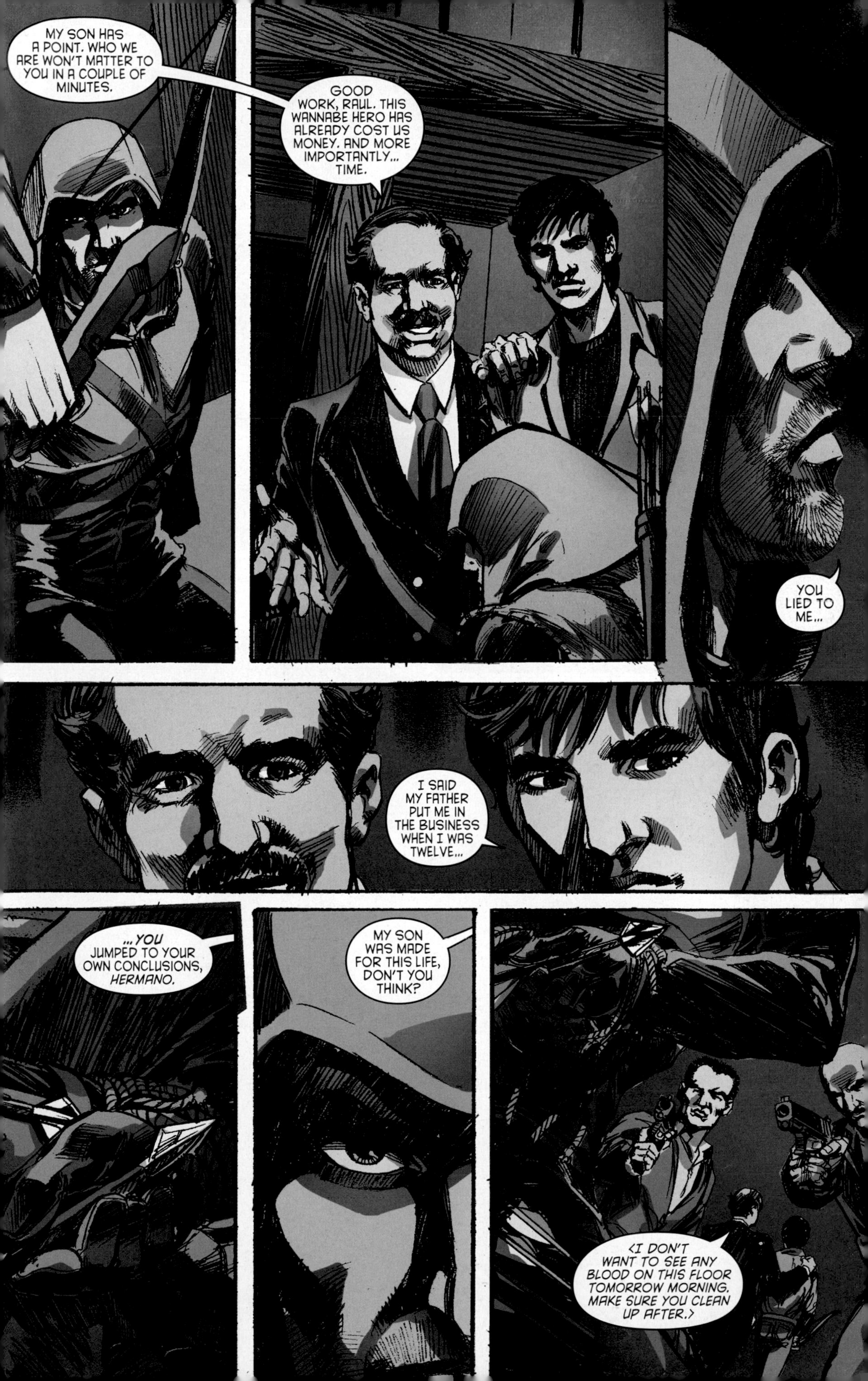
MY SON HAS A POINT. WHO WE ARE WON'T MATTER TO YOU IN A COUPLE OF MINUTES.
GOOD WORK, RAUL. THIS WANNABE HERO HAS ALREADY COST US MONEY. AND MORE IMPORTANTLY... TIME.
YOU LIED TO ME...
I SAID MY FATHER PUT ME IN THE BUSINESS WHEN I WAS TWELVE...
...YOU JUMPED TO YOUR OWN CONCLUSIONS, HERMANO.
MY SON WAS MADE FOR THIS LIFE, DON'T YOU THINK?
<I DON'T WANT TO SEE ANY BLOOD ON THIS FLOOR TOMORROW MORNING. MAKE SURE YOU CLEAN UP AFTER.>

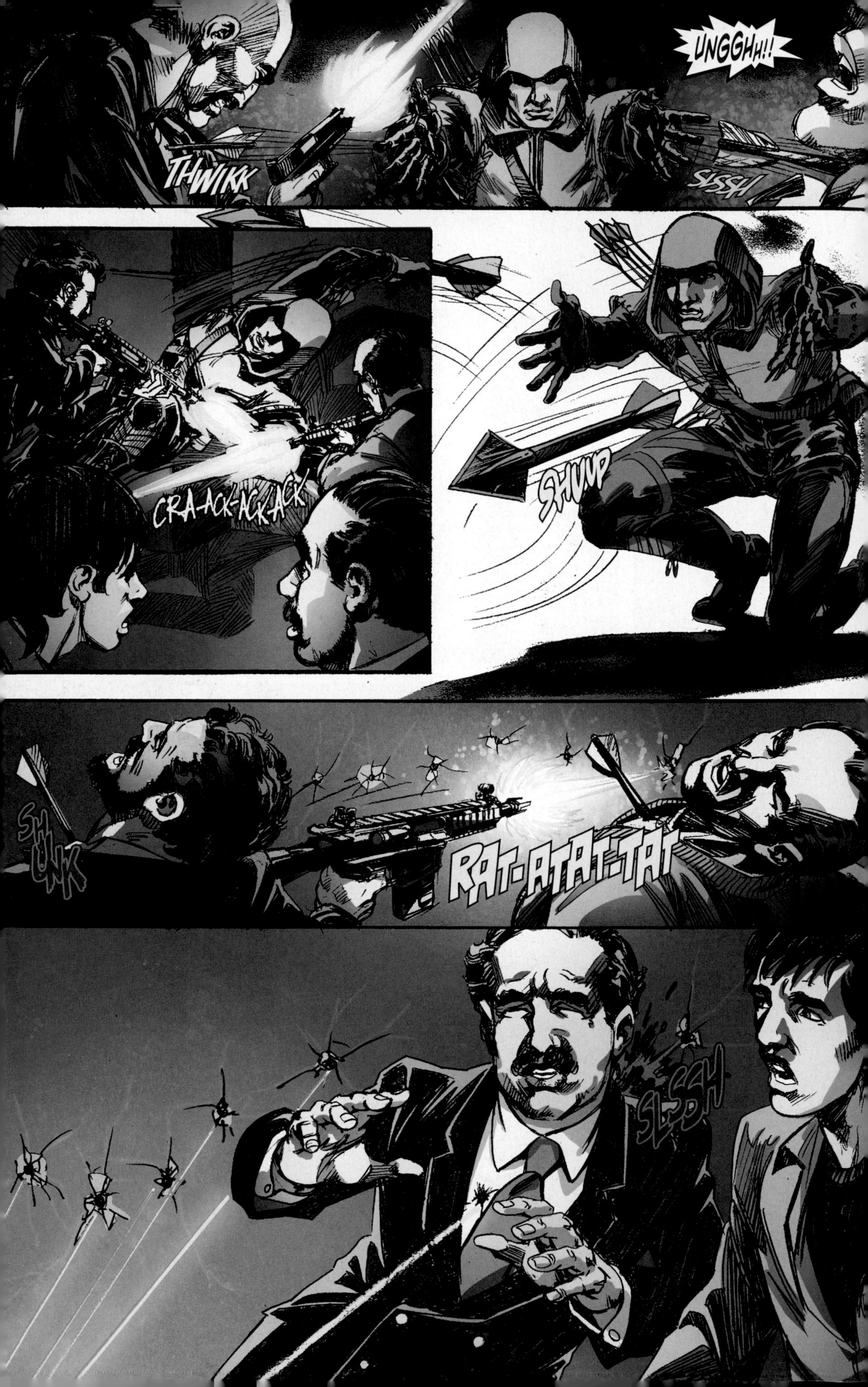
UNGGHH!!
THWIKK
SISSH
CRA-ACK-ACK-ACK
SHUNP
SHUNK
RAT-ATAT-TAT
SLSSH

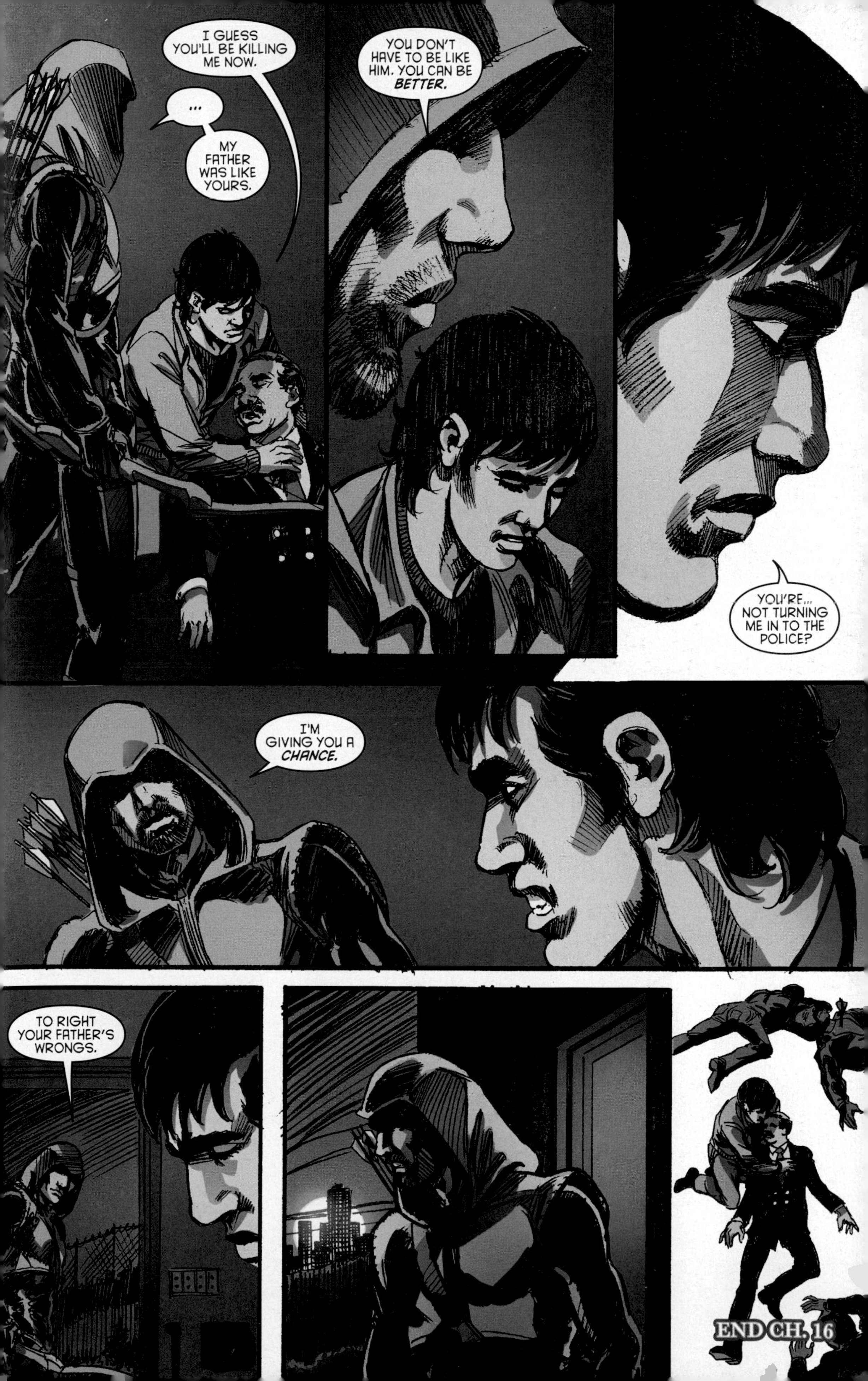
I GUESS YOU'LL BE KILLING ME NOW.
...
MY FATHER WAS LIKE YOURS.
YOU DON'T HAVE TO BE LIKE HIM. YOU CAN BE *BETTER.*
YOU'RE... NOT TURNING ME IN TO THE POLICE?
I'M GIVING YOU A *CHANCE.*
TO RIGHT YOUR FATHER'S WRONGS.
END CH. 16

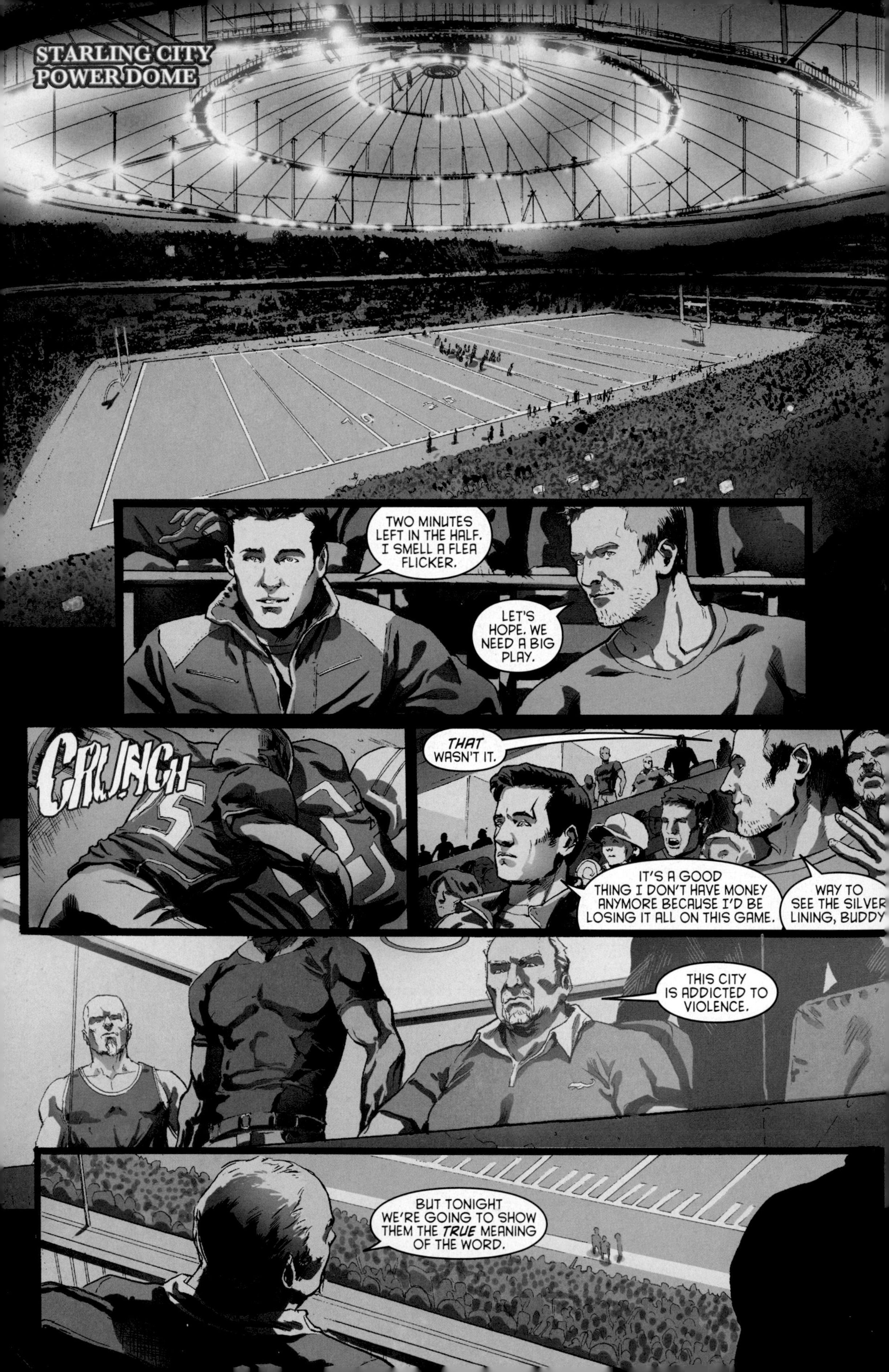
STARLING CITY POWER DOME
TWO MINUTES LEFT IN THE HALF. I SMELL A FLEA FLICKER.
LET'S HOPE. WE NEED A BIG PLAY.
CRUNCH
THAT WASN'T IT.
IT'S A GOOD THING I DON'T HAVE MONEY ANYMORE BECAUSE I'D BE LOSING IT ALL ON THIS GAME.
WAY TO SEE THE SILVER LINING, BUDDY
THIS CITY IS ADDICTED TO VIOLENCE.
BUT TONIGHT WE'RE GOING TO SHOW THEM THE TRUE MEANING OF THE WORD.

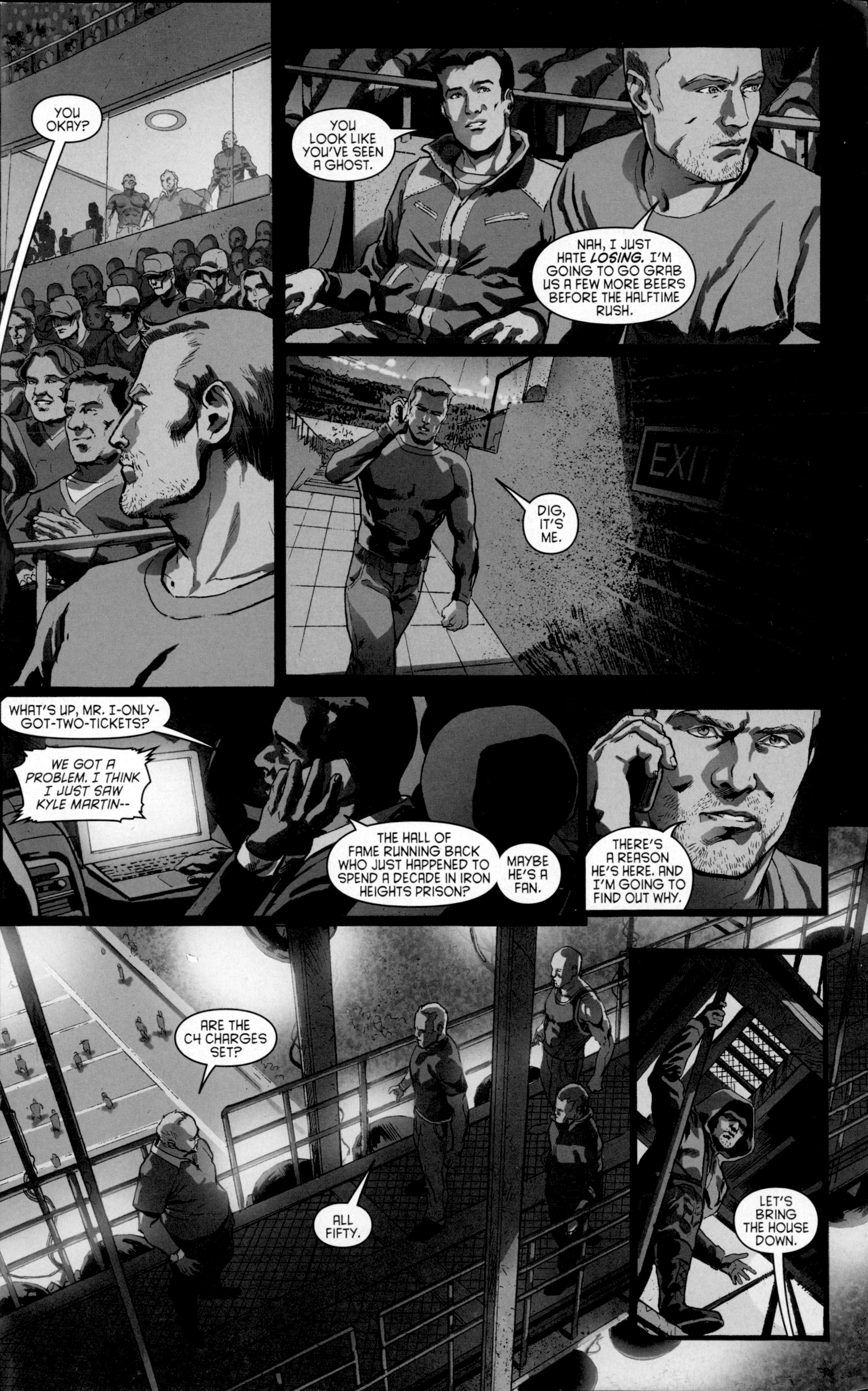
YOU OKAY?
YOU LOOK LIKE YOU'VE SEEN A GHOST.
NAH, I JUST HATE LOSING. I'M GOING TO GO GRAB US A FEW MORE BEERS BEFORE THE HALFTIME RUSH.
EXIT
DIG, IT'S ME.
WHAT'S UP, MR. I-ONLY-GOT-TWO-TICKETS?
WE GOT A PROBLEM. I THINK I JUST SAW KYLE MARTIN--
THE HALL OF FAME RUNNING BACK WHO JUST HAPPENED TO SPEND A DECADE IN IRON HEIGHTS PRISON?
MAYBE HE'S A FAN.
THERE'S A REASON HE'S HERE. AND I'M GOING TO FIND OUT WHY.
ARE THE C4 CHARGES SET?
ALL FIFTY.
LET'S BRING THE HOUSE DOWN.

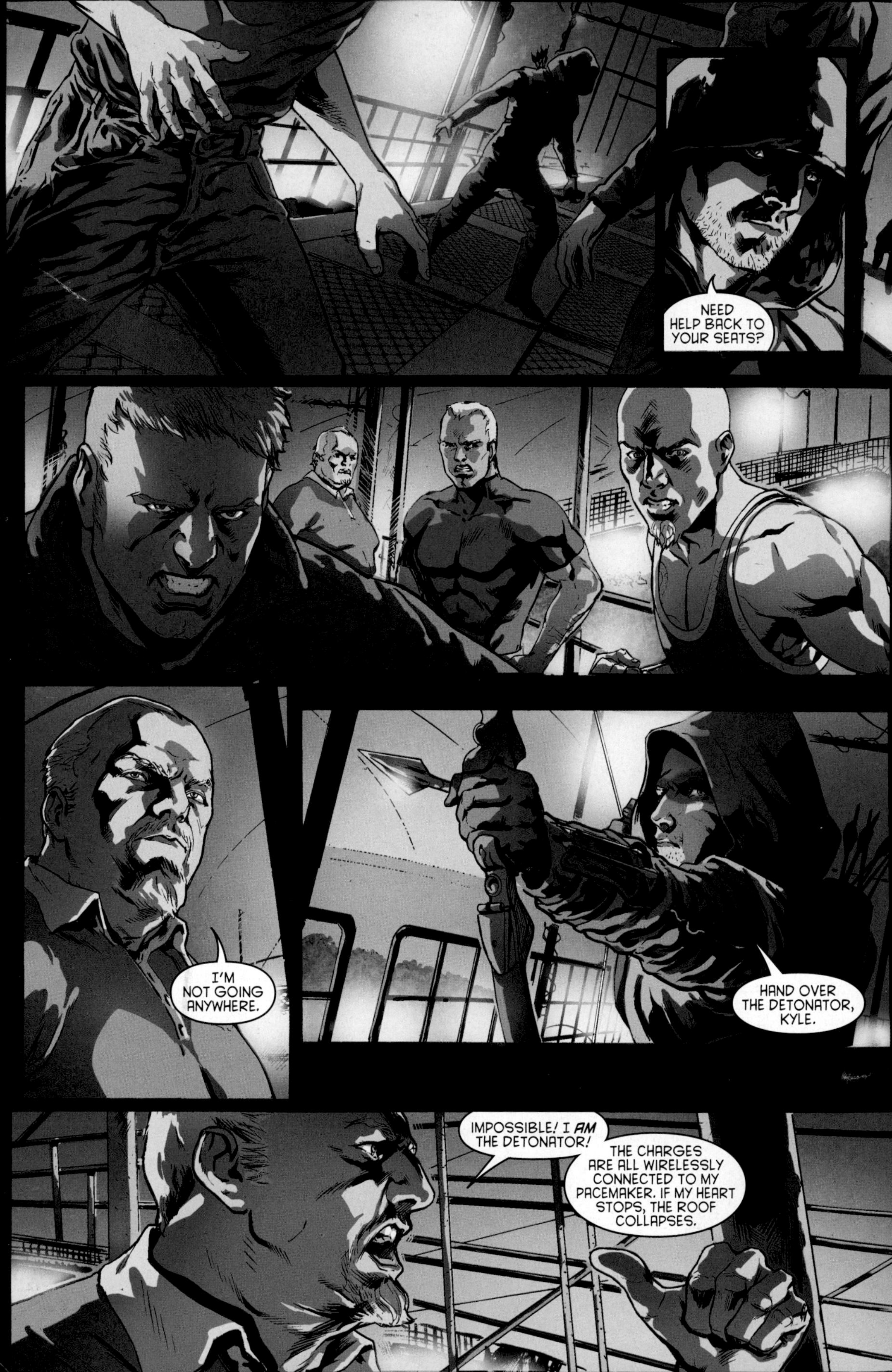
NEED HELP BACK TO YOUR SEATS?
I'M NOT GOING ANYWHERE.
HAND OVER THE DETONATOR, KYLE.
IMPOSSIBLE! I *AM* THE DETONATOR!
THE CHARGES ARE ALL WIRELESSLY CONNECTED TO MY PACEMAKER. IF MY HEART STOPS, THE ROOF COLLAPSES.

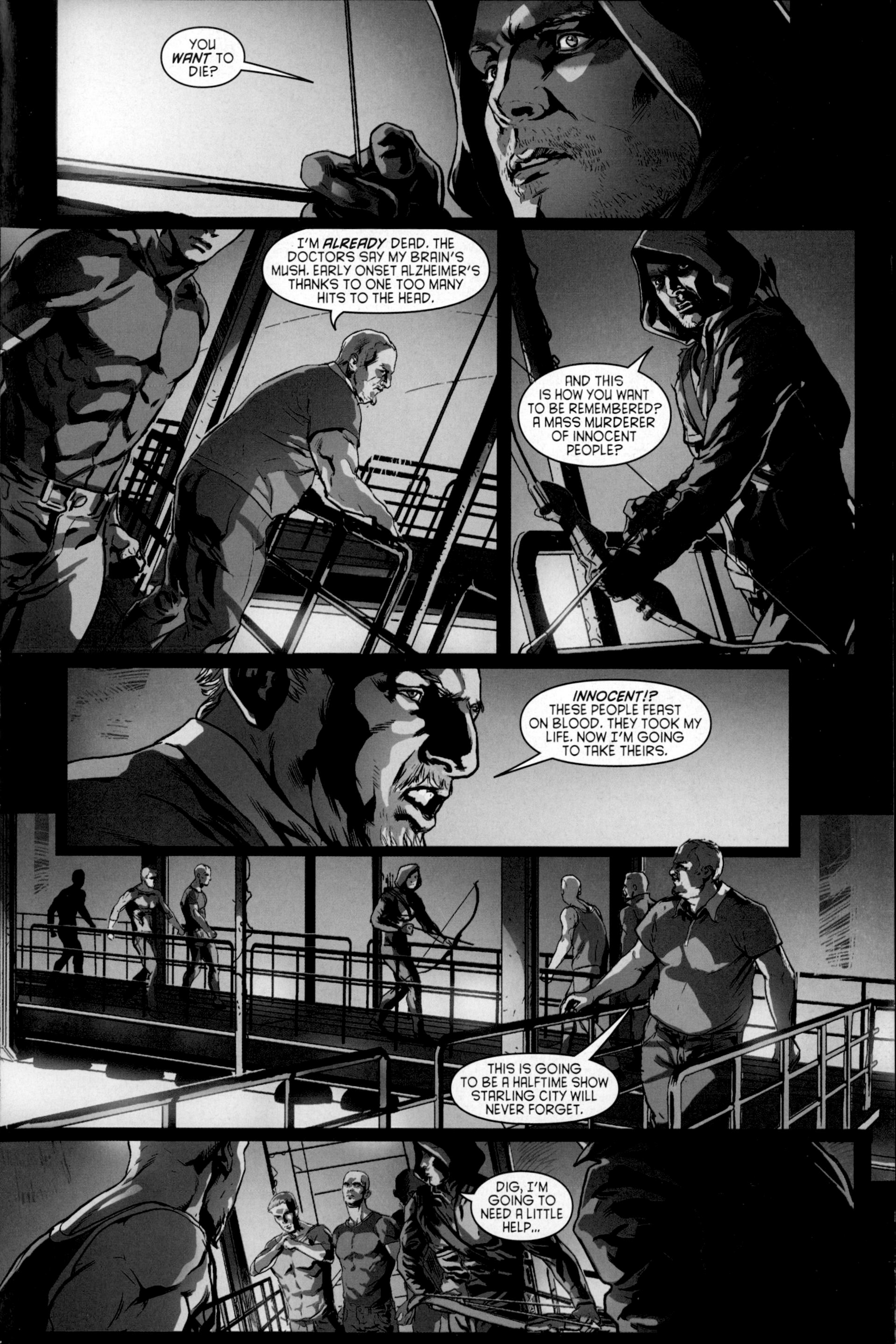
YOU *WANT* TO DIE?
I'M *ALREADY* DEAD. THE DOCTORS SAY MY BRAIN'S MUSH. EARLY ONSET ALZHEIMER'S THANKS TO ONE TOO MANY HITS TO THE HEAD.
AND THIS IS HOW YOU WANT TO BE REMEMBERED? A MASS MURDERER OF INNOCENT PEOPLE?
INNOCENT!? THESE PEOPLE FEAST ON BLOOD. THEY TOOK MY LIFE. NOW I'M GOING TO TAKE THEIRS.
THIS IS GOING TO BE A HALFTIME SHOW STARLING CITY WILL NEVER FORGET.
DIG, I'M GOING TO NEED A LITTLE HELP...

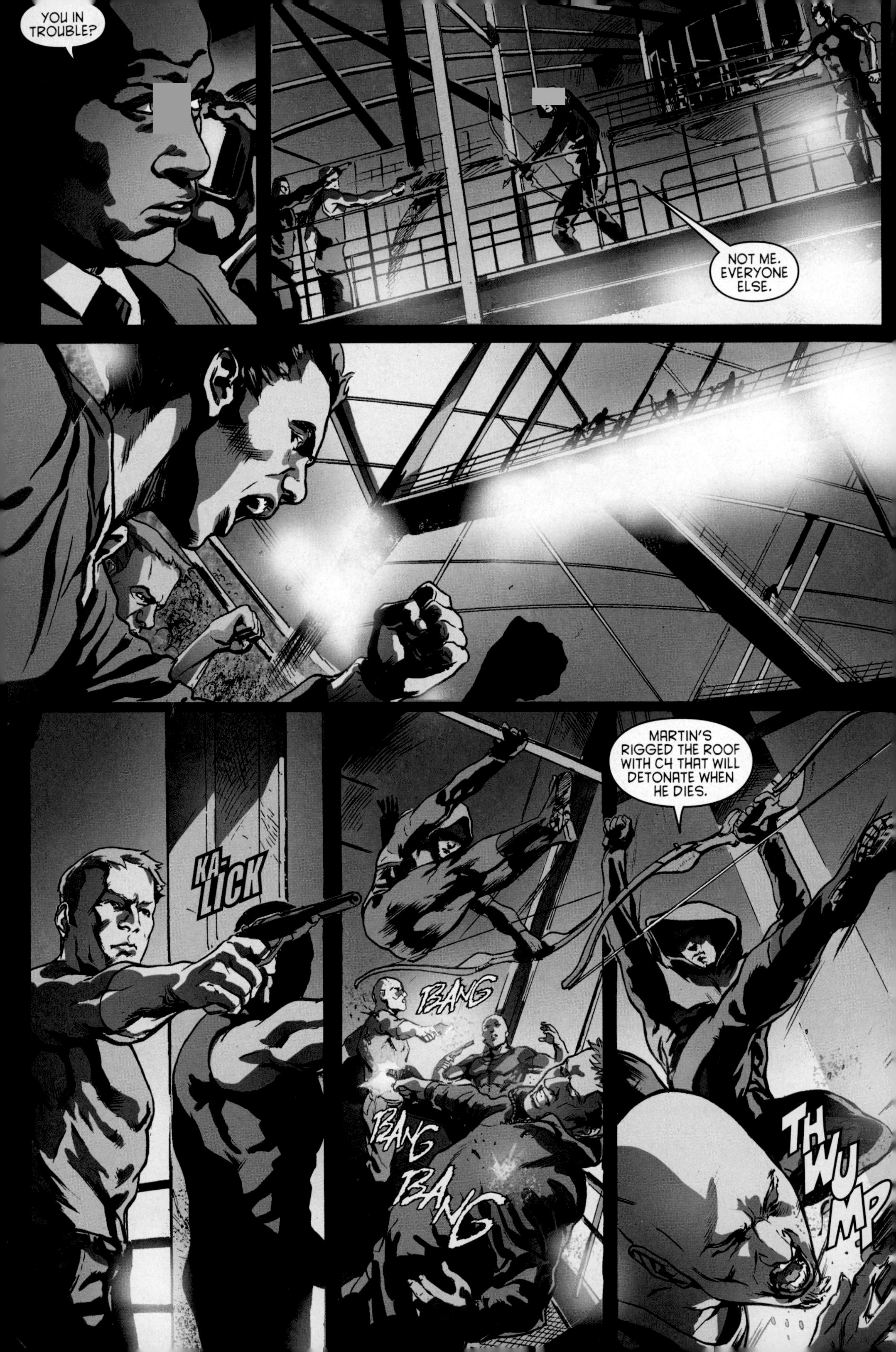
YOU IN TROUBLE?
NOT ME. EVERYONE ELSE.
KA-LICK
BANG
BANG
BANG
MARTIN'S RIGGED THE ROOF WITH C4 THAT WILL DETONATE WHEN HE DIES.
THWUMP

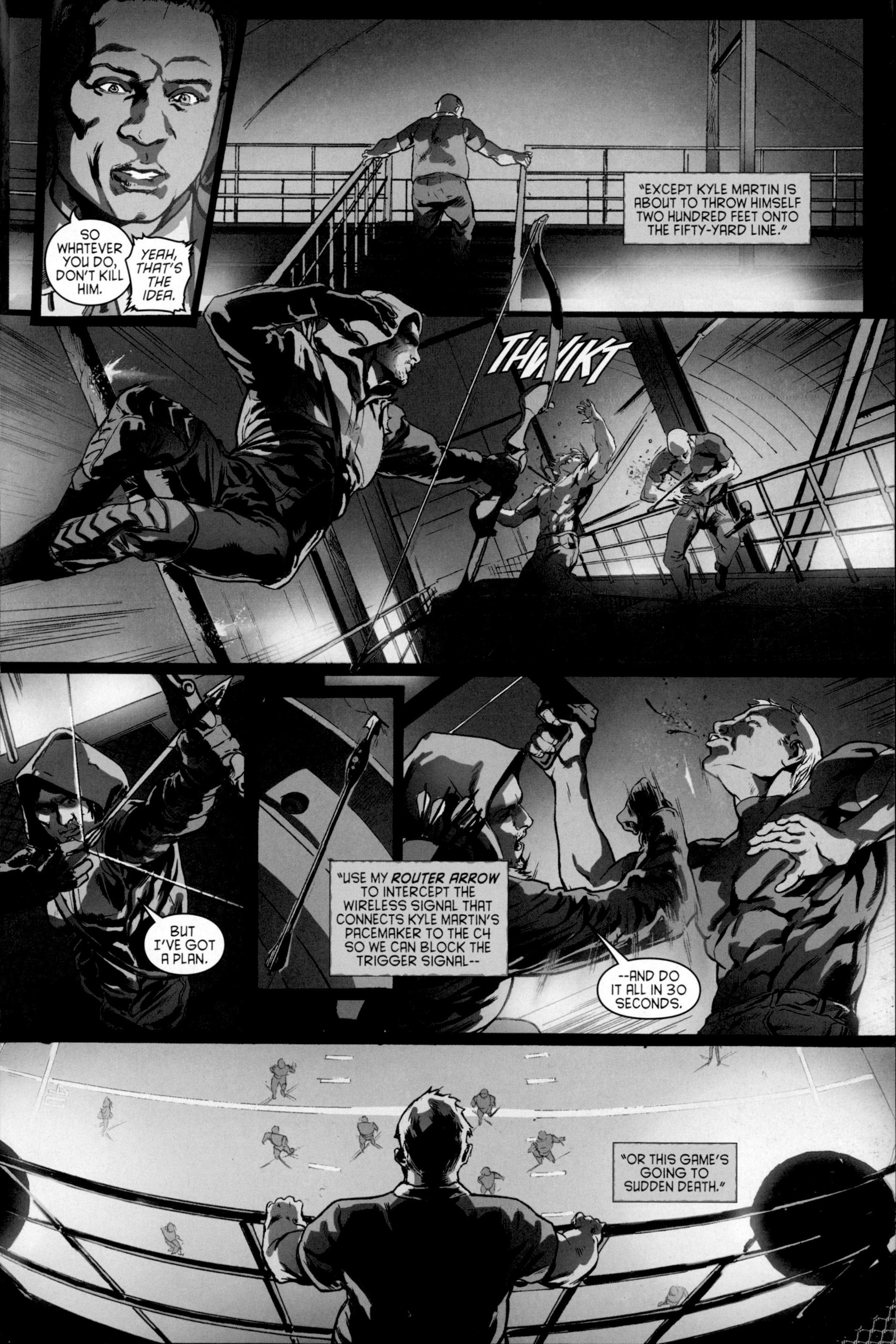
SO WHATEVER YOU DO, DON'T KILL HIM.
YEAH, THAT'S THE IDEA.
"EXCEPT KYLE MARTIN IS ABOUT TO THROW HIMSELF TWO HUNDRED FEET ONTO THE FIFTY-YARD LINE."
THWIKT
BUT I'VE GOT A PLAN.
"USE MY ROUTER ARROW TO INTERCEPT THE WIRELESS SIGNAL THAT CONNECTS KYLE MARTIN'S PACEMAKER TO THE C4 SO WE CAN BLOCK THE TRIGGER SIGNAL--
--AND DO IT ALL IN 30 SECONDS.
"OR THIS GAME'S GOING TO SUDDEN DEATH."

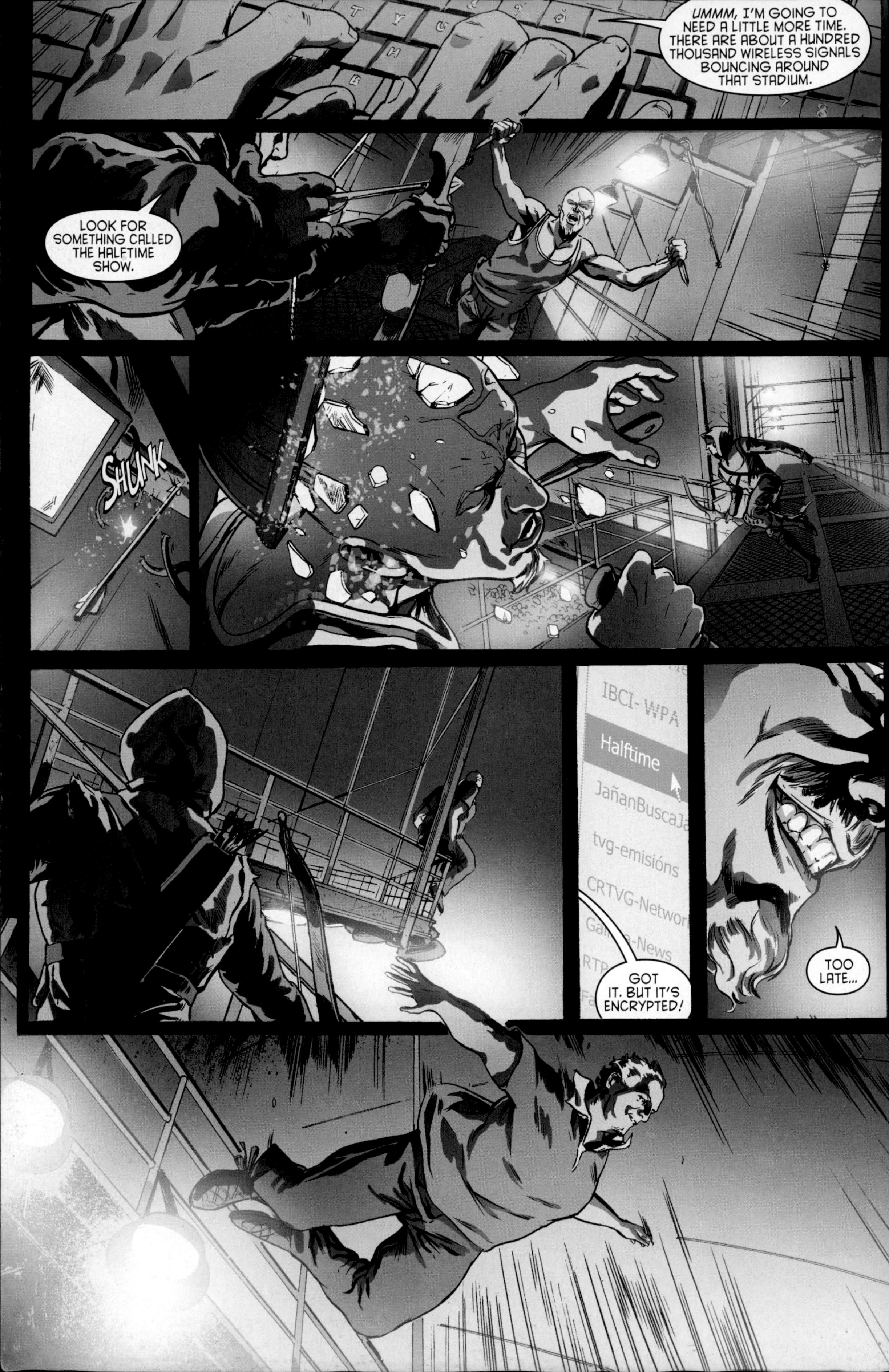
UMMM, I'M GOING TO NEED A LITTLE MORE TIME. THERE ARE ABOUT A HUNDRED THOUSAND WIRELESS SIGNALS BOUNCING AROUND THAT STADIUM.
LOOK FOR SOMETHING CALLED THE HALFTIME SHOW.
SHUNK
IBCI-WPA
Halftime
JañanBuscaJa
tvg-emisións
CRTVG-Network
-News
GOT IT. BUT IT'S ENCRYPTED!
TOO LATE...

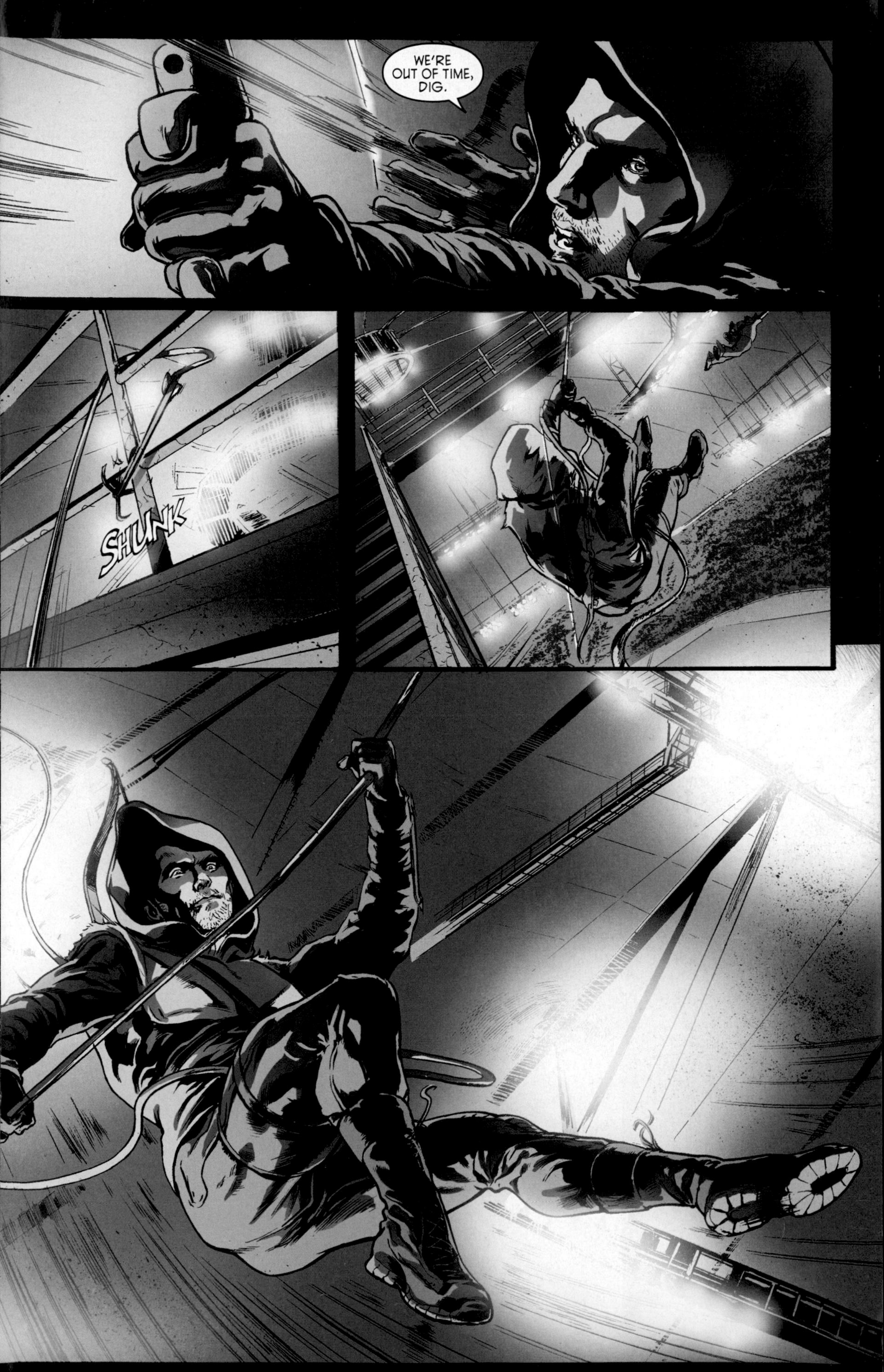
WE'RE OUT OF TIME, DIG.
SHUNK

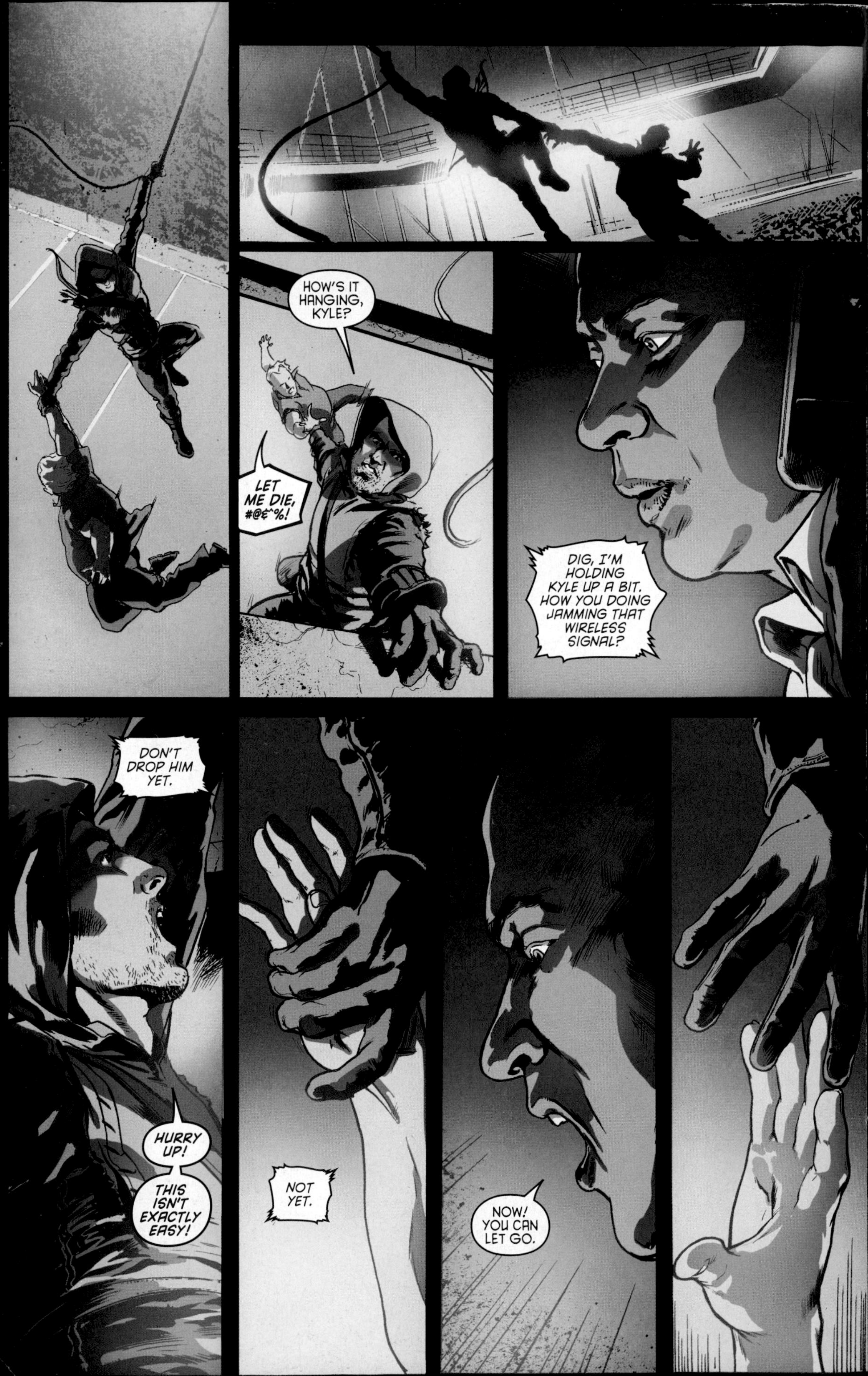

HOW'S IT HANGING, KYLE?
LET ME DIE, #@¢^%!
DIG, I'M HOLDING KYLE UP A BIT. HOW YOU DOING JAMMING THAT WIRELESS SIGNAL?
DON'T DROP HIM YET.
HURRY UP!
THIS ISN'T EXACTLY EASY!
NOT YET.
NOW! YOU CAN LET GO.

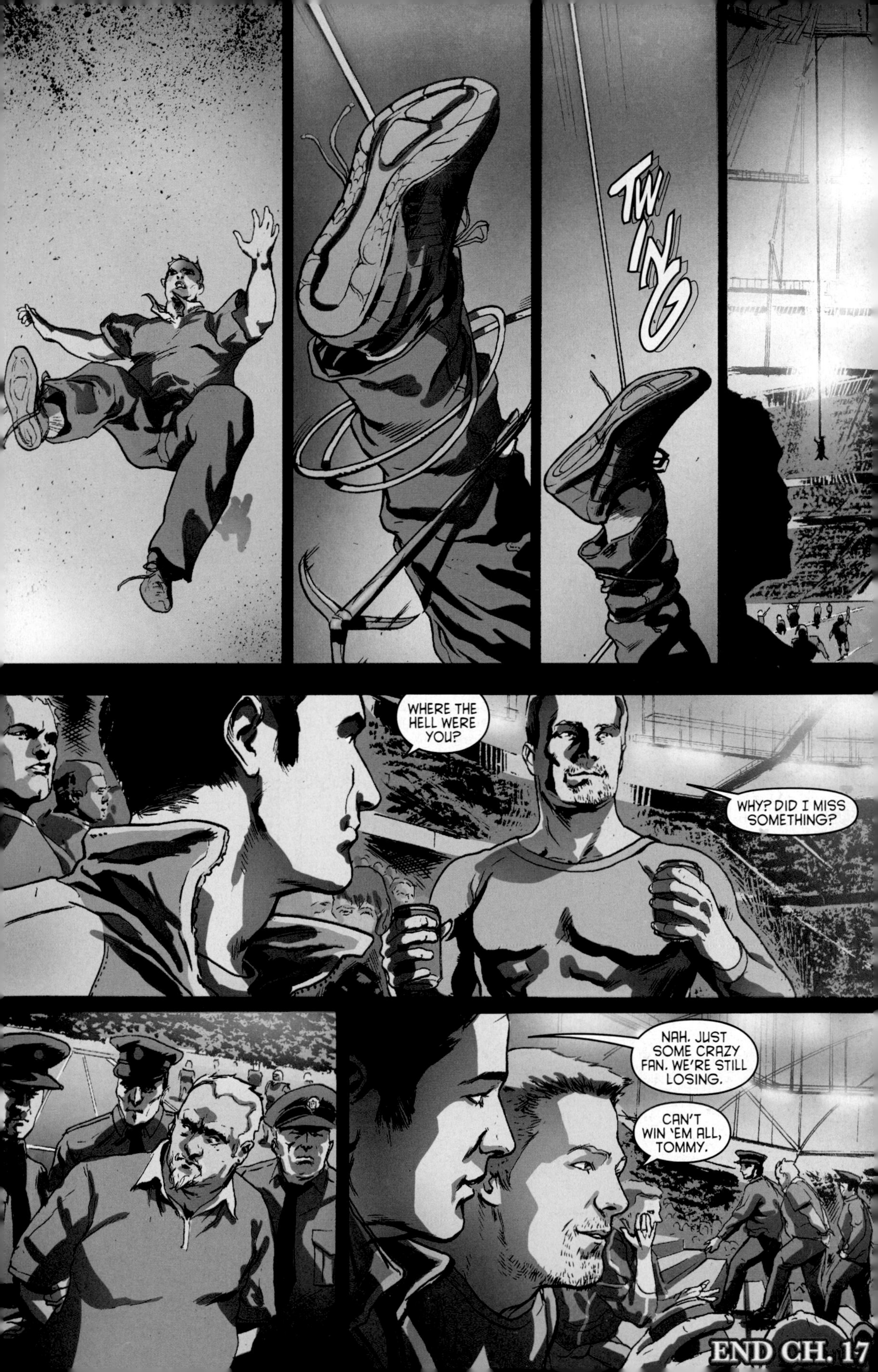
TWING
WHERE THE HELL WERE YOU?
WHY? DID I MISS SOMETHING?
NAH. JUST SOME CRAZY FAN. WE'RE STILL LOSING.
CAN'T WIN 'EM ALL, TOMMY.
END CH. 17

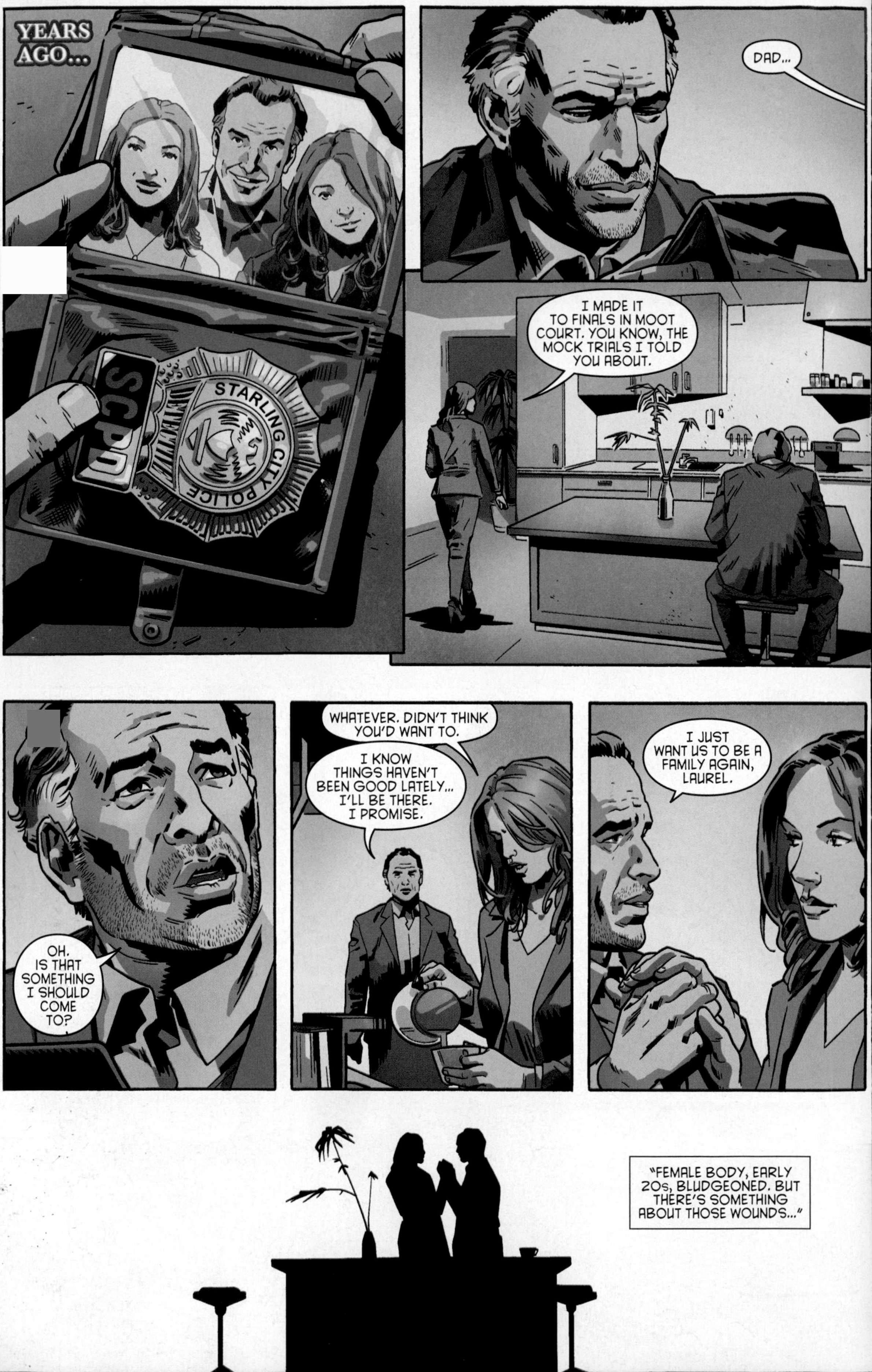
YEARS AGO...
SCPD
STARLING CITY POLICE
DAD...
I MADE IT TO FINALS IN MOOT COURT. YOU KNOW, THE MOCK TRIALS I TOLD YOU ABOUT.
OH. IS THAT SOMETHING I SHOULD COME TO?
WHATEVER. DIDN'T THINK YOU'D WANT TO.
I KNOW THINGS HAVEN'T BEEN GOOD LATELY... I'LL BE THERE. I PROMISE.
I JUST WANT US TO BE A FAMILY AGAIN, LAUREL.
"FEMALE BODY, EARLY 20s, BLUDGEONED. BUT THERE'S SOMETHING ABOUT THOSE WOUNDS..."

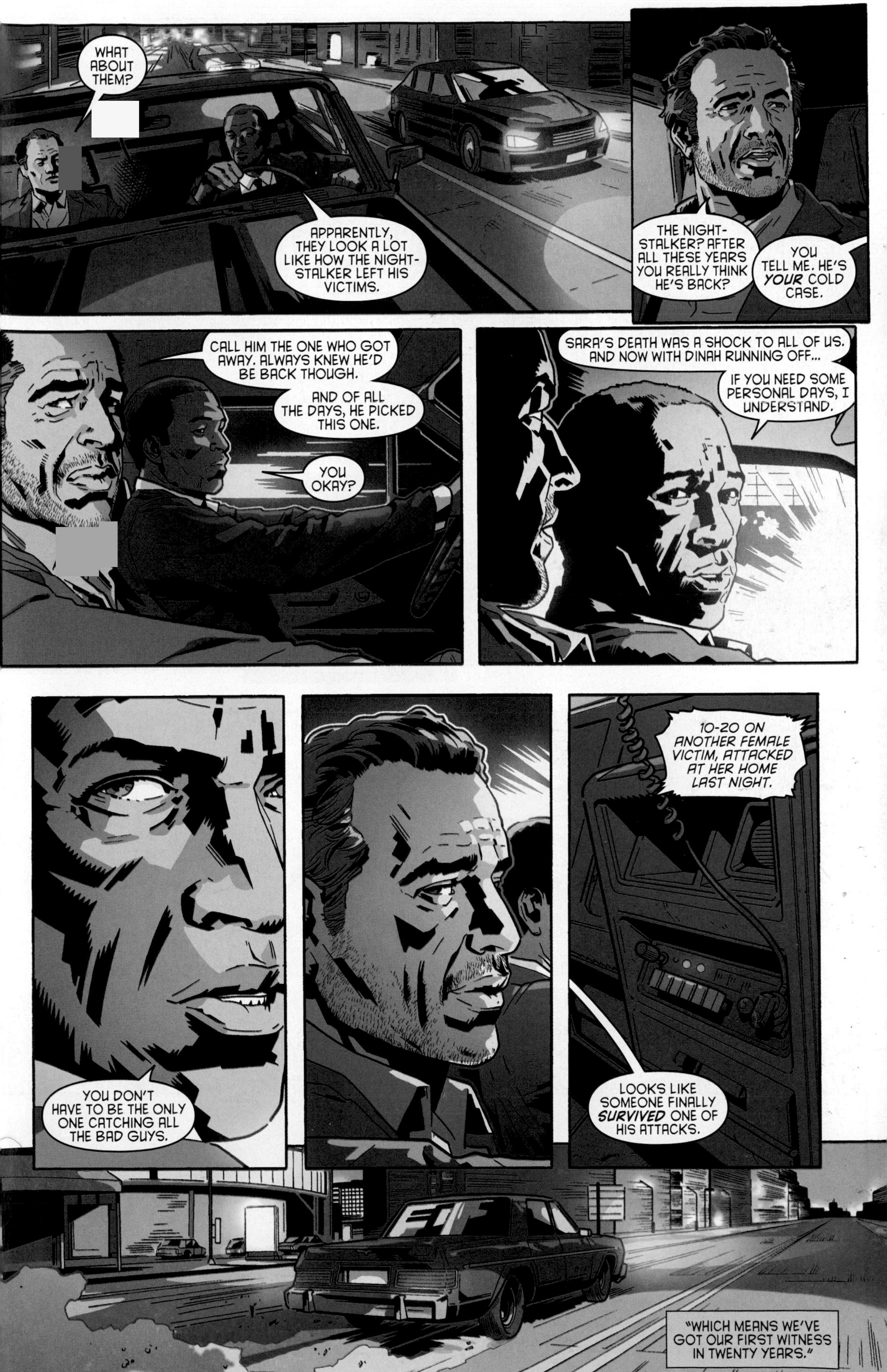
WHAT ABOUT THEM?
APPARENTLY, THEY LOOK A LOT LIKE HOW THE NIGHT-STALKER LEFT HIS VICTIMS.
THE NIGHT-STALKER? AFTER ALL THESE YEARS YOU REALLY THINK HE'S BACK?
YOU TELL ME. HE'S *YOUR* COLD CASE.
CALL HIM THE ONE WHO GOT AWAY. ALWAYS KNEW HE'D BE BACK THOUGH.
AND OF ALL THE DAYS, HE PICKED THIS ONE.
YOU OKAY?
SARA'S DEATH WAS A SHOCK TO ALL OF US. AND NOW WITH DINAH RUNNING OFF...
IF YOU NEED SOME PERSONAL DAYS, I UNDERSTAND.
YOU DON'T HAVE TO BE THE ONLY ONE CATCHING ALL THE BAD GUYS.
10-20 ON ANOTHER FEMALE VICTIM, ATTACKED AT HER HOME LAST NIGHT.
LOOKS LIKE SOMEONE FINALLY *SURVIVED* ONE OF HIS ATTACKS.
"WHICH MEANS WE'VE GOT OUR FIRST WITNESS IN TWENTY YEARS."

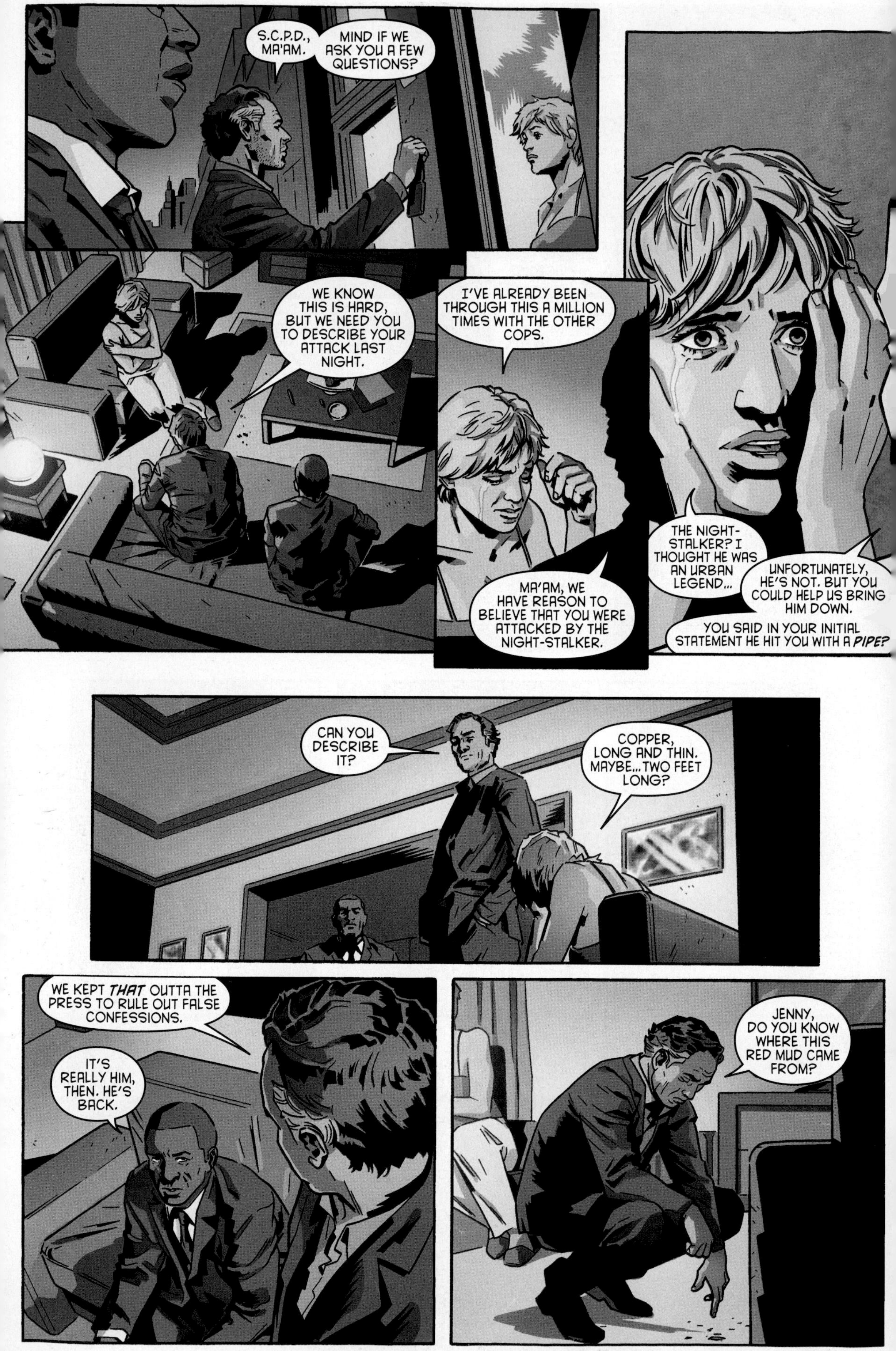
S.C.P.D., MA'AM.
MIND IF WE ASK YOU A FEW QUESTIONS?
WE KNOW THIS IS HARD, BUT WE NEED YOU TO DESCRIBE YOUR ATTACK LAST NIGHT.
I'VE ALREADY BEEN THROUGH THIS A MILLION TIMES WITH THE OTHER COPS.
MA'AM, WE HAVE REASON TO BELIEVE THAT YOU WERE ATTACKED BY THE NIGHT-STALKER.
THE NIGHT-STALKER? I THOUGHT HE WAS AN URBAN LEGEND...
UNFORTUNATELY, HE'S NOT. BUT YOU COULD HELP US BRING HIM DOWN.
YOU SAID IN YOUR INITIAL STATEMENT HE HIT YOU WITH A *PIPE?*
CAN YOU DESCRIBE IT?
COPPER, LONG AND THIN. MAYBE...TWO FEET LONG?
WE KEPT *THAT* OUTTA THE PRESS TO RULE OUT FALSE CONFESSIONS.
IT'S REALLY HIM, THEN. HE'S BACK.
JENNY, DO YOU KNOW WHERE THIS RED MUD CAME FROM?

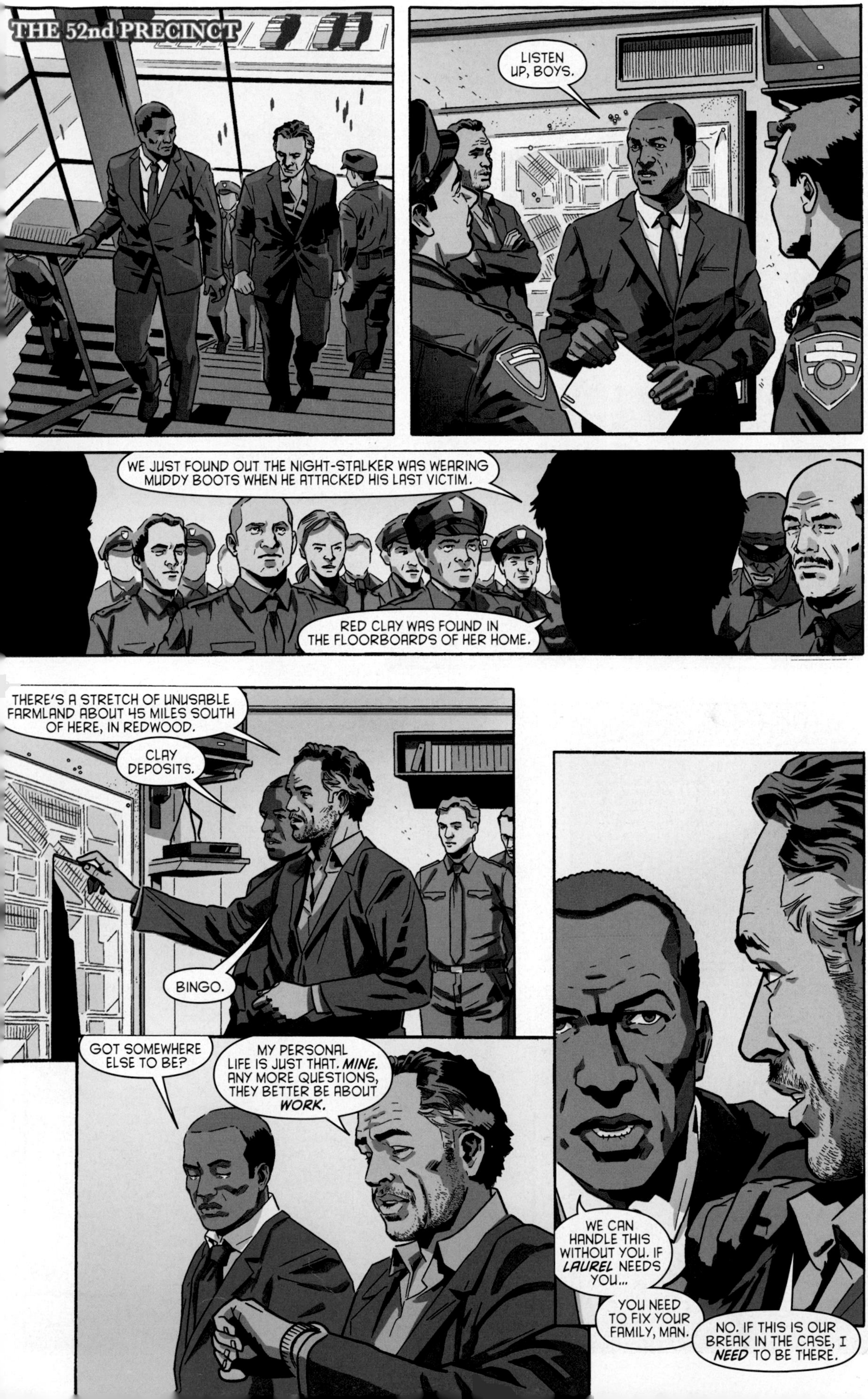
THE 52nd PRECINCT
LISTEN UP, BOYS.
WE JUST FOUND OUT THE NIGHT-STALKER WAS WEARING MUDDY BOOTS WHEN HE ATTACKED HIS LAST VICTIM.
RED CLAY WAS FOUND IN THE FLOORBOARDS OF HER HOME.
THERE'S A STRETCH OF UNUSABLE FARMLAND ABOUT 45 MILES SOUTH OF HERE, IN REDWOOD.
CLAY DEPOSITS.
BINGO.
GOT SOMEWHERE ELSE TO BE?
MY PERSONAL LIFE IS JUST THAT. *MINE.* ANY MORE QUESTIONS, THEY BETTER BE ABOUT *WORK.*
WE CAN HANDLE THIS WITHOUT YOU. IF *LAUREL* NEEDS YOU...
YOU NEED TO FIX YOUR FAMILY, MAN.
NO. IF THIS IS OUR BREAK IN THE CASE, I *NEED* TO BE THERE.

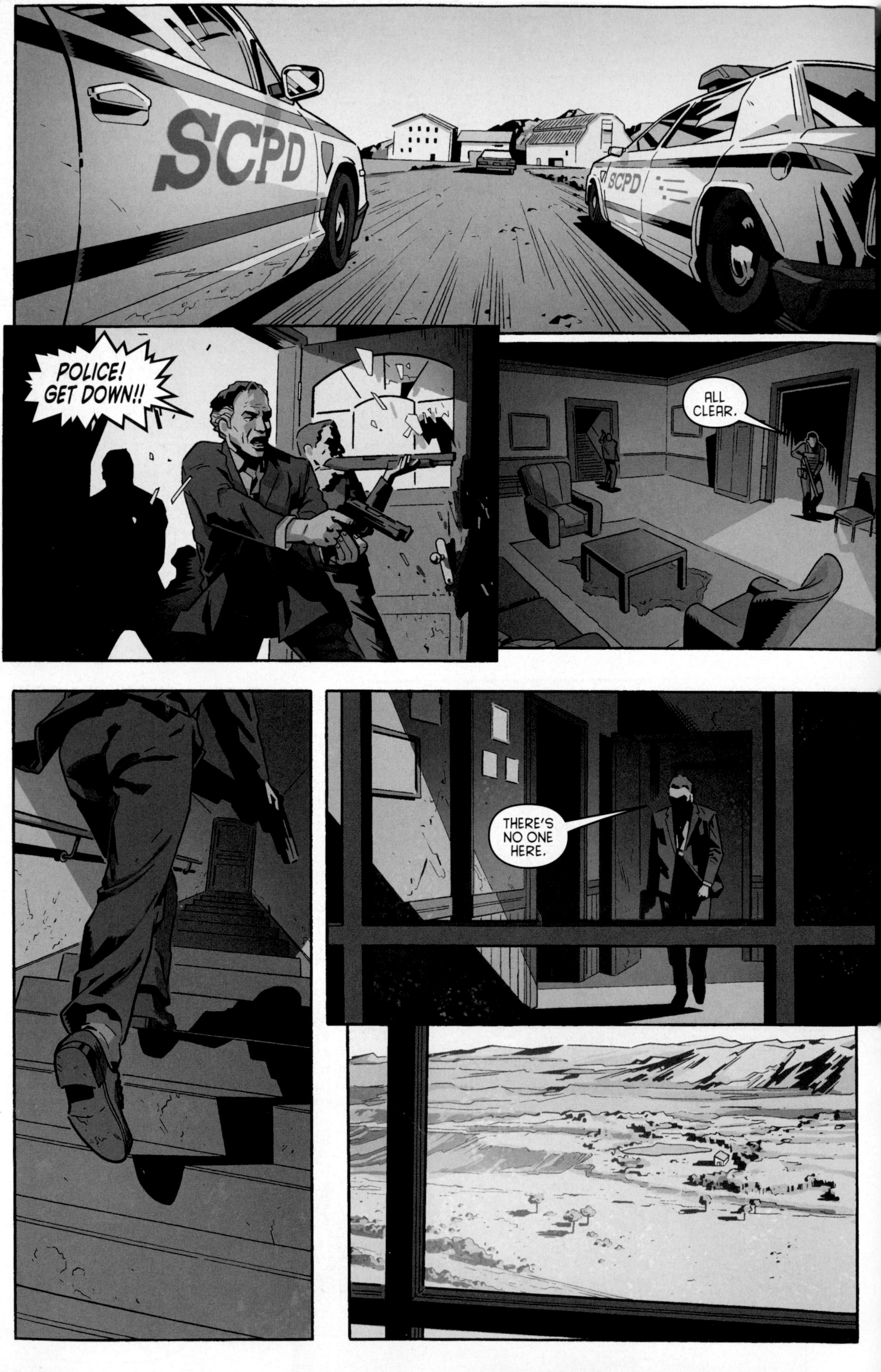
SCPD
SCPD
POLICE! GET DOWN!!
ALL CLEAR.
THERE'S NO ONE HERE.

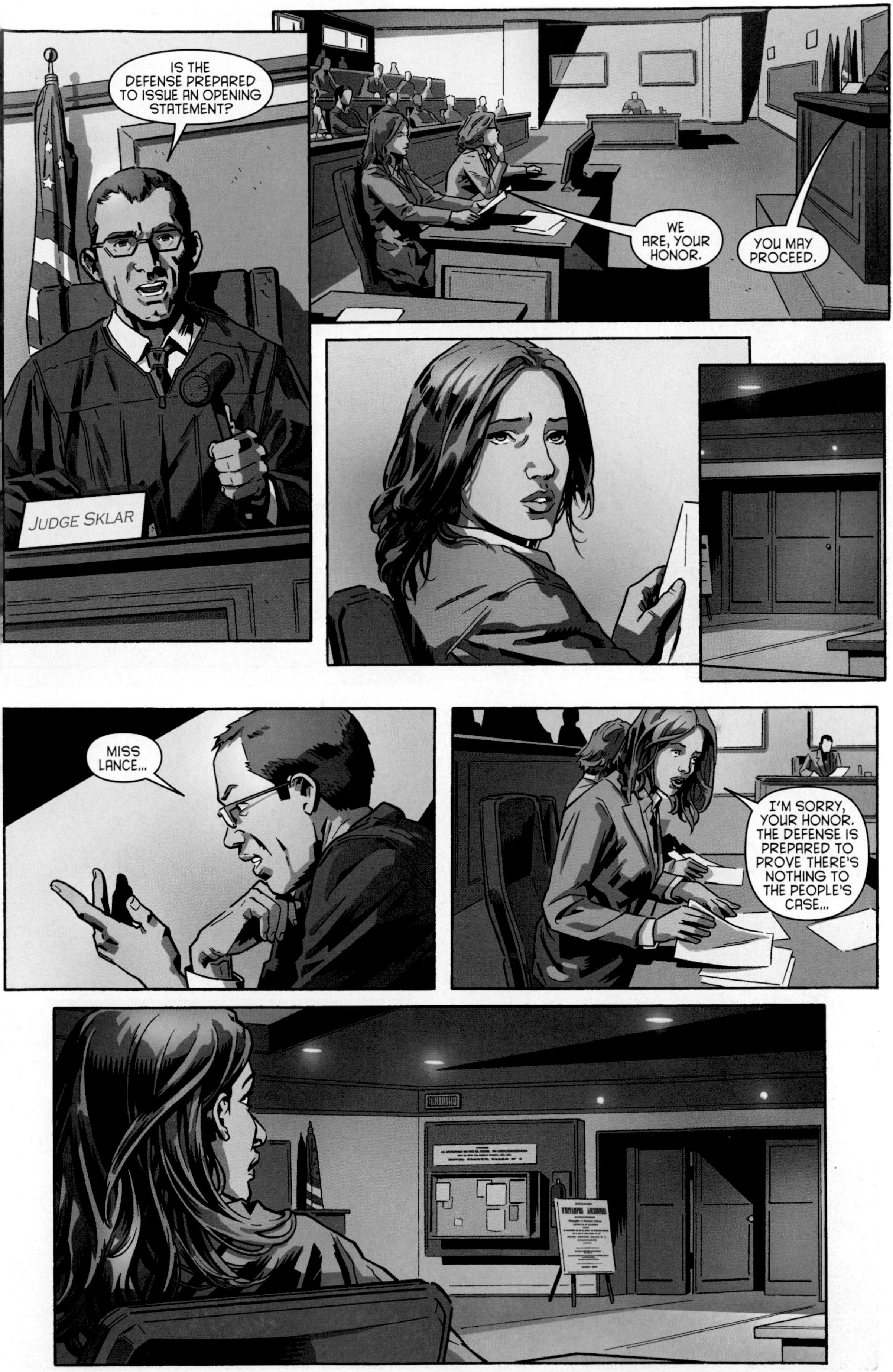
IS THE DEFENSE PREPARED TO ISSUE AN OPENING STATEMENT?
JUDGE SKLAR
WE ARE, YOUR HONOR.
YOU MAY PROCEED.
MISS LANCE...
I'M SORRY, YOUR HONOR. THE DEFENSE IS PREPARED TO PROVE THERE'S NOTHING TO THE PEOPLE'S CASE...

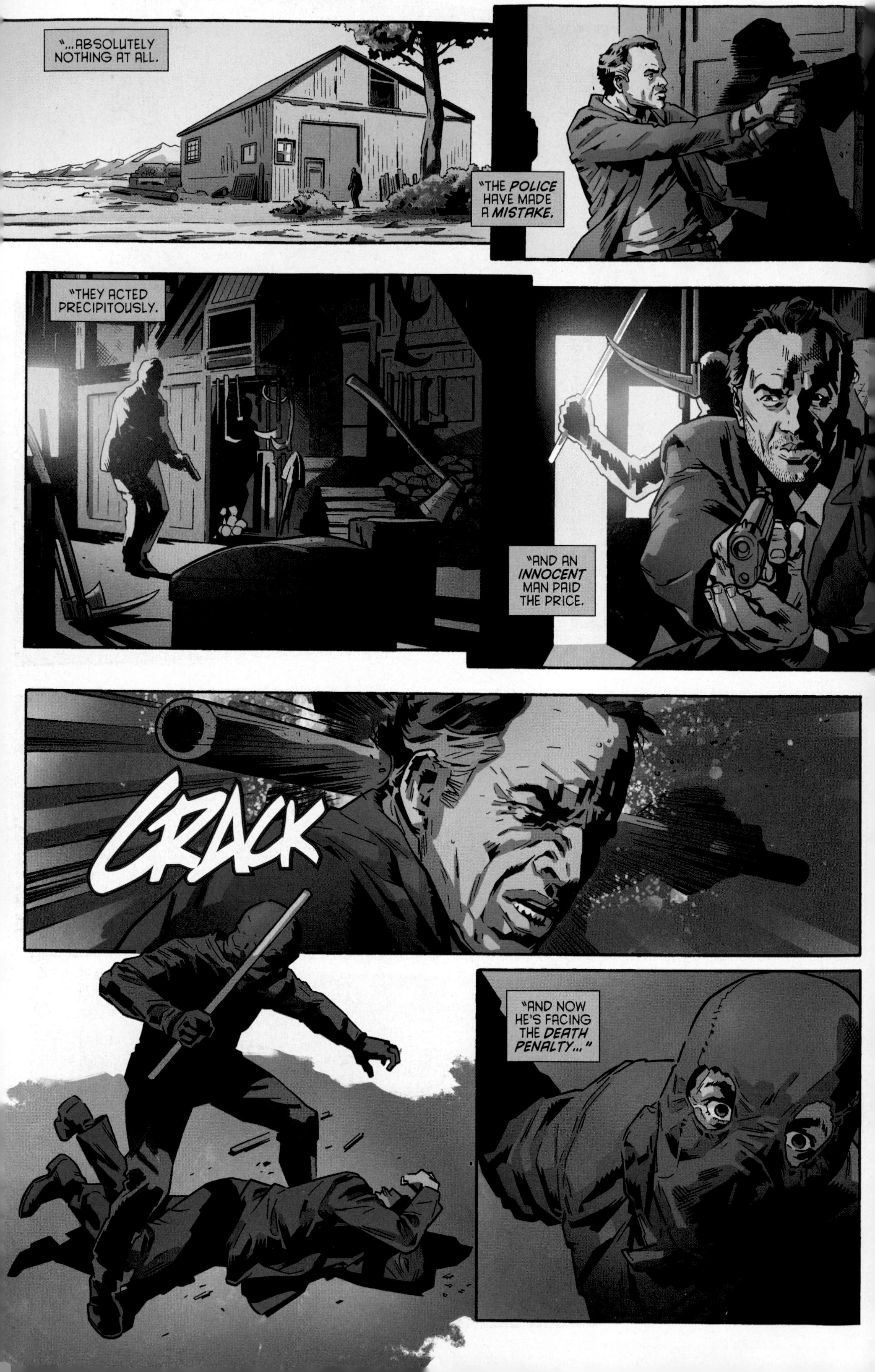
"...ABSOLUTELY NOTHING AT ALL.
"THE POLICE HAVE MADE A MISTAKE.
"THEY ACTED PRECIPITOUSLY.
"AND AN INNOCENT MAN PAID THE PRICE.
CRACK
"AND NOW HE'S FACING THE DEATH PENALTY..."

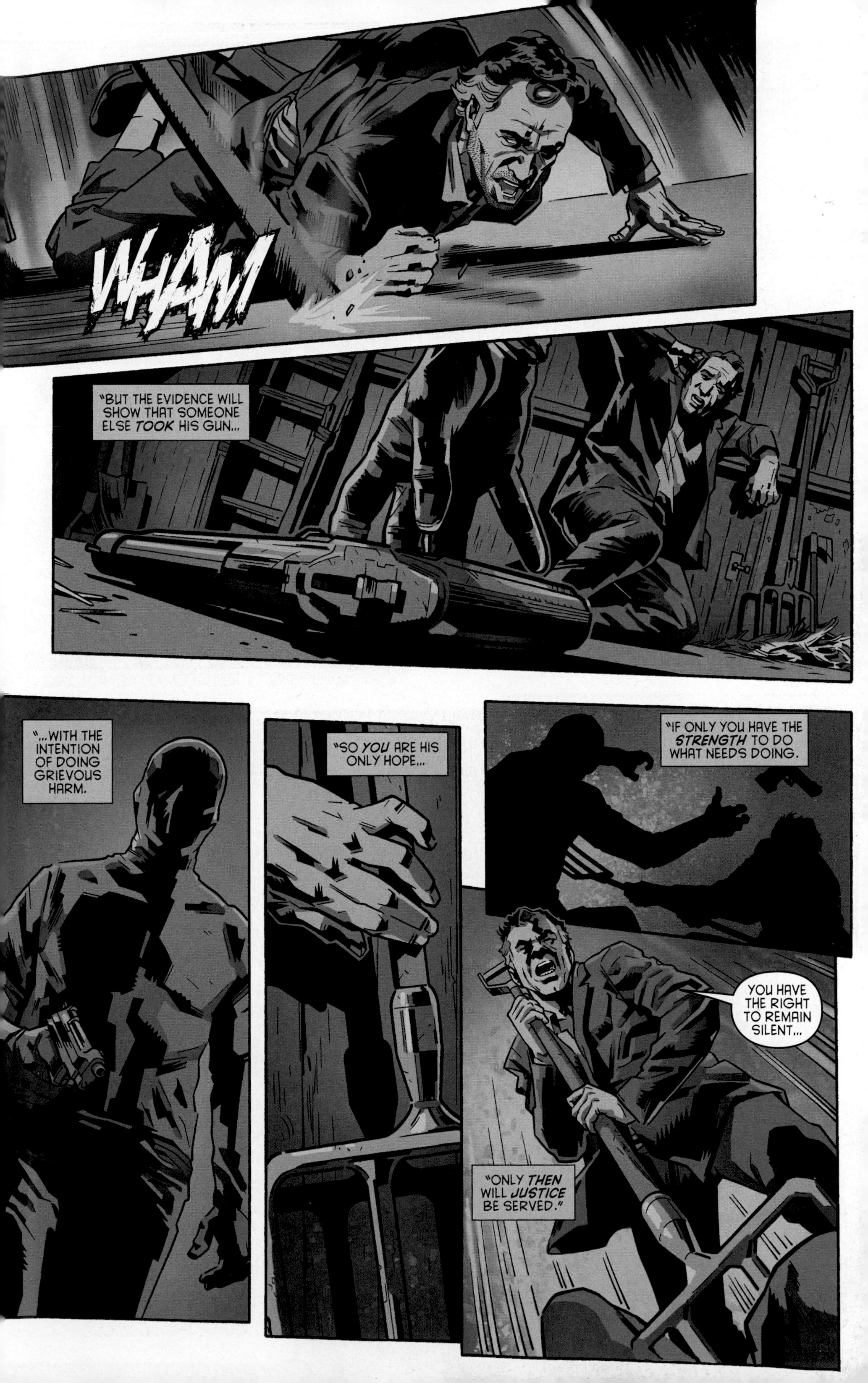
WHAM
"BUT THE EVIDENCE WILL SHOW THAT SOMEONE ELSE *TOOK* HIS GUN...
"...WITH THE INTENTION OF DOING GRIEVOUS HARM.
"SO *YOU* ARE HIS ONLY HOPE...
"IF ONLY YOU HAVE THE *STRENGTH* TO DO WHAT NEEDS DOING.
YOU HAVE THE RIGHT TO REMAIN SILENT...
"ONLY *THEN* WILL *JUSTICE* BE SERVED."

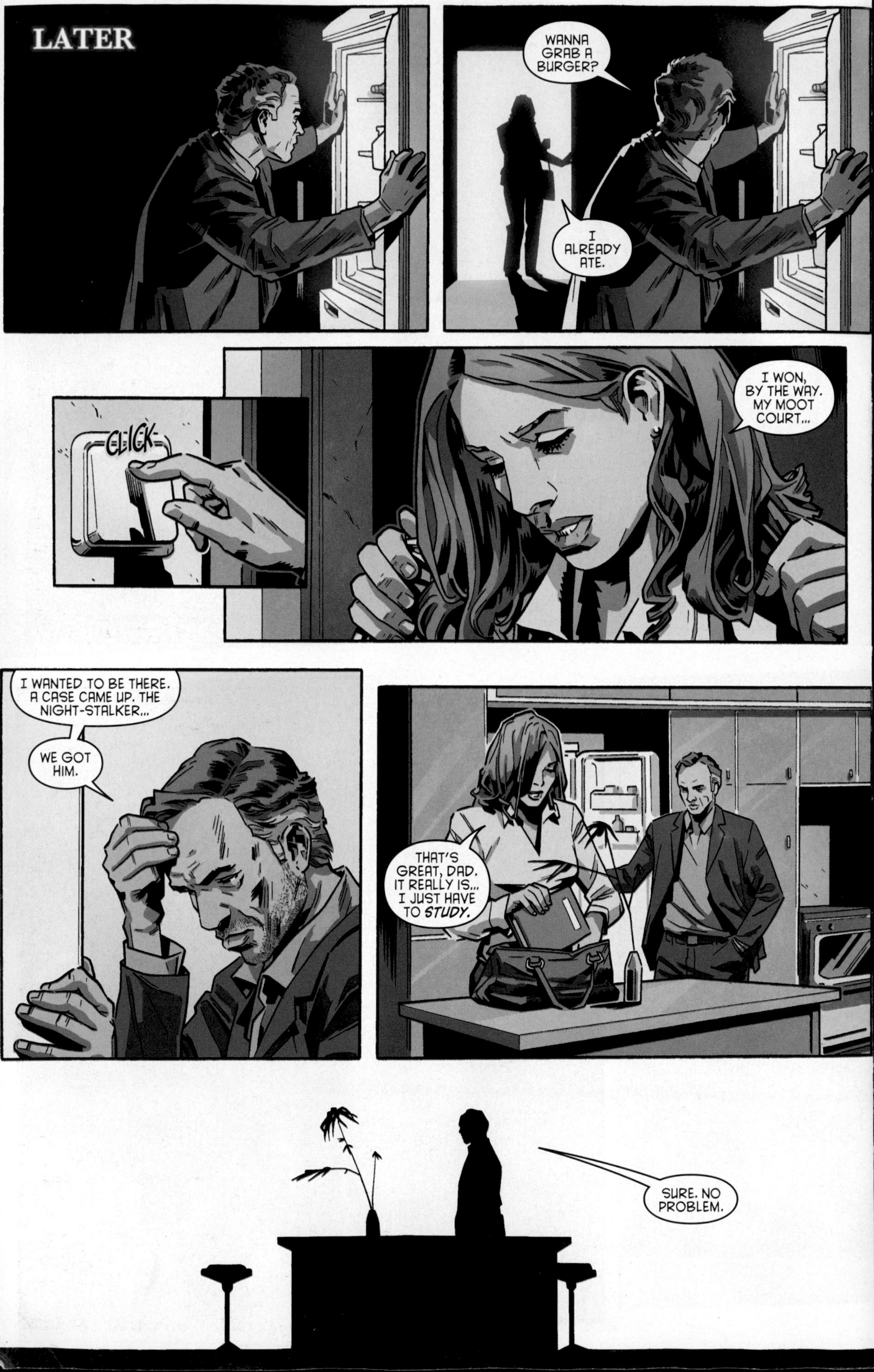
LATER
WANNA GRAB A BURGER?
I ALREADY ATE.
CLICK
I WON, BY THE WAY. MY MOOT COURT...
I WANTED TO BE THERE. A CASE CAME UP. THE NIGHT-STALKER...
WE GOT HIM.
THAT'S GREAT, DAD. IT REALLY IS... I JUST HAVE TO STUDY.
SURE. NO PROBLEM.

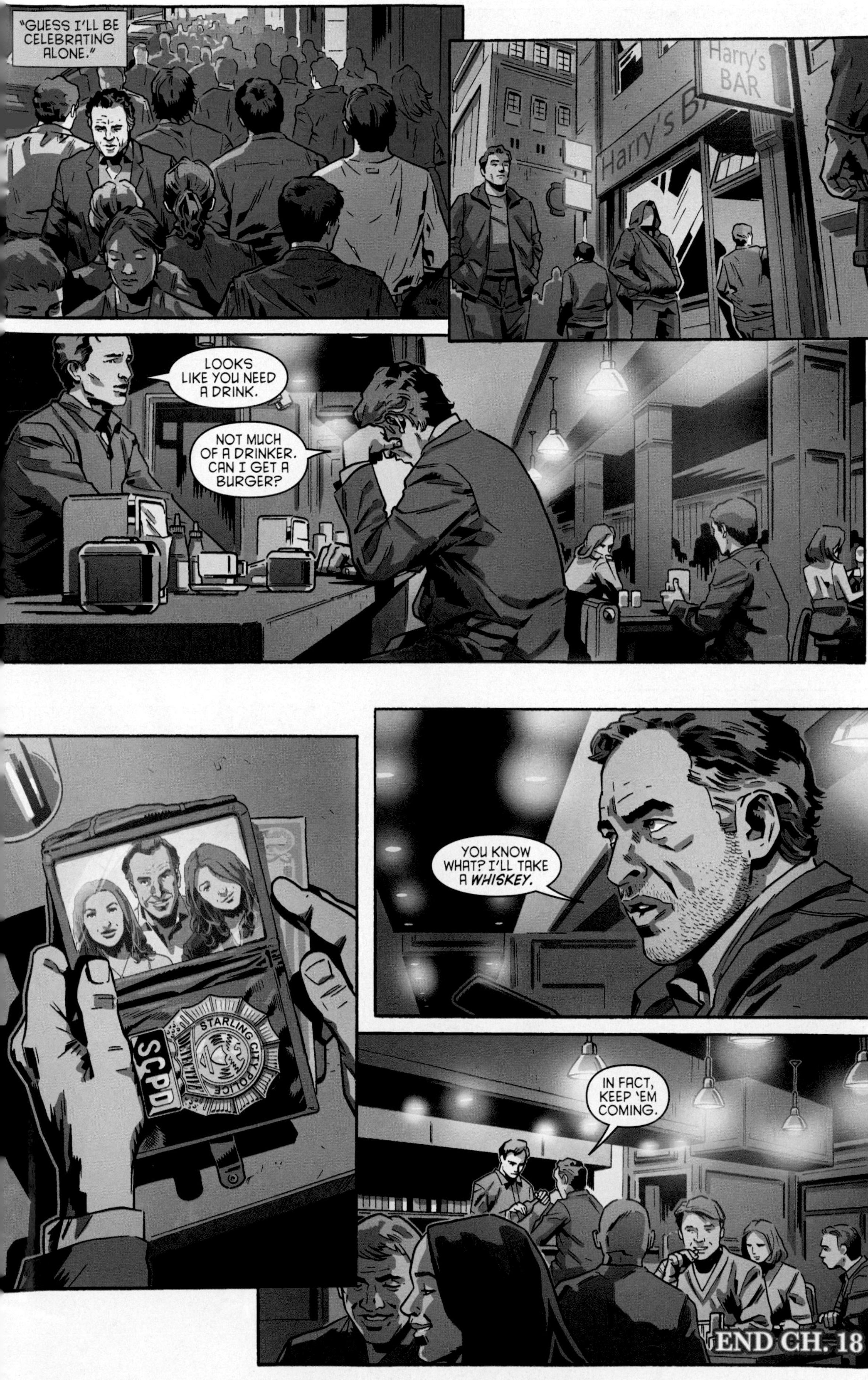
"GUESS I'LL BE CELEBRATING ALONE."
Harry's BAR
LOOKS LIKE YOU NEED A DRINK.
NOT MUCH OF A DRINKER. CAN I GET A BURGER?
SCPD
STARLING CITY POLICE
YOU KNOW WHAT? I'LL TAKE A *WHISKEY*.
IN FACT, KEEP 'EM COMING.
END CH. 18

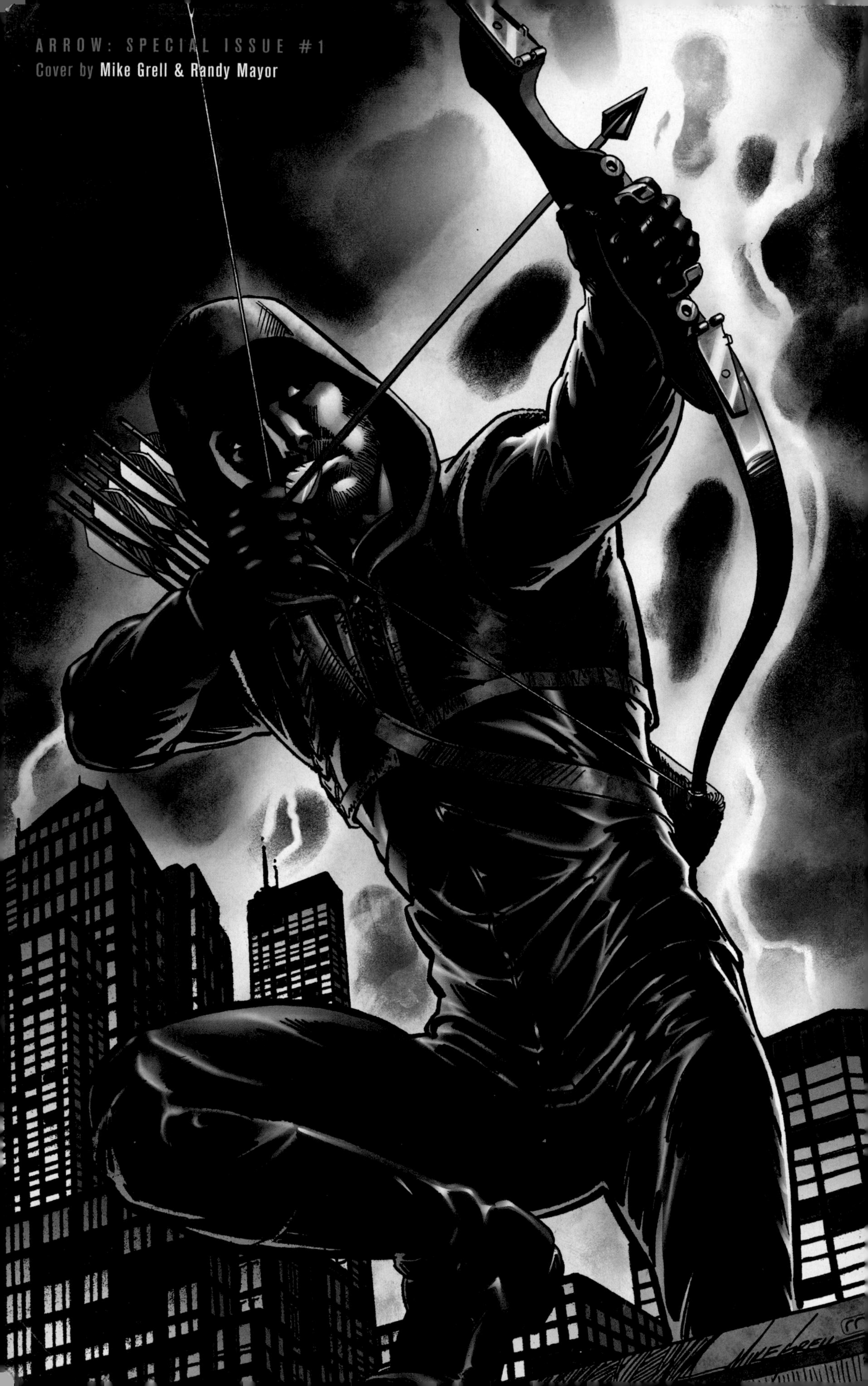

ARROW: SPECIAL ISSUE #1
Cover by **Mike Grell & Randy Mayor**

ARROW #1

Variant cover by **Mike Grell & Randy Mayor**

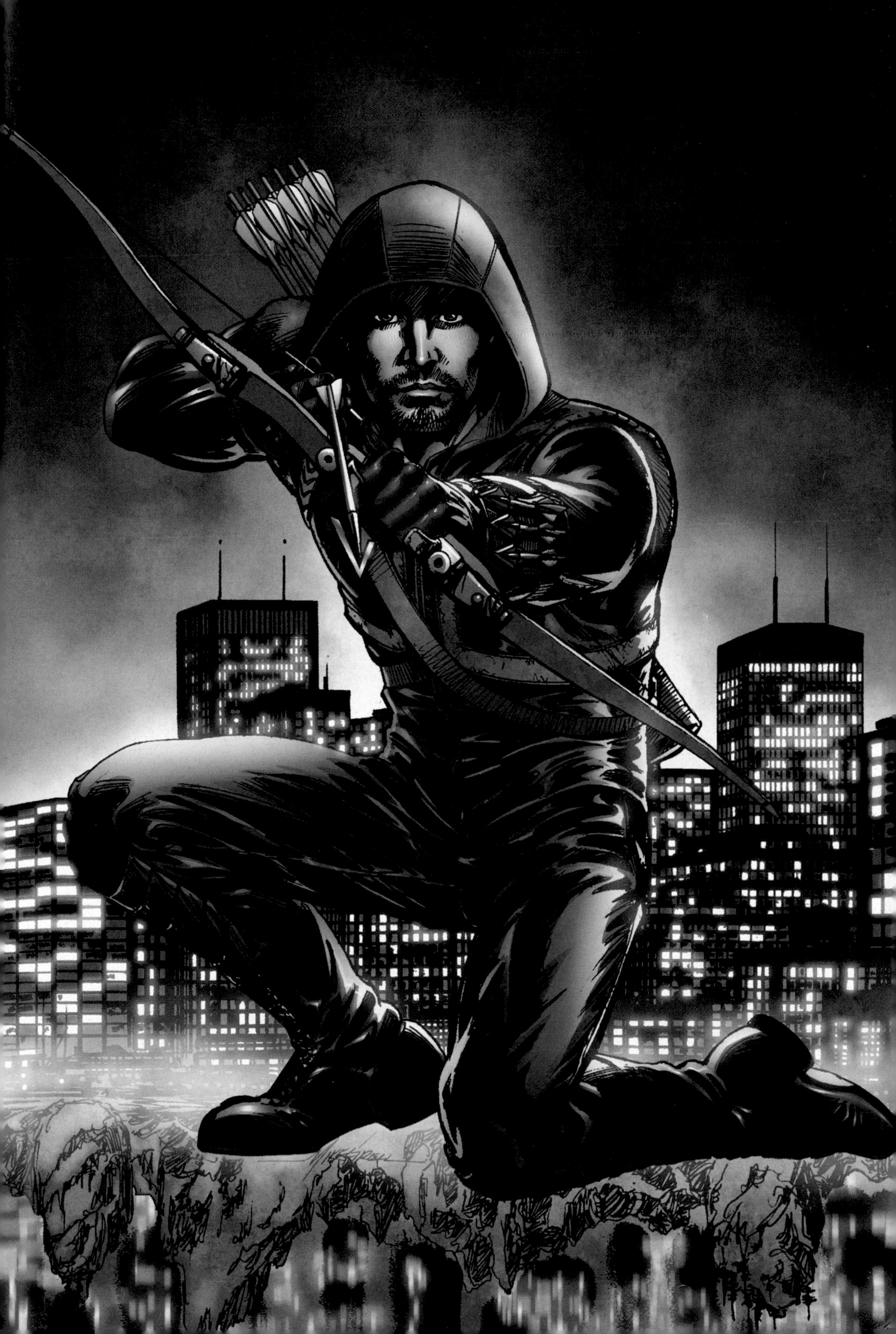

ARROW #2

Cover by Mike Grell & Randy Mayor

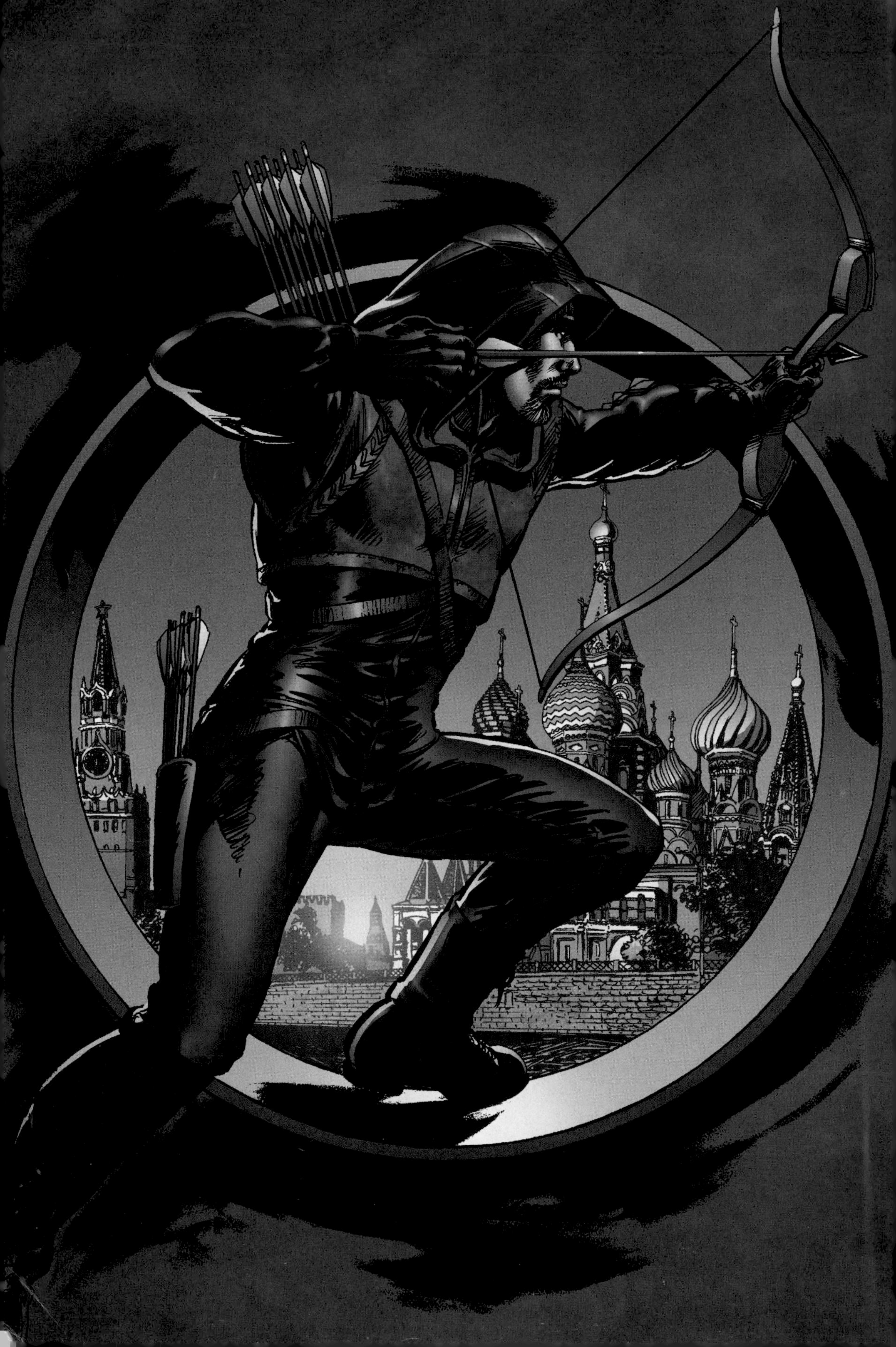

ARROW #3

Cover by **Phil Hester, Eric Gapstur & Randy Mayor**

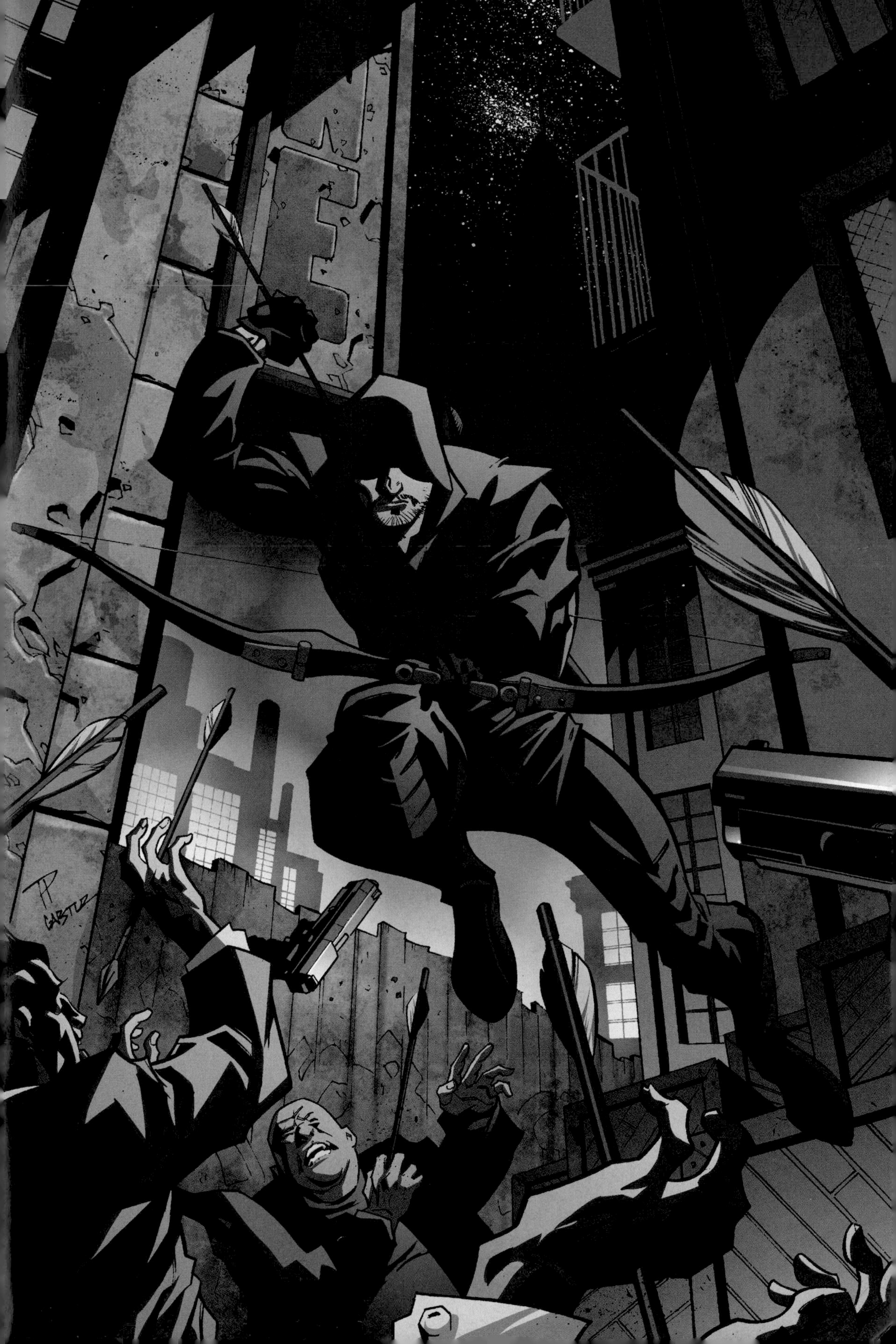

ARROW #4
Cover by
Jason Shawn Alexander & Lee Loughridge

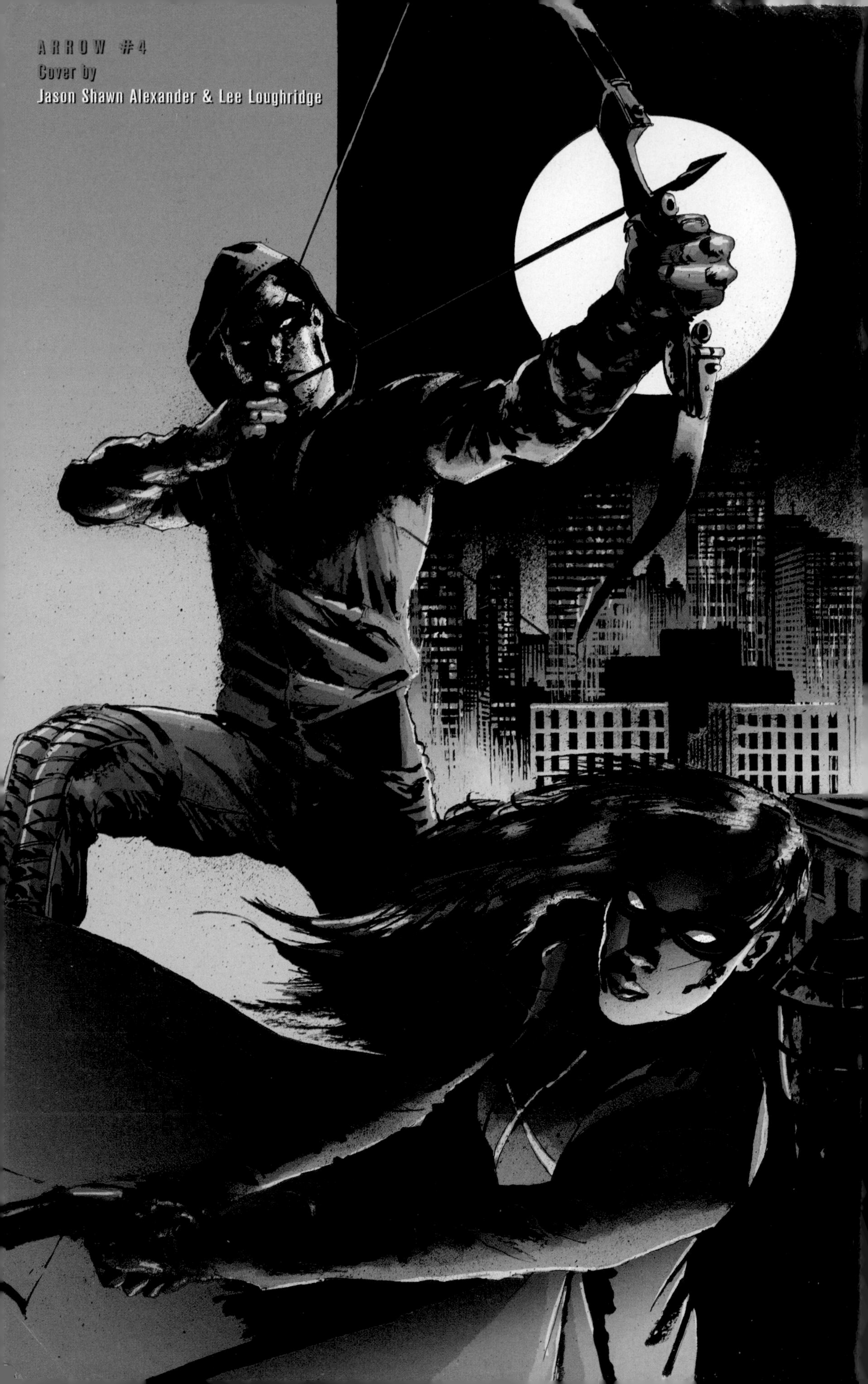

ARROW #5

Cover by Mitch Breitweiser & Elizabeth Breitweiser

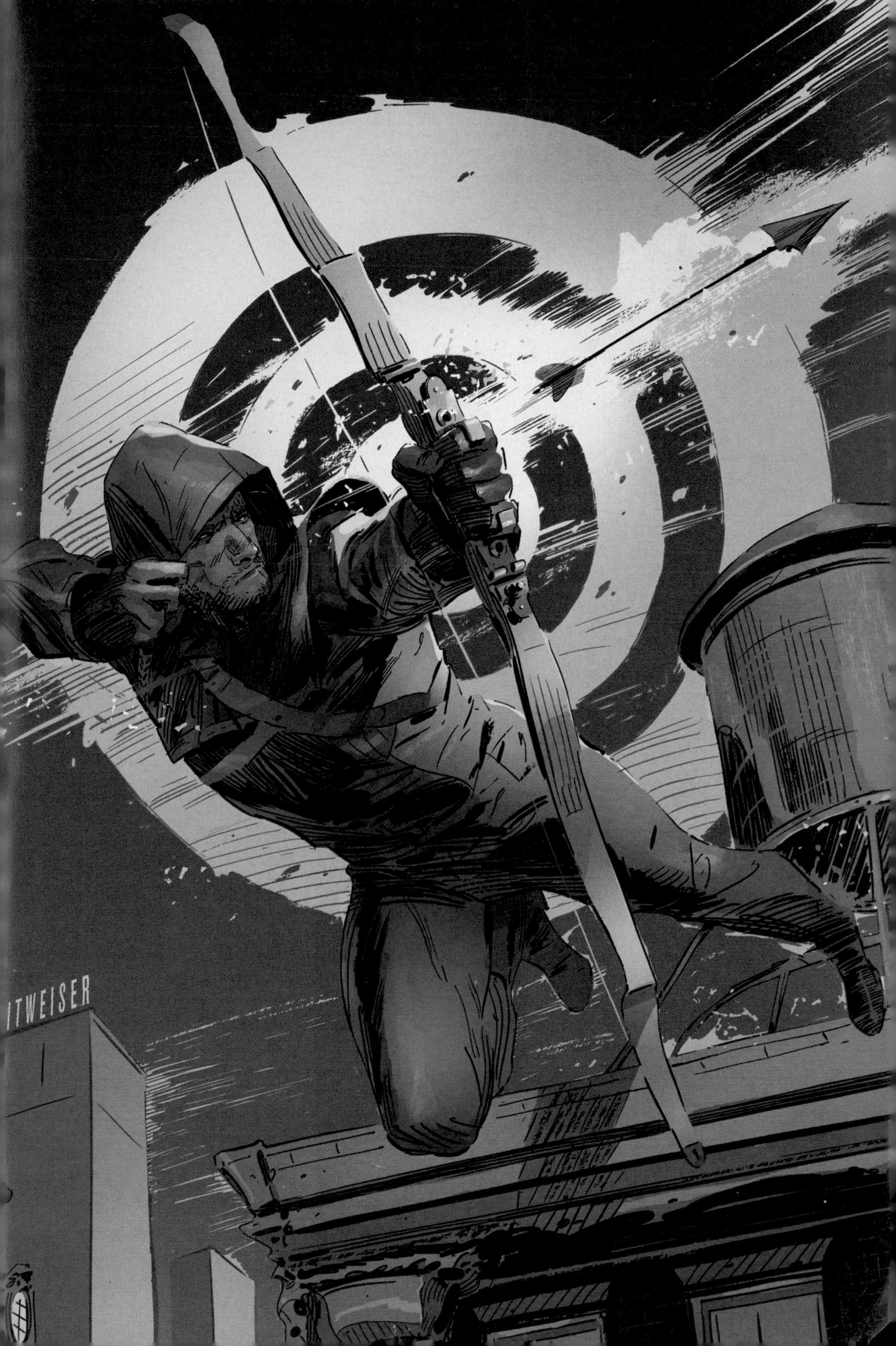

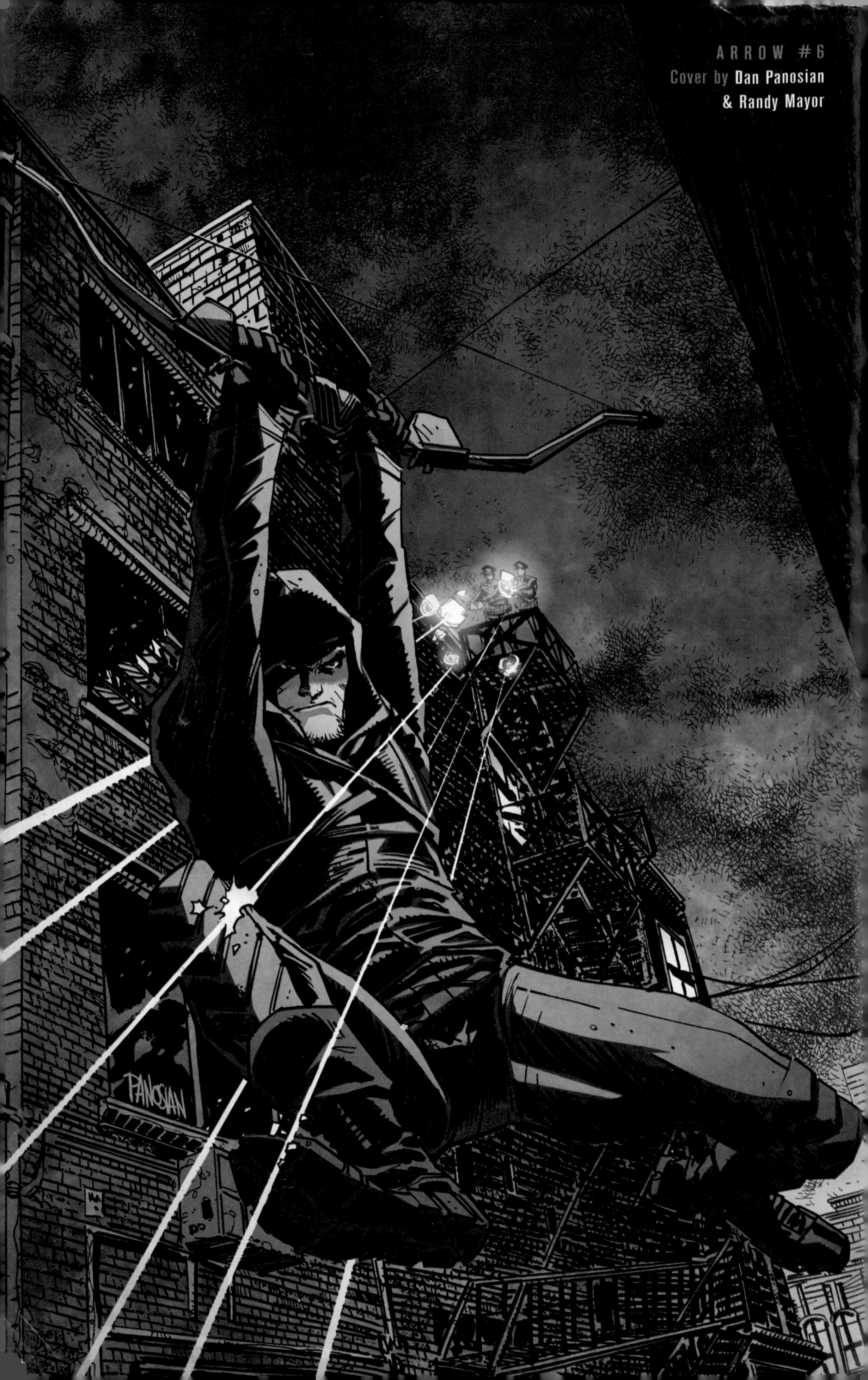
PANOSIAN

ARROW #6
Cover by Dan Panosian
& Randy Mayor

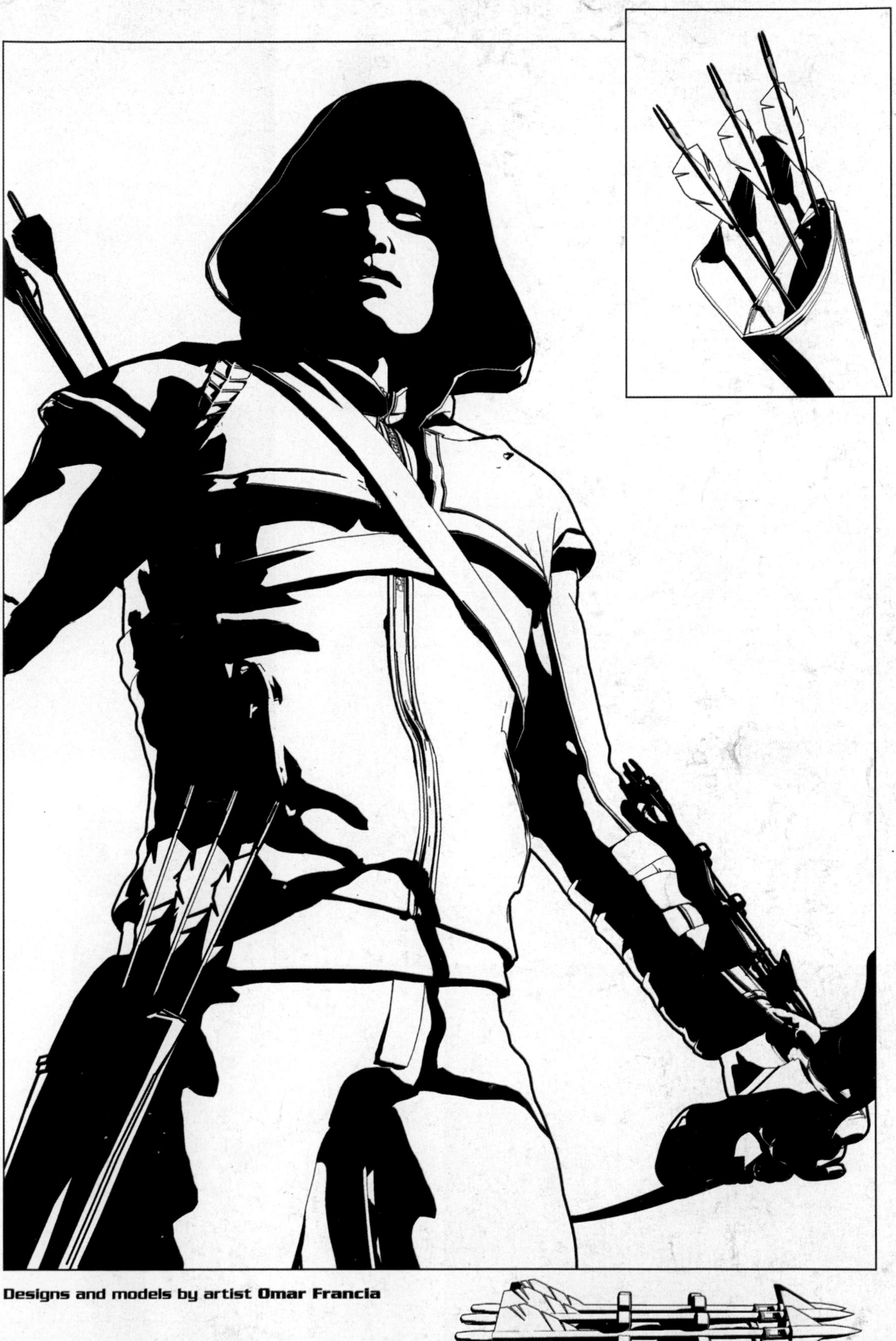

Designs and models by artist Omar Francia

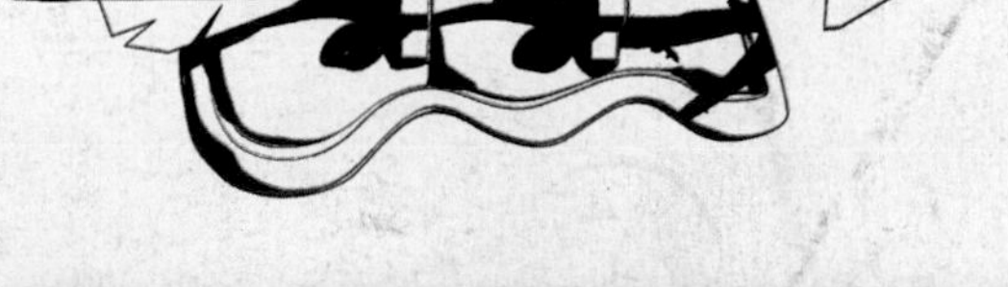

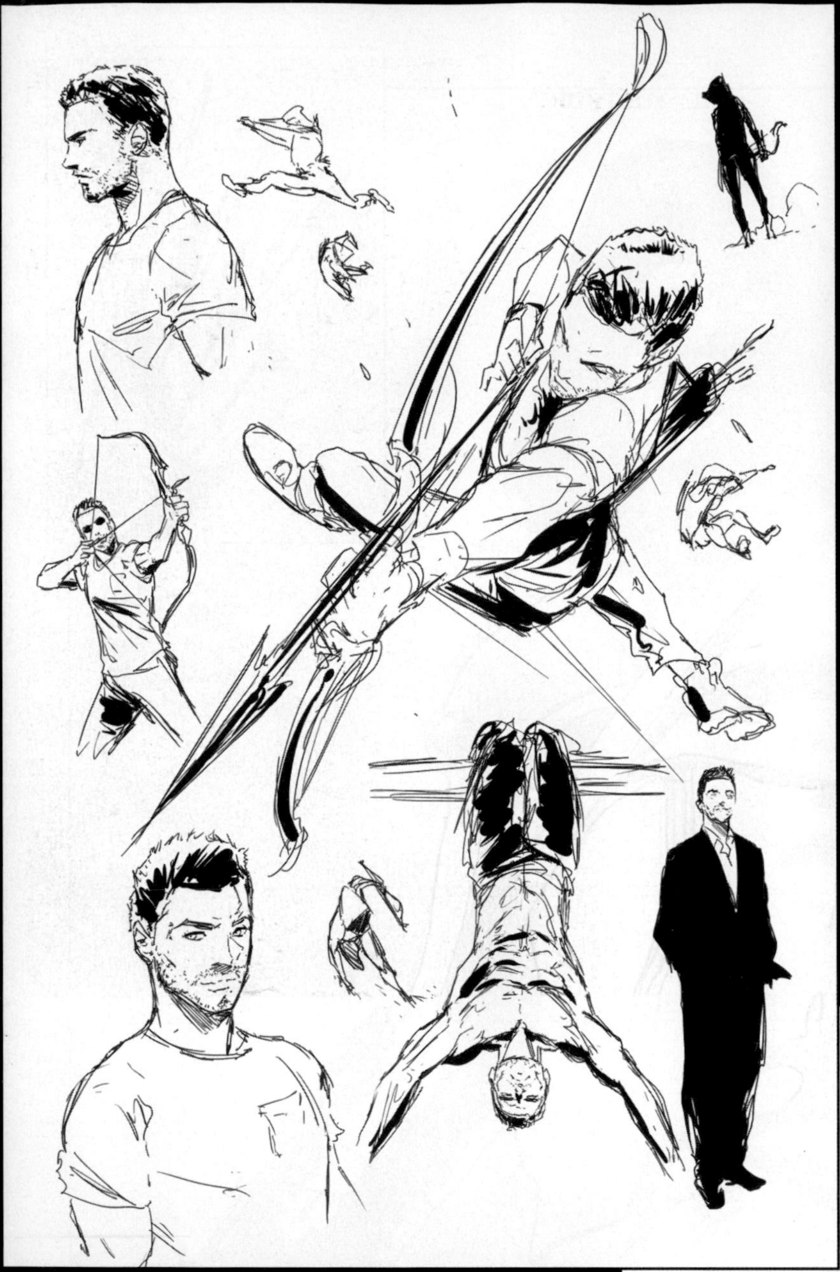

Designs by artist Jorge Jimenez

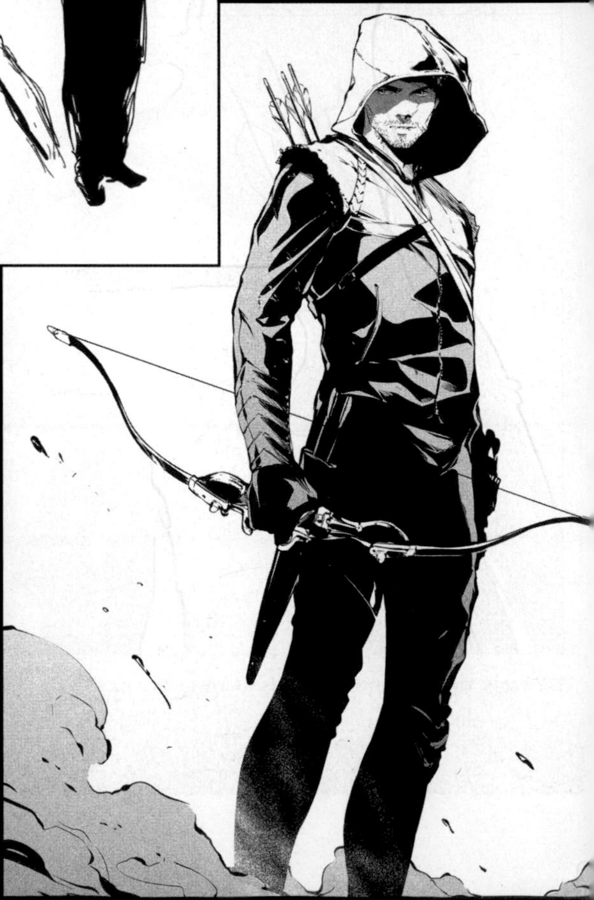

DEATHSTROKE

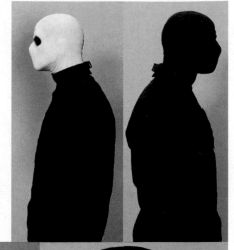

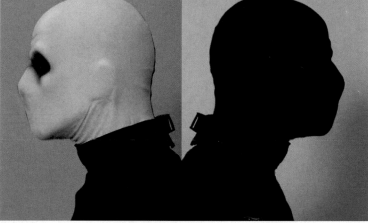

ARROW costume designs

Mask shown
cast to fit
stunt performer

When speaking role
cast a second mask
will be required

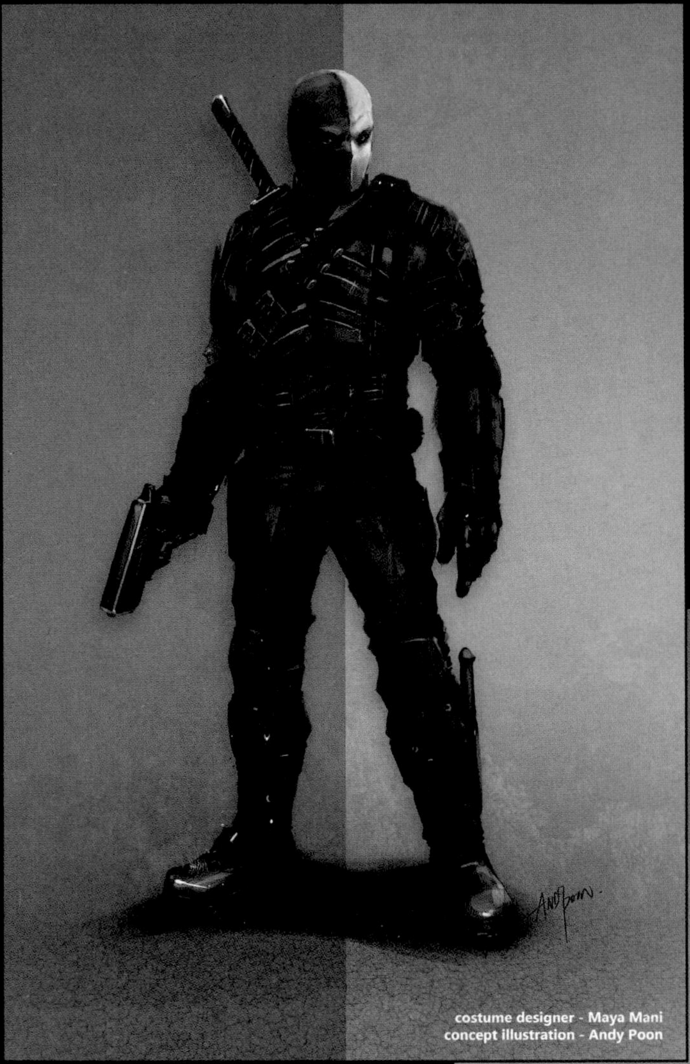

costume designer - Maya Mani
concept illustration - Andy Poon

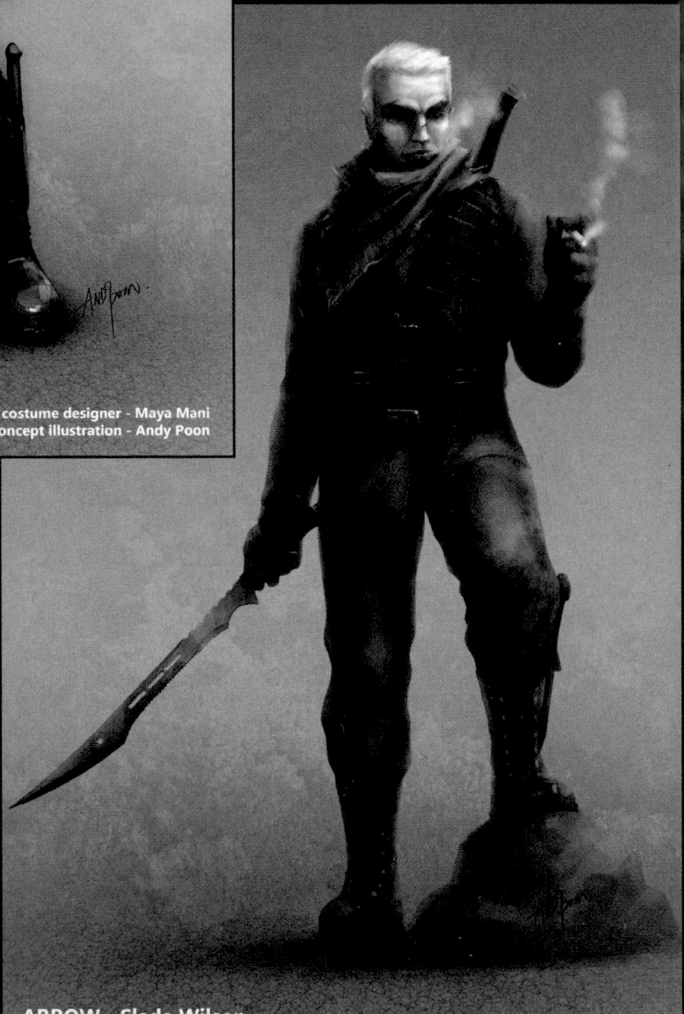

ARROW - Slade Wilson

costume designer - Maya Mani
concept illustration - Andy Poon

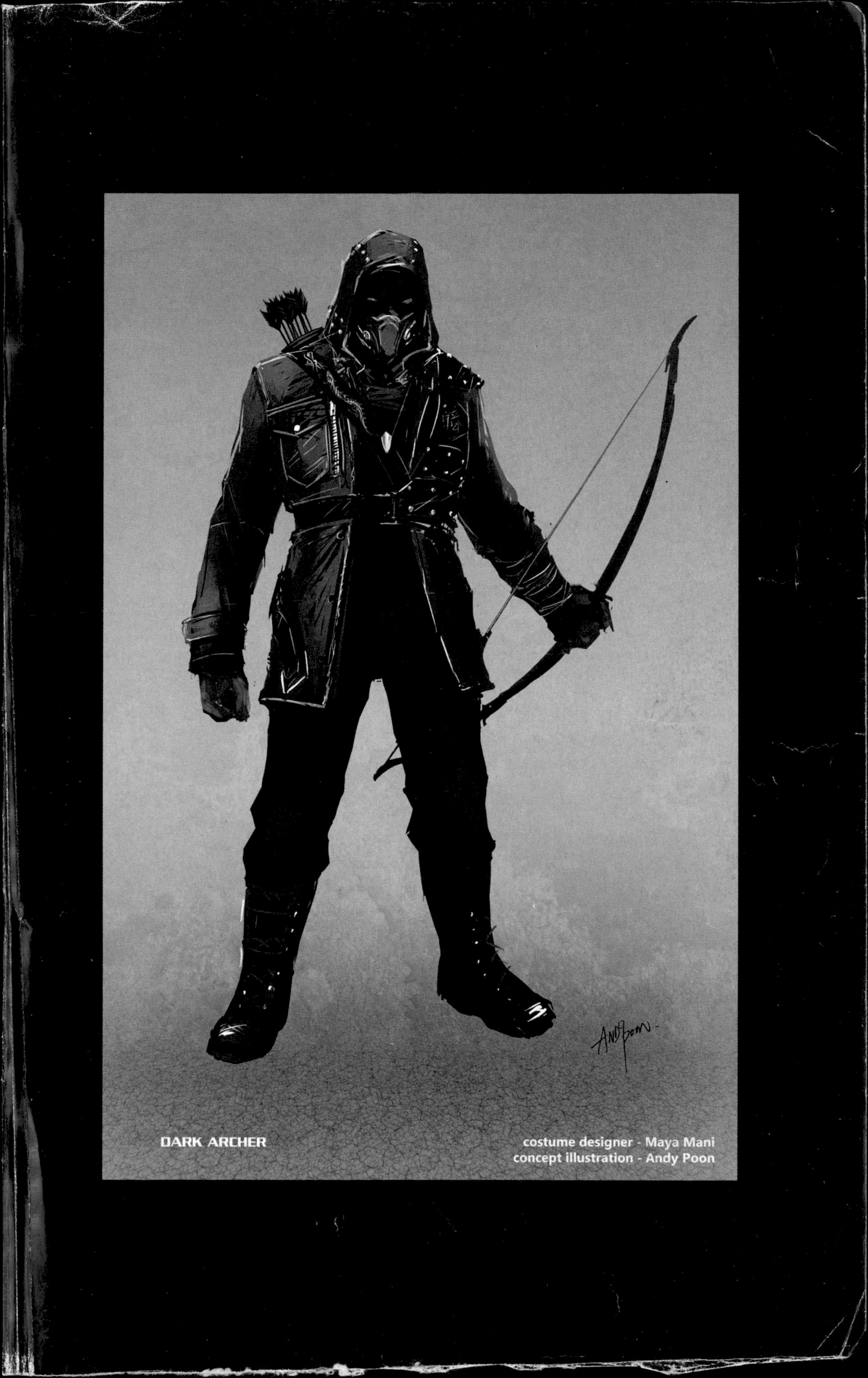
ANDY POON

DARK ARCHER

costume designer - Maya Mani
concept illustration - Andy Poon

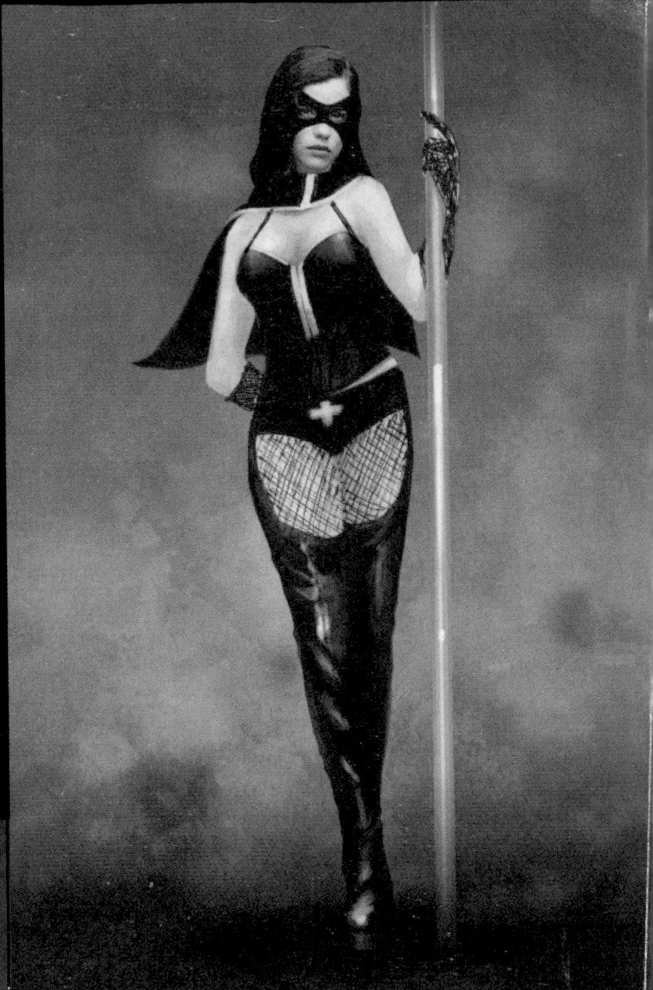

Huntress Dancer

costume designer - Maya Mani
concept illustration - Andy Poon

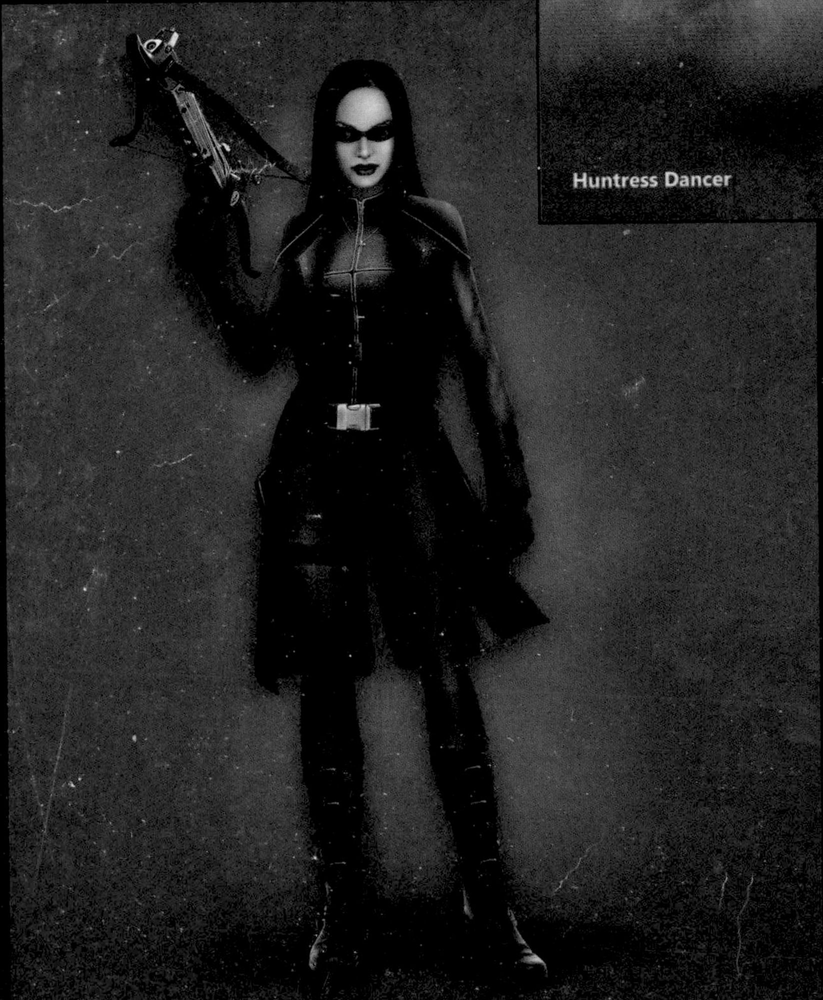

HUNTRESS

costume designer - Maya Mani
concept illustration - Andy Poon